NO TIME ON MY HANDS

By

GRACE SNYDER

as told to Nellie Snyder Yost

Illustrated with Photographs

Foreword and Epilogue by
Nellie Snyder Yost

University of Nebraska Press
Lincoln and London

First Bison Book printing: 1986
Most recent printing indicated by the first digit below:
7   8   9   10

Library of Congress Cataloging-in-Publication Data
Snyder, Grace, 1882–1982.
   No time on my hands.
   1. Snyder, Grace, 1882–1982.   2. Quiltmakers—
United States—Biography.   I. Yost, Nellie Irene
Snyder.   II. Title.
NK9198.S69A2   1986   746.9'7'0924 [B]   85-28959
ISBN 0-8032-9164-7 (pbk.)

Reprinted by arrangement with Nellie Snyder Yost

Originally published in 1963 by The Caxton Printers, Ltd., Caldwell,
Idaho

In tribute to Mrs. A. B. Snyder, North Platte's
most accomplished and widely-known quilt maker,
by
Alice Shipley Schott
Member of the North Platte Ladies' Quilting Club

She tells her stories not with gifted pen
And not with practiced touch upon the keys.
Her tales are told with needle and with thread;
Her manuscripts are quilts.
Her treasures these
Will be to leave to those she holds most dear;
Their loving pride will be her royalties.

Foreword

IN PUTTING this story together for my mother I have had the privilege of going back fourscore years and more, back to her birthplace in Missouri; the old house mouldered now, retaining little of the elegance that endeared it to my frail little grandmother. I have stood with her on the Nebraska prairie where my grandfather laid up his one-room soddy nearly eighty years ago. There is no trace of it there now, or has there been for many years. But in the grassy hillside below there is still a dimple to mark the spot where Pearlie's heifer calf fell through the dugout roof that long-ago August afternoon. Off to the north a little way there is a ragged gulch in a steep claybank, the unhealed scar where the footpath climbed the hill from the old well in the canyon below. A quarter mile or so to the southwest a straight, narrow strip of grass, different in color from the grasses on either side, ripples across the hills to the skyline. That strip, my mother tells me, is where Poppie plowed his fireguard that first autumn on the homestead. The guard long ago grew back to grass, but it has ever since been darker in hue than the rest of the prairie.

I have walked with her in old Walnut Grove cemetery, in the shadow of the tall cedar hedge. So many of the people who walked in the first pages of this story are sleeping there now. We stop awhile where "Poppie" and "Mama" are buried, on either side of a plain granite stone marked simply "McCance." Beside it, on a slender gray shaft, there is a small round picture of Florry in her wedding dress. That little likeness, inset under domed glass, has withstood the sun and storm of more than fifty years. Across the road are the graves of Grandma McCance and Aunt Dicy, of Aunt Bell and Uncle Rob and Uncle Tom. There, too, marked by a big marble stone, are the graves of Oss Brownfield, my mother's first beau, and his four wives.

Together we have strolled beside the looping Birdwood Creek, where she first met my father, and paused awhile beneath the ragged, broken old cottonwoods, listening to the sad whispering of their leaves and remembering— the story of the Birdwood years is so familiar that it seems as if I remember them too—all the disappointment and heartbreak that happened there. The ugly, weather-beaten little house is gone now, and the cellar cave where old Bill Sherman lived has long since fallen in.

It has been a fascinating experience, this journey into the long ago.

NELLIE SNYDER YOST
February 24, 1963

List of Illustrations

	Facing Page
Walnut Grove M. E. Church	112
By the sod house	113
Poppie's ball team	128
Grace, age sixteen, Florry, age eighteen	129
Bend in the Birdwood	240
Bill Sherman and his house on the Birdwood	241
Home of William F. Cody in North Platte	256
Grace and Bert Snyder	257
The sod courthouse in Tryon	336
The McCances, 1905	337
North end of Tryon, as it looked in 1908	352
Pictures taken in the summer of 1912	353
Ten Bar Ranch house, washhouse, and barn	464
Episcopal Church on the Dismal River	465
Covered wagon states quilt	480
Grace Snyder	481
The grape quilt	512
The bird of paradise quilt	513
Ribbons and trophies won on quilts	528
Our golden wedding day	529

NO TIME ON MY HANDS

Chapter One

I GREW UP on the high plains of Custer County, Nebraska, where, as a child of seven and up, I wished three wishes and dreamed three dreams. I wished that I might grow up to make the most beautiful quilts in the world, to marry a cowboy, and to look down on the top of a cloud. At the time I dreamed those dreams and wished those wishes, it seemed impossible that any of them could ever come true.

I was only three when we came to the Custer County homestead, yet the move, and the happenings of those first years, are clear in my mind—whether from my own memory, or from hearing my father and mother tell about them, I do not know. My parents passed on long ago, and my older sister, Florry, has been dead over fifty years, so there has been no one to talk with about these things for a long while. But, whichever way it is, I tell the story now as it began eighty years ago.

My father, Charles McCance, and my mother, Margaret Blaine, had gone to country school together in Cass County, Missouri. After their marriage they lived on a farm in the home neighborhood until the fall of 1884, when Poppie and a young bachelor friend, Joe Byler, went West to see for themselves the rich, free homestead country they had been hearing so much about.

Several of their Cass County neighbors had already

located near Cozad, a little town in the Platte River Valley, but when Poppie and Joe stopped there they found the valley land all taken. So they rode north into the high, rough chop-hills country, where they found the grass on the canyon bottoms richly substantial and the flat ridge tops well suited to dry farming. Poppie filed on a quarter section twelve miles northwest of Cozad, where his south boundary lay squarely on the line dividing Custer and Dawson counties, and Joe filed on a quarter several miles northeast, in Roten Valley.

Homesteaders had to be living on their claims within six months of the filing date, so Poppie and Joe hired an "immigrant car" the following March and headed for Nebraska. Poppie had to sell our only milk cow to pay for his share of the rough, dirty little boxcar, but his half of it held everything we owned: bedding, dishes, Mama's sewing machine, the cradle, our little iron cookstove, the marble-topped walnut bureau, Poppie's saddle, breaking and stirring plows, the wagon and harrow, gentle old Kit, her mule colt, Peg, and the big mule team, Toad and Tinker. Poppie and Joe rode in the car, too, eating and sleeping there and caring for their animals on the long, slow trip out from Missouri.

Mama and the baby and Florry and I stayed at Grandpa Blaine's while Poppie was getting a home ready for us in Nebraska. Florry was five, and the baby, Stella, was six months old.

The things that stand out clearest in my memory are the ones that frightened me, so I know that the remembrance of the day we came to Cozad is my own. As long as I live I'll remember that dark afternoon in May, 1885, when we got off the train in front of the dingy little yellow depot. Rain puddles pocked the muddy street stretching away in front of us, and it looked as if it might pour again any minute. A few planks and old boards, laid down at the crossing and in front of the stores, made a sort of footpath through the town.

Mama, weighted down by the fat baby and her heavy hand satchel, started off to look for a hotel. Florry and I followed close, holding fast to her long black skirts. A cold wind ruffled the water as we hopped from board to board. The pools looked black and deep, the boards frail and narrow; and I was terrified lest we make a misstep and fall into the water. Since that day, water, in anything bigger than a bathtub, has given me goose pimples.

Poppie came after us the next morning, driving Toad and Tinker to the big wagon. Poppie was medium-sized, trim, energetic, and ambitious. His neat brown mustache framed a wide mouth that was jolly when he smiled and straight and stern when he was cross. That morning, after nearly three months of lonely "batching," he was all smiles at sight of us.

It seems to me that I well remember the way Cozad looked when we drove through it on our way to the homestead. Its low, drab buildings seemed to hunker in the mud, as if barely able to keep afloat on the roily slough, and only one tree, a big cottonwood on the edge of town, broke the flatness of the whole wide river valley. In the entire town, then rounding out its twelfth year, there was at that time neither a piano nor a bathtub—not that it made any difference to us.

I do not remember the ride through the hills to Poppie's claim, but I can still see the homestead as it looked when we pulled into it that day—just two naked little soddies squatting on a bare, windswept ridge above a narrow, winding canyon. Not another building in sight, not a tree, not an animal, nothing but grassy flats, hills, and more canyons.

But Poppie was proud of the homestead, of the twelve-by-fourteen-foot buffalo sod house he'd built for us, of the snug little sod stable he'd laid up on the edge of the canyon just below the house, and of the few acres of prairie he'd broken out for his first cornfield. Some soddies, mostly those belonging to bachelors, went unfloored and unplastered all their days; but ours had a floor, and after the walls settled Poppie plastered them with a smooth, hard finish of canyon clay and water. A coat of whitewash every six months or so kept them clean and white.

To Florry and me it was all new and interesting, but to Mama it must have seemed poor and desolate. Mama was thin and frail, never weighing as much as a hundred pounds in her life. She had grown up among the green fields and woods of Missouri, where she lived in a big white house. She liked nice things, good food, pretty clothes, handsome furniture. I wonder, now, how she stood the hard life we lived, those first years in Nebraska. I know she must have been nearly crushed by the unexpected bigness of the prairie, the endless blue of the sky, our rough, homemade furniture, and the almost total lack of neighbors. She was never much of a hand to go visiting, yet she liked to have neighbors around her—and that first year we had only two, Tottens and Wahls.

Wahls, half a mile south of us, had come over from Sweden only that spring and didn't know much English yet; but Tottens, two miles east of us, were already old settlers. They had lived in a sod house the first two or three years but now had a new two-story frame house and a good well with a windmill above it. It was from their well that Poppie hauled our water in barrels.

But Mama was the kind who always did the best she could with what she had. She bleached flour sacks and embroidered them with flying red birds to make pretty curtains for the soddy's three little windows—a single sash, called a "half window," set into the middle of each wall except the south one, where the door opened onto a narrow yard that sloped down to the stable. She made little shelves, brackets, and comb cases out of cigar boxes and hung them on nails driven into the wooden pegs that Poppie pounded into the sod walls for her. On one hook above the walnut bureau she hung their marriage certificate. It was a big, gilt-framed certificate, decorated with colored scrolls, flowers, doves and cupids, and it gave an elegant look to the soddy.

Mama planted a garden on the patch of ground where Poppie had sliced up the sod for the house and stable. She carried our wash water from the big lagoon on the railroad section southeast of the house, where Poppie watered the mules and old Kit. But cooking was the hardest, she said, without milk, eggs, or butter to do it with. Only Poppie didn't seem to mind. With his appetite whetted by long hours of backbreaking work in the field, he was always hungry enough to eat anything.

From daylight till dark he plodded back and forth across the field, jabbing his hand corn planter into the tough sod and pushing the handles together to drop the seed into the ground. With each step ahead, he set one foot down hard on the gap left by the last jab, pressing the sod snugly over the seed.

When he finished the field, Mama asked him what he was going to do about a cow and some chickens. Poppie said he'd get them as soon as he had the cash, and that he could make good wages on the Burlington hi-line, where men and horses were in great demand—provided Mama didn't mind camping out for a while.

Mama said she could stand quite a lot for a cow and some chickens, and, anyway, she liked camping. That was one of the odd things about Mama; she could hardly endure living in the soddy, but she *liked* to camp out.

There was little more Poppie could do on the homestead until fall, for sod corn couldn't be cultivated, and weeds didn't bother it much anyway. So he rigged the wagon with bows and a canvas top, and laid boards across the overjet to hold a bedtick and bedding. He stowed the tent, a camp outfit, and the cookstove under the bed, and early one June morning we drove off behind Toad and Tinker, with old Kit tied to the endgate and her mule colt, Peg, tagging behind. At a ragged camp thirty miles south of Cozad, where the town of Eustis stands today, we pitched our tent among dozens of others and set up housekeeping for the summer. Poppie went to work with the mules and a "scraper" the next morning, helping throw up the high grade for the railroad that was building toward Cheyenne.

Early in August, Poppie said we had money enough to buy the things we needed, and that it was time to get back to the homestead and put up some hay for winter feed. We loaded our outfit and headed north, and at the end of the long day's ride Poppie stopped the wagon in front of a big patch of tall, ragged sunflowers and said we were home again. On the far side of the forsaken wilderness we could barely see the sod roofs of our house and stable. When we left them, ten weeks back, they had stood on bare, dusty ground.

Poppie started plowing fireguards the next day. Mr. Wahl had already plowed his and, dry as it was by then,

Poppie couldn't afford to lose any time getting ours done. Straight east and west on our north line, he turned the furrows that would, he hoped, stop any prairie fire that might sweep across the hills before the strong fall winds. From either end of the first strip he plowed two more, running south to meet the guard neighbor Wahl had turned on the county line between us.

Poppie's corn looked good when we got back to the homestead, and the garden had done well, too. Big onions crowded each other out of the sod, the bean bushes hung full of pods, fat watermelons dotted the patch, and the sweet corn was ready for eating and drying. Every morning for almost two weeks, Mama spread a new batch of corn, fresh cut from the cobs, on a sheet on the soddy's low roof and covered it with cheesecloth against the swarming flies. Several times a day, she climbed on a bench to turn and stir the sweet kernels, browning in the sun.

The big lagoon was dry when we came home, and Poppie had to haul all the water for the stock and for washing, as well as for house use. On the morning he made his first trip to Tottens to fill the barrels, he bought old Pearlie, a gentle little white cow with pretty, curving horns. A bit later, when he had time to lay up a little sod chicken house against the east end of the stable, he bought a flock of laying hens. Then Mama said it seemed like we were halfway living again, and Poppie took time to write a long-overdue letter to Grandma McCance, back in Missouri.

Sept. 6, 1885
ROTEN, NEB.

DEAR MA:

I take this opportunity to answer your letter. We are all well. It is misting today, has been cool and cloudy most of the time for

two weeks. Tell John [his eldest brother] the melon(choly) time
has come and we have all we can eat and they are good as well as
large. Tell Jake and Tom [cousins] if they come out for them to
plan to stay all winter as it will help their health. This is a real
healthy climate. There is a young man from Fort Scott in Cozad
who was like Tom, bad liver and dispepsia. He came out here for
his health and is as stout as anybody now.

Tell John that Cozad has a new elevator as big as the one in East
Lynne. Cozad is now more than twice as large as it was last fall, has
three hardwares, four drygoods, and one abuilding. They are building a large skating rink also.

It has been so cool that I haven't got any hay made yet. Have
some cut but haven't had any sun to cure it yet. We are a little afraid
of frost if this weather lasts much longer, and if we get much it
will catch our corn. I have more beans this year here than I and all
my relations ever raised in Cass County. I hired a man to bore me
a well a month ago. He was to have commenced three weeks ago but
he had a job where he was and hasn't got here yet. So I told him he
need not come for two weeks as I wanted to make hay now. Tell
the boys to write to me.

> As ever,
> CHARLIE McCANCE

Poppie finished his haying, snapped out his corn crop,
and began breaking prairie for a bigger field next year.
But, because the well man didn't get to us at all that
fall, he was delayed in everything he did by having to
stop two or three times a week to haul water. As soon
as the first hard frost killed the big sunflowers in the
yard, he began pulling them for fuel. He laid half a
dozen of the thick stalks in the V's of a sawbuck, tied
them together with twine, and sawed them into lengths
to fit the stove. When the sunflowers were gone we
burned the cobs from our corn crop, and then the stalks;
and so scrounged our fuel from the treeless prairie until
we came to own cattle enough to supply us with cow
chips, the "prairie coal" of the settler period. For fresh
meat we ate prairie chickens and big Canadian geese; and
later, after the geese had all gone south, Poppie could

step to the door on any moonlight night and pick off a
tender rabbit or two at the corn pile.

The weather stayed mild and open all that fall, and
Poppie and the mules, resting only on Sundays, plodded
back and forth on the flat, turning the tough sod to the
thinning sunlight. Even on Christmas they plowed their
steady furrows, stopping only when the first real days
of winter made the prairie crust flint hard, just before
New Year's Day.

Until the freezing weather drove Poppie from the fields
and gave him time to build a trundle bed for us, Florry
and I had slept on a "prairie feather" mattress, a straw-
filled tick laid on the floor at night. It was then, too,
after winter closed in, that Mama took time to show us
how to make the corncob dolls that took the place of
the real dolls we always wanted but never had.

The papa dolls, made from cobs the mules had stepped
on and split part way up, had two legs to put trousers
on. The babies—all our Cob families had lots of babies—
we made from the tiniest nubbins. Mama helped us dress
the dolls in scraps of calico and silk, in beads, braid, and
bits of ribbon from her scrap box, and Florry and I spent
hours on end in the cornfield and at the corn pile, hunting the longest and finest corn silks for hair for our lady
dolls. Dried sunflower heads, trimmed with bright barred
or speckled chicken feathers, made their fancy hats.

That year, and all the years afterward that we played
with dolls, we named the prettiest and most elegant lady
of the crop "Aunt Ollie," after Mama's pretty youngest
sister, who was dearly beloved by both of us.

Chapter Two

AMONG the new settlers who came to our neighborhood the spring after we did were Solomon and Lydia Yoder. They had been our neighbors in Missouri and their arrival made Mama happier than anything that had happened since we came to Nebraska. Mr. Yoder, having more cash than most homesteaders, built a good frame house on his claim, so they never lived in a sod house as most of the rest of us did. Another settler who located near us was a Mr. Wicklund, who had no horses, only an ox-team. Still another, Peter Anderson, who filed on the quarter joining us on the north, was a friendly young bachelor. Mr. Anderson often dropped in at our place at mealtime, and when I found out it was Mama's good homemade bread he hungered for I promised to bake his bread as soon as I was big enough.

While the buffalo grass was turning green again, on the prairie and on our soddy roof, old Kit had a knobby-legged mule colt one night. About the same time we found Pearlie licking a wobbly heifer calf when we went to bring her in from her picket pin one morning. Then Mama sent away for a setting of turkey eggs and began saving back the biggest and best shaped chicken eggs from each day's gathering. When our hens turned broody she set all the eggs in empty nail kegs behind the stable.

As soon as the frost went out of the ground, Poppie

stirred or "backset" the rotted sod of last year's cornfield for wheat. But he had no sooner broadcast the seed
and harrowed it in than trouble came from the sky.
Morning and evening big flocks of geese, flying north
to their nesting grounds, spilled down in gray waves onto
the fields to gobble up the precious seed. Until the flights
had all gone over, Poppie stood watch over our field with
his old muzzle-loading shotgun, blazing away at every
flock that circled low. Mr. Wahl, who had no gun, spent
the mornings and evenings in his field with his dog,
chasing the robbers away as fast as they came down.

Mama planted a bigger garden on the far side of Poppie's
new cornfield, where it would be out of range of the
chickens. She liked to garden, and during those first
years in Nebraska she said it seemed like every seed she
planted grew like mad in the rich, unspoiled land, where
insects and disease had not yet caught up with the frontier.
Later, when her gardens had lost that first fine vigor,
she declared that half a dozen assorted bugs came to sit
around every seed hill she planted, just waiting for the
sprouts to break through.

In due time little chickens and turkeys followed fussy
hens around the yard, and the new green of wheat, corn,
and beans covered the fields. Poppie said, for the hundredth time, that he had never seen such a land as this,
so rich, so fertile. But Mama said only that she wished
we had a well in our own yard.

Poppie had talked to a well man again that spring.
But with more jobs ahead than they could handle, all
the well men had raised their prices, and the gap between
the price of a well and Poppie's cash on hand seemed to
grow wider and wider. While there was water in the
lagoons it wasn't so bad. But after they dried up in hot
weather, and Poppie had to haul every drop that came

onto the place, then we used it sparingly indeed; saving the washday rinse water, the water we washed vegetables in, even the bath water, to pour into the chicken trough. But no matter how careful we were, the water barrels seemed always nearly empty, and sometimes we ran clear out before Poppie got home with the new supply.

On one of those days Mama screwed the coffee grinder down to its finest adjustment and poured pepper berries into the hopper and began to grind pepper. The little berries looked so good that I asked if I could taste one. "Mercy no!" she said. "They're hot as fire. They'd burn your mouth to a cinder."

But when she wasn't looking, I slipped a berry out of the sack and popped it into my mouth. Mama was right. It *was* hot as fire. It was fire itself. I danced and I cried and I howled. I held my mouth wide open and breathed in and out as fast as I could. But nothing helped, until Poppie pulled in with the water.

Water-hauling days, when Poppie loaded the four big barrels into the wagon and covered them with the wooden lids and a strip of clean canvas, Florry and I used to beg to go to Tottens with him. But Mama almost always said no.

Mama had a tremendously overgrown sense of pride, and she remembered too well the stylish clothes and handsome farm home of her girlhood. There, the big house had had front and back porches, and screens on the doors and windows, and it had a parlor where, except on special occasions, the blinds were always drawn and the door locked. Here, the rough ways of our frontier life, coupled with our lack of good clothes and houseroom, rubbed her where it hurt.

"I'll not have the neighbors thinking poorly of us," she'd say, "and I'll not have you girls going off the place

unless you're decently dressed in shoes and stockings."
Those years on the homestead, one or the other of us
usually *didn't* have decent shoes and stockings, so we
didn't go off the place very often.

We had fun, though, the few times we did get to go,
jouncing along in the wagon and singing with Poppie
above the rattle and bang of the empty barrels. Poppie
had a rich, deep voice and, like all his family, he loved
to sing. When we pulled up at the well, Mrs. Totten
would come out to visit with us while Poppie filled the
barrels, or maybe she would take us to the house with her.
And if the wind died and the mill wheel stopped turning,
so that he had to use the hand pump, we had a longer visit.

But, though we seldom went off the place, Florry and
I were not lonesome those summers on the homestead.
We had all of Poppie's claim, and the railroad section
besides, for a playground; and by midsummer, that second
year, we knew every hill and canyon, every plum thicket,
currant patch, and buffalo trail within a half mile. We
"took" homesteads for our cob dolls on each side of the
county line, and built dugout houses, roads, fences and
ditches in the claybanks. Then Florry and her Cobs, just
by stepping over the fireguard line, could come all the
way from Dawson County to visit my Cobs in Custer
County. In the same way, I traveled all the way to
Dawson County with the Custer County Cobs.

On the railroad section, near the big lagoon, we found
an ancient buffalo wallow. Except for a bare ledge on its
north side—where Poppie said the buffaloes had scratched
their necks until they wore the grass roots all away—
grass covered the big wallow and grew tall among the
bleached bones and skulls and horns scattered there. To
us it was a wonderful place, and we went there almost
every day to play among the bones.

Then Poppie came in from milking one summer morning and said he hadn't seen old Tom for two or three days, and that he'd hate to lose him because he was such a good hunter. "Oh," Florry and I said, "we'll find him." But, though we went hunting and calling through the canyons for days, we found neither hide nor hair of the big cat, dead or alive.

Mama did a lot of fretting about the way we disappeared right after breakfast, to play all day in the hills. She said she didn't see what we found so wonderful about "those hot, dusty canyons and that old wallow," and besides, there was no telling what we might run into. But to us the canyons and the flats were almost our whole world, even after the day Mama found the rattlesnake in the yard.

That happened one sultry washday when she was at her washboard and tub. When Poppie came in to dinner, she dried her hands and went in to dish up the meal. Mama finished eating first, stirred up the fire, set the teakettle over the front lid to boil water for starch, and went on to the yard to hang up a basket of clothes. She was nearly to the end of the clothesline, where a hen and a late-hatched brood of chickens sat in the shade of a clump of tall grass, when a chick screamed and the hen began to screech. The chick bounced out of the grass and ran to Mama. She snatched it up and yelled for Poppie to come quick and bring something to kill a rattlesnake.

Poppie dropped his knife and fork, jumped up and looked around, then he grabbed the boiling teakettle and sprinted for the clothesline. In the grass, the poor hen was flopping and clawing a big rattler and baby chickens were running in all directions. When Poppie ran up the hen took off, squawking and jumping, and he aimed the stream of boiling water at the snake. Even before the scalded rattler flopped his last flop, the chick in Mama's shaking hands was dead, its little body already puffed up and turning blue.

It might just as well have been Florry or Grace who ran onto the snake, out in those canyons, Mama said, or the baby, who had been toddling after the little chickens all summer.

Mama used to wonder, too, how sisters could be so different. Florry, she said, outgrew her clothes before she wore them out, but I tore mine off of me faster than she could sew them up.

Florry, grave-eyed and quiet, was a born lady. Pretty manners and care for her clothes came naturally to her, and she didn't mind wearing the deep sunbonnets Mama made for herself and us girls. (For to Mama, who believed soft white complexions were a woman's natural right, the harsh, burning prairie winds were pure torture.) Neither did Florry mind the thick buttermilk Mama made us rub into our faces at bedtime when, in spite of the bonnets, our skins still turned rough and brown. But I despised both the buttermilk and the bonnets; for I was a tomboy, with my hair a mop and my clothes in tatters from tearing through thickets and climbing over things, and I was delighted when Mama finally made me a pair of denim trousers and a jacket to match. I could travel a lot faster in that outfit than I could in long skirts.

When, late in the summer, Poppie finished shocking his good wheat crop and started digging a cellar in the canyon bank below the house, Mama asked him if he couldn't build another room onto the house while he was at it. For, she said, she didn't see how she could go through another winter with all of us cooped up in one little room. So Poppie hitched the mules to the breaking plow and sliced up the sod for a new room. He built it against the east wall of the old house, with a door where the window had been, and a full-length window, one that opened and shut, in the new south wall.

Joe Byler came to help Poppie lay up the new walls, and before the room was finished he told Mama that he was soon to be married to a girl from Pennsylvania who had come with her folks to a farm north of Roten Valley that spring. Mama told him she was glad to hear it, and to be sure to bring his bride to see us.

About the time they were ready to roof the new room, Mr. Wahl came to tell Poppie the neighbors were ready to thresh. All the farmers in our community worked together, following the machine from farm to farm until all the grain was threshed. A Swede owned the threshing machine and all the other farmers in the circle were Swedes, too, so Poppie, being the only "foreigner" on the list, always had to wait till the tail end.

For the next month Poppie drove away at sunrise every morning, riding on a bundle rack behind old Toad and Tinker. At dark they came home again, bone weary and caked with dust and sweat. But at last the big machine pulled in at our place. They staked it down behind the stable and hauled the turntable into place beside it, and all day Florry and I stayed as close as Poppie would let us.

We watched them hook four two-horse teams, nose to tail, to the turntable sweep where the driver, walking all day in the same spot on the platform turning beneath his feet, kept the teams circling at a steady pace to turn the thirty-foot tumbling rod that ran the "separator." Men on a long line of racks brought the shocked wheat from the field. The bundles, tossed steadily into the separator's maw, came out the other end in a yellow stream of grain and a big pile of fluffy, shining straw. Thick clouds of dust and chaff, mixed with the strong smell of sweaty men and horses, hung over the whole noisy, rumbling outfit.

I had never seen anything so exciting as this business of threshing. Once, to get a better look at the clattering machine, I dodged in and jumped over the rolling tumbling rod. "Hey! Get that little boy outta here before he gets hurted," the man on the turntable yelled at Poppie.

"I'm not a boy, I'm a girl," I stopped to yell back, just as Poppie yanked me away by the seat of my denim pants.

When the threshing was done, only a shining straw-stack, a scattering of tar boxes, and two deep paths, worn by thirty-two marching hoofs, marked the spot where the big machine had stood. The tar boxes, little drums with wooden heads, had held a thick grease used to keep the tumbling rod joints running smooth and free. Florry and I gathered up the drums, knocked the round heads out, and scoured them clean with dust and straw. Poppie bored holes through their centers and fastened them to cigar boxes for wheels. The Montgomery Ward catalog showed little wagons, some with sideboards and a tongue like a real wagon, but the only little wagons Florry and I ever had were the ones Poppie made us from the cigar boxes and tar-box ends.

After the threshing was done, Poppie roofed the new room with boards and sod and "floored" it with a thick layer of new straw, overlaid with a bright rag carpet, stretched tight and pegged against the walls. We moved the big bed, the trundle bed, the cradle and the sewing machine into the new room and Poppie bought a wide-bottomed, high-backed rocking chair to put in front of the full-length south window. In the evenings Mama sat there, busy with her knitting or mending, and if she wasn't too tired she sang to us, or told us stories. The stories we liked best were about her childhood in Missouri, before Aunt Ollie was born, when Grandpa and Grandma Blaine had kept a Negro mammy, Aunt Carrie, to look after Mama and her sister and two brothers. We dearly loved Aunt Carrie, and most of the songs Mama taught us were the ones the old mammy had sung to her so long ago. Our favorite was the "Pig Song."

> A jolly old mother pig lived in a sty,
> And six little piggies had she.
> And she waddled about saying "unh unh unh,"
> While the little piggies said "wee wee."
> Said one little pig to his five little brothers,
> Said one little pig, said he,
> "Let us strive for the future to say 'unh unh unh.'
> 'T is so childish to say 'wee wee.' "
> Now these little pigs grew skinny and lean,
> And lean they might very well be
> From trying so hard to say "unh unh unh,"
> When they only could say "wee wee."
> A moral there is to this little song,
> A moral you plainly can see.
> Don't try when you're young to say "unh unh unh,"
> When you only can say "wee wee."

I remember other things about that window, too. Two or three years later Dolly's black colt, Prince, came flying to the house, whirled, and backed up to rub off a savage deerfly that was stinging his rear. Prince didn't have time to pick his spot to rub, and so backed right into the window and broke out all the panes. I used to sit on that window's wide seat to watch for Poppie to come home from town. I could hardly wait for him to appear in sight over the last hill, except for one time, and that one time I dreaded it like the coming of Judgment Day. My first tooth had come loose after he left, and Mama had promised me that Poppie should pull it as soon as he came home.

It was well into the fall by the time the new room
was finished, but Florry and I, dreading the long winter
months when we'd be kept in the house, spent more and
more time in the canyons. One of the places we liked
best was an old buffalo trail that wound up a long canyon to the top of a big flat. Washed deep by the rains
of all the years that had passed since the buffaloes last
used it, it was steep and narrow, and so dim and shadowy
that we never dared follow it all the way to the top.
But we often played in its lower end, where the high
clay walls were full of dainty shells, brittle little skeletons
that crumbled to dust when we tried to dig them out.

We showed Mama the few tiny pieces we managed to
winnow from the dust, and she told us how, thousands
of years ago, this prairie had been covered by an ocean,
where the little snails lived. We spent more time than
ever in the old trail then, and one afternoon we crept a
little farther up the dim path than we had ever gone
before—and came upon a frightful, grinning THING.

We flew for home to get Mama; and when we climbed
the trail again, Florry and I hung back, letting her go
first. With her along, the THING didn't look so big, or
the awful grin so scary, when we came to it again.

"Why, it's poor old Tom," Mama said. "The coyotes
must've killed him."

There was little left of him but hide and bones and
the hideous grin that had scared us so. But after that,
we didn't care to play in the old trail any more. Instead,
we followed Poppie up and down the furrows of his new
breaking, enjoying the steady flow of the long sod ribbon
from the curve of the plowshare. Mostly, each new strip
fell smooth and flat against the one turned the round
before, but now and then it kinked and buckled into

little upside-down V-shaped hummocks, making little seats that Florry and I could sit on to rest awhile.

One afternoon a rattlesnake, stirred up by the plow, looped from under one of the kinks and crawled up the hill to dive into a hole. The hole, washed out by rainwater running into a gopher hole on the ledge higher up, turned out to be the entrance to an old den, a pit some five or six feet deep. Poppie climbed to the upper hole and looked in. On the floor of the pit, a big ball of rattlers was twisting and struggling into shape for winter hibernation. He got his gun and finished off the snakes, then he let us look into the awful hole—but he wouldn't let us sit on the little hummocks any more.

When the days turned too chilly for us to play outside any longer, Florry and I gathered the Cobs from the playhouses and moved them into the house, where they spent the winter in shoe boxes under the bed. Poppie finished his fall plowing and went over into Roten Valley, where he bought another cow, old Red, twice as big as Pearlie but not one whit a better milker. "We've got the start of a herd now," he said the evening he brought her home. "Two cows and Pearlie's heifer calf.

Flour sacks full of beans and dried corn hung in the kitchen corner that winter, and heaps of onions, turnips, pumpkins, cabbage, and potatoes filled the cellar cave. The potatoes were queer, flattish disks, so shaped because the "eyes," dropped in new sod furrows and covered by the tough sod of the next round, had found it easier to flatten out and grow sideways between the hard layers of earth than to grow round in the usual way.

Just before Thanksgiving the barrels came. For the first ten years or so that we lived in Nebraska, Grandpa and Grandma Blaine sent the barrels, three of them, every fall, and fine, spicy smells foamed out of them when

Poppie pried the heads off in our little kitchen. One barrel would be full of apples from Grandpa's orchard, and Mama would take the smooth red fruit in her thin hands and look at it with a faraway shine in her eyes.

I know now that the apples made her homesick for Missouri, for the orchards stretching away behind the big white house, for the fenced yard where lilacs, roses, and gooseberry bushes grew against the pickets. But to us girls the apples were just a special treat, to be handed out sparingly over the winter. And when the barrel was finally empty we would go to the cellar and lean over it, breathing deeply of the good apple smell that lingered long after the fruit was gone.

Another barrel would be filled with good molasses, fresh from Steven's sorghum mill where Poppie had worked as a boy; but the third, the one the "surprises" came out of, was always the best. There would be nuts in that barrel, from Grandpa's own nut trees, and sweet potatoes of his own raising; but the other two bundles, the ones Grandma and Aunt Ollie put in for Mama and us girls, were the ones we couldn't wait to see.

We would hang over Mama while she unwrapped Grandma's bundle, for out of it came a dress length of new calico for each of us. Every year Grandma cut each piece a little longer to accommodate our lengthening legs, and every second year she added a new piece for the baby girl who had learned to walk since she sent the last assortment. But better yet was Aunt Ollie's bundle of stylish hand-me-downs, her last year's jackets, dresses, and petticoats that Mama made over for us every winter. We always spread the lovely things out on the bed and made a big ceremony of looking at their rich colors, feeling their fine textures, and smelling their delicate perfumes.

Then we divided them up. Florry had first pick the first year, I had it the second, and so on down the line.

My new calico, that second year on the homestead, was a lovely piece, black, sprigged all over with tiny green leaves and red dots, and I liked it better than any dress I ever had. We wore the new dresses Christmas Day, when Tottens and Yoders came to our house for dinner.

We had a Christmas tree that year, a little wild plum bush trimmed with paper chains and strings of popcorn; and there were sixteen folks to sit down to Mama's good roast turkey dinner, too many to dine all at the same time.

Florence Yoder and the oldest Totten boy, both almost grown, ate at the first table with their parents and Poppie and Mama. But Howard and Charlie Yoder and the three younger Totten boys had to wait, with Florry, Stella, and me, for the second table. While hard knots of hunger grew and grew inside us, we had to sit back, smelling the good smells, and hoping there would be enough of everything left for us.

Homesteader children had to put up with a lot of hard things, but one of the hardest was waiting for second table.

Chapter Three

JANUARY, February, and March, always the longest months of the year, dragged by. Then, with the coming of April, the prairie greened and flowered again, Red and Pearlie had new little calves, and Poppie began breaking prairie on the big flat across the canyon for a bean and melon patch. And that spring the carefree days of hours-long play in the canyons ended for Florry and me. Poppie said we were big enough now to help with the chores, and Mama said it was a good thing, for it was time to start looking for turkey nests and we could help with that.

For plain outright aggravation there are few jobs to match that of trailing turkey hens to their nests. Guided by a stubborn wild instinct, the hens insisted on straying far from home to lay in hidden places, where snakes and skunks ate the eggs and coyotes snared the hens themselves off the nests when they started setting. For their own protection, we had to find the nests as soon as possible, and then go every day to collect the eggs. Mama had only eight or ten hens that spring, but later, when she kept twenty to thirty, finding so many nests turned out to be a tough job for Florry and me.

The hens would stroll the prairie for hours, acting as if they had nowhere to go and nothing to do. Now and then they'd stick their silly heads up high, looking and listening, and if they suspected we were watching them they'd go on strolling for hours longer. Sometimes we sat watching a hen for a solid half day, and then somehow missed her when she slipped, like the shadow of a cloud, into some patch of brush or tall grass and disappeared. Though we'd hunt and hunt all around the spot where we last saw her, the nest always turned out to be some other place, a long way off. We'd settle down then to watch for her to show up again, hoping we could find the nest somewhere nearby. But we never seemed to be looking in the right place. One minute the flat would be empty, the next the hen, her laying done, would be grazing along in the middle of it, nowhere near any shelter of any kind.

One afternoon, after we'd given up watching hens, we were playing in the tall grass at the head of a pocket when we found a nest with seven or eight eggs and a dead bullsnake in it. We went full tilt after Mama. The snake had been dead long enough to puff up three times his natural size, and Mama said the hen must have come along right after he found the nest and she had flopped him to death, and then left for good. Two of the eggs had been cracked in the fight but the rest were all right. Mama took the good ones to the house and Florry and I had to go on watching that hen until we found her new nest. A little later we found one of our hens sharing her nest with a pretty little quail hen, or maybe it was the other way around. As often as we could we hid out near the nest to watch the turkey slip into the thicket and sit down beside the tiny wild hen. Sometimes she covered her little neighbor with one careful wing; other times they just sat side by side, seeming to enjoy each other's company.

Mama went with us to each new nest we found, brushed

away the grass and leaves the hen kicked over it as she left, and gathered the eggs. She always left a chicken egg in their place because, if we left the nest empty, the hen would leave it and hide out another one. Sometimes Mama was too busy to make the daily rounds of the draws and pockets, in which case she gave us the keister —an old leather satchel used, in its better days to carry the baby's "didies" in—and sent us to bring in the eggs.

As fast as the hens turned broody, Mama brought them in from the canyons and set them in kegs and barrels in the yard. One hen had hidden her nest in the tall grass at the head of a little draw, so near the house that Mama said she didn't think the coyotes would dare bother her. To make sure, Poppie set a tall scarecrow above the nest. On a starlit night the scarecrow was ghostly enough to scare Florry and me every time we went outside; but not the coyote that ate the hen one night, leaving only a scattering of feathers around the nest to show what happened. "That coyote," Poppie said, "had plenty of gall. He ate the hen and then hung her entrails on my scarecrow, just to let me know what he thought of it."

Setting by setting, the turkeys' eggs hatched and the hens and their broods traveled together, the proud old gobbler pacing ahead of them, his chest stuck out and his long beard swinging. Ranging farther and farther away as the days went by, they always came back to the barnyard at sundown, where the hens hovered their babies on the ground and the gobbler kept his night watch from the stable ridgepole above them.

Our turkeys were all shades of tan and brown, ranging from one off-white hen to several chocolate-colored ones. One evening the nearly white hen was missing when the flock came in. Her babies were running every which way among the others and calling in a lost and frightened way. Mama said we'd have to try to find the hen before dark, so we went over the hills and down the draws, hunting as long as we could see, but we found no trace of her.

"The coyotes must've caught her," Mama said sadly, and began wondering how she was going to keep the little turkeys warm at night until they feathered out. But when we got back to the yard we found the gobbler down among the hens with his motherless babies all tucked under his bearded breast. The next morning the partly widowed gobbler led the little poults out to pasture with the rest, and all season he looked after them with tender care.

At Mama's urging, Florry and I hunted for days but we found no trace of the lost hen, not even a handful of feathers to show where a coyote had caught her.

When we had the business of locating turkey nests off our hands, Mama let us move the Cobs back to their homesteads. About the time we finished cleaning out the little dugouts and repairing the bridges, roads, and fences, Yoders came to spend a Sunday with us.

Florence was a pretty young lady of sixteen and Florry and I did not want to miss a minute of her company, so we did not go to the homesteads that day. But on Monday, as soon as we had time, we hurried to our nearest playhouse.

We found it in ruins, the ditches filled in, fences torn down, roads and bridges gone, and the house plugged with clay. Across the fireguard in Dawson County it was the same, and when we started cleaning out the dugouts we found all the poor Cobs standing on their heads in their houses.

I tell you, Florry and I were mad at the Yoder boys for a long time after that day.

Our new sister was born on July 24, the day after Poppie finished stacking his oats crop beside the stable. Florence Yoder came to take care of Mama and the baby and that, to Florry and me at least, somewhat made up for the disappointment that the baby wasn't the boy we had all wanted for so long.

The next day Poppie sent Florry and me to tell Mrs. Wahl about the baby, and to ask her to come over the next morning to do the washing and baking.

Wahls lived in a dugout, a snug little claybank house with a door and two windows on the front side of its single room. The first time we had gone to visit them, the fall after we came home from the railroad camp, a funny thing had happened. Mr. Wahl and the children, Mary, Ed, and Dora, spoke English fairly well by then, but Mrs. Wahl hardly spoke it at all, either then or later, so it was hard for Mama to visit with her.

Some other settlers from away over south had been there that day, too, and the little room was full of people when Mrs. Wahl picked up one of the visiting babies, carried it over to Mr. Wahl and whisked off its diaper. Laughing in an I-told-you-so tone, she had said something to him in Swedish, then sat down and pinned the baby back into its pants.

"The baby, she say girl, I say boy," Mr. Wahl explained matter-of-factly.

But Mama, who was so modest she probably never in her life saw all of her own body at once, had had a pink face all the rest of the afternoon.

Florry and I, the bearers of important news, hurried all the way to Wahls that sultry morning. Near the stable we passed an old cultivator where, on a board across the wheels, Mrs. Wahl had spread a clean white cloth covered with a thick wet paste of potato starch.

Mrs. Wahl, home alone that day, clucked in dismay when she understood that our new baby had turned out to be another girl. In the midst of promising us, by many nods of her head, that she'd be over to do the washing and baking, she suddenly yelled and took off across the yard, waving her arms and flapping her long apron. Startled, Florry and I took out after her.

Mrs. Wahl pulled up beside the cultivator and began flailing away at a skimmer calf. The calf spit out half a yard of cloth and fled bawling, its tail sticking straight out behind it. The poor woman, shaking her fists and screaming a flood of Swedish after him, stood in the middle of the mess of damp starch scattered on the ground. We shared her feelings, for Mama made her own starch, too, and we knew what a lot of work it was.

When the calf was out of sight over the nearest hill, Mrs. Wahl shook the cloth and spread it on the board again. Florry and I knelt to help her sort the starch from the sticks, grass, and dirt, listening all the while to fresh outbursts of Swedish scolding, mixed with the few bad English words she knew.

Poppie had hauled water that blistering day and all the barrels stood full when the sultry sun went down. We had used the last of our kerosene the night before and Poppie had to twist a penny in a bit of cloth and set it in a saucer of lard to make a lamp for Mama's room. He lit it and put it on the sewing machine, across the room from her bed, and came on to the kitchen for supper. The open door and the west window let in enough light for us to see, and while we ate we watched some ugly, threatening clouds pile up where the sun had just gone down.

We were still at the table when lightning began to rip the clouds apart. Then there came a tremendous crack of lightning, so near the thunder roared at the same instant and made us all duck in our chairs. While the thunder still rolled and crashed across the prairie, Poppie jumped up and ran to the door. He saw smoke coming out of the oats stack nearest the stable.

He yelled at Florence to bring a pail of water, and took out for the stable on the run. Florence jumped up to get the water and Florry and I lit out after Poppie, who was already yanking bundles from the burning stack and flinging them behind him. At his orders, Florry and I dragged the bundles farther back, out of reach of flying sparks. Florence kept heeling it from the house with pails of water for Poppie to throw on the fire, and Florry and I carried bundles as fast as we could. We soon had the fire out, and the only damage was a dozen or so scorched oat bundles.

Poppie said we'd got out of it pretty lucky, and that it was a good thing he'd hauled water that day since the storm turned out to be only a "duster," with hardly enough rain in the cloud to dowse a candle. Florence said yes, we were lucky, but we had used all the water on the fire and he'd have to haul more in the morning before Mrs. Wahl could do the washing—and then we smelled smoke again, only this time it had a bitter, stinging smell.

We all ran for the house as tight as we could go.

The kitchen was full of a choking haze. In the bedroom, where Mama was fighting for breath, the top of the sewing machine was all blistered and smoking. The cloth wick in the homemade candle had burned up the lard, and the red-hot penny had cracked the saucer in two and dropped onto the varnished wood, where it was just about to start another blaze.

We had come just in the nick of time; for poor Mama,

too weak and sick to get out of bed, was almost unconscious and the baby had nearly quit breathing.

When things had settled down again so that we knew
what we were doing, we named the baby Florence Ethel.

Grandma McCance came a few days later, and Florence
went home. From the talk that went on around us,
Florry and I gathered that Grandma had known there
was to be a new baby and that she had planned to be
with us when it came, but had somehow been delayed.

Grandma was little and thin and wiry, and she never
seemed to be still for so much as a minute. "I guess I've
got into the habit of workin' all the time because I've
always had so much of it to do," she used to say.

Three of her twelve children had died in infancy, and
her two eldest daughters were already married when
Grandpa McCance died of pneumonia in the winter of
1871. Of the seven left at home, Uncle John was only
fifteen then, Poppie fourteen, and the baby, Aunt Hester,
a year old. Somehow she had kept them together, scraped
a living from her little Missouri farm, and sent the younger
ones to college. Uncle John was still at home with her,
at the time she came out to see us, but all the others
were married, in school, or teaching.

Grandma took a liking to Nebraska as soon as she got
off the train in Cozad. She said Uncle John had been
wanting to come out ever since we left, and that she
believed it would be easier to make a living here than in
Missouri, and that, the way the country was settling up,
Aunt Bell and Aunt Hester wouldn't have any trouble
getting schools to teach. Poppie said that was so, and
that they would all feel better in Nebraska because the
dry air was so good for lung trouble and rheumatism.

Grandma spent a month with us, giving us a big lift
over a hard place. But by the time she left she had de-

cided to sell her place in Missouri as soon as Poppie could
get her a good farm near us.

We were all sorry to see Grandma McCance go; and
then, the very next week, we had a letter from Grandma
Blaine, telling us she was coming out for a visit. Mama
held the letter in her hand a long time, a stricken look
on her face. She was still weak and thin and tired, and
the baby, a frail, sickly mite, cried most of the time
and didn't seem to gain as she should.

When Mama said she'd have to have help to get ready
for Grandma, Florry and I begged them to get Florence
again. But Poppie said Florence was going to school in
Cozad and planning to be a teacher as soon as she finished
her education. So the new hired girl was Saphronie, a
giggly, flighty fifteen-year-old from a homestead over
west of us. She had been with us only a day or two
when Poppie shot the big owl.

"I didn't know they grew this big," he said, holding it
up by its outspread wings. "I guess I'll take it to that
new taxidermist in town and have it stuffed."

He hung his old muzzle-loader back on its wall pegs
above the bed we had set up in the kitchen for Saphronie,
and wedged the owl between the gun and the wall. That
night a terrible screaming woke us all up. Poppie jumped
out of bed and dashed into the kitchen, and the rest of
us rolled out and followed him. The screaming went
on and on, while he fumbled for a match in the match
holder. When its light finally flared up we had a glimpse
of Saphronie, standing in the middle of the kitchen in
her "shimmy" and long muslin underdrawers, her eyes
bugged out and mouth wide open, yelling bloody murder.
Another match got the lamp going, and then Poppie and
Mama closed in on the girl and got the racket stopped.

It turned out that the poor dead owl had come untucked and tumbled down on Saphronie's face, scaring her clear out of her senses. Poppie dug his owl out of the bedcovers and found a safer roost for it, and Mama got the hysterical girl quieted and back into bed.

Mama saw to it that Saphronie practically turned the house inside out, getting ready for Grandma, and the whitewashing, scrubbing, and dusting went on right up to the minute Poppie left for Cozad to meet the train. Then Mama turned on Florry, Stell, and me and scrubbed us almost to the quick—as if she hoped to wash off our sunburn and scratches—and hustled us into clean clothes from the skin out. Last, she put the wee fretful baby into the yard-long, tucked, lace-trimmed petticoats and dress that each of us in turn had worn, and that it took her half a day to iron.

Poor Mama. She knew how raw and bare our prairie home would seem to her mother, and she overtaxed her frail strength trying to make it seem better than it was. But Florry and I, scarcely remembering anything different, or better, were proud to show Grandma around. And Grandma, rustling and dainty in her silk dress and many petticoats, smiled at us and smoothed our wind-roughened hair with gentle fingers.

Yoders came to dinner on Sunday, and that afternoon plump, good-hearted Mrs. Yoder said to Mama, "Maggie, why don't you pack up and go home with your mother? 'Twould do you and that poor baby good to go back to Missouri and rest up and visit the home folks."

When Mama said, "Goodness no, I couldn't go and take all these children," Mrs. Yoder told her she needn't let that stop her, that she would be glad to keep Florry and me for as long as Mama wanted to stay.

Until then I hadn't wanted Grandma's visit to come to an end, but with the prospect of a visit to Yoder's ahead of me, I couldn't wait to find out when she intended to go home. Slipping around to her chair, I asked her; but Mama heard me and all that came of that idea was the good scolding she gave me for my lack of manners. For, she said, the baby was too cross and frail for such a long trip and she wouldn't try it yet awhile.

Poppie took Grandma to the train a few days later, and that afternoon Mama sent Florry and me to the melon patch to get a good melon for supper. It would frost any night now and spoil all that were left in the patch, she said.

Poppie had raised a fine crop of beans and melons on the new sod field across the canyon, and for weeks we had hauled the big, sweet melons home by the wagonload. The vines in the patch were withered and stringy now, and the melons small, but in a corner of the patch, under a whopping big tumbleweed, we found the biggest melon of them all. Waist high to the two of us, perfectly round and smooth, it had grown unseen all summer. We had carried other melons home by gathering them up in our aprons and toting them across the canyon on our stomachs, but this one was far too big for that. So we rolled it home. Across the field and down the near side of the deep canyon, across the bottom and up the far slope to the house. Several times we almost let it slip from our sweaty hands, and near the end of the trip we hardly had breath or strength to push it any farther, but at last we brought it safe to the kitchen door.

In all my life I have never eaten a sweeter, better melon.

Two or three days of damp, cloudy weather followed our trip to the melon patch, and when the sky cleared at sundown Poppie said we'd sure get a killing frost that night, it was so clear and still.

The next forenoon, after the heavy frost had melted,

Poppie took Florry and me to the bean patch and showed us how to pull and rick the dead vines. Before he left he warned us not to eat any of the melons left in the field beside the beans. They'd make us sick, now that they'd been frosted, he said.

Florry and I, working alone in the beans through the sunny October days, had a hot, tiresome, dirty job on our hands. One afternoon, when we had finished off the water in our bottle, we got so thirsty we went into the melon patch, broke open some of the best-looking melons, and ate the hearts. They tasted slick, and too sweet, and we felt bad about disobeying Poppie, but we ate enough to kill our thirst and then went back to bean pulling.

"You girls've been eating those frosted melons, haven't you?" Mama said as soon as we came in the door that evening. We looked at each other, wondering how in the world she knew.

"I can tell because your faces are cleaner around your mouths than anywhere else," she said, "and I just hope you aren't sick tonight."

But we were—cramping and throwing up most of the night, and unable to go back to the field until the next afternoon. When we left, Mama said she guessed we'd know better than to eat any more of the melons.

We pulled the last of the beans a few days later and then, because there was still quite a piece of the afternoon left, we stayed to play awhile in the melon patch —and so we found another mammoth melon. Late grown on the end of a vine that had wandered clear out of the patch, it had been protected from the frost by the heavy growth of grass and weeds that had hidden it so long and it looked fresh and crisp. We decided to break it open and try it. If it tasted slick, like those that had made us sick, we wouldn't eat it. But it tasted every bit as good as the earlier melons, so we ate all we could hold of it and threw the rest in the weeds where Poppie wouldn't see it when he came to haul the beans home.

Then we looked at each other. Sure enough, besides a guilty look, we each had a too-clean patch around our mouths. We fixed that by rubbing some dust into the sticky juice on our faces, and then went on home. But we must have overdone it a little; for as soon as Mama saw us she said, "You girls've been eating those melons again. Just wait till Poppie finds out."

We didn't get sick that time, but we got spanked for not minding.

Chapter Four

POPPIE mortgaged the homestead that fall, and sold the big mules, Toad and Tinker, for a good price. He put all the money into cows, "the fastest money makers in Nebrasky." The day he brought the little herd home, he said to me, "You'll have to be my herdboy now, Pete. Mommie needs Florry to help her in the house and you'll have to do it all alone. Think you can?"

I knew I could. I didn't like housework anyway, and to be Poppie's boy and have him call me "Pete," and to spend all my days out of doors—well, it seemed to me that was all I could ever want.

The next morning Poppie turned Red and Pearlie and the heifer calf in with the new bunch and helped me drive them to the shucked-out cornfield. All I had to do, he said, was keep the herd in our cornfield and away from Anderson's or Wahl's.

It was fun at first.

The fall days were warm and pleasant and the cows interesting. Cows are a lot like people. The new ones acted standoffish for a few days, staying by themselves. Then one of them decided *she* wanted to boss the herd, but little Pearlie, quick with her sharp horns and taking no back talk from any of them, soon showed her who was boss of *that* herd. Big, good-natured old Red didn't give a snap what the others did, so long as they left her alone; and the rest, except for a two-year-old heifer, soon found their proper places in the herd.

That heifer, contrary and mean from the first, gave me plenty of trouble. When I'd round up the herd to start home in the evening, she would dodge around me and cut back to the field; and several times, when I ran to head her off, she turned on me and shook her sharp, forward-pointing horns in my face. She had me worried, but I didn't want to say anything to Poppie. Now that I was his boy, I couldn't let him know I was afraid, but I did take to carrying a long, stout stick.

When the cornstalks were gone, Poppie had me take the herd to the strawstack in the middle of the wheat field. There the cows ate steadily into its south side, out of the wind, and needed very little herding. It was then that the days began to seem unbearably long and lonesome. It was colder, and I followed the sun around the stack, burrowing little nests into the straw to sit in and wishing I had Florry to talk to, or something to do with my hands. I thought about Grandma McCance and how, if she sat down for a minute to rest her back or her feet, she always picked up some darning, knitting, or sewing. But I didn't have a thing to do.

One evening, after the longest, lonesomest day yet, I watched Mama setting tiny, quick stitches into the diamond-shaped calico scraps she was sewing into a Lone Star quilt top. And right then I knew what *I* wanted to do. I asked her for some pieces to sew while I sat in the strawstack all day, but she said I was too young to do a good job. I *knew* I wasn't, and I just *had* to have those pieces. I begged hard and promised to be ever so careful, and she finally said I could try a little Four Patch. "But you'll have to do neat work and fasten the ends of your thread good," she said, "for I can't afford to waste thread and pieces on you if you don't."

She cut the little squares and showed me how to put them together in the pattern. After that, when the sun had warmed the air enough that I could take my mittens off, I sat in my straw nests and sewed on the little quilt, making my stitches small and neat so Mama would let me have more pieces. Young as I was, I knew that Mama's needlework, even her patching, was extra fine, and that it wouldn't be easy to learn to sew as well as she did. But it was during those days in the big strawstack, when I worked so hard to keep my stitches even and the block corners matched, that I began to dream of the time when I could make quilts even finer than Mama's, finer than any others in the world.

By the end of November the cows had eaten their way far into the stack, gouging out a good-sized cave, and when it was time to take them home at sundown they never wanted to leave it. I'd go into the cave, whacking their rumps with my stick, but by the time I could get the last ones headed out, the first ones would be coming back around the stack and crowding into the hole again. One cold evening they were more stubborn than usual, and no matter how much I ran and yelled and whacked, they outran me and dodged back into the cave. Finally, I pushed past them into the hole and began pounding on their heads with my stick. The older cows gave up and backed out together, leaving me suddenly face to face with the long-nosed, ornery heifer.

She saw she had me cornered and came straight at me, her eyes glittering in the dusk. I flattened myself against the wall of the cave and flailed away at her with my stick, but there was neither time nor room to hit her hard enough to stop her. Twisting her head sideways, she raked me from hip to armpit with a thin, sharp horn, then whirled and ran after the rest of the herd.

The heifer's horn had gouged deep enough to draw blood along the whole length of the stinging scratch, and Mama was upset when I showed her. That evening she told Poppie what had happened, and that he'd better do something about that heifer. He said he'd keep her in the corral until he had time to take her to town and sell her to the butcher. It was a big relief to me to know she wouldn't be in the herd any more.

A few days later Mama told us we could start wearing our last year's calicoes for everyday, now that the barrels had come and she had made up our new dresses. I was sorry to take mine for everyday, for I still thought it the prettiest calico I had ever had, but Mama said I wouldn't be able to get into it by spring anyway, the way I was growing. So I put it on, picked up my milk pail, and went to the stable to help Poppie with the milking, a chore I'd been doing ever since I had turned six in the spring.

Red and Pearlie were waiting by their feed boxes, just inside the corral. Down in the bottom of the canyon, the heifer was prowling along the lower side of the corral fence. Poppie came out of the stable and emptied a little can of grain into Pearlie's box. He told me to go ahead with my cow, and went back into the stable. I sat down to Pearlie and poked my head into her flank and started milking. A minute later I heard the heifer snort. I snapped around to look, and there she was, head down and coming straight for me on the run. Just in time, I ducked under Pearlie and rolled under the barbed-wire fence. The sound of ripping cloth was loud in my ears.

When Mama said there wasn't enough left of my pretty black and green dress to patch together, I cried harder

than I had over the hooking the heifer gave me. The
cut would heal, but my dress was gone forever. Later
that day Poppie put a rope on the heifer and led her off
to town behind the wagon.

It snowed that night, and the next morning Poppie
told me I wouldn't have to herd any more for a while,
that he'd keep the cattle in the corral and feed them
hay while the snow lay on. That afternoon Mr. Totten
came over to tell us that a turkey hen and a dozen
nearly grown young turkeys had shown up at his barn
that morning, and he figured they might be ours. Mama
asked him if the hen was almost white, and he said she was.

"Well, for goodness sake! I never thought we'd see
that hen again," Mama said. "She must've turned her
first brood over to the gobbler and hid another nest out.
It's a wonder the coyotes didn't get her, and all the young
ones too, but I'm surely glad to have her back."

A little over a month later the blizzard of January 12,
1888, roared down on us, just a little after noon on a
warm, hazy day. And from then on, storm after storm
packed snow into the pockets and heads of canyons and
piled it in high drifts on the rims above. By the first
of March the country was buried under such a depth of
snow that it didn't seem possible it could melt in time
to uncover the ground for spring planting. Then early
one morning a freshening breeze began to blow, and by
noon it was a chilly wind, sweeping hard and steady
across the softening drifts. It was unbelievable, Poppie
said, the way the big snowbanks shrank under the cold
wind, a true prairie chinook.

All afternoon the melt trickled to the low places,
making soft chuckling sounds. By dark the chuckles had
grown to a roar, the roar of tons of water rushing to
the canyon bottoms. Poppie said it sounded good to him,

that in a few more hours the snow would be all gone and the lagoons filled to the brim.

But it didn't sound good to me. I lay awake for a long time that night, listening to the sad sound of the wind at the eaves and to the ugly roar of the water. Even in my sleep, the sounds of wind and water seemed to fill the soddy.

By morning the wind had died and the water's roar had dwindled to a hoarse whisper. The prairie was brown and wet in the cool sunlight and only the ragged, dirty edges of some of the biggest drifts still showed in the deepest pockets. We heard later that the snow, melting too fast for the frozen ground to soak it up, had sent such a torrent of runoff water through the canyons to old Stump Ditch, three miles east of us, that the big ditch had been out of its banks for hours, all the way to the river.

March winds blew for days on end after the chinook, sapping the fields and prairie, and spring rains held off so long that finally only the big lagoon on the railroad section still held any water. With the prairie so brown and dry, the prairie fire that swooped out of the northwest one late March morning found little except the settlers' narrow fireguards to hinder it.

Poppie had started for the stable with his milk pail when he saw the smoke billow climbing the sky above the far hills. He called to me to come arunning and help with the chores, that a prairie fire was coming our way and he must help fight it. He headed into the wind a little after sunup, with a barrel of water and some old gunnysacks in the back of his wagon.

Mama and Florry and I kept an anxious lookout all forenoon. By noon the air was heavy with smoke and we could no longer see the sun through the haze. Up till then I had thought that drowning in cold, black water would be the worst way to die. Now I wondered if roasting alive in a prairie fire wouldn't be just as bad.

I asked Mama what we'd do if the fire came down our ridge. She said if the fireguard didn't stop it we'd have to take the stock and go to the middle of the big field, where there was nothing to burn. That sounded better, but just after that the wind suddenly died and the smoke began to thin. In a little while we could see the sun again. Mama said they must have whipped the fire out, and that Poppie ought to be coming any time now.

And then the wind came up again and blew harder than ever. The smoke closed in once more, and half an hour later the fire boiled over the top of the big hill northwest of us. We watched it licking through the tall grass at the head of the long pocket, the red flames leaping up and belching puffs of raw yellow smoke as they reached for Poppie's fireguard, halfway down the slope. In the corral the cattle began to bawl and mill, and I asked Mama if I hadn't better run and turn them out and start for the field. But she said not yet, that the fireguard might stop it. We'd wait and see.

The gray scar of the plowed strip looked awfully narrow in the face of that running fire. We watched it growling toward the strip, and then Mama said, in a steady voice, that the minute the fire jumped the guard Florry and I must run fast and turn the cattle out and head them for the field.

But fire burns slower downhill than up, and when it reached the furrows its drive was checked. And then we saw a new danger. The hard winds had piled old, dry tumbleweeds in the tall weeds along the edge of the fireguard and now, as the blaze quartered east along the strip, they caught fire and leaped up like something alive.

"The first one that lands on this side, you girls run for the corral," Mama said. But, one by one, the weeds dissolved in puffs of smoke before they could quite reach the dry grass on our side, and at the northeast corner of our place Pete Anderson's fireguard took over. We watched while the blaze moved out of sight beyond the swell of the prairie, and a little later Poppie pulled in, his clothes and face and hair black with smoke. They had whipped the main fire, he said, and settlers to the south would soon stop the stray headfire that had threatened us.

April 7, Mama's birthday, came on Sunday that year, and at breakfast she suggested we get ready and drive over to Yoders. It was young Charlie Yoder's birthday, too, she reminded us.

Poppie looked shocked. Not since we'd been in Nebraska had Mama been the first to suggest we go avisiting. Poppie loved to visit the neighbors, but when he'd ask Mama to go she usually said she'd rather not, that by the time she got all of us girls ready and then jolted over the hills in a lumber wagon, she was too worn out to visit when she got there. But Florry and I were even *more* shocked when Poppie said he didn't believe we'd better, that he'd been working the horses pretty hard and he kind of hated to drive them so far on the only day they had to rest. Mama sniffed and said she didn't think he'd been working them *that* hard. Poppie said, well, he'd see, and went on out.

Florry and I, hoping for the best, flew around doing up our chores. Mama washed and dressed the baby and put the rest of us through a tub of hot water back of the kitchen stove. In our best petticoats, we took turns at the bureau where she combed and braided our hair. When she finished, she told us to get dressed and pick up the dirty clothes and carry out the tub of water. Then she went to the window and looked out toward the stable. She said something about Poppie being so slow getting around this morning, but that maybe he'd show up by the time she was ready. Then she unpinned her black hair and bent over, brushing the long, heavy mass down in front of her face and combing it with quick strokes.

Florry and I were almost finished dressing when we heard a wagon rattling into the yard. Mama straightened up and looked out the window again. "Merciful heavens," she said, "there's Yoders, the whole family, and look at this house."

We looked at the house—at the tub of cold bath water behind the stove, at our dirty clothes sagging from the bed and chairs, at the litter of cob dust around the stove, left from firing up to heat the bath water.

"Poppie and his surprises!" Mama muttered, sweeping her hair into its usual neat coil on the back of her head and jabbing it fast with her pins. She scooped up an armful of dirty clothes, and Florry and I grabbed the tub handles and started through the door, dodging Poppie and Yoders and the birthday dinner they'd brought, all cooked and ready to eat.

Pretty black-eyed Florence told us that day that she was going to teach a three-months' term of school at Maline schoolhouse, beginning the next Tuesday, and she hoped Florry and I could come. Poppie said we should be in school all right, but a three-mile walk across the hills was pretty long for a six- and an eight-year-old and he didn't know if we could keep it up or not.

But to Florry and me the long walks through the dewy

mornings and sunny afternoons were pure pleasure. We loved the cheery whistling meadowlarks, swinging on dried soapweed stalks along the way, and the tiny, glistening white lilies and furry, three-pronged "pot legs" we found blooming in sheltered swales. We watched scared little striped ground squirrels whisking through the grass to hidden burrows. We caught tiny, bright-eyed sand lizards and carried them along in our cupped hands, liking the feel of their dainty, clinging toes and wondering at the changing colors running along their panting sides.

Just before we reached the schoolhouse we had to cross old Stump Ditch, bone dry except after heavy rains and big thaws. In a dog town on our side of the ditch, sassy prairie dogs bounced and chittered at us before diving headfirst into their holes, their short tails flipping like semaphores gone crazy. One cool morning we came onto a whopping big bull snake just sliding into a hole in the dog town. We grabbed his rear half and pulled, but he had such a purchase on the sides of the hole that our hands kept slipping on his smooth skin. About to lose him, we tried wrapping our hands in the skirts of the long capes we wore. It was easy, then, to yank him out on the prairie, where we "stomped" him to death. But when we told Poppie about it, he scolded us. Bull snakes lived on mice, ground squirrels, and other crop-eating rodents, he said, and were worth cash money to farmers.

In early May, Poppie told me I'd have to stay out of school and herd cattle while he got at his fieldwork. Before I took the herd out Mama had a little talk with me. The cows would be finding little calves any day now, she said, and I'd have to watch close and keep the herd together. I wasn't to let a single cow out of my sight, and if one started to stray I was to head her right back to the herd, otherwise she would hide out and the coyotes might get the new calf. I asked where they would find the little calves, and she said it would most likely be in the tall grass at the heads of the draws.

As soon as I took the cows out, they began to scatter all over the flat. They were only hunting the short spears of new green grass, but I thought they were hunting little calves. Every time one headed toward a pocket I ran like everything to get ahead of her and search through the tall dead grass. I wanted so much to find the little calf first but, though I ran myself to a frazzle those warm spring days, I never found a single baby calf.

Chapter Five

By THE spring of 1888 Poppie had more cornland than he could plant by hand, and more cattle than he could haul water for, after the lagoons went dry. A horse-drawn corn planter and a well would take care of his needs. But a drilled well, quickest put down and easiest to use, would cost a lot more than a dug well, and if he hired a well driller he couldn't afford a corn planter. The only way out was to dig the well and buy the planter.

The planter, which came first, was a wonder. It planted two rows at a time and had two seats on it, a high one over the wheels for Poppie, a little one down in front by the planting lever for me. Poppie tied a rag to a spoke in the right wheel, and every time it came to the top I pulled the lever that made the machine plant two hills of corn.

In the mornings it was fine. Nothing to do but ride back and forth across the field and pull the lever at the right time. Later, when the sun rode high and hot in the empty sky and the dust boiled up around us, the rag, turning steadily on the wheel, swam in front of my eyes. Then I rested my aching neck by turning my head the other way, and pulling the lever every time Peg lifted her right hind foot. And so, between the rag on one side and Peg's right hind foot on the other, I pulled the lever the thousands of times it took to plant the fields.

Poppie started digging the well as soon as the corn
was in.

In the high plains country it was a long way to water
and wells had always been the big problem. But any
way you looked at it, a man couldn't get ahead on these
dryland farms until he had his own well, Poppie said. A
man over on West Table had had to put an iron-cased
well down 444 feet before he struck water. It had cost
him over six hundred dollars and he had to mortgage
his place to pay for it, but it had paid off in the long
run. Dug wells didn't cost nearly so much money, but
they were dangerous and took a long time to dig.

Poppie said he could save a hundred feet of digging
and curbing by putting our well in the canyon below
the house, only then we'd have to carry water up the
steep hill. But Mama said that just having a well on the
place, after three years of hauling water and never having
enough to take more than a spit bath in, would seem
heavenly.

So Poppie put the well in the bottom of the canyon,
and dug himself below ground the first day. Then he
rigged a windlass above the hole and swung a pair of
big wooden buckets from the pulley—and from then on
until the well was done we worried about him. The
shaft might cave in on him, or a rope might break and
let a loaded bucket fall on him. There had been accidents
like that, and settlers still talked about how Sam Abernathy and Jim Cummings had met *their* everlasting in
Custer County wells a few years before.

Mr. Abernathy had been killed when he tried to slide
down the rope in his deep well to loosen the bucket that
had caught under the curbing at the bottom. He had
lost his hold, some way, and had fallen all the way down

onto the iron-bound rim of the bucket. But Mr. Cummings had had it even worse.

Astraddle a stick tied to the end of his well rope, he had gone down into the well to test for weak spots in the wooden curbing. He was within ten feet of the bottom of the two-hundred-foot hole when it caved in on him. His wife, backing the team hitched to the rope that let him down, had tried to pull him out. But the team couldn't even move against the weight of earth above her husband.

She had gone for help then, and all the neighbors for miles around had come. It seemed that twenty feet of the shaft had caved in, and he couldn't be dug out until the caved section was repaired. So, while some of the men drove to town after lumber for new curbing, the rest shoveled dirt into the well to fill the big hole above the cave-in.

The unbelievable part was that Mr. Cummings was still alive, and conscious, when they uncovered his head, *more than twenty hours after the well caved in on him!* His face had been pressed against a pipe that hung in the well to put a hand pump on, and a little air must have seeped down around it. They had hopes of saving him then, until they dug a little farther and found his legs were caught under the edge of the old curbing. They had to stop then, for fear the well would cave again and bury them all. The only thing left to do was to tie a rope around him and try to pull him out. It took twenty-five men, pulling on the rope, to get him loose, and they almost pulled him in two doing it.

The well had caved at eight o'clock on a Saturday morning. At two o'clock on Sunday afternoon they carried him to his house and laid him on his bed, where he died four days later.

When Poppie had help, Joe Byler or one of the nearer neighbors, one man stayed in the well to fill the buckets and the other hauled them up and emptied them. But when he worked alone he had to go down in the well and fill the buckets, and then climb up again to empty them. And he had to saw and fit a wooden curbing for the shaft as it went down. When he had dug himself so far down that it was dark in the bottom of the pit, he rigged a set of mirrors at the top to reflect light into the hole and went on digging.

A lot of things kept Poppie from working steady on the well. He had to stop to plant a patch of sorghum, and then to cultivate his other crops, and he could almost have dug the whole well in the time he had to spend hauling water from Tottens. And of course he never worked at it on Sundays. Grandma had brought her family up to too strict an observance of the Lord's Day for that.

Then there was another setback when a fierce wind struck one sultry night in July, howling and tearing at the house and waking us all. Poppie jumped out of bed and ran to shut the south window and the kitchen door. He was barely back to the bedroom when the darkness, black and thick as velvet, was ripped apart by a terrible blue flash of lightning. Then there was a cracking, tearing sound, and the soddy seemed to quiver.

Poppie lit the lamp on the bureau and opened the door to look into the kitchen. A blast of wind and rain set the flame in the lamp to dancing, and he shoved the door shut and put his back against it. "It was the roof," he said, "it's clean gone."

Poppie and Mama both went into the kitchen to try to take care of things, but they stumbled back to the bedroom a few minutes later, breathless and sopping wet.

It was no use, Poppie said, they couldn't do a thing, the way stuff was whirling around in there, but we'd be all right if the bedroom roof didn't go too. It didn't, and after a while the storm died away.

The kitchen was a sorry-looking mess when daylight came. Every last thing had blown off the walls, and all Mama's little shelves, brackets, whatnots, and pictures were either smashed to bits or gone entirely. A mixture of calendars, clothes, and window curtains was pasted to the floor and covered with mud. There didn't seem to be any place to start picking things up and putting them together again; even scrounging enough undamaged food out of the mess for breakfast, or finding enough dry fuel to cook it with, seemed a hopeless undertaking.

Mama went around in a kind of a daze, picking some of her torn and broken things out of the hash on the floor and sweeping out the worst of the mud. The hot sun was pouring down on our heads when Poppie, hard put to it to keep a cheerful expression on his face, offered thanks for the cornmeal mush and fried eggs we finally sat down to.

But the lagoons were full again, and Poppie wouldn't have to haul so much water for a while. Florry and I helped Mama carry water to scrub up and to wash the muddied clothes and curtains. When that was done, we walked with her over the prairie, picking up any of our belongings we could find. Under a clump of tall grass on the railroad section we found half of the marriage certificate, but no part of the frame or glass. Just that half, ripped from the rest, its doves and cupids hardly stained by the mud and rain.

Poppie spent the day hunting for the roofing boards that had blown away, but he found only a few, and most of them were cracked and splintered. So he had to leave the well to haul new lumber and tar paper from town to reroof the kitchen. And shortly after he finished anchoring the new roof to the soddy, cousin Tim came to stay with us awhile. Cousin Tim didn't delay the work on the well much, but he certainly didn't help it any.

He wasn't really our cousin, but an orphan boy Grandma McCance had raised up with her own big family. He had just finished a term at college, he told us, and thought he'd like to come out and see what the West was like. A slight, dark young fellow, he wore his best clothes for everyday and had no use for "dirty work." Most of the time he sat in our bedroom-front room and read his books. He dusted off his shirt sleeves and trouser legs if any of us girls, in our everyday clothes, brushed against him, and he made a great show of his book learning and fine manners. But Mama and I found it a strain to treat him as "company" after the day he spit tobacco juice across my bare feet. He also complained of "stomach trouble," claiming that light bread didn't agree with him and that he really should eat hot soda biscuits instead.

Mama made her own yeast, by boiling cornmeal and hop leaves to a thick mush and drying it in hard cakes, out of doors under cheesecloth in summer, in the oven in winter. The smell of the cooking hops always made me sick at my stomach and I dreaded my turn at stirring the long-simmering mash, but with the yeast Mama made big batches of featherlight, crusty bread. But now, to please cousin Tim, she began baking hot buscuits two and three times a day. She had more than enough hard work to fill her days as it was, so I don't know why she bothered—unless it was to keep him from writing the folks in Missouri that she didn't set a decent table. Mama's pride couldn't have stood that.

In August Poppie had to leave his well digging to cut

and shock his wheat, and by then the summer heat was bearing down unmercifully on the prairie. If it hadn't been for our visitor's tender stomach, Mama could have done most of her cooking with a small, "cool" fire. As it was the stove hardly had time to cool off after baking the dinner biscuits before she had to fire it up again for the supper batch. And by then the kitchen was so unbearably hot that we had to set the table in the yard, just outside the door, where a cooling breeze blew across the canyon as the sun went down.

The flies nearly drove Mama crazy but, since we had no screens anyway, they were little worse outside than in. In any case, it was my job to keep them off the table with a "fly-chaser" made of newspaper fringe sewed to a long stick. By waving the fluttering streamers over the table I could keep it reasonably clear of flies while we all sat down and Poppie asked the blessing. After that, everybody fended for himself.

To Florry and me, eating outside was like a picnic every day. While the slow dusk settled on the prairie we lingered at the table; until Poppie, mindful of chores still to be done, pushed himself up and went to bring the mules, Peg and Lee, to water at the old tub at the corner of the house by the water barrels.

Peg was the mule colt we had brought from Missouri. Lee was her brother, born to old Kit the next spring after we came to the homestead, and we never could understand what made them so different. When she finished drinking, Peg, always friendly and sociable, would hurry to the table to beg for scraps. She ate everything we offered her, even the bacon rinds she detested. Those she always gulped down in a hurry, then stuck her bony old head up high in the air and wiggled her ears and curled her long upper lip in a horrible leer of disgust.

But Lee, never kind or friendly toward anyone or anything, would neither taste nor smell any scrap we ever offered him.

It was about this time that I ran a rusty nail in my foot and had to turn the herding over to Florry until I could walk on both feet again. Poppie went after water, that first afternoon I stayed at the house, and I wanted to go along. But Mama said no, and put me to pounding broken dishes and old buffalo bones into "grit" for the chickens, a job I could do sitting down.

The foot-long section of old railroad rail we kept by the chicken house for the purpose lay in the full glare of the hot sun, but it was too heavy for me to move so I squatted down beside it and went to work. The chickens came clucking around me, snatching at the china slivers that slid off the iron as I hammered on pieces of old dishes. The bones were harder to do and I always put them off to the last, hoping I'd run out of time before I got to them.

After a while Tim came outside, carrying his book and a chair. The house where Mama worked must be getting too hot for *him*, I thought, watching him settle down comfortably in the shade of the east wall and tip his chair back against the house. I picked up a bone, laid it on the iron and hit it a whack. It flattened but did not break.

Beyond the chicken house where I worked, the yard sloped gently to the edge of the canyon, fell off steeply to a second bench, then slanted on down to the canyon floor. In the bank above the bench Poppie had built a little dugout shed, roofed with brush, straw, and sod, for the milk cows. I was still whamming away at the bone when Pearlie's yearling heifer wandered down the slope and onto the dugout roof. I had seen the cows on the shed roof before, and I thought nothing of it now—until the roof, probably weakened by the big rain the month before, suddenly went down with the heifer.

I yelled for Mama and then hobbled to the shed, where the bawling heifer was scrambling out of the brush and dirt. She was panting and scared, but unhurt as far as we could see. Mama was relieved; she counted on this calf of Pearlie's making us another good milk cow. Just then Tim came sauntering down to see what the racket was all about. He walked all around the heifer, gave her a delicate thump or two, then dusted off his hands and said he wouldn't be surprised if she was "injured internally."

As soon as Poppie got back we took him to see the yearling. She was dozing in the shade of the stable, and Mama said she couldn't see that she looked or acted any different than usual. But Tim was sure she was beginning to bloat, "a positive sign of internal injury." If she was butchered right away, before she bloated any more, she wouldn't be a total loss, he suggested.

Because he'd had so little schooling himself, on account of his father dying so early, Poppie had a great respect for education, the kind that came out of books, and the older he grew the more he seemed to respect it. Since Tim had had the benefit of higher education and talked like a learned man, Poppie was inclined to give weight to his ranting about internal injuries and overstrained intestines. By dark he had butchered the heifer.

We put the meat in the cool, dark cellar, away from the flies. In spite of the heat, it kept in good condition until we could use it all. Mama, however, never did believe the heifer had really been hurt, but only that cousin Tim wanted some fresh beef to go with his hot biscuits.

Early in September, Poppie struck water at a depth of 150 feet. He fitted a set of trapdoors, hinged at the sides and opening in the middle, over the well and hung a tall wooden bucket from the windlass pulley. The bucket filled through a valve in its bottom as it settled into the water. When it swung clear of the water on its upward trip, the valve closed and the bucket, coming against the trap doors, lifted them open. Old Peg, hitched to the well rope, furnished the power that lifted the big bucket. Poppie had me lead her out across the canyon until the bucket cleared the trapdoors, and then back her up to let it down into the well again. But after the first few trips, the smart, willing old mule learned to do the job all by herself. When she heard the doors bang shut beneath the bucket, she'd wiggle her long ears and back up a step or two, letting the bucket down on the doors so Poppie could empty it into the tank for the stock, or into the barrel for the house. Then she'd back up until the rope slacked, and wait for Poppie to tell her to "get up" again. Old Peg was the first automatic power we ever owned.

The well was a great time-saver for Poppie, but because of the long, steep climb up the hill with heavy water buckets, we still had to be careful with water at the house.

Chapter Six

COUSIN TIM hired out to teach the three-months' fall term at the Maline school, and Poppie said he'd furnish transportation to the schoolhouse if he'd take Florry and me along. The transportation was old Peg and a two-wheeled cart.

School started early in October and the weather stayed fine until near the end of the month. Then there came a cold, frosty morning that sent old Peg trotting down the road like a two-year-old. Tim pulled her up sharply at the edge of old Stump Ditch, where the road went down at a sharp angle, made a short turn to the left at the bottom, then climbed steeply to the rim on the far side.

Peg took the down trail at a walk, her usual pace, but at the bottom she suddenly broke loose in all directions, kicked up her heels, bucked around the short turn and upset the cart. I had a glimpse of spinning arms and legs, of dinner pails going one way, lids another, and sandwiches flying every way. A wheel scraped hard on my shinbone, then Peg loped on up the far slope, dragging the uptipped cart. I sat up, howling with the pain of my skinned shin. Florry's nose was bleeding a bright stream, Cousin Tim, his good clothes full of dirt and "kuckle" burrs, was pulling his head out of the claybank.

He scooped up his cap, shook the clay out of it, and

lit into scolding me as if the upset had been all my fault. We brushed the burrs and clay out of our clothes and hair and cleaned off our sandwiches as best we could and stuffed them back into the dinner buckets. Then we climbed to the rim, set the cart right side up, and went on to school.

At supper that evening Poppie said the cane was ready to strip and cut. The cold snap that had put too much zip into old Peg that morning had sweetened the sap just right.

When a Mr. Hodson built a sorghum mill down on the river valley the fall before, Poppie had decided to raise his own sorghum if he could. The strip of cane he planted in the spring had made a fine growth, but whether or not we were to have sorghum from it depended on the fall weather—a cold snap at the right time turned the sap sweet and good, a too-early freeze ruined it entirely.

Poppie went to the cane field the next morning, a stripper (a sharpened length of lath) in each hand. He went up and down the rows, striking at the cane stalks with hard, down-slicing blows that stripped them of most of their leaves. Then he went over the field with a corn knife, cutting the tall cane for Florry and me to gather into bundles to be hauled to the mill.

To us, the sorghum Mr. Hodson pressed from our own cane had a sweeter, richer flavor than that that had come up from Missouri in the barrels of other years. The first time Poppie spooned the thick, dark sweetening onto his pancakes, he said it seemed like *anything* would grow in this country, and that he planned to put out an orchard as soon as he could get to it. "I've been reading about a Jules Sandoz, up in the northwest part of the state, who raises all kinds of fruit on his place," he said, "and if he can do it there, we can do it here."

Just after that, our whole community was turned upside down by the senseless murder of Hiram Roten and Bill Ashley. The Ashley and Roten families lived about half a mile apart in Roten Valley, only a few miles from us, and Poppie knew them well.

On the morning of November 9, Mr. Roten had hitched his team to his wagon. He told his wife he was going over to see Bill Ashley, and that they might go on to Cozad. He drove away, and she never saw him alive again. When he didn't come home that night she began to worry. The next morning she took her three little girls and her baby boy and walked over to Ashleys. Mrs. Ashley hadn't seen the men either, since they drove away the morning before, and she was worried, too. They spread the alarm then, and before the day was much older most of the neighbors were out looking for the missing men.

Poppie was with a posse that stopped at the Al Haunstine place that day, a mile or so from the Ashley homestead, to tell Al the news and get him to go along and help in the hunt. But there was no one at home there, and the stove was cold.

The mystery deepened fast. The two men hadn't been to town, or to any of the neighbors. No one for miles around had seen them, or the team and wagon, since they drove out of Ashley's yard.

There had been bad times in Custer County, back in the seventies when the big cattlemen had tried to keep the first farmer-settlers out. The violence had reached its peak when some of the ranchmen hung and burned two of the settlers; but that old trouble had been settled years ago and the hills had been peaceful for a long time. So no one knew what to make of the disappearance of

Mr. Ashley and Mr. Roten; for neither of them had had any serious trouble with anyone in the community, so far as anyone knew.

For three days the posses rode, and then some tired men on their way home heard horses whinnying in an old abandoned sod house about three miles from the Roten place.

They found Hiram Roten's team, frenzied with thirst, tied inside.

The next morning some of the men went back to Haunstine's place. Al and his wife were still away, but the bodies of the missing men were there—Haunstine's hungry hogs had rooted them out of a strawstack near the stable—and both had been shot in the back.

Al Haunstine, a member of a highly respected Custer County family, had a nice wife and had never been in trouble before, so far as his neighbors knew. People just couldn't believe that he could have murdered anybody, but a day or two later the Custer County sheriff took him off an eastbound train, down near the eastern edge of the state, and brought him back to the Custer County jail in Broken Bow, charged with the double murder.

In his confession Haunstine said he had had an argument over some school matters with Ashley and Roten, who were both on the school board in their district. And for such a small thing he had killed in cold blood, and left two young families fatherless. He had then taken the team to the empty sod house, he said, and hitched his own team to the wagon, which he and his wife had driven away. In a town near Omaha he had sold the team and wagon, after which he sent his wife to her folks and boarded the eastbound train himself.

The whole thing was especially hard on our family because Joe Byler's pretty wife Ida was a close relative of the murderer. We all loved Ida Byler, and she and Mama had been fast friends since the day Joe first brought her to see us, nearly three years before, so we all suffered with her and Joe through the long, bad time that followed the crime.

For Al Haunstine's hanging, the first and only execution ever held in Custer County, was turned into a shameful exhibition. We didn't go, of course, but hundreds did, as if it was a circus. The sheriff tried to keep the affair as decent as possible by having a high board wall built around the gallows. But as soon as the condemned man was taken onto the scaffold, someone gave a signal and the crowd swarmed in and tore down the fence.

The execution date had been postponed several times, and feeling had seemed to run higher and higher with each postponement, until it began to be said that the murderer should hang twice because he had killed twice. To make sure of it, someone partly cut the rope. When it broke the first time the trap was sprung, Haunstine had to be taken up and dropped through a second time —but that was more than two years after the murders.

At the double funeral, held in the Roten house the day after the bodies were found, the neighbors set the next Saturday to shuck out the Roten and Ashley cornfields.

The sun was just coming up, the morning of the big shucking bee, when Poppie turned our team into the road to Roten's place. To Florry, Stell, and me, bouncing along in the back of the wagon below the swaying bangboard, the day was a grand and unexpected picnic. Two or three wagons were already in the field when we pulled up in front of the house, in plain sight of the two fresh graves on the hillside beyond. Other wagons were coming

from every direction, their high bangboards looking like
sails scooting across the prairie. Poppie hustled us out
of the wagon and pulled across the road into the field.
Mama herded us into the house, each of us carrying
dressed hens, pies, or fresh bread, her contribution to
the community dinner. Women and children kept coming, until the walls of Mrs. Roten's two-room soddy
fairly bulged.

A little before noon, while Maggie Roten and I were
playing just outside the door, Mama and Mrs. Roten
stepped out of the steaming kitchen for a breath of fresh
air. Out in the field the ears of corn beat steady tattoos
against the bangboards; across the yard Joe Byler was
pulling up to the crib with a load of corn.

"Why, it's good of Joe to come and help," Mrs. Roten
said. "Most men in his place wouldn't have."

"Joe always does what's right," Mama said.

The men came in to eat in relays, one tableful after
another, but Joe was not among them. Mrs. Roten asked
where he was, and one of the men said he guessed Joe
had brought his own lunch along. The widow then went
out, crossed the road to Joe's lonely wagon, and asked
him to come in and eat with the other men. But Joe
thanked her and said he'd better not, that he only wanted
to help out what he could.

At home that evening, Mama told Poppie that some
of the women had told her how they'd made money the
year before by dressing out their turkeys and shipping
them to Omaha. She said she thought we ought to try
it too, provided the weather turned cold enough to keep
the carcasses from spoiling.

Florry and I had been dreading the day when we'd
have to give up Nip and Tuck, the two nearly black
turkeys Mama had given us for pets in the spring. We

had already tried to persuade her to let us keep them over for next year, but she had said no, that black turkeys were the poorest market variety because they were hard to pick and didn't look pretty when dressed, and that they would only produce more like themselves if we kept them. So Mama's plan upset us like everything —it would be bad enough to see our pets hauled off alive to Cozad, but it would be unbearable to see them go, naked and dead, on the long trip to Omaha.

The weather did turn cold, and one December night Florry and I had to help catch and pen the turkeys for the next day's slaughter. While they dressed my pet, the pretty gobbler Tuck, I sat out behind the house and bawled.

Poppie hauled the barrels to Cozad and shipped them off to Omaha, and Mama seemed well pleased with the size of the check that came back the next week. At Tottens, Christmas Day, three lovely wool toboggans (hoods), bought with the extra turkey money, came off the tree for Florry, Stell, and me. Florry, lady that she was, appreciated hers, and Stell had loved pretty things from the time she could toddle; but I would rather have had Tuck, alive and strutting.

Chapter Seven

GRANDMA McCANCE moved out from Missouri in March, to the farm Poppie had rented for her near our place. She brought quite a family with her, Uncle John and the two youngest girls, Aunt Bell and Aunt Hester, and her sister, Aunt Dicy Garner.

Grandma was only fifty-eight, but she seemed as old then as when I last saw her, years later, and she had probably looked old for a good many years before I ever saw her. Early marriages, big families, and years of hard work turned most of the women I knew old long before middle age. Grandma, though often stern and cross with others, was always kind to me. She had no use for lazy or wasteful people, so I think she favored me because I liked to work.

"If there's one thing more'n another I simply can't abide, it's time on my hands," she used to say. Grandma's hands were thin and brown and spotted, their soft, paper-dry skin crisscrossed with high, dark veins, and the fingers twisted and knotty, but she would look at them with grim satisfaction—anyone could see she'd never had any time on *her* hands.

Uncle John, on the other hand, got a great deal of fun out of life. Big, jolly, and good-natured, he was always singing and joking, good times or bad. Long after he was gone from this world, his neighbor, Gus Matz, recalled a stinging zero morning when Uncle John had come to draw water from his well. Even with numb, blue fingers, while he struggled with the slippery, ice-crusted bucket, he was singing away at the top of his voice, Gus said. And I remember the morning he stopped at our place and hauled a big, fresh-killed coyote out of his wagon. "Oh, Maggie," he called to Mama, "come out here, I want to show you some condensed chicken."

Aunt Bell and Aunt Hester were young and slim and pretty, and we all loved them. We loved Aunt Dicy, too, although she was old and anything but pretty, having long ago lost all her teeth and most of her hair.

Somewhere back in the hard years after Grandpa died, Aunt Dicy had come to Grandma as a legacy from her own mother. On her deathbed, Great-Grandma Garner had asked Grandma to take Aunt Dicy home with her, and to take care of her as long as she lived.

Long before that, when Grandma herself was only two years old, the Garners had lived in a big house built over a tanning vat. The owner of the house was a poor crazy woman who wandered the place at night, and who, one midnight, had fallen into the tanning vat. Great-Grandma Garner, hearing her screaming and threshing around in the tanning fluid, had gone down and helped her out. Aunt Dicy, born very soon after that, had always been "queer," and everyone said she had been "marked" that night.

Whatever the cause, Aunt Dicy couldn't seem to keep out of water. When she saw a puddle, she'd look worried and begin to mutter, "Dicy mustn't get in the water, Dicy mustn't get in the water." Then she'd lift her skirts and paddle right through the middle of it, even if she had her good shoes on.

Aunt Dicy's full name was Lovisa Garner. She had

learned to spell it by syllables, the way spelling was taught one hundred years ago. Florry and I loved the way her nose and chin hopped up and down to meet over her toothless gums when she clipped off the sounds, like this: "L-o lo, v-i vi, s-a sa, Lovisa; G-a-r gar, n-e-r, ner, Garner; Lovisa Garner." We liked to hear her sing, too. The few songs she knew were sad and mournful, but it made her happy to have us ask her to sing them. Our favorite began this way:

> The ship went down in the howling storm,
> And the waves rolled o'er his lifeless form.
> La, la, loo. La, la, lay.

The song had a lot of verses, with this sorrowful chorus repeated over and over:

> A sailor boy and I, his bride,
> A-weeping by the ocean side.
> La, la, loo. La, la, lay.

As soon as Grandma was settled, Cousin Tim came to visit her. Florry and I couldn't see that he had improved any since he had stayed with us, and it made us furious to see the sly way he teased and tormented gentle, simple Aunt Dicy behind Grandma's back. But we didn't have to stew about it too long, for Tim soon decided he'd had enough of homesteading and went back to Missouri, leaving us to our ignorant, unlearned ways.

Poppie took him to town to catch the train; he had to go in that day anyway, after the new windmill and force pump he had ordered.

Poppie tried to put at least one major improvement on the place every year. The first year it had been the buildings and old Pearlie, the next it was the second room and old Red. The third year it was the range herd; last year it had been the corn planter and the well—and now the windmill. But when he got home that evening he had a strange thing to tell us about old Lee.

They had been jogging along on the valley, about half a mile from town, he said, when all at once Lee began to bray and pull to the side of the road. He went on jigging around and pulling sideways, and Poppie couldn't figure what ailed him—until he looked past the mule's swiveling ears and saw old Kit, grazing on a stake rope out on the flat. It had been more than two years since we had sold Kit, and Lee hadn't seen her in all that time; yet he knew his mother, and made such a fuss over seeing her again that we all felt a bit more kindly toward him —for a while.

Poppie set the mill and pump above the well, laid an underground pipe from the pump to a barrel on the canyon rim above, and so brought water almost to the soddy door. From then on, we didn't have to be so stingy with it, and Mama even planted a row of four-o'clocks beside the house, where we could water them handily.

That fall Mr. Wahl made arrangements with Poppie for me to herd his cattle with ours, first in his shucked-out cornfield and then in ours. It would be easier, he said, than for me to try to keep our cattle out of his stalks—but I think the main reason was that, with me looking after both herds, he wouldn't have to herd at all.

When I hazed our cattle into Wahl's cornfield, that first morning, I kept an anxious eye on Pearlie; for I knew there was apt to be trouble when the two herds met. The little cow had always been boss of our herd, but the boss cow in the Wahl herd was almost twice her size, and I didn't know how my pet would come out in the tussle that was bound to come. Several of the sub-bosses in the herds had some sharp skirmishes during the day, but Pearlie and the big cow kept to their own sides of the field, letting each other strictly alone.

But at sundown, while I was busy cutting my cows out of the herd, the big cow rushed Pearlie. Taken completely by surprise, she didn't have time to turn and fight, or even to get out of the way, and the big cow hit her hard, almost upsetting her, and raking a long strip of hair and hide from her side with a sharp horn.

I guess I felt worse about the cowardly big cow's mean trick than Pearlie did. I was so mad, and I felt so bad about the ugly blood-caked welt on Pearlie's side, that I walked home with my arm around her neck, bawling, and telling her I knew she could whip the big cow if she'd just be careful and keep on the lookout for her. And that's exactly what she did; for when the herds met the next morning Pearlie was ready for the big cow and did some hide-raking herself, enough to whip the other cow out and make her glad to keep to her own side of the herd. The "boss" business settled, the two herds quieted down and grazed peaceably together, except for an occasional minor set-to.

I had taken to riding Pearlie to and from the fields, and on warm days I sometimes dozed on her back while she grazed with the herd. I was asleep on her back, face down, one day when she took a sudden notion to hook another cow—and ran right out from under me to do it. I hit the ground headfirst, and so hard that I saw stars of all colors, but I didn't blame Pearlie. I was proud of her position as boss of the herd, and I knew she had to work at it to stay there.

No one was surprised when our new baby, born that November, was another girl; but she was the first of us to have blue eyes, like Mama's folks, and Mama said she was the prettiest baby she'd had yet. We named her Nellie M.

Florry's full name was Flora Alice, the "Alice" for Mama's oldest sister. Mine was Grace Bell, for Aunt Bell, and Poppie's favorite song, "Grace Darling." But when Stella was born Mama said she wasn't going to have any more of us named for close relatives—hand-me-down names, she called them. So Stella May and Florence Ethel were new names in our family, and so was Nellie. Poppie had wanted to add Margaret, but Mama objected; for that was *her* name, and Grandma McCance's too, so they compromised on Nellie M.

Our hired girl that time had freckles and long, heavy, bright-red hair. She was a good worker, though, and Mama meant to keep her a couple of weeks after she got up, but on her first day out of bed she discovered that all of us girls had *lice* in our hair. Mama knew where they came from; for Florry and I had been sleeping with the hired girl in the kitchen bed, and she made things fly then.

First, she told the girl she wouldn't need her any longer. Then she went out and told Poppie to get her off the place as fast as he could. They were hardly out of sight before she was whacking off our braids, close up to our heads. Then, with a pan of kerosene and a fine-toothed comb, she went to work on us in earnest.

To me, the lice were an unexpected blessing. I had always begrudged every minute that it took to comb and plait my long, heavy braids, and I loved the feel of my new, short, "boy" haircut. But I was glad Mama didn't cut her own hair. She had beautiful hair, black as a crow's wing, and so long and heavy that it hung to her knees in shining, rippling waves when she let it down. She wore it puffed out a little around her thin face, and coiled it in a big knot on the back of her head. I always thought it was her prettiest feature.

She played it safe though, and gave her own head several kerosene treatments. The smell that haloed us all for a while was pretty rank.

Chapter Eight

POPPIE proved up on the homestead, that fall of 1889, and sold it and bought an unimproved quarter section in Roten Valley, just across Stump Ditch from the schoolhouse. A Mr. Ericson, recently come from Sweden, made a cash payment on the homestead and took over the mortgage.

We wanted to move as early in the spring as possible, so, as soon as the ground thawed out, Poppie built a sod house and stable, a small frame chicken house, and a new wire corral on the new place. Early in April he hired the first well men he could get hold of, a Mr. Foster and his two sons, to put down a bored well.

The three Fosters, all tall men, stayed with us on the homestead while they worked on the well. They had to sleep in the kitchen bed, and Frank, only a trifle shorter than his father, said he didn't ever get to use much of it. John, tallest of the three, slept cornerwise in the middle of the bed, Frank said, and their father took the next roomiest section on the front side, leaving only the little corner on the back side for him.

Poor Frank had to put up with the little corner for quite a while, for they had a bad time with the new well. Poppie had planned to put it halfway between the house and the stable but, after a week's work, that spot turned out to be no good. They tried another place, which was no good either, and the well they finally finished was close by the kitchen door—but a long way from the stable.

Because of the trouble with the well, we were still living on the homestead when I went to bed on the night of April 22, hoping, as I had hoped on every April 22 since we had been in Nebraska, that the next day—my birthday—would be warm and sunny. If it was, Mama would let us go barefoot, although she seldom thought the ground warm enough for that until after the first of May. But once in a long while, if the season was early, April 23 turned out to be *the* day; and I knew, as soon as I woke up on my eighth birthday, that it was one of the good days.

The first day of going barefoot was almost as good as Christmas, or the Fourth of July. There is almost no describing it; the good feeling to tender, bare soles of cushiony new buffalo grass, or of the fine, warm dust of a cow trail. Our feet, turned loose from heavy, high-topped shoes, seemed to run and jump and dance of their own accord. After the first day we'd have to cripple along on the sides of our feet, or the heel of one and the toes of the other, until we grew protecting calluses, but even that didn't dim the joy much.

That morning, as soon as we finished our chores, my sisters and I celebrated by putting on a barefoot parade. We gathered up some old pans and kettles and lids, and sticks to pound them with, and marched around and around the soddy in the dust, banging on the pans and singing "bowlegged, bowlegged, bowlegged," as loud as we could. I have no idea why we picked that word, but we were having a fine time until Mama came out and stopped us. She said "bowlegged" was not a nice word for girls to use.

We moved to the new place on a warm afternoon a
week or two later.

Poppie unloaded the furniture and set up the stove and
beds, then hurried back to the old place to milk the cows
and catch the turkeys and chickens off their roosts. Mama
and Florry and I flew around, unpacking dishes and food
and making up beds.

The new house had a bedroom, a sitting room, and a
big kitchen. One corner of the kitchen was boarded off
for a fair-sized pantry, a halfway-up partition across
another corner made a little bedroom for Stell and Dovey.
"Dovey" was Mama's pet name for Ethel. When she was
a baby, the first cooing noises she made had sounded just
like the little prairie turtle doves, Mama said.

But, the same as on the homestead, there had to be a
bed in the sitting room, and Mama didn't look very
pleased when she made it up that day. More than anything else, she wanted a parlor, one without a bed in it.

When Mama and Florry began fixing supper, I went
outside to take a good look at our new home. I didn't
like what I saw. The old place had had a homey, well-
used look. This one was all new and raw. The sod walls
of the house and stable were smooth and dark, unpocked
by bird's nests and mouse runs, not yet dried to a light-
grey color like those on the homestead. The chicken
house smelled of fresh pine pitch and didn't look as if
it belonged here yet. The new well, with only a hand
pump on the pipe, looked stumpy and queer in the empty
yard. The new posts and barbed wire in the corral fence
were unsullied by rust and weather, and the level, springy
patch of buffalo grass inside was unmarked by hoofs.
The floor of our old corral had long been deep with dust
—or mud—depending on the weather.

I walked down the slope to old Stump Ditch, looping

away from where I stood to the crossing where old Peg had upset the cart with us. Across the ditch the Maline schoolhouse squatted in the weedy schoolyard. In the old prairie dog town on the ditch bank a pair of little prairie owls claimed squatters right to a burrow. They fluffed their feathers and made big eyes at me, daring me to come any closer.

I watched them for a while, then scuffed back up the hill to the yard, leaned on the pump, and watched the sun go down.

As the shadows lengthened the little owls began their evening song, their sad, gentle voices mourning the setting sun—and suddenly I was homesick. Everything here was too neat and still and empty. I wanted to go home, back to the old soddy on the edge of the canyon. I wanted to be milking old Pearlie and feeding the bucket calves. I wanted to eat supper and go to bed in the old house. I didn't see how I could ever go back into that new house again.

The next morning I went back to the homestead with Poppie and Florry. Poppie loaded the last of the machinery into the wagon and turned the pigs and cattle out of their pens. Florry and I helped him haze them up the road, while Peg and Lee followed with the wagon. At the top of the hill I turned to look back. The soddy looked so little and lonesome, and beyond the empty farmyard I could see the sunny claybanks where the little dugouts were already crumbling to dust. It made me sad to think we wouldn't be playing there any more, but I knew we were getting pretty big for that kind of play, anyway; and that it was time now to be looking ahead, not back, so I turned and hurried after Poppie and Florry.

As soon as we were straightened around in the new house, Mama had Grandma and her family over for Sunday dinner. They came in the big wagon, Uncle John driving and Grandma, Aunt Dicy, Aunt Bell, and Aunt Hester riding on kitchen chairs in the back. Just to be with Aunt Bell and Aunt Hester made any day perfect for us girls anyway, they were so pretty and gay, and wore such stunning hats and dresses; and, as always when Poppie and his folks got together, there was lots of singing.

Before the afternoon was over Poppie said that, since the Swedish people hadn't been having Sunday school at the Maline schoolhouse for quite a while, he thought we ought to start one. Aunt Hester said she hoped we could, that she had missed church and Sunday school more than anything else out here, and that it was too far to drive from their place to Walnut Grove for services.

We had never been to the big new church at Walnut Grove either, although it was only four miles down the valley from our new place. Mama said she simply didn't feel up to combing and dressing so many girls, fit to go to church among the valley's best-dressed people. But we knew she wouldn't mind our going to Sunday school at the schoolhouse. She wouldn't have to be so particular about our appearance, just to send us across the ditch to be with the same children we went to school with during the week.

Almost everybody in the district came to the new Sunday school. Most of the children were Swedes, all wanting to learn the American language and customs as fast as they could, and glad to come to the services. Poppie was elected superintendent, and Aunt Bell and Aunt Hester volunteered to teach classes. Aunt Bell ordered enough Sunday school papers for everybody, and the people brought whatever kinds of hymnbooks they had at home. Methodist, Lutheran, Christian, it was hard to find enough songs alike in those books so that everybody could sing at the same time. So, as soon as the collections brought in sufficient money, we ordered enough new books, all alike, to go around. After the books came, Poppie, John Maline, and Hilda Berg met at Grandma's every week to practice to the tunes Aunt Bell and Aunt Hester played on the little organ they had brought from Missouri with them.

A few times, the summer before, Poppie had taken Florry and me to Sunday school at the Roten schoolhouse, five miles up the valley from the homestead. It was there we had first heard about the big annual Sunday school picnics, where all the little Sunday schools from all the little schoolhouses in the hills banded together for a big dinner and program. The picnic was in a different district each year, and the men of the host school always built a shelter of tall poles, roofed with leafy plum brush, for the program and dinner.

A year ago the picnic had been in a branch canyon off Roten Valley, a long way from our place, but Poppie had taken us, and Mama had gone along. Just before we reached the plum brush pavilion, we had passed a patch of glistening sky-blue flowers with a cloud of yellow butterflies dancing above them. I had never seen anything so pretty, and as soon as we were out of the wagon I asked Florry and Stell to run back with me to pick some of the lovely wild flowers. We had our hands full of the pretty blossoms before we noticed the thick, yellow juice oozing from their stems, smearing our hands and the fronts of our dresses.

So we threw the pretty flowers away and went to Mama for help. Stell told her I was the one who had wanted to pick the flowers, and Mama said she might

have known I'd mess myself up the minute she turned
her back. Then she took us off to the wagon and poured
water from Poppie's big field jug onto her handkerchief
and began to scrub. But the yellow sap wouldn't wash
off, and Mama said we'd be pretty-looking things the
rest of the day.

It wasn't the way I looked that bothered me as much
as it was the way I *smelled*. The sickly sweet odor floating up from my hands and clothes was turning my
stomach. It didn't seem to bother my sisters, but by
noon I was too sick to eat a bite of the big picnic dinner,
or to watch the program afterward. The whole lovely
day had been ruined for me.

This summer, as soon as the new Sunday school was
going well, Aunt Hester, who was very good with "songs
and pieces," started us practicing for the part our school
was to have in the big Sunday school program, and Poppie
went to work on our banner. Every program began
with a grand parade of all the schools, led by old Mr.
Cummins with his fife, and his sons, Jim and Henry,
with their drums, and each Sunday school marched behind its own banner.

The banners were big, lightweight frames, covered with
cloth or paper on which were printed the names of the
schools, their slogans and favorite scripture verses. The
school with the handsomest banner always carried off the
honors for the day. Competition was keen and a lot of
work went into those banners. Poppie made the frame
for ours by bending a strip of metal into the shape of a
big *U* and hanging a smaller shield-shaped frame inside it.
Aunt Bell covered the smaller frame with white muslin,
printed our school's name and slogan on it, and topped the
whole thing off with lovely ribbon rosettes and streamers.

This year, too, the picnic was quite a way from our

place and we started off in good time. An early morning shower had cleared away in time to promise fair
weather and the prairie looked as if it had been all scrubbed
up just for this day. Curlews circled and screamed above
all the sparkling lagoons along the road and the hillsides
were covered with creamy spikes of soapweed. We soon
came to a part of the country I had never seen before.
We drove over a wide, flat tableland and through a
range of low, rough hills, and then the winding road
dropped suddenly into a canyon where the picnic shelter
stood.

Whether they went to Sunday school or not, practically
everybody in the whole country turned out for these
big Sunday sociables, and nearly everybody was there
when we pulled in. The parade was beginning to form
and Aunt Hester, crisp and pretty in white lawn, hurried
us girls into line behind our school's fine banner. Mr.
Cummins blew a warning note on his fife and the long
line straightened and tightened. Then the three-piece
"band" struck up a marching tune and the big parade
was on.

All around the picnic grounds we marched, cheered
on alike by our families and by the folks who didn't
belong to any Sunday school. Our beautiful banner swung
back and forth in its frame, its lovely streamers fluttering in the warm breeze. It was easy to see it was the
finest in the parade, and all of Maline Sunday school
strutted right proudly behind it.

It was a good thing we had our little victory then,
for we certainly had our "comedown," a little later.

The pavilion was furnished with benches, facing a platform, and everybody taking part in the program sat on
the front benches, ready to go up to the platform when
the time came.

We had all worked hard on our parts, especially on an "action song" half a dozen of us girls were to sing. Pretty little Sadie Southworth had the leading part in that one, and Aunt Hester had gone over it with us so many times that it seemed we couldn't help but do it right. When it came time for us to sing, Aunt Hester was to go up on the platform and begin playing our tune on the organ that had been hauled in from some settler's house for the program. After the first bar, Sadie was to stand up and sing, "Come, little children, join in our band." At that, the rest of us were to stand up and march behind her to the platform, singing as we went. There, lined up in a row, we were to finish the song.

That's the way it was supposed to be. But Sadie, excited and too eager, got up at the same time Aunt Hester did and sang out sweet and clear, "Come, little children, join in our band." We had done all our practicing without music anyway, so the rest of us stood up and stepped out behind Sadie, singing brave and loud. We reached the platform right behind Aunt Hester, lined up and sang on. And poor Aunt Hester, with never a chance to play a note for us, just sat at the organ, her back stiff with embarrassment, while we finished the song. We were all just too mortified for words.

Chapter Nine

ALL SUMMER I had been coaxing at Poppie to let me go to town with him on one of his Saturday trips. I hadn't been to Cozad again since the day we got off the train there, five years before, and when he finally gave in and said I could go I really whizzed around. I helped pack the eggs in pails of oats, and carried big balls of butter from the barrel at the windmill spout, then, dressed in my best, I climbed into the wagon with Poppie and we headed for town.

Poppie whistled and sang the miles away, but I could hardly wait for the town to come in sight; and when it did it seemed to be all whirling windmill wheels, with sunlight sliding off their blades. As we came nearer, I saw a man on horseback coming out of town leading a cow. He stopped beside a little shack ahead of us and the cow started swinging her head from side to side in the oddest way, then she got down on her knees and began to bawl. The low, mournful sound spread over the flat and sent shivers up my backbone.

I asked Poppie what on earth the cow was doing, and he said the shack was the slaughter house and that the cow could smell the blood of other cattle that had been butchered there and was afraid. I remembered the heifer that had hooked me. Poppie had sold *her* to the butcher, and I wondered if she had knelt here and bawled in fear.

I turned my face away from the bawling cow as we drove by, but I couldn't shut out that awful, despairing sound.

Poppie drove on around behind Darner's store, un-hitched and watered the mules, and tied them to the wagon to eat the grain and hay he'd brought along. I helped carry the butter and eggs to the store, but after my first look at Mr. Darner, a man so big that all by himself he made the store seem crowded, I stayed close to Poppie. The storekeeper had bushy, hornlike black eyebrows and a heavy topping of coal-black hair. He looked fierce and dangerous; but after a bit, when he gave me a stick of candy, I saw the jolly twinkle in his deep black eyes. I felt easier then, and began to look around.

There was a fine smell to those old-time general stores; a mixture of dried fruit, vinegar, strong cheese, shoe leather, smoked ham, dill pickles in open barrels, new cloth, molasses, fresh-cut plug tobacco, rope, overshoes, and a hundred other things. I watched Mr. Darner scoop up and weigh the coffee beans, sugar, and prunes that Poppie read off his list. The big man's handiness with wrapping twine was fascinating. Flipping the string around the package, and then around his huge little finger, he snapped it loose from the big cone hanging overhead and tied off the knot, all with one easy motion almost too fast to see.

After a little I left Poppie and sidled past a tall spit-toon to the dry-goods side of the store. There I pressed my face against the glass front of a tall showcase and feasted on the grand jumble inside: foot-long fancy-headed hatpins, jet belt buckles, beaded dress trimmings, laces, insertions, ribbons, cardboard cubes of colored glass-headed pins.

Then Poppie came over with his arms full of packages

and said we'd better go eat a bite. At the wagon, he stowed his armload under the seat and hauled out the water jug. We sat in the shade of the wagon box and ate store cheese, crackers, and gingersnaps, washed down by long swigs from the jug.

When we finished, Poppie said he had to go to the blacksmith shop, so I followed him back to the street.

I had been uneasy for the past hour, wanting to ask Poppie a very personal question and not knowing *how* to ask it. But before I could say anything, he told me the blacksmith shop wasn't a very nice place for girls and that I'd better just sit down on the edge of the sidewalk and wait for him. Then he hurried up the street and out of sight, and I sat down on the edge of the wooden walk and looked around. Earlier in the day there had been two or three women on the street; now it was nearly deserted—and there wasn't a woman in sight. But maybe one would come along, and even if I didn't know her I could ask her what I needed to know.

It was a long time before Poppie jogged back into sight. I stood up, ready to hurry ahead of him to the wagon, when a man came out of a store and Poppie stopped to lean on a hitch rail and talk a while with him. I waited, jigging from foot to foot in misery, until he finally came on again. I helped him hitch up, then scrambled up to my side of the seat. Poppie climbed in, picked up the lines, then reached for the jug.

"Want a drink before we start?" he asked. I shook my head. All *I* wanted was to get started. He uncorked the jug, took a long drink, corked it again and set it back among the bundles under the seat. "Giddap," he said at last.

The mules jogged along, half asleep, Poppie whistled and hummed, and I thought we would *never* get out of sight of the town. As we pulled into the first hills on the edge of the valley, Poppie turned to me. "Well, Pete, did you have a good time?" he asked.

I began to howl like a puppy that's had its tail stepped on.

"Now what in the world's the matter with you?" Poppie demanded.

"Well, I have to go *out*."

"*Oh*," Poppie said, pulling the team to a quick stop so I could climb out over the wheel.

Toward fall Poppie built a frame entryway onto the back door of the house. Besides keeping out a good deal of cold wind, the hoodlike little room was a handy place to store extra fuel and kindling and to hang up things like the washboiler, the lantern, and the stove cleaner.

Now Poppie was a good hand to put off finishing the things he started. The spring he ditched water up the hill to the house, over on the homestead, he had left the deep ditch for the pipe uncovered for quite a while and a little pig had fallen into it. Its mother made an awful fuss, running around counting the the rest of her brood and squealing bloody murder. Florry and I tried to get the piglet out of the ditch, but every time we climbed to the top with the squalling, wiggling baby the old sow rushed us, her tusked mouth wide open, and we'd have to drop back in the ditch fast. Florry finally got a long pole and drove the sow away so I could climb out with the lost little pig.

This time, before Poppie got around to hanging the outer door on the entryway, the cats moved in and took up sleeping quarters on the cob barrel and Nell, my little herd dog, bedded down on the floor beside it at night. Nell, a gentle, friendly little dog, but now about to have pups, had turned cross and short-tempered of late. One evening, after she curled up in her place, she bit a cat that passed her on its way to the barrel. The cat squalled, and Mama told me to make Nell get out and leave the cats alone. But when I tried to put her out she sprang at me and bit my face. I screamed and ran back into the kitchen to spit a lower front tooth and a mouthful of blood into the cob basket.

Mama cleaned me up and poured peroxide into the deep cuts, and Poppie shot poor Nell after I went to bed. The cuts healed fast, leaving barely noticeable scars, but I missed my little dog and the help she had given me with the herd.

When school started I showed Lillie Maline my scars and told her how I got them. Lillie was about my age and I liked her, but of all the girls at school she was hardest for me to get along with. We didn't speak to each other for a week, the time we quarreled about Jesus' nationality; she said He was a Swede, and I said He wasn't.

Lillie was crazy afraid of three things, thunderstorms, trains, and mad dogs. She wanted me to be afraid of them too, and now she thought she had me. Nell was mad, she told me. I said I knew it, she was mad at me for trying to put her out. Lillie said she meant the dog had "gone mad," and asked if she wasn't frothing at the mouth. I said of course she wasn't, and Lillie said she would have been if my papa hadn't killed her so quick, and that I would soon go mad and froth at the mouth and show my teeth and dig at people with my fingernails. I told her I wouldn't do any such thing, and I wouldn't talk about it any more. But every forenoon for the next three weeks she looked me over good for signs of madness—and seemed considerably disappointed when none showed up.

About a month after Nell bit me the root of the broken

tooth began to "gather," and my face swelled up as big as a bucket. Home remedies did no good, and there came a night when I was tormented by hideous yellow strings, running endways from me like the strings on a zither, their ends fastened in an invisible sounding board. A flock of fuzzy knots went up and down the strings, whirling and twisting with a low, moaning hum, coming toward me and sliding away so fast I couldn't tell which were coming and which were going, and I could never get away from them. Poppie and Mama were up with me most of that night, and by daylight Poppie was on the road to town with me.

Dr. Fochtman's morning fire had hardly taken the chill off his office when we came in. My ulcerated jaw wasn't ready to lance yet, he said, and wouldn't be for two more days. "If it hasn't broken by then, bring her back and I'll lance it," he told Poppie.

Poppie wanted to buy me a cup of hot milk before we started the cold, rough ride home. I couldn't remember ever eating in a restaurant. Any other time I would have loved it, but I was too sick even to think about it. Again that night the whirling, fuzzy knots slid up and down the humming strings, driving me wild until, just after daylight, the ulcer broke. The pain drained out of my jaw with the pus, leaving an enormous ache I hadn't felt until then—it was in my stomach and I was *starved*.

Mama had fussed over me and made my favorite desserts, custard and "blamange," and I didn't have to help with the dishes or do anything else I did not want to. So, after the pain was gone, I loved every minute of my sick spell; for I couldn't remember when Mama had ever babied me before.

I used to watch her petting and making over the newest baby, or frail, nervous little Ethel, and ache for the affection she never had time to show us older ones. But my top place in the sun of her tenderness didn't last long. In spite of myself I was well again in two days, just in time to go to the first literary meeting of the winter.

All the communities had been having Grange suppers and "literaries" for several years, but this was the first winter that we got to go to them. Even when Mama didn't feel like going, Poppie took us girls. One of the Grange suppers was held in a schoolhouse away over northeast, in a section of rough country called "Little Kentucky" because its settlers had come from the mountains of Kentucky. Everybody took food for the suppers, and any left over was auctioned off to raise money for the Grange treasury. At the auction one night, Poppie bought a baked chicken, and Mama roasted *him* plenty when she cut the chicken up for dinner the next day. It had been baked *whole*, everything there except the head, feet, and feathers, and we had to throw it out.

We liked the literaries best. Big crowds always turned out, and everybody took part in the lively programs. Debating and singing rated highest, and Poppie was very good at both. His voice took on a ringing authority as he pounded home his points, arguing just as well "against," as "for," no matter which way he really believed. He used to be asked, over and over again, to sing the ballads he did so well, and I always felt so proud when he stood up and sang, his deep, rich voice filling the schoolhouse to the very eaves. Of all the good old songs he used to sing, "Fair Charlotte" was my favorite.

> Fair Charlotte lived on the mountainside
> In a wild and lonely spot.
> No dwelling there for ten miles round,

Except her father's cot.
On many a cold and winter's night
Young swains would gather there.
For her father kept a social board,
And she was very fair.
On New Year's night the sun went down,
Far looked her wishful eye,
As she stepped up to the frozen pane
To watch the sleighs go by.
How brightly beams her laughing eye,
As a well-known voice she hears.
And dashing to the cottage door,
Young Charlie's sleigh appears.
"Oh, daughter dear," her mother cried,
"This blanket round you fold,
For 't is a dreadful night abroad,
You'll catch your death of cold."
"Ho no, ho no," fair Charlotte cried,
And she laughed like a Gypsy queen.
"To ride in blankets muffled up,
I never shall be seen.
My silken cloak is quite enough,
You know 't is lined throughout,
And then I have my silken scarf
To twine my neck about."
Her bonnet and her cloak was on
And she stepped into the sleigh.
And away they went o'er the mountainside,
And o'er the hills away.
At a village fifteen miles away
Was to be a ball that night.
Although the air was piercing cold,
Their hearts were warm and light.
What a creaking noise the runners made,
As they passed o'er the frozen snow.
There's music in the frosty bells
As o'er the hills they go.
"Such a dreadful night I never saw,
My reins I scarce can hold."
Fair Charlotte said in a feeble tone,
"I am exceeding cold."
Charlie cracked his whip and urged his team
Much faster than before.

Until at length five weary miles
In silence they passed o'er.
Spoke Charles, "Full fast the freezing ice
Is gathering on my brow."
Fair Charlotte still more faintly said,
"I'm growing warmer now."
Thus on they rode through the frosty air,
Through the glittering cold starlight,
Until at last the village lamps
And the ballroom came in sight.
They reached the door and Charles sprang out,
And offered his hand to her.
"Why sit you there like a monument
That has no power to stir?"
He called her once, he called her twice.
She answered not a word.
He asked for her hand again,
And still she never stirred.
He took her hand in his. 'T was cold,
And hard as any stone.
He tore the mantle from her face,
And the cold stars on it shone.
Then quickly to the lighted hall
Her lifeless form he bore.
Fair Charlotte was a frozen corpse,
She spoke to them no more.
He took her to her parents' home,
And they no harsh word spoke,
For they saw by the sadness on his face
That Charlie's heart was broke.

Chapter Ten

SPRING came early and it seemed like, overnight, the last of the snow was gone and a clean, sweet new smell rode the strong winds. Meadowlarks sang their hearts out all day, and broody hens ruffled their feathers at us when we went in the chicken house to pick the eggs. In the sitting-room window, the pair of canaries Mama bought at Christmastime fussed over the matchbox nest she had tied in their cage. Down in the old dog town, the little owls began to scold every time we passed on our way to and from school, one screeching at us from the burrow, the other from the top of the corner fence post.

During the spring school term, while Poppie had to be in the fields, I herded our cattle mornings and afternoons and went to school only between recesses. After the grass began to green up it was hard to get the cattle to leave it, and one morning, when I had more trouble than usual corralling the herd, it looked like I was going to be late for school. I finally panted into the house, yanked my school clothes on and ran out again, pretending not to hear Mama calling after me that I had forgotten my bonnet. A minute later I wished I had minded her; for the owls came at me like twin furies, clawing, pecking, and flopping against my bare head so hard that I fairly ran for my life.

When I puffed into the schoolyard, just ahead of the

recess bell, Florry told me the owls had stormed at her
and Stell, too, only they had had their bonnets on. On
my way home at afternoon recess, I ducked my head,
covered it with my arms, and ran as hard as I could, the
fierce little pair flopping me all the way past the dog town.

Mama seemed to know all about the habits of wild
things, especially birds, so while I changed back into my
herding clothes I asked her what made the little owls so
savage. She said it was because they had started to build
their nest, and that they would be on the fight until
they had raised their family. So, for the rest of that school
term, we wore our bonnets—and were even grateful for
the protection of the long-hooded old things as we scooted
past the dog town with the owls beating a tattoo on their
cardboard slats.

When the baby owls began to come out to take the
sun in front of the burrow, we tried to tarry long enough
to get a good look at the solemn little things, mostly eyes,
as far as we could see. But the old owls would come at
us in such a rage that we always took to our heels as hard
as we could. When they'd chased us out of their territory, they'd fly back to their posts and sit down to put
their feathers straight again, their little faces bobbling
like everything while they scolded about the trouble we'd
put them to.

The week before Easter, Miss Buckley, our teacher,
took sick at school and had to be taken to her home in
Cozad. Poppie made his usual trip to town on Saturday,
and came home with the news that she was dead. She
had died twice that day it seemed, once in the forenoon,
and again in the afternoon. The first time, after the
neighbor women had her partly laid out for burial, she
had come to and lived nearly half a day before passing
away again.

We had no more school that term, so I went back to herding all day.

Easter morning Poppie called us all out to the corral to see old Dolly's newborn colt, little black Prince. Dolly and Peg had the wobbly colt between them, while Lee, his lips curled back from his long yellow teeth and his little pig eyes glaring, walked around and around them, watching for a chance to sneak past them and get at the colt.

Lee, as different from Peg as a saint from a sinner, enjoyed torturing every living thing on the place. Peg, who loved all baby things, had all her life stood between him and the other animals, taking his wicked kicks and bites to protect them. Poppie said Peg had been having a time of it to keep Lee away from the colt, then he put a halter on the big mule and tied him in the barn. We laughed at the way old Peg acted about the colt, as proud of him as if he was *her* son. "She's just like a nice old grandma," Mama said; and for the rest of the kind old mule's life we called her "Granny."

Poppie planted a field of broomcorn that spring. The Swedes had had good luck with it the year before and he figured it would pay him to try it, too. The day he went to town to buy the broomcorn seeder he came home with a new mare, Daisy. Daisy, he told us, was quick and lively and we were not to fool around her, for she wasn't broke to ride and she wasn't safe for kids. I was terribly disappointed because, more than anything else, I wanted a good saddle horse.

Dolly, wide, fat, and heavy-footed, was anything but a riding horse, and Gypsy, the pretty little iron-gray Oregon mare Poppie had bought the spring before, had turned out to be dead lazy. When we drove her in double harness we had to prod her at every step to make her keep up, and when I rode her I wore myself out kicking her to keep her moving at all. But Daisy now—she was good-looking and full of snap, and I had to figure out a way to ride her.

When the corn stood high enough to cultivate, Poppie told me I'd have to help him. Stell could take over the herding, he said, and I could drive Daisy between Dolly and Gyp, where she'd have to behave herself. The next morning he helped me get my outfit started for the south field, nearest the house, before he headed out to the north field with the mules. Daisy pranced along between slow-footed Dolly and lazy Gyp and I felt sorry for her—but I saw right then how I could break her to ride.

At noon I unhitched the three mares from the go-dig, snapped the tugs to the britchen strap hooks and climbed on old Dolly for the ride to the house. The mares were all cross-checked together, and it seemed to me that if I was to slide off old Dolly onto Daisy she couldn't do much about it, anchored as she was between the other two. At the feel of my weight on her back she snorted a time or two and pranced a bit livelier, but that was all.

At first, I'd climb back onto Dolly before we got to the house, but one day I rode Daisy all the way home. Poppie was watering the mules at the tank. At first he looked startled, then stern, and then he grinned. "Looks like you've got yourself a new riding horse," he said.

Ever since we moved, Poppie had been trying to find time to haul the tank down to the corral. But it wasn't until that second summer, after we had the corn laid by, that he got it done. To get below frost level, he had to dig the long trench for the pipe a good four feet deep, so it took him quite a while to get it dug and the pipe laid and the tank moved.

On a Saturday morning not long afterward, Mama

told Poppie she was going to have an early dinner and
go to town with him. Mr. Darner was having a one-
cent calico sale from one to three that afternoon, she
said, and she wanted to get there before the goods was
all picked over.

The weather had turned scorching hot, and I was fairly
steaming inside my long-sleeved, high-necked dress when
I brought the cattle in that forenoon. The water in the
tank sparkled clean and cool in the blazing sunshine,
and I thought how good it would feel if I could only
get in it. We had been coaxing for the last week to go
"swimming" in the tank. But Mama, who wouldn't even
take all her clothes off at one time in the privacy of her
own bedroom, had been shocked at the very idea. We
told her we'd wear old dresses while we were in the water,
but she still said no, that we were getting too big to strip
off that near naked where Poppie or someone might see us.

After dinner, when we were carrying the butter and
eggs to the wagon, I whispered to my sisters that, as soon
as the folks were gone, we could go swimming in the tank.
It would be all right, I said, because Poppie would not
be around to see us. But a few minutes later, Mama
looked down from the seat and said, "Now don't you
girls go swimming in that tank. It's too near the road
and somebody might come by and see you."

They drove away, and we sat down to talk things over.
It seemed that all that Mama was afraid of was someone
seeing us in the tank, but if we kept a sharp lookout
for wagons coming down the road we could take care of
that. On the other hand, we'd have to swim in our bare
skins—if we wore old dresses Mama would be sure to
find them and know they'd been wet. But if we undressed in the house, and ran out and got in the ditch,
which Poppie hadn't filled yet, we'd be out of sight all

the way to the tank and back. The plan seemed fool-proof.

At first the water felt freezing cold and we did a lot of splashing and spluttering before we got wet all over. We kept a careful watch on the road, though, and things were going fine until I backed up to the tank rim and sat down on a wasp that had just lit to get a drink. The sting hurt like everything, and the girls all laughed so hard over the fuss I made that we all forgot to watch the road. When we finally saw the wagon, it was almost to the corner of the corral.

It wouldn't have been so bad, even then, if we had thought to duck to our chins in the water. But, guilty and scared, we hopped out of the tank, dragged little Dovey out after us, and dived into the ditch. All the way to the house we could see the shocked faces of the three ladies in the wagon—and the man, rocking back and forth on the front seat and laughing so hard his shoulders shook. We were a sad bunch of girls, all the rest of that afternoon; for we knew Mama would find out about it someway, and we knew we'd "catch it" when she did.

That year turned out to be an extra good one for broomcorn, so good that, along in the fall, Poppie said if he could get the crop all tabled and topped before frost he'd make enough out of it to get the things he needed, and a new cookstove for Mama besides. It was time we had a new stove. The tired-looking old one we had brought from Missouri was about burned out; both its oven doors sagged on warped hinges, its four lids were cracked and bent, and, anyway, it was too small for a family the size of ours.

So Poppie dropped everything else, hired a man, and went to work on the crop; for if the mature green corn

NO TIME ON MY HANDS 107

froze in the field it would make a poorer quality, lower-priced straw.

Everything about broomcorn harvesting was hard work. Day after day, Poppie and his man walked backward down the rows from dawn till dark, bending the stalks at right angles so the long, bushy heads lapped each other in the middle to make the "table." The second time over the field, they "topped" the bent stalks and hauled the heads home. Each day the sharp stalks ripped their jacket sleeves to ravelings, and every evening Mama basted the backs of old overall legs to the sleeves, replacing the shredded patches she'd sewed on the night before. But, well ahead of the first hard frost, the big crop was laid up in a long, neat rick beside the stable, all the heads pointing north.

Then, for weeks, Poppie, Florry, and I followed the broomcorn thresher on its rounds of the community. This machine, too, was owned by one of our Swedish neighbors, so of course we were last on the list, and the weather was turning chilly by the time it pulled in at our place.

The broomcorn "scraper" was a simple thing, only a pair of four-foot-long rollers, studded with iron spikes, and set one above the other like the rolls of a wringer. A team of horses, walking around a small turntable, furnished the power that turned the rolls. Two men carried straw from the rick to a long table by the machine; boys and girls on the crew "evened" the ends against a board on the edge of the table, then passed it on to two men at the machine. These two gripped the bunched stalks by the cut ends and held the heads against the cylinders until all the seed was pounded out. The sharp spikes jerked a good deal of the straw from their hands and whirled it through the rollers to the seed pile on the other side. When enough had gone through to be worth salvaging, the driver stopped the machine and yelled, *"Pluka pika"* ("Pick up, boys"), the signal for us to get onto the seed pile and pick up the loose straw.

Everybody hated broomcorn threshing, but it was hardest on the boys and girls. The men on the crew wore scarves and goggles, but we had no such protection. The dust and chaff, flint-hard and rough-edged, sifted into our eyes and down our sweaty necks, where it itched and stung all day. But the miserable, gritty job was finally done; and the straw, stacked in smooth, even piles, was ready for the baler.

Poppie sold the straw in November, and brought the new stove home one chilly afternoon. It stood on high, curved legs—Mama wouldn't have to stoop to do the cooking now—with its back to the wall and its single oven door in front. It had a reservoir on one end, a hearth shelf on the other, six lids on top, and was altogether the prettiest stove he could find in town, Poppie said. He showed us how to work the damper, the little handle between the reservoir and the oven. Turned up, it heated the oven, down, the reservoir. We set it to heat the freshly filled reservoir and poked in cobs and chips until the fire roared.

After supper, Florry and I hustled the dishpans onto the table. Everybody watched while Florry opened the reservoir lid to dip up steaming-hot water—but there was no steam, and no hot water. "That's queer," Poppie said, "it's had plenty of time to heat." But it hadn't heated, and we washed dishes with water out of the teakettle, as usual.

The oven, we discovered then, wouldn't heat either. So Poppie had to take the beautiful, useless stove back to town. The one he brought back in its place wasn't so handsome, but its oven baked wonderful bread and its reservoir turned out steaming-hot water.

Aunt Bell taught our school that term. She stayed with us during the week and rode horseback to Grandma's on Friday evenings. I was all out of quilt pieces when school started, as I was most of the time, and Aunt Bell promised to bring me a bundle of scraps when she came back the next Sunday evening.

On Saturday morning I climbed on old Dolly and took our herd away up the valley where the grass was good. Poppie had gotten me another herd dog, little black Kringa, and I left her on guard while I stretched out on Dolly's broad bare back, with my face against her neck. I was thinking about the new quilt pattern I wanted to try with the pieces Aunt Bell was to bring me, when Dolly suddenly threw up her head. The gentle old mare sometimes had spells when any little thing, a weed waving in the breeze, a scrap of paper, or a skittering jackrabbit made her forget her age and act like a bronc for a minute or two. So I grabbed a handful of mane and sat up in a hurry. Far to the north, past her pointing ears, I saw a smudge of smoke creeping down the valley.

For a year or two those smoke clouds, signaling the slow approach of enormous steam engines, had been a common sight at this season of the year. In our part of the country, the big engines had almost replaced horse-power outfits like the one that had threshed our first wheat crop, five years before.

Dolly and I watched the machine chugging down the valley, pulling a big water wagon, and I figured the driver was on his way to our place after water for his engine. The outfit crawled out of sight behind a hill and Dolly went back to grazing. I lay down on her back again and shut my eyes—then a horrible screech suddenly split

the quiet forenoon wide open, and before the first echo
came back from the nearest hill Dolly had jumped right
out from under me. I landed flat, and so hard that it
seemed I'd never breathe again.

Until then, I had liked to hear the engines whistle.
All through threshing season they seemed to play a game
with each other, each engineer trying to be the first to
blow his whistle in the morning. For weeks on end, the
shrill screeches woke the roosters, and Poppie said the
engineers must stay up all night, building up steam to
blow at daylight. One morning we had counted five
whistles, each in a different key, seeming to talk to one
another in a language all their own.

By evening, my chest and stomach were sore all the
way down from the fall I'd had. When I came in with
the cattle, Mr. and Mrs. Smith were just driving away
from our place. The Smiths lived quite a ways north of
us and went by every Saturday, driving a pair of tiny
mules to a topless old buggy. The mules, hardly taller
than the buggy box, and little more than half as long as
the tongue, could barely keep the neck yoke from dragging the ground as they jogged along. Mr. Smith was
little and skinny, Mrs. Smith was short and fat, and on
the steep drop into old Stump Ditch the buggy had run
down onto the little mules hard enough to pitch Mrs.
Smith out over the dashboard. Pushed on by the weight
of the buggy against their rumps, the mules pulled the
front wheels right over her before Mr. Smith could stand
up and haul back on the lines to stop them. Then, when
the backward pull on the lines overcame the forward
push of the buggy, the mules reversed themselves and
backed the wheels back over Mrs. Smith. The poor lady
was pretty well mauled by the time Mr. Smith got her
on her feet and boosted back into the buggy. So they

had stopped at our house to clean her up and assess the damages which, like my sore stomach, were more painful than serious.

The girls were still giggling about the Smith mishap, and when I told them about Dolly jumping out from under me they laughed harder than ever. All but little Nellie. She came to me, patted my arm, and said "Poor Gheet, poor Gheet."

"Listen to her. She's trying to say 'Grace' and 'Pete' at the same time," Florry said. From then on, I was "Gheet" to the family.

I was waiting for Aunt Bell when she rode into the yard Sunday evening, stepped down from her sidesaddle, and handed me a neat bundle. How good Aunt Bell was, and how lucky. She had beautiful clothes, and a sidesaddle, too. She made all her own clothes, and I had already made up my mind to make mine as soon as I learned to sew well enough, and to get myself a sidesaddle as soon as I could manage it.

We put her horse away and went in the house, where I looked through the bundle of pretty scraps. My fingers itched to be at them, but I knew Poppie wouldn't let me take a stitch on Sunday. So I put them away and got out the Montgomery Ward catalog to look up the price of sidesaddles again.

The next week Mama came down with a heavy cold and had to stay in bed. Poppie was helping a neighbor at the time, so he brought sixteen-year-old Mary Durland to stay with her and the two little girls while the rest of us were at school. I was herding mornings and afternoons again, and going to school between recesses. One morning that week, when I started the cattle across the flat at sunup, as usual, it seemed to me that I had never seen such a beautiful fall day. The valley was all gold and hazy and the bright blue sky looked as if it had just been polished. But there was a queer *feel* to the air, a feeling like waiting for the thunderclap after the lightning flash.

By the time I hurried off to school at recess, the day had turned sultry and close. At noon we tried to play pullaway, but gave it up because of the heat. Aunt Bell came to the door two or three times and looked uneasily at the clear bright sky. "Queer it should be so hot, this time of year," she said.

About one o'clock heavy black clouds began rolling up from the northeast, blotting out the sun and sky. At two, when we could no longer see to study, Aunt Bell dismissed school and told us to hurry home ahead of the storm. But we had hardly left our seats when the clouds broke wide open and the storm fell upon us. For the next hour, wind and rain shook and pounded the schoolhouse, lightning crackled in bright green flashes, the air smelled of sulphur, and the thunder roared without letup.

We all huddled around Aunt Bell. Lillie Maline was almost insensible, the rest of us not much better off. Aunt Bell tried to hearten us, but the howling of the gale drowned her voice. The storm stopped as suddenly as it started, and for a little space there didn't seem to be a sound. Then we heard a deep, ugly growl—old Stump Ditch was flooding again.

We hurried outside. The clouds were rushing away to the southwest and a pale, shamed-looking sun shone on the flattened grass. From the schoolhouse we could see a little way down into the ditch, where it made an elbow turn below the schoolyard. As yet we couldn't see the water, except on the other side, toward Malines, where a wide, shallow flood poured down the draw toward the ditch. We all ran down to the crossing. The ditch

WALNUT GROVE M. E. CHURCH

BY THE SOD HOUSE

Standing, left to right: Aunt Lizzie and Uncle Jonathan Famuliner, Uncle John McCance, Ralph Boling (an orphan boy), Johnny Famuliner, Uncle Will Blaine, Aunt Hester, Roy Woodruff, Uncle Tom, Aunt Bell, Earnest Woodruff (her fiance), Mama and Poppie. *Seated:* Aunt Mary Stauffer and baby; Charlie, Emma, and Tom Famuliner; Grandma McCance; Florence and Effie Famuliner; Aunt Dicy; Stella, Florry, Grace, Ethel, Elsie, and Nellie McCance.

was already half full and rising by the minute, dirty, tumbling, and foam-topped. The sight of it gave me a pain in the pit of my stomach, and I was glad when Aunt Bell said we might as well go back and finish our lessons.

When we came out again, an hour later, the ditch was brimful. Heavy froth topped the bucking waves and big splashes leaped over the bank on the far side of the elbow turn, clawing at the crumbling dirt and falling back into the flood. We sat down on the porch to wait, while the water roared by on both sides of us. After a while trash began coming down the ditch, old boards, tin cans, stove-in kegs, all tossing and turning on the water. Then an old rocking chair came by, rolling over and over. And next a bridge, from a crossing up toward the head of the ditch, with a tail of barbed wire and posts twisting behind it and catching at weeds and grass along the banks.

The sun slid on down to the hilltops and long shadows lay across the soaked valley. With all the raging fury of old Stump Ditch between us and our homes, there was no possibility that we, or the three Durlands, would sleep in our beds that night. And very little more that Bergs and Holmes and Malines, from the other side of the valley, would sleep in theirs; for the water coming down the long draw on the east barred their way.

We had no light, no supper, and no beds, and we dreaded to see night come down. And then we saw Mr. Maline coming. The water was almost up to the wagon box and his team leaned hard against the sweep of the current. He pulled up beside the schoolhouse, and while the children from his side of the valley climbed into the wagon, he said something to Aunt Bell.

"Now, don't worry," she told the rest of us when the

wagon drove away. "Mr. Maline will be back in a little
while with supper and bedding for all of us."

We sat down on the porch again and watched the early
stars come out. Florry and I wondered about Mama, and
if Poppie had made it home before the ditch flooded. If
he hadn't, the cows would still be shut in the corral
without a bite to eat, I thought. Then eight-year-old
Burt Durland began to howl, "I'm hungry. I'm awful
hungry."

"I know," Aunt Bell told him. "We're all hungry,
but Mr. Maline will soon be here, and then we can eat."

We fell silent again, until Frances Durland said suddenly, "Listen to the frogs, they're saying 'knee-deep,
knee-deep, better go 'round, better go 'round.' "

Sure enough, they were, thousands of them, come out
to enjoy the rain.

"Only it's more than knee-deep, and we can't go
'round," Aunt Bell said. And we all giggled and felt
better.

Just before full dark, Mr. Maline splashed back across
the draw, bringing a lantern, several quilts, bread, a pail
of hard-boiled eggs, and a big pot of hot black coffee.
Things seemed better right away. We sat around Aunt
Bell's desk in the little circle of yellow light, eating bread
and eggs and drinking coffee. Florry, Stell, and I felt
pleasantly wicked about the coffee—Mama never let us
drink it at home because it would make our teeth black.

Then we spread the quilts on the floor and went to
bed with our clothes on. All night the flood roared down
old Stump Ditch, and every time I woke up I could see
the old rocking chair, riding the foamy water and turning and turning.

By morning the water was more than half down in

the ditch, and dropping steadily. On the far side of the dog town, I could see Poppie turning the cattle out of the corral. I whistled with relief, and ran back to the schoolhouse to help roll up the quilts and finish off the bread and eggs.

Chapter Eleven

MAUD ELSIE, another of the dark McCances, was born the eighth of the next April, one day too late to be a birthday present for Mama. She was a plump, good baby and Mama called her "Precious," a pet name the rest of us had shortened to "Presh" by the time she could sit alone. Poppie hired Mary Durland to help with the work until Mama got her strength back, and that, as it turned out, took all summer.

Stell and I switched places that spring, she working the corn planter lever for Poppie while I herded the cattle. Most of the time I followed the herd afoot; for Dolly, growing old and soon to have another colt, was taking it easy, and Poppie needed the other horses in the field.

I had turned ten in April, and that summer the prairie had a new meaning for me. Its quivering life was all around me, to be felt and seen and listened to. I found that when I lay flat and still on my stomach, my ear to the ground, I could hear the grass growing, all its little roots pushing and digging like everything. And if I held my breath, it even seemed that I could hear the very small sound that time itself made as it went by. I liked to lie on my back, too, watching the whipped-cream cloud puffs sailing across the sky to pile up for the sunset, and trying to imagine what it would be like to look down on them from above. Sometimes my longing to fly above the clouds was strong enough to hurt; as my longing for a "boughten" doll with real hair, or for a sidesaddle like Aunt Bell's, sometimes hurt. But, like the doll I was almost too old for, or the saddle I couldn't have because it cost too much, I knew I'd never get above the clouds either.

One of the finest times of the day came at sundown, when the cattle grazed toward home and the early dew began to fall and the cleanest, freshest smell in all the world came up from the cropped grass. But all the hours seemed interesting now, and I spent a lot of them watching the lively affairs of the prairie creatures. I watched thick, dark bugs kick wet balls of dirt along a cow trail. Every little while they stopped to spit on the balls, then kicked them along in the dust again, rolling them up until they were bigger than themselves.

One day I saw a terrible battle between a yellow jacket and a grasshopper. I don't know what started the fight, for they were hard at it when I first saw them. But the wasp, curling his rear half under him, was stinging the hopper so hard it made me squinch; and the grasshopper, holding the wasp fast between his powerful front legs, was crushing its head with his tough old jaws. They tumbled over and over, stinging and pinching for dear life. The battle ended in a draw, both of them stone dead, clasped to each other's bosom in a grisly hug. How silly of them to fight—surely the prairie had been big enough for both of them.

One afternoon a big butterfly, swinging on a tall grass stem, reminded me of the cocoon I had found on a withered sunflower stalk one snowy evening the past winter. I had wrapped the papery little case in a scrap of old silk and tucked it away in my quilt-piece box, where I forgot all about it until the day I saw the butterfly in the pasture. That evening I brought out my piece box. Due to my perennial lack of quilt pieces, the box was usually full of bird feathers, weed-seed pods, pretty colored grass stems, dragonfly wings, and all the other odds and ends of the season's gleaning on the prairie. I dug out the bundle and unwound the silk. At the end of it I found the butterfly, a dead, dry husk. At the proper time, Nature had called him from his long sleep and he had broken through the walls of his own prison, but halfway through the layers of the winding sheet I had given him he gave up. Poor butterfly, never once unfolding his bright wings to the sunlight; how I wished I had left him in the snowy cornfield, safe on the sunflower stalk he had picked for his winter bed.

On the south slope of old Stump Ditch, just out of range of the savage little owls, I found a precious thing one day. A clump of strong new grass had raised one edge of a wide, flat cowchip a few inches, and under the cozy lean-to a pair of meadowlarks had built a nest and filled it with five pretty eggs. Whenever I could, I sat where I could watch the family. The neat little mother on the nest paid no attention to me, the father, so pretty in his yellow vest and black necktie, sang to us both from the top of the nearest fence post.

I was probably more impatient than the parent birds for the eggs to hatch; for then they had never a daylight minute to rest. The father, too busy to sing any more, helped his mate carry bugs from sunrise till dark, and whenever I found them both away for a minute I took the babies in my hands. Growing so fast that their naked skins were stretched thin over patches of pure yellow fat, they opened their mouths and begged for food while I held them. Dear, ugly, greedy meadowlark babies—they were just starting to feather out when the big hailstorm struck.

The storm came down at the end of a sultry afternoon in late May. Mama stood at the window, watching the egg-sized hailstones pound her garden into the ground. "Dear me, this'll kill a lot of little birds and prairie chickens," I heard her say. I lay awake a long time that night, worrying about my meadowlark family.

I hurried to the nest at sunup. The big chip was gone, beaten to pieces and washed away; the mother and all her fat babies were dead, their poor little bodies torn and battered in the grass. The father was nowhere around.

There was more bad news, too. Old Lee had broken loose in the night and, in spite of all poor Granny could do to stop him, had chewed old Dolly's new little mare colt to death.

During the next week I found dozens of dead birds on the prairie, but those that had survived the storm started right in building new nests and raising new families. And so, a little later, I found a ground sparrow's nest, a wee dainty thing, tucked under a thick tuft of grass in a little scratched-out place on the ground. There was one egg, a lovely, jewel-like thing, and I couldn't help picking it up. But the shell was so thin and delicate that, in spite of my care, I cracked it ever so little. I put it back then and went away, sorry I had ever touched it. When I came back the next day the parent birds were gone and ants crawled over the cold, broken little egg. I felt like a murderer—and I never bothered birds' eggs again.

But, anyway, after Poppie put me to go-digging corn with the mules in June, I didn't have any more time for birds' nests and prairie mysteries. I had never worked Lee and Granny before, but I managed fine until about an hour before quitting time. By then they were tired and wanted to go home, and every time I pulled out into the road to turn around they'd keep on going toward the house. Granny wasn't hard to turn back but Lee was plain dirt mean about it. Twisting his ugly old head around until he could get the bit in his teeth, he'd have Granny and me halfway home before I could get him sawed around and headed for the field again.

Toward the end of the month, Florry, Stell, and I began coaxing Poppie to take us to Cozad to the big Fourth-of-July celebration. Mama still had to stay in bed a good deal and we knew she wouldn't feel like going, but we hoped Poppie would take us girls anyway. He finally said he would if we could get the corn all laid by before the Fourth.

From then on, I prodded Lee and Granny up and down the rows at double time and cut their rest between rounds almost in half. Now and then poor Granny looked around at me, a now-what-have-I-done-to-deserve-this look in her eye. "It's only until the Fourth," I'd apologize. But when Lee gave me the same look, I'd give *him* another poke with my driving stick. "You're getting just what you deserve, and you know it," I'd tell him, thinking of Dolly's poor little colt.

We finished the corn in time, and Poppie took Florry, Stell, and me to the celebration. A few days later we heard that some of the girls we ran around with that day in town had come down with whooping cough. By August, when Mama's brother, Uncle Will Blaine, and Poppie's brother and two of his sisters and their families, came out from Missouri to visit, all six of us girls were whooping good.

Grandma arranged to have a family group picture taken while the relatives were there, and they all came to our house for the sitting. Grandma and Aunt Dicy, in their good black dresses, looked as smooth and shiny as a pair of jet buttons, and it seemed like Sunday, with all of us standing around in our best clothes, waiting for the photographer to come from Cozad.

Poppie and the other men set chairs and a plank bench in front of the house, and Mama brought her cages of canaries out and hung them where they'd show in the picture. Then the photographer came and set up his tripod and his black-hooded camera. Aunt Lizzie's family had all had whooping cough but Aunt Mary's baby hadn't, so they put us six whoopers at one end of the line and Aunt Mary and the baby at the other. Aunt Bell had invited her "intended," Earnest Woodruff, over to be in the picture; and his younger brother came along, so they included him, too.

Grandma had bought the relinquishment to a quarter section that joined our place on the north, and that summer Poppie and Uncle John built a five-room, shingle-roof soddy for her there. But Grandma bossed the job.

"Dig the cellar here," she told them, pointing out the place on the sunny south face of a low hill, "and build the house across the front of it. I'm tired of running clear to the south forty every time I want a ham out of my cave. And I want my sitting room *and* my kitchen both on the front. A woman spends most of her time in the kitchen, so why stick it way 'round in the back?"

They built her house the way she wanted it, with a big kitchen and sitting room across the front and three bedrooms behind, against the hill. The big bedroom, shared by Aunt Bell and Aunt Hester, opened off the sitting room, and Grandma's smaller one opened off the kitchen. The little middle room, built across the cellar door, belonged to Aunt Dicy—and to all the other odds and ends of the household. For Aunt Dicy wasn't fussy. As long as her room had a bed, and a hook for her clothes, she was satisfied.

Grandma papered her house with the plainest paper she could buy, and covered its floors with new woven rag rugs. Poppie said the rugs reminded him of all the carpet rags he had helped sew "winter evenings, back in Missoury, where nobody at Ma's house ever wasted any time." Mama said that Grandma, being the boss in her household, got her house built the way she wanted it; while women with husbands had to put up with whatever their menfolks thought was the cheapest and the quickest.

Pretty Mary Durland was with us all that summer, on account of Mama's poor health; and on Sundays, and sometimes on weekday evenings, too, young Earnest Love came a-courting. In the evenings we all carried chairs to the yard and sat a while, singing to the sweet music Earnest played on his little accordion. He called his sweetheart "Molly," and "Molly Darling" was the song he played and sang for her. Then Poppie would ask him to play "When You and I Were Young, Maggie," and he would sing that one for Mama.

He meant to cheer her, singing for her the song he loved so well, but it seemed to me it only made her more homesick for Missouri; for there was nothing resembling the "mill and the creaking old mill wheel" anywhere near our upland prairie home.

Of all the songs we sang in the cool of those summer evenings, my favorite was "Barney McCoy." I loved his wistful plea, "Will you go with me, Nora darling?" Her sad reply always broke my heart:

I'd go with you, Barney, darling,
If my mother and the rest were there.
For I know I would be bles't,
In that dear land of the West,
Living happy with you, Barney McCoy.

But I knew she should have been brave enough to leave her folks and go with Barney, anyway. I would have.

As the summer drew to a close, Mary told Mama that she and Earnest planned to marry in September and she must soon go home to get ready for her wedding. Mama still looked as if the first good breeze that came along could blow her clear out of the county, but all she said was, "I don't see how I'm going to get along without you, Mary."

A week later Mary spent a part of her summer's wages for a length of lovely blue foulard and went home to make her wedding dress. She was married at home, with only her family and close relatives there, but we heard later that she didn't get to bed at all the night before the wedding. By the evening before her wedding day, she had her dress all done except for the full, tucked, and braided sleeves. She worked on into the night, making the sleeves, but when she was ready to set them into the dress she found that she had made them both for the same armhole, and it was morning by the time she finished making and fitting another sleeve.

After Mary left, Mama told Poppie she didn't know how she was going to get the washings done after Florry started to school.

Poppie said he'd been thinking about that, too, and that he believed a washing machine would just about take the place of a hired girl.

The washing machine was a nine days' wonder at our house. A handle on top turned a three-legged "dolly"

under the lid, and after fifteen minutes in the machine
a whole tubful of clothes came out as clean as if each
piece had been rubbed that long on the washboard. At
first, Florry, Stell, and I fussed over whose turn it was
to push the handle back and forth, but by the time we
had put out a few family washings, none of us wanted
to do it.

Along with the machine, Poppie brought home the
first glass canning jars we had ever seen. Mama had
always canned her vegetables in tin cans, and sealed the
lids on with hot sealing wax. The new jars had screw-
on lids and were a lot easier to use. Besides that, they
looked so pretty on the cellar shelves, the red and green
and yellow jars of tomatoes, snap beans, and corn shining
like jewels in the dim light in the cave.

On a hot, muggy Saturday morning, that October,
I was helping Poppie clean the chicken house when Mary
and Dora Wahl came walking in to tell us that Johnny
Belstrom had died and his family was holding the funeral
as soon as the neighbors could gather. Poppie told them
he'd be over as soon as he could get ready. He started
for the house and I ran along beside him.

"Poppie," I said, "I've never been to a funeral."

"Well, if Mama don't care, you and Florry can go to
this one," he said.

For a wonder, Mama didn't care, and half an hour
later we left, on foot, for Belstrom's, half a mile across
the hills.

Johnny Belstrom had come over from Sweden about
the time we moved to Roten Valley. He had lived with
his brother Eric on the Belstrom homestead until the past
spring, when he bought the quarter section between us
and Eric's and put in a crop and built a little red granary
beside the field. Just lately, we'd heard that he and a

young Swede woman from away up the valley were going to get married just as soon as he could put up a sod
house.

At Eric's, some of the neighbors were standing out
in the yard, talking about the way Johnny died. It had
happened the day before, when Johnny, a big, heavy-set
young man, was hurrying through his dinner so he could
get started to Cozad to meet some relatives who were
coming in on the afternoon train. He was about through
eating when he suddenly dropped his knife and fork and
and looked at his brother in surprise. "Eric," he said, "I
don't feel good. Maybe you better go meet the folks."

Then he fell off his chair onto the floor, with thin
streams of blood running from his mouth and nose. They
said he was dead by the time they got him on his bed.

More neighbors came right away, and then the minister drove up in a buggy. Mr. Belstrom came out of
the house and said they'd have to have the funeral in
the yard on account of the smell getting so bad in the
house. Poppie and some of the other men carried the
coffin out and set it on four chairs in front of the house.
Then the family and Johnny's girl came out and the
minister began to read out of his Bible. It was noon,
just twenty-four hours since Johnny died.

After the service we all walked by the coffin, the family last. There was a glass window in the top half of
the coffin lid, and Johnny's face had swelled until his
nose pressed flat against the glass. He had turned a dark
bluish color and, even out of doors, the smell was so
bad that everyone hurried by. Johnny's girl lingered the
longest, crying into her handkerchief. Mrs. Maline finally
led her away, and some of the men fastened a cover
over the glass and put the coffin in a wagon. The fam-

ily and some of the neighbors climbed into other wagons
and started for the graveyard at Walnut Grove.

Until that day, I had never seen a dead person, and
all the rest of the fall I thought about death a good deal.
I was alone all the daylight hours with the cattle, and
all around me the prairie was dying. The sound of death
was in the wind that never stopped blowing across the
whitening grass, or rustling the dead weeds at the edges
of the fields. There was a forlorn, lonesome note in the
bawl of a calf for its mother and in the honking of wild
geese down the pale sky. On still days the whistle of a
train, far down on the river valley, seemed to carry a
terrible grief in its faint, lonely wail.

I thought about Johnny, too, wondering what had become of all his memories and thoughts, right up to the
noontime when he died, before he could even think about
that. Where were his thoughts now, and all the things he
had known? Did they just stop when his mind stopped, or
did they go on somewhere? I knew souls went to heaven,
but where did thoughts go, or did they just come to an
end and be wasted? With death so much in *my* thoughts,
I took a liking for grazing my herd near two little graves
in the corner of Maline's pasture. I felt so sorry for the
two little girls buried there, even though I'd never known
them. They hadn't had time to do much living, and it
seemed to me I was keeping them company, sitting beside their graves while I sewed quilt pieces, when I had any.

Late in the fall, when Mr. Belstrom sold Johnny's
goods at public auction, Poppie bought the little red
granary. He moved it over to our place and located it
beside the big new frame granary he had built that summer to store his wheat in. Crops had been good again
that year and Poppie had stored all his grain, intending

to hold it until prices went up in the winter, and so make a good profit on his season's hard work.

The wedding that finished out that interesting year took place at high noon on December 28, a Wednesday—the most favored day of the week for weddings—when Aunt Bell and Earnest Woodruff were married in Grandma's new sitting room. Aunt Bell made her own wedding dress, a lovely cream-colored brocade that set off the rich, heavy coils of her dark hair.

Poppie's sister, Aunt Anna Williams, and her family came out from Iowa for the wedding, and after the ceremony the minister and the grown-ups sat down to the big wedding dinner. All of us young McCances, along with our Williams cousins, had to wait our turn at the second table, and before we'd had time to eat much, we had to quit and rush out in the yard to help wave Aunt Bell and Uncle Earnest off in their new buggy.

Uncle Earnest's place was away up in the head of Roten Valley, and I knew I wouldn't be seeing them very often any more. I knew, too, that I was going to miss Aunt Bell like everything.

Poppie loved surprises, and late that winter he pulled a big one off in high style.

When the price of wheat went up in February, he began hauling his grain to town. He hauled the last load on a Saturday, and the stars were shining when he pulled in home, whistling like a teakettle on a red-hot stove, and unhitched behind the stable. All the rest of the evening he whistled and hummed in high good humor. We supposed, of course, that it was because he'd made a good profit on the wheat.

The next morning Florry, Stell, and I were still scrubbing, combing and buttoning up when Poppie, in his Sunday clothes, left the house with his Bible. He always

went to the schoolhouse early, to lay out the songbooks
and the Sunday school papers, but it seemed to us he
was earlier than usual that morning. But we knew he'd
be cross if we were late, so we hustled into our wraps
and scooted out the door—just as Poppie, straight as a
ramrod on the front seat of a brand-new spring wagon,
drove Gypsy and Daisy out from behind the stable.

The new carryall was a beauty. Its two padded black
patent-leather seats were soft as air, and its long buggy
box rode like a breeze above its elliptic springs.

Poppie's pleasure in it was all the greater because Mama
was happy with it, too. From then on, she went places
with us oftener, partly because the handsome two-seater
rode so much easier than the big wagon, partly because
she knew it looked nice and she could be proud of it.

Before spring work started, Poppie built a corncrib,
facing the granary, and roofed the wide driveway space
between them. The driveway, which was fairly weather
tight after he got around to hanging a heavy roller door
at each end of it, made a fine shelter for the spring
wagon, where we could put it in out of the weather and
keep its black paint and patent leather from chipping
in the sun and rain.

POPPIE'S BALL TEAM

Front row: Bill and George McCarter; *middle row:* ———— Munger, Art Williams, Gib McCarter, other two not identified; *back row:* Poppie and Herbert Totten.

GRACE, AGE SIXTEEN; FLORRY, AGE EIGHTEEN

Chapter Twelve

BY THE beginning of my eleventh year I was herding cattle again, but that spring I had a new dream to help pass the long days away.

In my geography book at school there was a picture of a cowboy on horseback, watching a big herd of grazing cattle. I had never seen a genuine, live cowboy; for in Roten Valley there were only homesteaders and their sons, riding farm horses. But in my dream the cowboy, riding a fine tall horse and leading another, always came galloping up to me. Then I would step easily into the new sidesaddle on the led horse and ride off with him to help look after the cattle herds on his big ranch. At that time there was no romance in my dream. The important thing about the cowboy was that he brought me a saddle horse and a new sidesaddle.

Of course I knew the new dream was almost as far-fetched as the one about floating above the clouds, or even the one of making the finest quilts in the world. For, since Aunt Bell had moved away, I hardly ever had any pieces to practice on.

One warm afternoon that spring I took the cattle up a long canyon northeast of Grandma's place. Near its upper end I turned the herd over to Kringa, pulled my bonnet off, and stretched out in a thin strip of shade along the canyon wall. I watched the drifting clouds for a while, then, to stop the ache inside me to be up there with them, I turned on my stomach, folded my arms under my head, and switched to my cowboy dream.

Now and then Kringa left the herd and came to nuzzle at my head to see if I was all right, or dropped down beside me to pant a bit. I knew my good little dog would keep the cattle in the canyon, so I dreamed and dozed the afternoon away, until a sudden coolness in the air reminded me that it was evening.

As I sat up and reached for my bonnet, Kringa dashed off up a little side canyon after a rabbit. A minute later I heard her barking, short, sharp little yelps that meant she had found something she didn't like—a skunk maybe, or a snake. She often killed snakes, even rattlers, by jumping at them and wearing them down until she could grab their necks and shake them to pieces.

I ran up the little canyon to see what she'd found. It was a queer little canyon, level as a floor except for some lumpy little hillocks, sticking up like thumbs here and there. Each one was round on three sides and flat on the fourth, with long grass hanging down over the flat side. Kringa, barking and snarling, was running back and forth in front of the grassy side of one of them, and a smooth, ugly buzzing came from behind the grass. She whined at me when I came up, and then began jumping at the cornered snake.

The rattler struck at her each time she jumped, but she was quicker, jumping away just in time — all but once. Maybe the overhanging grass made her misjudge the distance. Anyway, the snake struck her in the face, with a horrible dull, meaty *thud*. I ran to the plum thicket at the head of the pocket, then, and broke off a limb big enough for a club. After I had pounded the rattler's flat, ugly head to a pulp, game little Kringa grabbed the snake and gave it a good shaking. Then we hurried to round up the cattle and start them home. Her little black face was already beginning to swell, and she kept whining in a hurt and worried way. By the time we reached home she could hardly see or breathe.

Poppie made a deep puddle in the dusty ground beside the tank and put poor Kringa right into the mud. We kept handfuls of the mud plastered on her poor little face, but her head went on swelling until it seemed the skin would split wide open. She couldn't open her mouth and her breath came in short, whining jerks. Her agony was awful, and it went on for hours and hours. But by morning she was dead.

The cows knew, that first morning, that Kringa was gone and they gave me a bad time, scattering in all directions and heading into cocklebur patches in spite of all the running and yelling I could do. Kringa had been so good about driving them out of the burr patches for me. Afterward, she'd sit by me and pull the burrs off herself, then wait while I helped with the ones on her back that she couldn't reach. When hers were out, she'd run her little black nose all around the hems of my dress and petticoat, pulling out the burrs I'd picked up on the fringes of the patches. But now, by the time I plowed through the thickets and chased the cows out, my skirts would be stiff with the miserable burrs, and there was no good little friend to help me pull them out.

So I had trouble aplenty until Poppie got me a new dog, Rover, a big, young dog, and the most ambitious thing I ever saw. He wasn't much help with the cattle, but he was fun. Always on the move, he would be chasing something, or digging for something, or maybe just wearing himself out piling up cats. We had four kittens that summer, and when we weren't out with the herd he'd be doing his best to keep them in a pile, out in the orchard Poppie set out that spring. He worked so hard at it, carrying one kitten after another to the pile, but while he was going after the last two the first two would be scooting back to the house. Poppie said it looked like he'd learn, after a while, that piling up cats paid off about as fast as pouring water in a basket with a sieve.

Next to Christmas, the Fourth of July was the big day in our lives. We started planning for it right after the Sunday school picnic, and we looked back on it until time to start planning for Christmas again. Poppie enjoyed the big celebrations in Cozad as much as my sisters and I did, and Mama went along when she was able.

Every summer Mama made us new dresses for the Fourth, but this year, for some reason or other, she was late getting started and it was less than two weeks before the Fourth when she began making them. "It'll be a miracle if this old machine lasts 'til I get these dresses made," she said that morning, and, sure enough, it broke down a little later. It was the same old machine she had brought from Missouri, and no amount of polishing and varnishing had ever quite covered up the blisters that scarred its top the night the lightning struck the oat stack, but she had sewed piles and piles of underwear, shirts, dresses, and aprons on it since that July. She had cleaned, tightened, and repaired it dozens of times, but this time it seemed beyond her power to make it sew another stitch.

At noon Mama told Poppie she'd have to have a new machine before she could finish our dresses. Poppie sat down and thought about it for a minute, then he said, "Can't you fix it again, enough to make it work for now?"

"That machine's away over twenty years old," Mama

said. "It was old when I started to use it, and I've fixed it up and made it work ever since we've been married. I simply can't make it work any more."

I didn't like to hear Mama use that tone of voice to Poppie, but this time I was on her side, and I was glad when she went ahead and made out the order to Montgomery Ward. She wrote "please rush" across the top and bottom and handed it to Poppie. Without another word, he sat down and wrote the check.

We sent the order off with George Powell early Monday morning.

George was our mail carrier. He left Callaway, far to the north of us, early every Monday morning, driving a long-legged horse to a light, two-wheeled cart. His first stop was the Over post office; Roten, in the head of our valley, his second. He passed our place soon after breakfast, went on to Level post office, a few miles down the valley, and pulled in to Cozad well before noon. The next day he carried mail from Cozad to Callaway, and the day after he came back again.

"If the new machine comes by Saturday," Mama said, as George's outfit loped off down the road, "I'll still have time to make your dresses by the Fourth. If it doesn't, you'll have to wear your last year's dresses." In that case, short and faded as they were, we knew Mama would very likely not go at all, or let us go either.

Florry, Stell, and I knew that Mama knew the machine hadn't a chance in a hundred of getting to Cozad by Saturday, that she had just used the emergency to get the new sewing machine she needed. But, even though we knew it, from the moment the order left our hands we never stopped hoping the new machine would come in time.

That was a long, anxious, gloomy week, but Saturday

morning came at last. Poppie took the back seat off the
spring wagon, mostly to make us girls think he expected
the sewing machine, and jogged off on his regular weekly
trip to town. Long before his usual time to come home,
we heard the harness jingling and all of us ran out into
the yard where we could see the road. The mules were
coming at a lively trot and Poppie was beaming when
he pulled up in front of the house with the crated machine in the back of the wagon. Good old Montgomery
Ward! He had made sure we would have our new dresses
for the Fourth of July.

We headed for Cozad early, that morning of the Fourth,
driving the mules to the spring wagon. Gyp and Daisy
would have made a better-looking driving team, but Lee
and Granny made better time and we wanted to be there
early. Under the seats we carried a bag of grain for the
mules and a tubful of picnic lunch—including one of
Mama's five-layer cakes, three white and two yellow, with
custard filling between the layers and whipped cream,
shredded coconut, and black walnut meats on the top
and sides.

Down on the valley, our turnout joined the long procession of wagons, buggies, and carriages heading for the
picnic grounds on the east side of town. Poppie let us
out in front of the big pavilion, where some people were
watching two men put down a well. The well had always
been there for other celebrations, but this was the first
time I had seen them put it down. It didn't take long.
All they had to do was screw a short piece of pointed,
perforated pipe onto another short piece of ordinary pipe.
Then they drove the pointed end a few feet into the
ground, screwed a pitcher pump onto the top end and
started pumping water. To me it was a miracle—water,
without weeks of hard work. But, like everyone else, we

took a drink from a tin cup chained to the pump head, and to my surprise the water was both cold and good. Then we hurried off to watch the parade.

Old Mr. Cummins and his sons played in the good-sized band that led the parade. Next came a long line of fancy-top buggies, surreys, and carriages with big brass side lamps and fenders over the wheels. Every rig had been polished like glass and all the wheels twinkled with colored ribbon and paper woven in the spokes. The horses, curried and brushed till they glistened like satin, were decked out in bridle plumes, colored harness rings, ribbons, and showy fly nets.

The people in the rigs were as gay as their turnouts. The ladies wore hats covered with plumes, flowers, fruit, and ribbons and had fringed summer lap robes spread over their knees. The men wore satin sleeve holders and stiff straw hats, flicked tasseled buggy whips, and let their right feet dangle outside their rigs.

New wagons and farm machinery followed the pleasure rigs, and no parade was complete without at least one new binder—the last word in laborsaving machinery. Fine big work horses with enormous feathered feet pulled the machines. I always liked to watch the horses. The driving teams were so light-stepping and proud, the work horses so powerful and steady.

Footraces, three-legged races, fat men's races, and sack races were run off after the parade. The tug-of-war was next. The strongest men in the crowd, eight or ten to a side, lined up facing each other on the rope. At the word "go" they dug in their heels and strained back on the rope. Sometimes it went on for quite a while, every man grunting and sweating and pulling as hard as he could. The tug was over when one side yanked the other over the center mark.

Then came the greased pig contest and the greased pole climb, both for boys. A fat shoat, smeared from his snout to his tail with axle grease, was turned loose inside a circle of boys. They all went after him as hard as they could, and when enough grease had rubbed off on the boys and enough dust had settled on the pig, some boy would finally manage to hang onto him for keeps; for the pig was his prize.

Every year about a dozen boys lined up to draw for turns at climbing the fourteen-foot greased pole for the silver dollar on its top. One after another they'd tackle the pole, gripping it hard with their hands, elbows, and knees, and shinnying up as far as they could. The first boys didn't have much chance, as they played out too soon, but each one wiped off a little more grease when he slid back to the ground.

This year a skinny boy, littlest of the lot, drew a chance toward the end of the line. He filled his pockets with fine dust while he waited his turn, and by then only four or five feet of messy, slippery grease was left on the pole. This was more grease than any of the other boys had been able to climb over, but the little fellow spit on his hands and tackled the job. Just below the grease he stopped, dug into his pocket for a fistful of dust and went on. Helped along by several more dustings, he made a nonskid trip to the top of the pole and grabbed the dollar.

By then it was noon and everybody headed for the pavilion, where the women were unpacking lunches and making lemonade in big crocks and buckets. Mama and Mrs. Totten were putting our dinners together at one end of a long bench, and when we all got together we ate all we could hold.

After dinner there was always a two-hour program

of songs and speeches: the Gettysburg Address, the Declaration of Independence, and several patriotic talks. And then came the most exciting part of the whole day—the big water fight.

Two horse-drawn fire engines were lined up in the middle of Main Street and, when somebody fired a pistol, two teams of volunteer fighters went for each other with the fire hoses. There were a lot of men on the pumps and a lot of force behind the water squirting through the big hoses. The fighters all wore slickers, waterproof hats, and rubber boots so, by the time one outfit finally had the other on the run, the bystanders were a whole lot wetter than the fighters. Of course Mama and most of the other mothers kept all the girls back out of range of the hoses, but we enjoyed the water fight anyway.

By five in the afternoon the celebration was all over except for the fireworks in the evening. Farm families who lived near town hitched up and started home to do chores so they could get back in time for the fireworks. We lived too far away to do that, or to stay for the fireworks and go home afterward. But, with the sun no ways near down, it seemed too early to leave. We knew Poppie thought so, too, when he said, "Let's drive out to the river and ride across the new bridge before we start home."

Florry, Stell, and I, glad for anything more that would stretch the wonderful day out a little longer, yelled "Oh, let's do!" So Poppie hitched up and brought the spring wagon around. When he'd stowed our belongings under the seats and counted us all in to make sure no one was left behind in the crowd, he headed the mules south on the river road.

Florry and I hadn't seen the river since the summer

we forded it on the way home from the railroad camp,
when it had been almost dry, and we had never seen the
long new wooden bridge. Lee, born and raised in the
upland hills, had never seen a river, and Granny probably didn't even remember tagging her mother across
the Platte, that summer eleven years ago.

Before we had gone two wagon lengths onto the bridge
we knew the whole thing was a mistake; for Lee and
Granny were scared out of their wits by the water flow-
ing by down below, and by the hollow sound of their
feet on the planks. Right away they both decided to
walk in the exact center of the bridge. Braced against
each other, they inched along, snorting and shivering.
Poppie talked to them and urged them on. The rest of
us hung on to the sides of our seats, and to each other,
and tried not to look down at the muddy water.

Part way across the long bridge, we began to meet
the rigs that were coming back to town for the evening
celebration. Since the bridge was wide enough for only
one wagon at a time, three or four "turnouts," or double
width sections, had been built into it for passing—but
our mules wouldn't think of using them. So all the rigs
we met had to pull to the farthest edge of the turnouts,
tight against the rail, while we edged past them in the
middle of the bridge.

After a long time we reached solid ground on the
far side of the river. The mules stood there at the end
of the bridge, shaking like they had St. Vitus's dance.
Poppie let them quiet down a little before he turned
them around and headed for the bridge again.

"Oh, Poppie, can't we go 'round it this time?" Dovey
begged.

"I'm afraid not," Poppie said. "This river begins in

Colorado and ends in the Missoury, and we'd never get home in time to do chores if we did."

But going back wasn't quite so bad. Lee and Granny still kept to the middle of the bridge but they walked a little faster, knowing they were headed toward home. And this time all the rigs were going our way, so we didn't have to pass anybody on the turnouts.

Chapter Thirteen

ONE AFTERNOON toward the end of July I was scuffing along the road from Grandma's back to our place. I had enjoyed my visit with Grandma, but I still missed Uncle John. Grandma said she missed him, too, though she was glad he was married and doing for himself, which was his right, she said, after all the years he'd stayed with her when she needed him.

Uncle John had taken a homestead over northeast of Walnut Grove that spring, and married Irene Kirkpatrick, daughter of a settler from the east side of Roten Valley. Poppie and Mama had taken Grandma and Aunt Hester and gone to the wedding. Florry, Stell, and I had wanted to go but I had to herd cattle and Florry had to stay home with the little girls.

But, all in all, this summer had been a good one. Poppie's wheat, already cut and shocked, flanked the road on my left, his biggest field of corn grew tall and green on the right. There had been plenty of rain to make the wheat crop extra good, and the corn crop looked like it was going to be a bumper. Pastures and crops everywhere looked good, and Poppie and the neighbors talked of replacing sod buildings with frame before long, and of buying more land and livestock, or new machinery and furniture.

The trees in Poppie's orchard stood head high, and

with part of the cash he got from the sale of his summer shoats he had bought a new binder in time to cut the wheat. The wheat would pay off our debts, he said; the money he'd get from his steers in the fall would see us through the winter in good shape; and he'd be able to hold back his entire corn crop to winterfeed the extra young sows he was going to keep.

A few weeks back, the Swedes had finished a new schoolhouse over in the Wahl district, near our old homestead, and they had started holding Sunday school there. Of course the Swedes all began going over there, and there weren't enough people left to have Sunday school in the Maline schoolhouse. So Aunt Hester began driving our light team to the spring wagon and taking us three older girls to Sunday school and church at Walnut Grove. We loved going with our pretty aunt to the big white church. There the long hitchracks out back were crowded with saddle horses and teams and the church was always well filled. After church, while Aunt Hester visited with her friends, we walked with the other girls our age among the headstones beginning to dot the cemetery across the road. Johnny Belstrom's, bought with the sale money, was the biggest one there.

The minister, Mr. Matthews, lived in the little white parsonage beside the church. Because he hadn't been away from his native England very long, we found him hard to understand and had to guess at half he said. Poor Mr. Matthews, he knew so little about horses, but with all the valley in his parish he had to use a horse and buggy to get around among his congregation. His church members took turns loaning him a horse and buggy, but he never learned the proper way to hitch the two together. Time after time he started off from the parsonage barn, only to have the harness he had just put on

the horse come apart someplace and leave him sitting in
the buggy, somewhere on the road, while the horse trotted
on back to whatever stable it belonged in.

I was nearly halfway home when a barred Plymouth
Rock hen suddenly darted from behind a wheat shock
and ran across the road into the cornfield. That hen
really surprised me, out there all by herself. She wasn't
ours, I knew, for Mama wouldn't bother with barred
Rocks. She said they were too cross to make good mothers,
fighting and breaking their eggs and killing little chickens.
She didn't belong to any of our near neighbors either;
for their flocks, like ours, were mixtures of all kinds,
speckled, spotted, streaked and striped.

I told Mama about the hen when I got home, and she
said I'd better go back to Grandma's next day and see
if she knew to whom it belonged. But Grandma didn't
know. She said someone must've lost her out of a sack
or crate on the way to town and that I'd better catch
her and take her home with me before a coyote got her.

On the way home I hunted in the cornfield until I
found the hen, and kept after her until I ran her down.
I tucked her under my arm—and all the rest of the way
home I made big plans. I had never really owned any
live property before. The pet turkeys had belonged to
us only until they grew up and went into the common
barrel, but this hen was *mine*. She'd be easy to tell from
the rest of our flock, and I could set her and raise more
chickens, and set those and raise more, and before long
I'd have enough money from my chickens to buy myself the new sidesaddle I wanted so much.

It was late by the time I got home, so I turned my
pretty hen loose and hurried to do my evening chores.
When I came in from milking, Mama told me the hen
wouldn't know enough to go to roost with the other

chickens this first night and that I'd better hunt her up and put her in the chicken house. But, though I hunted everywhere until full dark, I couldn't find her.

At daylight I started hunting again, and after a little I found a handful of black and white feathers under the granary—all that a sneaking skunk had left of her. I had looked under the granary twice the evening before, but in the dusk I hadn't seen her. I felt so bad about it all. I was not only as far as ever from owning a side-saddle but, if I had left the hen in the field, she might still be alive.

A little later I made friends with a late-hatched, half-grown white rooster from Mama's flock. He was so friendly and seemed to like me so much, and I took to carrying him with me while I herded. After an hour or so on the prairie he'd have his craw so full of grasshoppers he could hardly see over it, and then he'd sit beside me and visit, clucking and chirping at a great rate as long as I'd answer him. He was a very polite chicken that way.

And then, early in August, the hot winds began to blow. In other summers we had had the hot winds for a day or two—but now they blew on and on without letup. Day by day the corn shriveled until, by the end of the month, the stalks stood white and lifeless. The prairie turned brown and brittle and the land seemed to pant for breath under the burning sun.

To add to the punishment of that terrible drouth-ridden August, typhoid fever broke out in the neighborhood. When Poppie heard about it he said we'd have to stop going to church or anywhere else as long as there were any cases around. So we didn't even go to the funeral when little Katie Helen Matthews was laid to rest in the cemetery across the road from her father's parsonage.

One of our neighbors, a North Carolinian, barely pulled through the fever. His wife was named Elizabeth and his two girls Liz and Dell. He owned a breechy old dun cow. No fence in the neighborhood could stop or hold that cow, and whenever he saw that she had crawled or jumped the home fence he yelled at the girls, "Liz (or Dell) go git that dun cow in, and don't stop to git yore bunnit neither." While the poor man was out of his head with the fever he had repeated over and over for days, "Elizabeth, the Devil, an' the old dun cow, Elizabeth, the Devil an' the ole dun cow, Elizabeth. . . ."

In September, when, outside a few irrigated gardens, not a green thing was left anywhere, the winds stopped blowing and the weather turned cool and pleasant. Poppie and I snapped out a skimpy pile of corn, and Poppie looked at the nubbins and said he guessed he'd have to sell all the little pigs as soon as they were weaned, but that he'd keep the sows. There should be corn enough to get them through the winter, he thought.

Nearly everybody had to give up the big plans they had made in the early summer, but then, they said, you had to expect a bad year now and then. No country had all good ones, and "next year" would be different. Poppie went ahead and paid off his debts with the wheat money; but the steers, poor and thin because of the drouthy pastures, brought such a low price that money soon began to be tight at our house. Like most of our neighbors, we had to cut corners wherever we could. Mama let out the hems and waistbands on last year's dresses for us to wear to school, and patched the patches on our everyday clothes. The only new dresses we had were the ones she made from the cloth that came out of the Missouri barrels.

Aunt Hester taught our school that term, and for the

first time since my second year, I went to school all day.
Because of the drought, Poppie had no fall work to do.
So he took over the herding during school hours.

One nice morning soon after school started, Florry,
Stell, Dovey, and I went early to the schoolhouse and
sat down on the porch to wait for some of the others to
come so we could play a while before school. A few
minutes later we saw a girl coming down the road from
Bergs. We were surprised, for Bergs had only boys. The
girl came to the edge of the schoolyard and stopped.

She had wide blue eyes and fair, smooth skin. Her
heavy, waist-length yellow braids were tied with broad
blue ribbons and the ends hung free and bushy below
the bows. It was the prettiest hairdo we had ever seen.
Her dress was crisp and new, and she wore shoes and
stockings. We wouldn't start wearing ours until the
weather turned cold.

Then Aunt Hester saw the girl and came out on the
porch. "Good morning," she called, "won't you come
on in?" The girl didn't move or answer. She looked
about ready to cry. Aunt Hester went over, then, and
tried to talk with her, but it seemed that she didn't speak
English and she wouldn't come any closer.

When some of the Swede girls came and talked with
her, she told them her name was Esther Shogren and
that she had just come from Sweden to live with her
aunt, Mrs. Olaf Berg. The Berg boys, like all the big
boys in the valley, didn't start to school until all the fall
work was done, so Esther had had to come all alone that
first day, and she had been so frightened she was almost
sick.

Esther could read and write very well in Swedish, but
she had to learn everything all over again in English. I

helped her all I could, for she was about my age, and from the first I loved Esther and her pretty ways.

During the six years we had been going to school in Roten Valley, there had always been more than twice as many Swedes as Americans in the school. The Swedish children soon learned passable English, but it took us longer to learn their language—and until we did they had a lot of fun talking about us, to our faces, in Swedish.

There were some language mix-ups, too, like the time one of the Berg boys, who was a big cutup anyway, was clowning more than usual. I said, "My, but he's *loony*," and at that, the Swede girls almost had hysterics. I begged them to tell me what was so funny about "loony" but they only laughed harder than ever. Finally, one of them whispered a translation, which didn't explain much, but left me with an idea that it was something you didn't talk about in mixed company. To this day, I'm not sure what it meant.

But if our mistakes in Swedish amused them, theirs in English were just as funny. One of the Swede girls came to school one morning wearing a pair of new shoes that pinched her feet. She limped up to Florry and leaned hard on her shoulder and said, "Oh, please let me use you to leg." Another time, when we came to school, there was a bad odor in the schoolyard. "My goodness, I smell skunk!" I said. One of the Swede boys sniffed hard, and then said, "Huh, I don't feel no smell."

Later on that winter two grown young Swedes, just over from Sweden, came to school for a while to learn to read and write English. Aunt Hester was perfectly willing to teach them, but she did have to put a stop to their chewing tobacco and spitting the juice on the schoolhouse floor.

The weather stayed mild and dry all through November. So one pretty Sunday we drove up to the head of Roten Valley to visit Aunt Bell and Uncle Earnest. It was the first time I had been there and I thought Aunt Bell had a beautiful house. It was only two rooms, but the furniture was all new and her dishes all matched.

After dinner Aunt Bell gave me a big bundle of pretty quilt pieces, and altogether we had such a good time that it was almost sundown when we climbed back into the spring wagon to go home. As we drove away, we kept calling good-byes back to Aunt Bell and Uncle Earnest until we turned onto the main road, and right after the last good-bye the sound of a gunshot came clear and loud across the prairie.

"Oh, oh, somebody 'boomed' a prairie chicken," Mama said.

Two mornings later Poppie came running to the house with the *Callaway Courier* that he had just taken out of the mailbox. "Look at *that*," he said, and spread the paper on the table.

The headline, in big black letters, read "DEAD IN HIS BOOTS," and the story filled most of the front page. A man named Hardy Mullholland, it said, had been shot and killed just before sundown on Sunday evening by a Mr. West, who lived near the head of Roten Valley. The two men had quarreled a few days earlier, and Mr. West had ordered Mullholland off his place and told him not to come back. But on Sunday evening Mullholland had gone back, and West had come out with his gun in his hands and told him to stop where he was. When Mullholland came on anyway, Mr. West fired at his feet. And when that didn't stop him, he had raised the gun and fired again. That second shot, the one we heard as we drove away from Aunt Bell's, was the one that had killed a man.

Under the headline, "A LITTLE COLD LEAD," the *Cozad Local* carried the story the next day. And both papers, later on, carried accounts of the trial at Broken Bow, where Mr. West was acquitted.

December came in cold and blustery—and with it new trouble for us. For one wintry evening none of our turkeys came home to roost. Mama said it seemed like misfortune always came double, or worse. First the drouth, and practically giving our pigs and steers away, and now the whole flock of turkeys gone. She said she supposed the coyotes had been after them, but she didn't see why they had to wait until almost the night before time to dress and ship them. Florry, Stell, and I felt awful about it, too, for we knew the new overshoes, mittens, caps, hair ribbons, candy, and gum Poppie and Mama gave us for Christmas came out of the turkey money.

But the turkeys weren't lost after all, at any rate not entirely. A neighbor came driving them home the next evening.

"Didja lose some turkeys last night?" he asked.

"Yes. Not a single one of our bunch came home," Poppie told him.

"Well, I guess they musta come in with ourn," the neighbor said. "We shut ourn up last night so we could butcher out the gobblers and ole hens today. Afore we got through butcherin' I told the ole lady we was aputtin' too many gobblers in the barr'l, so we counted up, and, sure enough, we had about twict too many. We figgered then that somebody's flock musta come in with ourn, so I've brung you back what gobblers're left, and yer hens, and enough of ourn to make up fer what we killed of yer gobblers."

He went away, and we went out to look the turkeys over.

"We've got the right number back, all right," Mama said bitterly, "but they're all late young hens and skinny gobblers. All the fat gobblers and big old hens went into the barrel over yonder. Our turkey check'll be pretty slim this year, I'm afraid."

All our checks were pretty slim that winter. Because of the poor pastures, the cows dried up earlier than usual and Mama had to stop making butter to sell. Even the egg money didn't amount to much. We had started shipping eggs to an Omaha produce firm the winter before, and Mama had taken part of her pay in factory-cured bacon, which we liked so much better than our own home-cured side meat. But now the price of eggs fell off with every case we shipped, and the price of the good bacon went up to two and a half cents a pound, and then to three. When it got that high Mama said we'd have to do without it, that it was too dear for us to buy any longer, tight as money was.

Nearly all of January, that winter of '94, was dry and cold; and on a bitter Saturday morning near the end of the month little Esther Holmes died of pneumonia. Mrs. Holmes and some other Swedish ladies laid her out in a little homemade coffin and the men carried it down to the empty granary, where her little body would keep marble cold until the funeral the next afternoon.

The next morning Mr. Holmes and all the children walked past our place on their way to Sunday school over in the Wahl district. Mr. Holmes went first, holding his Bible against the front of his long thick coat. Joseph came next, then Louis, Hannah, Anna, John, Phillip, Ellen, and Lydia. And it seemed to me that Hannah and Phillip had left a little gap between them—where four-year-old Esther had walked on other Sundays.

Except for Mrs. Holmes, who wasn't able to walk so

far and always stayed home with the latest baby anyway, all the family had walked the two miles to Sunday school every Sunday since the summer before. Mr. Holmes had good work horses, but he said they should have their day of rest, too. And, anyway, that four-mile walk did not seem a hardship to the family, and on that bitter Sunday, even though little Esther lay a corpse in the granary, they went faithfully to worship as usual.

The cold, dry winter turned into a warm, dry spring, and the spring term of school was about over when a young man who taught a school up toward the head of Roten Valley stopped one noon to visit our school and talk shop with Aunt Hester. The day had started out unusually warm for that time of year, and by last recess it was so hot that all of us girls went around to the east side of the schoolhouse to sit in the shade. I suggested we play school to pass the time away. But Lillie Maline didn't want to, so we just sat there, slapping at gnats and trying to think of something else to do.

Through the open window above our heads we could hear the visiting teacher telling Aunt Hester about a fight he'd had with the big boys in his school. He had been to Lexington that morning to see the county superintendent about it and he sounded pretty discouraged.

"That's too bad," Aunt Hester said, "but I wouldn't know how to advise you. My scholars all get along so well together that I really don't know what I'd do if there should be any trouble among them."

What Aunt Hester didn't know, until it boiled over that very minute, was that a fine kettle of trouble had been brewing all day in her own school. Ever since she came to school that morning, Lillie had been feeling jealous because she thought all the rest of us played better with each other than we did with her. So she sat on

the outside of our little circle and pouted. Her little
dog, Uno, had followed her to school that day, and when
he pushed up against her, just then, and tried to lick
her face, she slapped him away.

"Why, Lillie, you should be ashamed of yourself,"
gentle Esther Shogren told her.

"I shouldn't either," Lillie snapped back at her. A
right good quarrel followed, with some most unlady-
like remarks flying back and forth, and with more of
us getting into it every minute.

Aunt Hester, her pretty face pink all over, broke up
the fuss by coming to the door and ringing the bell hard.
The young man, looking a little less discouraged, bid
her good-bye and rode away.

Chapter Fourteen

BY PLANTING time the ground was hard and cracked with drouth. But farmers, always hopeful, plowed and seeded as usual, and then waited for spring rains to green the winter-pale pastures and start the seed in the dusty fields.

But almost no rain fell, that terrible year, and what little there was came on winds so hard that it hadn't time to soak into the baked ground, but ran instead down the slopes into the cracked lagoons, where it was licked up in a day or two by the blazing sun and the hot, never-ending wind.

In spite of the drouth, the hardy buffalo grass started in the bottoms of the swales and draws, making a little feed for the livestock. When school was out and I took over the herding again, Uncle John came over, bringing his little bunch of cattle and offering to make a bargain with me. "Gheet, if you'll herd my cattle with yours, this summer, I'll give you that bob-tailed calf, there," he said.

The calf was a nice red heifer, born on a January night so cold her ears and most of her tail had frozen and come off. She was an odd-looking little beast, I know, but to me she was beautiful. I named her Bess and loved her all her life. Once more I owned some livestock, and again I could plan to buy myself a sidesaddle.

Of course I didn't ever intend to sell Bess, but one of her calves would take care of it. Bess wouldn't even have a calf for two years, though, and by the bargain I'd made with Poppie—to give him every other calf for pasturing my cattle—it was going to be quite a while before I had any calves to sell.

All that hot, dry summer I gave Bess special care. I hunted out the greenest spots in the dried-up pastures for her, and brushed her pretty coat to keep the burrs out of it. She hadn't enough tail left to switch flies off herself, so I helped her out by swinging a fly-chaser of weeds over her back and legs for hours at a time. But all the cattle had a hard time of it that summer. Already thin from a winter of short rations, they seemed to grow thinner by the day as they walked and walked, snatching a few spears of grass here and there, hunting for patches of better forage.

Mama went ahead and planted her usual big garden, but only the radishes and lettuce grew big enough to use. When the rest of the garden withered and died in the scorching heat, Poppie fenced a little patch between the windmill and the chicken house and spaded in a load of droppings from the hen roosts. We seeded the plot to summer vegetables, beans, beets, carrots, potatoes and tomatoes. The seeds, planted in such rich ground and watered every day from the mill, sprouted almost overnight, and grew like Jack's beanstalk the rest of the summer.

Poppie's sows had farrowed big litters that spring, but before the pigs were old enough to wean, the little pile of corn was gone and there was nothing left to feed them. So Poppie turned all the pigs out and put Florry and me to herding them on the scarce forage of the wheat fields, so weedy by June that there was no possible hope for a crop there. While Stell and Dovey herded the cattle on the dry prairie, Florry and I tried to keep the pigs in the faded wheat fields, where they dug their tough snouts into the caked ground and rooted out every tiny shoot and stem—and seemed to get longer nosed and thinner flanked every day. Under the scorching sun we ran and ran, turning the poor starving creatures back from the cornfields, where the young corn still seemed to draw a little nourishment from the parched ground.

Each day seemed hotter than the one before. The sun came up blazing, sailed all day through a glittering, brassy sky, and set in a smothering blast of heat that lasted all through the night. The burning winds moaned endlessly across the prairie and there was seldom even a thunderhead to break the sameness of sun and heat.

One hot July morning Mama and the little girls picked a part of a tubful of chokecherries from some scattered little patches in the draws. She said the cherries were runty little things, mostly skin and seeds, but they'd make a bit of spread for our bread next winter.

Poppie wasn't at home that day, so Florry and I, putting off as long as we could the afternoon horror of herding pigs, dallied over the dinner dishes. We had just finished when the Gypsies came, ten or twelve wagonloads of them, pulled by poor, bony old ponies. The last two wagons pulled out of the plodding line and stopped in front of our door. The tired ponies hung their heads to their knees and panted, while a fat woman and a half dozen ragged children spilled out of the wagons and crowded into the kitchen.

None of us girls had ever seen Gypsies before and we backed away, half afraid of such bold, dark-skinned people. Mama had just emptied several pans of fresh bread onto the table, and the Gypsy woman gathered

her full skirt into a bag with one dirty hand, snatched
a loaf of hot bread with the other and dropped it into
the pouch. She reached for another loaf, but Mama darted
to the table, slid the rest to the back and stood in front
of them.

Then the woman began to beg for a chicken, "Jus'
one cheeken for poor seek woman in wagon. Poor seek
woman got leetle baby."

"Our chickens are so poor they wouldn't even make
good soup," Mama told her.

"Oh, yes, make good soup for poor seek woman," the
Gypsy begged.

So Mama told Florry and me to go catch her a hen.
The little Gypsies went with us and all of us surrounded
a hen. The poor thing wasn't hard to catch; for all
our chickens were so thin and scrawny that if a brisk
breeze blew against their feathers from behind it took
them scooting across the yard as if they had sails on.

When we went back to the house the Gypsy woman
was at the tub, shoveling chokecherries into her mouth
by the handful and begging for some to take with her.
Mama filled a tin can and gave it to her, but she went
on eating out of the tub until Mama pushed it into the
corner and stood Florry and me in front of it. When
she saw that she had gotten all we had to give her, the
Gypsy clucked her brood to her and waddled out. They
all tumbled back into the rickity wagons and headed
south, following the rest of the seedy outfit.

A day or two later a shabby little man with bushy
hair and thick mustaches rode up on a rawboned horse
to invite us to preaching at Walnut Grove the next Sunday afternoon. He was a traveling preacher, he said, and
he was having a special service in order to deliver an
important message to the people of our community.

When Poppie told him we'd try to come, he heeled his poor old horse on down the valley.

The church was well filled on Sunday afternoon when the little man got up to preach. "Behold! I am Alpha and Omega," he shouted, "and I am come to tell you of the wrath to come." He went on and on, yelling and ranting against "Lucifer the dollar, the root of all evil." Once he started to reach into his pocket for a sample of the terrible Lucifer, but missed his pocket and rammed his hand down inside the loose waistband of his suspendered trousers instead. There was a minute of embarrassed silence all around, before he finally located the pocket and pulled out the dollar.

After raving on for nearly an hour on the evils of Lucifer—to an audience that was lily white so far as that particular sin was concerned that summer—Alpha and Omega took up a collection and closed the meeting. The poor old fellow counted and pocketed the little handful of extra Lucifer he had gained, then climbed on his crowbait horse and rode off down the heat-hazed valley.

As the days dragged on the leaves of the stunted corn began to roll and turn white in the deadly heat. Only our little garden, where the water ran all day between the rows, looked green and natural for this time of year.

Then, near the end of July, there came a day hotter than any we had yet lived through. At breakfast Mama looked so pale and sick that Poppie said he would help me herd the pigs until noon and Florry could stay at the house and help with the work there.

While we herded the squealing, starving pigs toward the almost bare wheat field, Poppie squinted at a pale hint of a cloud poking above the northwest rim of the the sky—the first cloud we had seen in weeks. "There's still a chance to save some of the corn if we get rain in the next day or two," he told me.

The cloud got bigger, blacker, and uglier all forenoon. At noon Poppie shook his head and said he didn't like the looks of it, that he was afraid a bad storm was coming up. "Florry," he said after dinner, "you'd better herd cattle this afternoon and let the little girls stay at the house. And Gheet, I have to go up the valley a ways but I'll help you take the pigs to the field first. Now you girls watch that cloud. If it starts to come up fast, you hurry home."

The afternoon was sultrier than the morning, the still air seemed thick and hard to breathe, and the cloud looked more threatening than ever. I watched it uneasily while I circled the restless pigs, keeping them together the best I could in case I had to start for the house in a hurry. Then, late in the afternoon, the cloud suddenly began to bloom across the sky, like a black shawl flung out by the wind, and I knew it was time to go.

The pigs, scared, too, by the "feel" of things, for once were willing to head for home and we came in flying. Florry had just corralled the cattle and Poppie was unhitching the mules from the spring wagon in front of the stable. Florry came running to help me pen the pigs, and Poppie yelled "Hurry, girls, get to the house. This looks bad."

We were halfway to the house when a wind as hot as a red-hot stove whirled out of the cloud and almost knocked us off our feet. Then Poppie caught up with us and yelled at Florry to help Mama and Stell get the little girls to the cellar, and at me to shut the windows while he shut off the windmill. "Then run for the cellar," he said. He was yelling at the top of his voice, but we could barely hear him above the terrible roar of the wind.

I flew through the door to the nearest window. Mama, Florry, and Stell each grabbed a little girl and ran for the cellar. The wind had come so suddenly that Mama hadn't had time to shut the windows, and while I jerked at the stubborn sash I could see Poppie pulling at the shutoff lever on the windmill. The mill wheel was screaming at full speed and whirling and whipping like a crazy thing, so that it was all he could do to get the lever down. Dust, leaves, and dry grass filled the air and the wind seemed to screech against the awful, greenish purple cloud; then the storm shut out the last bit of light and I couldn't see anything at all.

I banged the last window shut and ran outdoors. The wind knocked me back against the entry wall and I couldn't get my breath. Then Poppie caught my hand and pulled me along toward the cellar. Behind us there was a rip and a bang as the entry tore loose from the house. Then the boiler lid, snatched from its nail beside the boiler, flew past my ear with a screaming whistle. All at once we stumbled against the cellar door, and Poppie pulled it open and pushed me down the steps.

Poppie was panting, and his voice sounded loud in the sudden stillness when he asked Mama if the rest of them were all right. She said they were, but that she'd been pretty worried about Poppie and me.

We huddled there in the dark, musty-smelling cellar for quite a while. The roar of the storm was faint down there, under the thick dirt roof, and we couldn't tell what was going on outside. After what seemed like a long time, I asked Poppie if he couldn't look out now and see if the storm was over.

"Not yet. If I open the door too soon the wind might explode the roof right off this cave," he said.

But a little while later, when he raised the door and

peeked out, he said the wind had gone down considerably and the clouds were breaking a little. Then, relief in his voice, he reported that the red granary was over on its top again but that seemed to be about all the damage he could see.

Early in the spring another high wind had turned the little granary over on its top but hadn't hurt it much. So if that, besides the wrecked entryway, was the total damage done by the storm it wouldn't be so bad. Poppie waited a little longer, then opened the door and stood up. The storm was blowing over fast now, and it was getting light again.

"Oh, oh! That wasn't the red granary I saw, it was what's left of the big granary," Poppie said in a shocked tone of voice.

"Oh, no!" Mama exclaimed. We had all been so proud of the big granary.

We all came out of the cellar. The sun was about to go down behind a few scattering clouds and the yard was an awful-looking place. The big granary was a pile of wet rubbish. The corncrib still stood, but it was twisted all out of shape, and the broken shed roof that had joined it to the granary had tumbled into the driveway. If Poppie had had time to put the spring wagon away it would have been smashed to splinters. The chicken house was torn apart and dead chickens lay all around, their feathers blown wrong-end-to so that they looked as if they had their skirts up over their heads. The entryway was nowhere in sight, and the red granary, on its top all right, had been scooted along until all its shingles had ripped off.

We walked over to the wreckage of the big granary. Somewhere under the piled-up, broken boards a kitten was crying. The mother of the week-old kittens was sitting on top of the pile, lifting one paw and then the other, curling it against her breast and putting it down again. She went on doing that, over and over, and paid no attention to the blind, crying kitten—she had been a good mother, too. We began pulling the splintered boards away, and deep in the pile we found the kittens, all dead but the one that was crying.

Then Poppie dug into the ground with the end of a split board. "See," he said, "dry dirt! That rain hardly dampened the ground. Unless we get more in a day or two, there'll be no show for a crop of any kind this year."

In the last light of that awful day we found one of the heavy roller doors from the driveway. It was out in the road southeast of the house, its rollers caught on the top wire of the yard fence. To land *there*, it had had to pass between the house and the cellar at a level low enough to catch the wire.

"Lucky for us, Gheet, that it didn't sail by while we were running for the cellar," Poppie said.

By bedtime it was all clear again, and Poppie told Florry to run out and turn the windmill on. "There'll be no more rain tonight, so we'd better keep the water running on the garden," he said.

Florry came back a little later, crying and rubbing her arm. When Poppie asked her what had happened, she said she didn't know, that there was fire on the windmill and when she tried to turn it on something had hit her arm, hard, and knocked her hand away. She looked scared—and I knew she was more afraid Poppie wouldn't believe her than she was of what had happened at the windmill.

But all Poppie said was, "I know, that happens once in a while. You watch while I turn it on." When he touched the iron rod that released the wheel and fan, a long bright spark flashed from the end of it, knocking his hand away. He used a stick, then, to unhook the rod and turn the mill in gear. "The storm charged the metal part of the mill with electricity," he explained, "and when we touched the rod it discharged a little."

Chapter Fifteen

IT WAS harvest time again, but there was nothing to harvest. For days on end after the storm the sun blazed on in a sky without a cloud. The grass in the swales and draws that had, in other years, afforded winter feed, was already grazed into the ground. The cornfields were nothing but weedy patches of stunted, scrawny stalks, with hardly a dozen ears to the forty acres anywhere. In the lagoons, where water had stood a time or two earlier in the summer, the barren stalks stood a little taller, but that was all. There was nothing substantial anywhere to cut for winter feed.

The day after the storm Poppie had turned the pigs loose to root and rustle where they liked, for there was nothing left in the fields that they could damage. A few days later he began killing the young pigs, one by one, and feeding them to the few hens the storm had left us. But, even after the skinny starvelings were all killed, the lean sows could barely stay alive on the scanty forage left in the burned-out valley. "I'd hoped to get our winter's meat out of them," Poppie said of the poor, long-nosed, panting creatures, "but there's hardly enough lard on the bunch of them to fry one skillet of meat."

With the pigs turned loose, I went back to herding cattle, keeping them out of our own and the neighbors' dried-up cornfields. I grazed them mostly on the dusty

slopes of the railroad section south of our place, and
there one day, in the weedy bottom of a little draw, I
stumbled over the remains of our washboiler. Mama and
the girls had spent hours looking for it after the storm;
but the big wind had rolled it across the prairie so hard
and so fast that it was as round as a bushel basket and
no good for anything.

Only our little irrigated garden yielded anything like
a normal crop that fall, and even there the potatoes and
tomatoes had "gone all to vines" and bore no crop. Over-
encouraged by too much water and too rich soil, they
had grown so long that Poppie, holding the end of a
vine as high as he could reach, could hardly take all the
slack out of it.

All up and down and across the country it was the
same. Some families, certain that nothing but starvation
was ahead, sold for what little they could get and pulled
out. Those who stayed—and most in our valley did—
knew they looked a hard winter in the face.

In spite of the discouraging turn of affairs, most of
the settlers tried to be cheerful. The *Cozad Local* raised
a good laugh when it came out with a story about the
fish in a creek down on the valley kicking up so much
dust that the people's health was endangered—until the
town council called out the fire department to play water
on the fish and sprinkle the creek enough to keep the
dust down. Then there was a story going around about
a poor farmer who was turned off his farm, after working all spring digging a well on it. Shortly after he
moved to another dry farm in the next county, the big
wind had pulled his well up by the roots, carried it over
to his new farm and transplanted it between his house
and barn. The same wind had caught a well-known teller

of tall tales with his mouth open, and a particularly big gust had blown him inside out before he could shut it.

In September Poppie knocked a little sled together out of boards from the wrecked granary and fastened a sharp plowshare to its left side (Poppie was left-handed) just above the ground. Then I rode old Granny and guided her down the corn rows, and Poppie, riding the sled behind us, picked up the withered stalks as they fell before the plowshare and piled them on the sled beside him. We hauled the few loads back to the stable and piled them there, and when we were done he looked at the measly stack of dusty fodder a long time. Finally he said, "We'll have to sell the cattle, Gheet." It must have cost him a lot to say that, but I was stunned.

"All of them," I asked, "even Bess?"

"Even Bess. There's no feed, and they'll starve if we try to keep them over. We'll have to save this little dab of fodder to feed the teams next spring while we put in the crops."

So I went over all our place with a heavy corn knife, cutting every tiny stray wisp of corn I could find, and every withered bit of grass or weeds that had, so far, escaped a hungry creature. I tried so hard to bring in enough extra fodder to claim the right to keep Bess, but it was no use. In all that burned valley there wasn't enough extra feed to keep one little bob-tailed heifer through the winter.

Poppie went to town the next day to sell the cattle, and that afternoon an old peddler came to our house. Nearly every summer a peddler tramped through the valley, a different one each year, but all sharp-faced, dark, and foreign-looking. The patient look of their backs, bent beneath the heavy packs, was always belied by the sharp impatience of their quick, darting eyes. The packs were mostly full of glittering, bright-colored trash: cheap fancy buttons, braids, and laces, sleazy ribbons, back and side combs with glass "sets." Mama always dreaded the peddlers' coming because she could seldom get them out of the house without buying something she didn't want and couldn't afford.

The peddler that afternoon was already inside the open door before we even knew he was on the place. Mama tried right away to tell him she hadn't any money and couldn't buy anything, but he went ahead and opened his battered old suitcase. There wasn't much inside it, just a scanty jumble of gray-looking lace, some shoddy beads and broaches, a few combs with broken teeth and missing sets. Of a pattern with everything else in the land, the peddler and his stock were worn, shabby, and hard up.

In broken, stuttering English, he tried his best to "do beezness," but Mama told him over and over that she had no money. Finally he slammed his goods back into the case and banged it shut. Then, glaring at her as if she had taken up his time on purpose, he snatched hold of his old pack and stomped off down the road through the shimmering heat.

Poppie came home that evening, more beaten and discouraged than I had ever seen him. "Maggie, I don't know what we're going to do this winter," he told Mama. "I couldn't sell the cattle. I couldn't even *give* 'em away. Everybody else is trying to sell, too, and nobody has any feed or any money. There's a money panic on in the East and there's hardly a dollar in the whole country."

A little later, the men of Roten Valley held a meeting at the schoolhouse to decide what to do about their livestock. Then they did the only thing left to do—just turned all the cattle and workstock loose on the prairie, to get through the winter the best they could. So I didn't have to sell Bess after all, but it was small comfort to me—for if the winter turned out to be a bad one there wouldn't be a cow left alive by spring.

Mr. Ericson, over on our old homestead, had never managed to own any cattle; so the old strawstacks of other years still stood in the fields there. Poppie made a deal of some kind for them and we hauled the straw home, a hayrack load at a time. It was poor feed but it kept our milk cows giving milk through most of the winter; toward spring, though, the milk was so thin it hardly raised enough cream to color Poppie's and Mama's watered-down coffee.

In late September Aunt Hester used the money she had saved from teaching to take Grandma to Chicago to the World's Fair. At our place Poppie, with nothing else to do, went to work building a little stable out of the lumber he had salvaged from the wrecked granary; while Mama patched and "made over" and patched some more, trying to get us girls ready for school in October.

For by then, like almost everyone else in the community, we were down to our bottom dollar and supplies were running low. Poppie would have gladly "hired out," but no one had anything for a hired man to do, or money to pay him with if he had. But, hard up as we were, we weren't as bad off as some of our neighbors; for Grandpa Blaine had written that, along with the barrels, he was sending extra supplies: wheat for Mama's chickens, and coal and flour. Even so, Poppie said, we'd likely have pretty slim pickings before another spring rolled around.

And then, as if times were not already hard enough, the seventh McCance baby picked that autumn to arrive. Florry, Stell, and I hadn't even known one was expected,

so we were in for a big surprise when we came home
from school one afternoon and Poppie, beaming like a
new-polished plowshare, met us at the door with the
news that we had a baby *brother.*

A boy at last! It was hard to believe, but his coming
made that October day the brightest of all that hard
year. The next morning Poppie sent letters off to Grandma McCance in Chicago and to Grandpa Blaine in Missouri, telling them about our boy, and none of us could
seem to get enough of just looking at him.

We hadn't named the baby yet when Poppie wrote
his letters; for we had long ago given up picking out
boys' names for the new babies at our house, so we were
caught unprepared. We had no more than decided on
a name that suited us all, than Grandma McCance came
flying into the kitchen, breathless from hurrying all the
way from Chicago.

"What did you name that boy?" she asked, not even
stopping to say "hello."

"Charles Roy, but we'll call him Roy," Poppie told her.

"Thank goodness," Grandma said, sitting down and
heaving a big sigh. "I was so afraid I wouldn't get here
in time. When your letter came, I said to Hester, 'Hester,
we must get home as fast as we can. Charlie's have a
boy and like as not they'll name him "James" if I don't
get there to put a stop to it.'"

Grandma had come to have a deathly fear of the name
"James." Her own father, James Garner, had died very
young. Then she had named a baby son of her own
"James," and he had died in his first year. She had named
her next son "James," too, and he had lived only a few
months. A few years later Grandpa James McCance had
died while yet a middling young man; so Grandma was
convinced that any McCance named "James" hadn't long

to live. Since Mama's father, Grandpa Blaine, was another "James," Grandma had been so sure that Poppie'd
name his first boy for both grandfathers that she had
rushed home from the Fair to save the baby from the
curse.

"There wasn't any danger," Mama told her. "I was
determined all the time that he'd have a brand-new name."

A few days later Mama had a letter of congratulation
from her oldest sister, back in Garden City. It was the
first letter she'd had from Aunt Alice in all the years
since we left Missouri; and she put it away in the top
bureau drawer, back of the little red velvet box that
held her keepsakes. "I'm going to keep it," she said. "I
may never get another letter from Alice, the way she
puts off writing." She never did.

Roy was a sweet, chubby, good-natured baby, and in
spite of the extra love and attention we all gave him he
stayed that way. But it was hard on Poppie that his
first boy was the only one of all his children he couldn't
pay for at the time the doctor made the long trip out
to our house. Years later, after we had laid him to rest
at Walnut Grove, we found among Poppie's papers the
ten-dollar promissory note he gave Dr. Fochtman the
day Roy was born. The payments, scratched on the back
of the note, fifty cents or a dollar at a time, covered most
of the next two years.

Early in November the *Cozad Local* carried a notice
that relief for the drouth-stricken settlers was on the
way, that several carloads of flour, coal, food, and clothing
were due any day, and that each school district should
hold a meeting and appoint a board to distribute the
supplies. On the next mail, Poppie received notice from
the depot in Cozad that the goods, billed direct to us
by Grandpa Blaine, had arrived in the Garden City re-

lief car, an entire carload of supplies sent by Cass County
folks to their friends and relatives in the Cozad community.

At our district's meeting, held at the schoolhouse that
same week, a plan of operation was set up and a board of
three, Poppie, Olaf Berg, and another neighbor, appointed
to administer it. According to the plan, the head of any
family seeking aid must have a list made out and signed
by all three board members before it would be honored
at the relief headquarters in Cozad. Any member of the
board, through what he knew of the applicant's circumstances, could "cut down," or "strike off" items from
the list before signing it.

Most of the Roten Valley people were honest and careful in making out their lists. A few tried to "chisel"
more than their fair share, while others in real need were
too proud to take "relief" at all. Some families took
the free supplies but tried to keep it secret; others went
openly on relief and didn't care who knew it. And some
complained about everything, insisting their neighbors
didn't need, or shouldn't have, the supplies they drew.
Only the local boards and the Cozad officials knew for
certain who received aid, so of course there was a good
deal of prying and jealousy; and any woman or girl who
came to church or to the literary in a dress new to the
community was sure to be suspect.

At school one day one of the girls slipped around and
asked me, straight out, if we were "on relief." "No," I
told her, more thankful than ever that Grandpa Blaine
had sent enough to see us through the winter.

Besides our own supplies, Grandpa had also sent an
extra barrel of molasses for Poppie to divide among our
neighbors. As soon as it was known that we had molasses
to give away, a neighbor or two began showing up at

our door nearly every day, bucket in hand. But when the relief barrel was empty, Poppie hadn't the heart to tell the bucket brigade so—and went on handing out molasses until our own barrel was empty, too.

Most of the relief clothing shipped in from the East was practical and usable, but not all; for out of those bales came some furbelows never seen in our valley before—things like long-trained evening dresses and silk, satin, and velvet gowns.

"Fancy us wearing those doodads out to milk the cows and slop the pigs." Some of the women laughed. But others snatched at the doodads, taking all they were allotted and begging for more, and made them over into school dresses for their daughters. And so it came about that the daughters of some of the "reliefers" wore silks and velvets to school for a winter or two, and were far better dressed than they had ever been before.

From the pretty calicoes Grandma sent, and from Aunt Ollie's castoffs, Mama made Sunday dresses for us as usual, but for school we had to wear our too-short, patched, faded last year's dresses. So all that winter we simmered under the smug gazes of our silk-clad schoolmates.

During a short, hard cold spell shortly after New Year's, Poppie and I both came down with the "grippe." We were still too sick to leave the house when a poor old woman from the north end of Roten Valley pulled in to stay all night with us. She had turned her stock out on the prairie that fall, too, she said, and when she ran out of supplies and had to go to town for her "relief" she'd had a hard time catching up a team. She finally managed to snare an old mare and a big, lubberly colt, both so poor they couldn't move off a walk, and had been all day getting to town and back again as far as our place.

Poppie told her to put her team in the new stable, finished except for hanging the door, and lean the door against the opening to break the bitter wind. With the one halter she had with her, the old woman tied the young horse up and left the old mare loose in the stable. The next morning she found the door pushed down and the mare gone.

"If I'd 'a' had a lick o' sense I'd 'a' tied the other one," she scolded herself. "The colt wouldda stayed wherever the old mare was."

Poppie tried to talk the old woman into remaining with us another day. By then, he told her, he'd be able to get out and catch her another horse. But she said there were no two ways about it, she had to get on home that day. So he told her that, if the colt was gentle enough, there was a way to hitch him so he could pull the wagon alone. She said he was gentle enough, that he didn't have the "gumption" to be anything else.

So Poppie told her how to thread the halter rope through the ring on the other end of the neck yoke, then tie it back to the hames on the colt's harness, so as to hold the neck yoke level. She did the way he said; then the poor lopsided outfit crawled off up the valley, the woman hunched against the razor-edged wind, the colt shambling along at a pace that would barely get them home by sundown.

Except for that cold spell, the winter turned out to be one of the mildest ever known in central Nebraska. Once, an early morning snowstorm left a few little skifts of snow behind scattered clumps of withered bunchgrass. By noon it had all melted and the days were bright and warm again. And that year we learned the true worth of buffalo grass in an open winter—the cattle, browsing the short curly spears, stayed in surprisingly good condition, better at least than anyone had expected.

Socially, it was a good winter, too. With almost no outside work to do, folks neighbored and visited more than they ever had, and good crowds turned out for all the Grange and Literary meetings. A new song, "Nebraska Land," outgrowth of that terrible year of drouth, caught on and everybody learned it by heart and sang it at the tops of their voices at every meeting.

> We have reached the land of drouth and heat,
> Where nothing grows for us to eat.
> For winds that blow with scorching heat,
> Nebraska Land is hard to beat.
>
> Oh, Nebraska Land! Sweet Nebraska Land!
> While on your burning soil I stand,
> And look away across the plains,
> And wonder why it never rains.
> Till Gabriel doth his trumpet sound,
> They'll say the rain has gone around.

At one literary, Florry and I sang all seven verses and choruses of "The Drunkard's Lone Child." Other top favorites were "The Gypsy's Warning," "Two Little Orphans," "The Death of Little Blossom," and "Give Me Three Kernels of Corn, Mother."

But it was little Leonard Maline, a first grader with a deep bass voice, who stopped the whole show when he stood up at one literary meeting and boomed:

> Times are hard an' girls are plenty,
> So don't get married till yer twenty.

Chapter Sixteen

THE MILD winter of '94-'95 warmed into an early spring and gentle rains soaked the long-dried fields in time for plowing and planting. Good crops grew again on the rested land and new grass covered and healed the drouth scars on the prairie. Homesteaders, their faith in Nebraska restored once more, got busy with new plans —to be carried out as soon as their debts were paid.

That spring, too, Mama said Florry and I were too big to go barefooted any more. Florry didn't mind; she felt like a young lady anyway, and was willing to look and act like one. With me it was different. I was as tall as my older sister and I wanted as much as she did to be grown up, for it would mean we could go more places without Mama. Now I learned it meant giving up some things, too. But, in spite of my longing to turn my toes out again to the feel of warm cow trail dust and cool green grass, I minded Mama and wore my shoes and stockings—even after the day I went with Poppie to the ball game and a low foul ball hit my shinbone a savage whack and peeled a dollar-sized patch of skin off it.

Poppie had played on the Roten Valley ball team almost ever since we came to Nebraska. Each community had its own team, and good crowds always turned out for the Saturday afternoon games. (Sunday games were unheard of in those days.) Mama hardly ever went to

the games, and she didn't often let us girls go, either,
so I didn't dare let on at home how much my skinned
shinbone hurt. But for days the bruise leaked into my
thick-ribbed cotton stocking, gluing it fast to the sore
spot. Every evening I soaked it loose with tender dabs
of a wet washcloth. Barelegged, the sore would have
healed a lot faster, and it wouldn't have hurt nearly so
much.

Rains came when we needed them, all that summer,
and soon it was hard to believe the country could ever
have looked so bare and desolate as it had the year before. Then, toward the end of September, Aunt Irene
and Uncle John came over to tell Mama they had heard,
at a picnic, that the wild grapes were thick as flies in the
big canyons south of Brady Island. It was thirty miles
over there, they said, and they were taking a camping
outfit and would be gone two nights; and they wanted to
know if Mama wanted to go with them.

Of course she wanted to go; for if there was anything
Mama liked better than camping out it was picking wild
fruit.

They started early the next morning, driving a tiny
mule, Pete, beside a big work horse. Mama left Roy
with Florry, but Aunt Irene and Uncle John took their
year-old son, Irvie, along. The weather was bright and
sunny that day, and the next, but the third day was
cold and wet; and when they drove into our place that
afternoon Aunt Irene was wearing a quilt instead of her
jacket, and she and Mama were both so cold and frazzled
they could hardly climb out of the wagon.

The first day of their trip had been fine, they said.
They had found a good campsite and set up their tent,
but at supper Mama had advised against giving little
Irvie water from a strange well so they gave him coffee

instead. Uncle John was still laughing about it. The coffee made him drunk, he said, and he had giggled and cut up so much all night that nobody could sleep.

All the next day they had climbed up and down the steep hills, picking buckets and buckets of grapes, and when they came back to camp they found another party of fruit pickers camped close by. And *that* evening the poor little mule, Pete, took a spell of colic and groaned outside the tent till daylight. After the second sleepless night they turned out early, shivering in the cold drizzle that had settled over the canyons in the night, and Aunt Irene couldn't find her jacket.

"Those campers looked sneaky to me, right from the start, so I had a good idea where it went to," she said.

They had packed up as fast as they could and pulled out on the long, wet trip home—and it didn't help poor Mama any when we had to tell her that Dovey fell off the corral gate while she was gone and broke her collarbone.

Florry, Stell, and I went to our first party that winter, a Valentine party Aunt Hester gave for the young folks in the valley. Florry was sixteen then and I was fourteen, Stell was only twelve and Poppie and Mama thought she was a little too young, but she put up such a howl to go along that they gave in. Florry and I couldn't blame her for that—a first party is exciting to look forward to.

We dressed up in the new red plaid dresses Mama made us and walked across the fields to Grandma's house, the first time we had ever gone anywhere at night without an older person along. Aunt Hester had decorated the living room with dozens of red hearts and ribbon streamers, and baked a lot of little heart-shaped pies. She played the organ for the games, "Skip to My Lou," "Old Dan Tucker," "Spin the Platter," and "Button,

button, who's got the button?" And Aunt Dicy kept
smiling her wide, toothless smile and tapping her feet
and bobbing her head in time to the music. Even Grandma, who considered more than a very little fun a waste
of time — if not actually sinful — seemed to enjoy the
evening.

And I know I did. Oss Brownfield chose me for his
partner for all the games that evening. Oss was fifteen
and good-looking, and I felt so grown up that night that
I didn't believe I'd mind not going barefoot when summer came again.

Ten days later, while the hearts and streamers were
still up, Aunt Hester and Charlie Bischoff were married
in Grandma's living room. Aunt Hester's wedding dress
was a beautiful pearl-gray brocade that glistened like frost
in the morning sun.

The minute the ceremony was over Grandma said,
"Grace, you come along and help me," and she rustled
out to the kitchen and tied a big apron on over her
black dress. Then she stooped to fill the stove with cow-
chips. Maybe Grandma was getting too old to manage
a big dinner any more, or maybe seeing her "baby"
married had flustered her; anyway, before she realized
what she was doing, she took the lid off the teakettle
instead of the stove. She caught herself just in time.
"My, my, I almost popped these chips into the teakettle!
Wouldn't that've been something?" she scolded. "My,
my" and "pop" were the only slang expressions Grandma
ever used, and very seldom even those, so I knew she was
upset.

Uncle Charlie had a farm over southeast of Walnut
Grove, and he and Aunt Hester went there to live. Later
that spring Uncle John built another big room onto

Grandma's house, so he and Aunt Irene could move back
to look after her and Aunt Dicy.

And that spring we moved again, too, this time to
the Rowan farm in McCarter Canyon, where there was
more pasture for our growing herd of cattle. Poppie
leased our own place to Mr. Ericson, who had lost the
homestead during the big drouth, and we moved the
week after school was out.

Our new house was a tall, narrow, T-shaped affair. It
had three bedrooms upstairs and two downstairs, besides
a front room and a kitchen-pantry-dining room with a
lean-to tacked on the back. Houses like it, big, naked,
ugly, and built to last forever, sprouted all over the country in the nineties, cluttering up the prairie for years
afterward. Their upstairs rooms were icy cold in winter
and hotter than ovens in the summer, but they were a
step up from soddies and they stood for progress.

With so many bedrooms we didn't, for the first time
since we came to Nebraska, have to have a bed in the
front room. But we still had a problem with that room.
It was big in all directions—its ceiling was nine feet
high—but it had so many windows and doors there was
almost no place left to set the furniture. There was a
door to the kitchen, one to each bedroom, and *three to
the outside,* one on the west, one on the south, and one
opening onto a tiny afterthought of a porch that was
tucked into the angle of the T. All three of them opened
onto the same dreary patch of bare, shadeless, windswept
yard.

Mama would have liked to make that front room into
a real parlor, one she could keep locked except on special
days, but we had to pass through it to get to the bedrooms, so of course she couldn't.

The kitchen, a dark, gloomy room, was another big

mistake in that house. A dark, musty little pantry was crowded into one corner, between the outer wall and the steep, narrow stairway to the upper floor. One of its two long, narrow windows was shaded by the useless little porch, and its walls and ceiling were lined with dark wainscoting, those deep-grooved boards so popular in the nineties which were so hard to keep clean. The front-room walls were lined with it too, up to chairback height, and dirt, smoke, and grease filled all the grooves in both rooms.

We scrubbed every inch of that wainscoting clean, but Mama said we wouldn't have to wash the plastered walls above the wainscoting in the front room, that we'd cover the smoke and grease there with new wallpaper.

She bought pretty flowered paper and we worked hard for two days, pasting it on the high walls and ceiling. The night we finished, Florry, Stell, Dovey, Nellie, Presh and I all went in for a last look at the pretty walls before we went upstairs to bed.

The sight we saw when we came down the next morning was shocking. The greasy plaster had shucked every shred of the drying paper loose in the night. Some of it hung down over the wainscoting, the rest humped across the floor in stiff, dirty strips. Mama just stood and looked at it, the way she had looked at the homestead kitchen the morning after the big wind took the roof off.

"Never mind," Poppie said. "The girls'll help you clean it up and wash the walls, and I'll get some more paper and help you put it on."

He bought new green window blinds too, the first blinds we had in Nebraska, and they gave Mama quite a lift. She made pretty curtains of white cheesecloth to hang over them, and we were all proud of that front room when she finally got through with it. She put a new woven rag carpet down over a thick padding of clean, fluffy straw, and hung a "yard of fruit" still life above the door to the kitchen.

She had squeezed enough change out of the butter money to buy three of the yard-long pictures. She hung the other two, a "yard of pansies" and a "yard of kittens," above the bedroom doors, and finished the room off with the big family pictures, hanging those wherever the four windows and six doors left wall space enough to accommodate them.

Poppie built a little sod milk house beside the windmill in the backyard, where cold water ran through a wooden tank to cool the crocks of milk and butter. At milking time we took the milk directly to the milk house, strained it, and washed the milk things. Besides making the work easier, it helped keep flies away from the house.

Early that summer a Mr. and Mrs. Joe Williams, on their way to Colorado in a covered wagon, stopped to visit us. Poppie and Mama had known Mary Rundel in Missouri, before she married Mr. Williams, but they hardly recognized her in the pale woman, far gone with tuberculosis, who had to be helped out of the wagon.

The next evening, while Mama and I were washing up the milk things in the milk house, she said it was a pleasure to have company, now that we had a spare bedroom to put them in and a decent room to sit in to visit with them. Then she said she was afraid poor Mary had waited too long to make this trip, that it might have helped her a year ago but now she'd never live to see Colorado. At that minute, a blast of wind swooshed through the doorway, where Poppie hadn't yet got around to hang the door, and stirred up a choking whirl of dust from the dirt floor. Then a heavy hand seemed to slap hard on the sod roof above us.

The windowless little room faced east, so we hadn't seen the big hailstorm, boiling up from the southwest while we worked. For a few minutes hailstones the size of eggs bounced in the yard, and wind and rain screamed by the door; then the storm rolled off to the north and Mama and I ran for the house. In the kitchen the girls and Mrs. Williams stood shivering by the front-room door, watching Poppie and Mr. Williams sloshing around through the mess in our living room.

The hail had smashed the big south windows and the storm had poured right on in. Poppie and Mr. Williams had pulled the new blinds down over the broken windows, trying to keep the rain and hail out, but the jagged stones had slashed the blinds to ribbons and turned the pretty cheesecloth curtains into torn, dirty rags.

That was a bad country for big hailstorms, and for lightning and thunderstorms, too. There was another bad hailstorm later that same summer, the day Grandma had her big family picnic.

Always a great hand for family gatherings, Grandma had written to Aunt Libby in Missouri and Aunt Anna in Iowa, asking them to come home for a reunion. The rest of her large family were already in Nebraska by then. Aunt Mary Stouffer, after her visit in '92, had persuaded her husband to come out to Custer County and buy a farm. Uncle Tom and Uncle Rob had come, too, and had been teaching neighborhood schools for the past year or two.

Grandma had her picnic in the new park at Gothenburg, a little town west of Cozad. It was August and the day was blazing hot, so hot that, even at a walk, the teams sweated all the way to town. At the park, while we spread the picnic dinner on a long cloth laid on the grass under the little cottonwoods, Poppie and the uncles went on downtown and bought some watermelons and a big chunk of ice. A little later, from her place at the head of the cloth, Grandma looked down the line at all her children and grandchildren, smiled a little and said, "My, we make a crowd nowadays, don't we?"

Not a leaf on the cottonwoods was stirring by the time we finished packing up the picnic things, and the seats of the rigs were so hot that we sat as light as we could on the drive downtown to the picture gallery; for Grandma wanted a "family group" picture, since it might be the last time she'd ever have them all together. The rest of us all went along to watch the photographer pose Grandma and her nine sons and daughters on fancy wicker chairs and set off the magnesium flares for the shots.

The gallery was on the ground floor in a two-story building, and the room where the pictures were taken was in the back and had no windows. The photographer was quite a while, diving in and out from under the black cloth cover on his camera and getting things set to suit him, and while we were in the back room the hailstorm came down on the town from the north. Because of the rooms above, we didn't even hear its roar as it passed over, but when we came outside again the street was inches deep in hailstones and nearly every glass store front in town was smashed. The trees were stripped leafless and the air was cold, even though the sun was shining again.

"Well, well," Uncle John said, "if we'd just of waited a little we wouldn't a had to buy any ice to cool our melons."

We headed home then, across the beat-up hills, and

the farther north we drove the worse the damage seemed to be. Gardens were pounded into the ground, corn-fields, just coming into roasting ears, were cut to short bare stubs. At every farm we saw broken windows, ruined roofs, dead chickens, cattle and horses with cut and bloody hides.

"I wonder what it looks like at our place," Poppie said, finally, and Mama said she dreaded to go on and see.

But within the next mile we could see that the storm had eased off a little, and with each mile after that the damage was less and less. At home we had had no more than a good rain, which we needed.

Another bad storm, a year or two later, came on a hot Sunday evening. Poppie and Mama had gone over to Uncle John's that afternoon, and just before they left Poppie asked Florry and me if we were looking for any beaux to take us to church that evening. We said we weren't, so he told us we could do the chores up early and ride horseback to Walnut Grove if we wanted to.

By chore time, an ugly black cloud was coming up in the northwest, but we hurried through our work any-way, and I saddled Gyp and Daisy. Though I had been using Aunt Bell's sidesaddle since her babies began com-ing, I hadn't given up hope of owning one of my own someday. In the spring and fall, when the new Mont-gomery Ward catalogs came, I still turned first to the saddles to pick out the one I wanted. I still dreamed about my cowboy, too, but Montgomery Ward didn't list cowboys and I didn't know how I was going to get one.

By the time I had the horses ready, the whole north-west sky had come to a rolling boil and the air was hot, still, and heavy. We knew better than to go and leave the younger children alone in the face of such a storm, but Poppie wasn't there to tell us we couldn't, so we went, riding hard for Walnut Grove.

The first gust of wind blew out of the purple-black cloud as we tied our horses to the crowded hitchrack behind the church, and dollar-sized raindrops splattered the yard dust as we flew for the door. By the end of the first hymn the storm was going full blast. For the next hour the crack of lightning, the roar of thunder, and the beat of the rain all but drowned out the preacher's voice.

After church, when we all came out into the mud and the dark to go home, Gus Matz found his driving mare dead between the broken shafts of his buggy, struck down by a bolt of lightning. It was a miracle that the bolt had spared the rest of the long row of horses, tied to the same hitch line, ours among them.

Because it was so hot when we left, we hadn't brought any wraps along. But it was more than the cold, wet wind that kept us shivering all the way home. We knew we were going to get a good scolding when we got there, and we knew we deserved it.

In that part of the country lightning killed a few cattle and horses in their pastures every summer, and set a barn or a feed stack afire here and there. The church steeple at Walnut Grove was struck by lightning several times, too. One time, when a bolt started a lively blaze in the church, the minister and his wife went to work to put it out. About halfway through the job the poor woman, who was subject to bad headaches, clutched her head and said she felt one of her spells coming on.

"Wife," the minister yelled at her. "This is no time for spells. Fetch me some more water." So she put off the spell and brought the water.

Chapter Seventeen

THE FALL little Roy was three years old Mama took him and went back to Missouri again. A week or so later Poppie, who hadn't been back to Missouri since he came out to the homestead twelve years earlier, got Dave Zook and his fifteen-year-old daughter Grace to stay with us while he went to bring them home. Mr. Zook, one of Poppie's old Missouri neighbors, lived on a farm south of Cozad, where his wife and two of his children had died in a measles epidemic soon after they came to Nebraska.

While Poppie and Mama were gone we went up to Aunt Bell's and picked a lot of ripe tomatoes. Ours had been killed by the early hailstorm, but Aunt Bell had more than she could use and Florry wanted to surprise Mama with a nice lot of canned tomatoes when she came home. But the surprise was all ours.

Florry had never tried canning by herself before and she must have slipped up somewhere; for a few days after she finished them the jars began blowing up. Those that hadn't already blown up were sizzling and spewing around their tops when we discovered what had happened, so we had to dump them too, and then spend the rest of the day cleaning tomatoes off the cellar roof and wiping up the mess.

On the Sunday before Poppie and Mama came home,

Mr. Zook and Grace went home for the day. The girls and I drove the spring wagon to church at Walnut Grove, as usual, and when we came home we found a wedding party waiting in the yard. There were two couples, the one that was getting married and the other that had come along to "stand up" with them. They were from a neighboring community and we scarcely knew them—but we did know, good and well, that Poppie didn't approve of them, or of the "wild" crowd they ran with.

But they had come a long way, and they still had several miles to go to reach the home of the justice of the peace, up at the head of McCarter Canyon. So Florry and I asked them in to dinner, and they invited us to go along to the wedding afterward. We knew Poppie wouldn't like it if we went, but we thought it would be fun, so we agreed to come along.

It didn't seem like a wedding at all, no family, no preparations, no minister. Just the fat, bald-headed little justice, in dirty overalls and rolled-up shirt-sleeves, mumbling a few words out of a torn book, while his wife, a big, frowsy woman with bulging eyes, looked on. But those most concerned seemed to think it was all right. As soon as they were married, the bridegroom fished a box of cigars out of his buggy and offered the justice one.

"No, thanks," he said, "I don't smoke, but th' missus does."

The newly married man passed the box to the big woman. She took a cigar and lit it, then she puffed out a cloud of smoke and boomed, "Jim, the first good news I hope to hear from you is that you have a ten-pound baby boy." She winked and slapped her fat leg with the flat of her freckled hand and laughed like it was all a big joke. Even the wedding party seemed a little

page 186

embarrassed by such good wishes, offered a bare fifteen minutes after the ceremony.

Of course Poppie heard about it, and Florry and I would have been in trouble, except that he got notice about the same time that the new organ and bicycle he had bought in Omaha, on his way to Missouri, were at the depot in Cozad.

Poppie had known all along that Mama wouldn't like it because he bought the bicycle—not when there were so many things we *really* needed. But he wanted it so much, and he figured that if he surprised her with a fancy new organ for her front room, she wouldn't say much about the bicycle. It worked. Poppie, thankful that she let him off the hook easy, did the same for us girls.

Everybody was buying bicycles that year. Both men and women had taken to wheels, and bicycle clubs were all the go. The papers played up the new fad with pictures and stories, and in the cities some of the lady riders had even invented a new outfit, the "bicycle bloomer," to wear while riding their "wheels."

But Mama, like most of the other women in our community, didn't think much of the bloomer. Neither, it seemed, did the editor of the *Dawson County Pioneer*, who printed this description of it:

The much talked about bloomer bicycle outfit for ladies is simply a pair of trousers very baggy at the knees, abnormally full about the pistol pocket and considerably loose where you would strike a match. The garment is cut decollet at the south end and the bottoms are tied around the knees to keep the mice out. You can't put it on over your head as you would a skirt, but you sit on the floor and pull it on just as you would put on your stockings, one foot in each compartment. You can easily tell which side to have in front by the button on the neck band.

I was fifteen that winter, with my sixteenth birthday
coming up in the spring, and for a long time it had seemed
that everything I most wanted to do depended on the
day I turned sixteen. Oss Brownfield had asked to take
me to several parties, but Poppie always gave me the
same answer, "Not till you're sixteen." He let me go to
the parties with Florry and her beau, a neighbor boy
named John Houk, but that wasn't the same as going
with my own beau.

It was the same with the silk sunshade I wanted so
much. Florry had saved the extra butter money the
year before, and by the Fourth she had had enough to
buy a lovely parasol with a colored silk shade and a fancy
handle. I had begged for one, too, for I had been as tall
as Florry for the last three years, but Mama said I'd have
to wait until I was sixteen.

Then, about a month before my birthday, we gave
our first party. There were two reasons for the party:
Mama's pride and Poppie's conscience.

Mama, seldom well and always tired, dreaded the extra
work a party meant for her, but we had gone to parties
in nearly every home in the neighborhood and she couldn't
have us obligated any longer. Poppie hoped the party
would make up to us girls, especially me, for the loss of
Pearlie and Bunt.

When young Earnest Totten's wife died and he had
to have a good cow to supply milk for his motherless
baby, he had asked to buy Pearlie back. We knew she
had to go, but Mama and all of us girls shed bitter tears
when Earnest led her away. But when, only a few weeks
later, and not long before we gave the party, Poppie
sold Bunt, we really had the blues.

Bunt was a little black, snubnosed heifer Mama had
bought with her extra egg money when we lived in Roten

Valley. She had grown up to be the best milk cow we ever had—and Poppie hadn't meant to sell her. It had been a sort of accident. A Cozad man had asked him what he'd take for her, and he had named a price so high he was sure it would choke the buyer. But when the man said, "If she's worth *that* much, I'd better take her," Poppie had to come home and tell Mama he'd sold her cow.

I felt even worse about it than Mama did, for to me a good milk cow was worth a lot more than money. So, when Florry and I asked if we could have a party, Poppie fell right in with the idea, and even made a special trip to town to get a gunnysack of oranges to serve with the five-layer cakes Florry and Mama baked for the party.

We played all the old, lively "play party" games that night, with Poppie leading the singing, and playing the games, too, and before the party was over Oss Brownfield asked me to go with him to the Adle party. The Adle party, the *big* one of the year, was set for two weeks *before* my sixteenth birthday. I wanted so much to go to it with my own beau, but I had to coax for all I was worth before Poppie finally said I could go with Oss.

Adles had the finest house in the community, a tall, many-angled, two-story affair with second story balconies and gingerbread porches and colored glass panes in the front door. All the young folks for miles around came to that party, and the parlor was so crowded there was no room left to skip and swing to the singing and clapping. So the Adle boys asked their mother's "leave" to move the big base burner out of the room. She said they could, provided they would set it up again in the morning. A dozen or so big boys hustled the tall heater outside, but when they took up the wide stove board that protected the floor beneath it, Mrs. Adle was horrified at the winter's dust that had seeped underneath it. She rushed away for her broom and dustpan, but the swept square still looked smudgy so she asked us to wait while she brought her mop and pail and scrubbed up the dingy spot.

The party finally got under way—with old Grandpa Adle, nearly ninety and quite feeble, watching from his big chair in the corner. Later, far past his usual bedtime, he tottered to his feet and went outside. He came in again, carrying an old iron teakettle, and we parted ranks and let him through. There was an embarrassed silence while he shuffled across the parlor to the stairway door and climbed slowly to his bedroom above, his teakettle chamber bumping the wall as he went.

Most of the families in our neighborhood bought new top buggies that spring, too. Ours was plain black, but some, a cut above the plain ones, had red or yellow wheels and fancy upholstered seats. After my birthday, Oss took me to parties in his father's fine new buggy, but on Sundays, when his father and sisters drove it to church, he had to come for me in a one-horse cart. John Houk, though, owned the red-wheeled model he took Florry out in, and anyone could see he was proud of his buggy and high-stepping team.

John was calling on Florry one Sunday afternoon when a friend of his, owner of another new red-wheeled job, followed him to our place and stopped in to compare rigs. While we were admiring his fine new buggy he asked me to go for a little spin with him and try it out. I told him I'd see if I could, and went in the house to ask Poppie.

But Poppie said no. "Fred's all right, so far as I know," he told me, "but his older brothers and sisters are considered 'fast' and I don't care to have you seen with any of the family." The fact that Fred later became a minister didn't help me out a bit that day.

Later in the summer another good-looking young fellow stopped in to ask me to go to church with him the next Sunday, but Poppie didn't approve of his family either. One of the hardest things I ever had to do was to go out and tell him I couldn't go—and watch the hurt, disappointed look that came over his honest face. With so many girls in his family, I suppose Poppie thought he couldn't be too careful, but it was pretty hard on us.

Right after my birthday I began saving the extra butter money each week, and just before the Fourth I went along to town with Poppie to pick out my parasol. One of the popular two-hour, one-cent calico sales was going on at the store that afternoon, and the dry-goods side was jammed with women. Uncle John was there, too, backed into a corner, sweating and miserable. When he saw me he waved a scrap of calico and began pushing his way out of the crowd. "Gheet," he panted, "Sis (his pet name for Aunt Irene) wants me to try and match this, but I'll never get within reach of that counter by three o'clock. You see if you can get in there and match it for me."

I took the sample and edged into the crowd. I didn't find any calico like Aunt Irene's sample, but I came away with my parasol. It had a gay, ruffled silk shade and a bright celluloid handle and was altogether the prettiest thing I had ever owned.

On the Fourth, Poppie took Florry and me to Cozad in the buggy. Mama, who hadn't felt well all summer, stayed home with the younger girls and Roy.

It was a scorching day, and Poppie said he'd leave the buggy near the pavilion for us to sit in while we watched

the races, that we'd need considerable more shade than
we'd get from "those fandangled little parasols."

He found a gap in a good location, backed the buggy
into it and took the team away. We walked around a
while, greeting our friends and twirling our pretty parasols gracefully, but we were glad to sit in the buggy to
watch the contests. At noon we left our folded parasols
in the seat while we helped unpack and set out our picnic dinner in the pavilion.

And after dinner, when we were gathering up our
dishes, a big, fat, redheaded girl climbed into our buggy
to get out of the boiling sun and sat down on my parasol
and broke the handle square in two. The girl was so
hot and miserable, and she looked so scared because of
what she had done, but I couldn't feel very sorry for her.
I was feeling too sorry for myself.

The Fourth of July committee had gotten up a new
kind of entertainment for that afternoon, a big sham
battle instead of the usual water fight. That Fourth of
1898 was only thirty-four years away from the end of
the Civil War, and a good many of the men at the celebration had fought in the war, so we knew the battle
would be exciting.

Florry shared her parasol with me and we hurried with
the crowd to the battlefield, a pasture at the edge of
town, where the two camps faced each other across the
flat. One side had set up a little cannon in front of its
line, and both sides had thrown up earth breastworks
and dug in for a hot fight. The shooting began as soon
as the crowd was settled on the sidelines. Now and then
a man sneaked up through the grass and fired the cannon
and ran back again. Boys were shooting firecrackers all
over the place, too, and the noise and smoke and dust
hanging over the battlefield and the spectators was ter-

rific. Before long—what with the shooting and yelling and the "dead" men on the field—the whole thing began to seem almost too real for fun.

Then a man from behind one line ran past us, a good-sized open box in his arms. He had almost reached the battlefield when a boy on the edge of the crowd tossed a lighted firecracker into the box. The explosion fairly shook the ground beneath our feet.

Out on the field men were flung to the ground. A thick cloud of smoke and dust covered everything and a bitter smell set us all to coughing and sneezing. When the smoke lifted a little we could see men running toward a man on the ground. All the "dead" men had gotten up and were running, too. Then a canopy-topped carriage dashed onto the field and the man on the ground was lifted into it. Two or three other men climbed in with him and the carriage rushed away toward town.

Everybody started back to the pavilion, and bits of news about the accident began seeping through the crowd. Several men had been hurt, someone said, but the man on the ground had had his arm blown off and wasn't expected to live to reach the doctor's office. But someone else said that wasn't it at all, and then told a different story, so we didn't know what had happened until we met Poppie back at the buggy.

We asked him who it was had his arm blown off, and he said it was Charlie Streit, a farmer south of town, only he didn't have his arm blown off. Instead, the box of gunpowder he was carrying had blown up in his face and burned him terribly. He had breathed a lot of the gas, Poppie said, and the doctor was afraid his lungs were burned, deep down. A Cozad man, Hy Allen, and Blacksmith Poffenberger had been burned pretty badly, too, he said.

All in all, that was a tragic Fourth. Mr. Streit died two weeks later, leaving a widow and several small children, and I never got to carry my new parasol again.

In August George Famuliner, one of our Missouri cousins, came out to spend a month with us. Then John Houk came over one evening to ask Florry, George, and me to go to North Platte with him. Buffalo Bill's Wild West Show was to be there September 3, he said, and he thought we ought to go.

North Platte, forty miles to the west of us, was the biggest town in western Nebraska. Florry and I had never been there, or had we ever seen a show like the great Wild West, with real cowboys, Indians, and all, so of course we wanted to go. At first, Poppie said it was too long a drive to make in one day and we'd be too late getting home at night, then he gave in and said we could go, provided Mama didn't care. But Mama wouldn't say, one way or the other. The best we could get from her was an uncertain "wait and see." *Even on the morning of the second day of September she still said we'd have to "wait and see."*

"But Mama," Florry said then, *"what* are we waiting for? We *have* to know today, so we can tell the boys."

"All right," Mama told us, "I'll let you know this evening."

But late that afternoon, when John and George came for our answer, Poppie sent them right on to Cozad after the doctor; and a few minutes later I was kiting across the fields in the buggy to bring Grandma. By the time I got back with her, Dr. Fochtman had gone back to town and the new baby girl was asleep.

Grandma took right over and ordered us all off to bed, and Poppie, Florry, and I, limp as old dishrags after all the excitement, were glad to go.

Upstairs, Florry sagged onto the bed. "I never dreamed that was why Mama wouldn't say if we could go or not," she said.

It seems hard to believe, but neither did I. Mama hadn't been well for so long, and the Mother Hubbards she always wore for everyday made her look the same all the time anyway. And besides, in our family we never talked about the babies until they were on hand, so, even though Florry was eighteen and I was sixteen, we hadn't known that a baby was due at our house. But that night we couldn't help wishing she'd waited a couple of days longer to be born—we had so wanted to go to North Platte to the Wild West Show.

We named the baby Esther, but Mama called her "Sweetheart," a pet name the rest of us soon shortened to "Heart." She was barely a month old when the old washing machine played out, and on the way home from town with the new one the spring wagon fell apart. We couldn't complain, though, Poppie said, for both of them had given us an awful lot of mileage.

Chapter Eighteen

CROPS were good, that summer of 1898, and Poppie and I started to shuck out our corn early in the fall. But before we had been at it long, Poppie got a bad boil on the back of his neck and Mama caught a heavy cold that she couldn't seem to throw off. When Poppie couldn't stand the pain of his boil any longer, he had me take him to town to have it lanced. He felt a good deal better for a day or two, and then the boil began to spread and grow into a carbuncle; and before we were through with that we had to make half a dozen trips to the doctor. Once we went on a Sunday forenoon. The doctor was out when we reached his office, so Poppie said we might as well eat while we waited for him to come back.

At the restaurant Poppie ordered us each a glass of sweet cider. He tasted his and said, "M'm, I wouldn't call this 'sweet' cider. You'd better not drink it, Gheet." I had tasted mine too, and liked the tangy bite of it, but I set it back as he asked. By the time we were through eating, he had finished his and mine too; but if there was any real kick to that cider he was the one who needed it, worn out as he was with his long tussle with the boils.

And by the time Poppie was well again, we were all worried about Mama. Her cold had left her with a hard, racking cough that none of our home remedies seemed to help, and she hardly appeared to have strength enough to get through the days. So, as soon as he was able, Poppie took her to the doctor, and they found out she had a bad case of catarrh, and that she wouldn't get much better as long as she had to breathe the dust of a farming country.

All of this had kept us out of the field so much that it was well into November before we finished shucking corn. On the day that we brought in the last load, Poppie said, "Well, Gheet, that job's done and you can start to school in the morning."

But I had it figured different. Because Florry hadn't had to miss nearly as much school as I had, she had finished the course offered by the Dawson County schools and wasn't going to school anymore. Since she wasn't going, I didn't want to go, and I told Poppie so. Then I said, "I've always worked outside and I don't know much about housework. If I stay home this winter I can learn to cook and keep house; and anyway, with Mama so poorly, and the new baby and all, Florry needs my help. Besides, school has been going so long, now, that I'd be way behind the rest."

Poppie heard me out, then he said, "Gheet, I don't want to see you do as I did. When I was your age, I thought I knew more than Ma and my teacher put together. So I decided I'd had enough schooling, and that I could help Ma more by quitting and going to work. I don't want you to make the same mistake, and be sorry all your life like I have. They've got an extra-good teacher this year and it won't take you long to catch up. Now you think it over good."

I started to school the next day.

The McCarter Canyon school was a large one, especially after the fall plowing and corn shucking were done and the big boys started. The schoolhouse was two miles north of our place, a long way for little Presh and Nellie to walk, so they rode the tiny mule, Pete. Renee and Nellie Shaulis, little Ethel Matz, and Bob, Jake, and Mary Ann Waller, all living south of us, usually came along by the time we were ready to start for school. We'd boost Ethel Matz and Nellie Shaulis, the littlest ones, onto Pete with Presh and Nellie, then we'd all set off together, with hardly any of Pete showing under so many little girls. Later in the fall, when the five big Anderson boys, Halbert, Alfred, Harry, Albert, and Eddie, started, we all rode with them in their high-sided lumber wagon, behind a team of big mules.

Our Nellie, small for her age, with big blue eyes, soft brown hair and gentle ways, was a favorite with the whole school. But it was her classmate of the first year, big John, already seven years in the second grade, who really shined up to her. The fact that she could already read better than he could made no difference to John. He only sat and grinned at her while she recited lessons still too hard for his clouded mind, a big, silly grin of honest worship. The next year Nellie went on into the third grade, leaving big, simple John to turn his wide, wet smile on Presh, who moved up to second.

The teacher, my second and last year in the McCarter Canyon school, was Mrs. McKenny. Thin, gray, and nearly sixty, she was determined that her scholars should learn all that she could possibly cram into their heads. Only John, smiling all day at the line of little girls passing through his second grade, seemed beyond her reach.

Mrs. McKenny demanded absolute respect and obedience from her school, and it was just too bad for the boy or girl who failed in either. One morning she wore a pair of new button shoes to school to "break them in." Toward the end of the day, when she couldn't stand the pinching any longer, she unbuttoned the shoes and slipped them off. One of the big boys, catching sight of her bony, black-stockinged feet beneath the table, snickered out loud. With a few scorching remarks about boys so rude as to belittle their elders, and betters, Mrs. McKenny trimmed him down to frying size in a hurry. It isn't likely he ever saw anything funny about a woman's stockinged feet again.

After the custom of the times, all our teachers used the after-recess quarter of every Friday for "speaking," "ciphering down," or "spelling down." Aunt Bell had preferred ciphering down, but Aunt Hester had liked the speaking best. Every one in her school had to learn a piece "by heart," usually a poem from the "readers," or a "memory gem" from the "spellers," for Friday afternoons. Once, to "hack" Aunt Hester, Lily Maline, who didn't care much for poetry anyway, stood up in her turn and recited:

> Once there was a little rattlesnake,
> That ate so mucha muttoncake
> It made his little belly ache.

My sisters and I had learned most of our poems from the bundle of *Youth's Companions* that Aunt Ollie tucked into the "surprise" barrel every fall. Then one summer Poppie and I farmed the old Freeman place in Roten Valley for Uncle John. There was no house on the Freeman place, only a big old barn with living quarters partitioned off in one corner of its haymow. No one had lived there for years, so one day I went poking around in the cobwebby old rooms, and in a little room under the eaves I found stacks and stacks of old magazines. I carted the whole pile home—for most of the papers had whole pages of songs, ballads, and poems—and after

that I read poetry in all my spare time, and memorized
a lot of the pieces for Aunt Hester's Friday afternoons.

Mrs. McKenny, though, leaned to the all-school spell-
downs. On my first Friday in school, Frank Brown
spelled the whole school down. (Frank was about my
age and, like me, he had had to stay out and help his
father pick corn.) The next Friday I won the spelldown;
and from then on Frank and I battled it out with big
words, each of us trying to be the first to win twice in
a row.

One chilly evening, near the end of that December,
we were just sitting down to supper when there was a
loud knock at the door. Dovey, Nellie, and I began hitching our chairs closer together and Florry got up to set
another place at the table. Poppie called "come in" and
the door opened—but we already knew who was there.
Old Bill Sherman always came at mealtime, and he always
banged on the door that way. Old Bill swung his ragged,
greasy cap in a wide circle, bowed his dingy bald head
down to his knees, and sang out, "And Abou, old bald
head, led all the rest."

Old Bill, middle-sized and middle-aged, wore his hair
and whiskers long—to save barbering expense—and seldom
cleaned up or changed his clothes. He owned a fine farm
on the valley, where he sometimes lived in a dugout;
and though he was known to have a good deal of money
in the bank, he spent most of his time tramping around
the country, eating off his neighbors, and driving a sharp
bargain wherever he could. He dealt in hides a good deal,
and the neighbors swore he could follow his nose straight
to the owner of any dead critter, to ask leave to skin it
for the hide.

He had once taken a horse in on a deal, but before
he could turn it to any new advantage to himself it took

sick during a spell of bitter winter weather. Old Bill
took the horse right into the dugout with him, and tried
to doctor it, but it died on a zero afternoon. It was too
late to skin it before dark, and he had no light of any
kind (too expensive), so, since the carcass would freeze
solid if he dragged it outdoors, he left it beside his bunk
all night and skinned it comfortably beside his fire the
next morning.

A native Pennsylvanian, Old Bill was well educated
and well read, and he could, and often did, recite Shake-
speare and other poets by the yard; yet for ordinary conversation he talked like a cellar bum. He was descended
directly from a judge, a minister, and a famous sea cap-
tain who had come from Essex, England, in 1634. Besides that, he was first cousin to a New York congressman and to General William Tecumseh Sherman. Old
Bill himself had enlisted in the Union Army at eighteen
and fought through three years of the Civil War, and
by the time he came to Cozad in 1889 he was already a
man of means—and a bum by choice.

By scrounging cast-off clothes wherever he could, and
going barefooted most of the year, he managed to keep
himself dressed at no expense to himself. People said it
was easy to tell the time of year just by counting how
many shirts Old Bill was wearing. When the fall days
began to turn cool, he'd put an extra shirt on over the
remains of the one he'd worn all summer, and with each
new cold snap he'd add another shirt and another pair
of pants. By genuinely cold weather he had accumulated
a good many smelly layers, but as spring came on again
he shed the extra layers by simply letting them wear
out and drop off.

Old Bill had come to our place that evening to tell
Poppie he'd heard he was looking for more pasture, and

that he'd like to rent him a good place he owned up on the Birdwood, about sixty-five miles to the northwest of us. Poppie listened with a quickening interest to Old Bill's description of the Birdwood, a long, twisting creek, often deep but never dry, formed by the meeting of East and West creeks in northwest Lincoln County. The creek, he said, meandered southward through a grassy valley for some twenty miles, to join the North Platte River a little way east of the town of Sutherland. The rangeland, both along the creek and in the hills, was the finest in the world and there was plenty of it; for few people lived in that section of the country. There were big trees on the banks of the creek near the house, and the land all around it was well grassed. "Y' couldn't ask fer a purtier layout," he told Poppie.

Poppie asked him how far the place was from school and town.

"Sutherlan's about thirteen miles d'rectly south, an' it's mebbe a mile an' a half t' school," Old Bill said.

"It's a long move from here," Poppie said, "but it sounds like what I'm looking for." Then he turned to Mama. "It's mostly grass country, and we'd be getting away from the dust that keeps you coughing here, Maggie. What do you think?

"How big is the house?" Mama asked.

"Well, it's ony four rooms," Old Bill admitted, "but two of 'em are fair sized."

Poppie sighed. "I guess it won't do then," he said. "It'd be pretty hard to crowd ten of us into four little rooms."

"But these purty girls a yourn'll be marryin' off b'fore long," Old Bill said, leering at us, "an' there won't be ten o' ye much longer. But I'll tell y' what I'll do, y' rent th' place t'night, an' nex summer I'll jine a good-sized room onta that house."

They closed the deal that evening.

I hardly knew what to think about moving to the Birdwood. I'd been having a good time the past year, going to parties in the Walnut Grove community with the lively crowd of young folks in the valley. From what Old Bill had told us, it would be different on the Birdwood, a thinly settled country; but he had said it was ranch country—and where there were ranches there were bound to be cowboys.

But, however I felt about it, the deal was made and we would be moving, come the first of March.

Chapter Nineteen

TOWARD the end of January a measles epidemic broke out in Cozad.

Poppie had had the measles when he was a boy in Missouri, but Mama and the rest of us hadn't had them. And we'd better not get them either, Poppie said, for if they ever got started in our family we'd be half the summer getting through with them. So, when a family just the other side of Walnut Grove came down with them, Poppie said we'd have to stop going to church and Sunday school.

Early in February the weather turned bitter cold. Andersons put a thick layer of hay in the bottom of their big wagon, and the rest of us brought quilts along to wrap up in for the freezing ride to school. And every evening Poppie asked us if any one at school was sick that day; for whole communities had been exposed to measles because one child had taken sick in school.

The battle of the spelling words was still going strong between Frank and me and, with the first of March coming up fast, we were both trying harder than ever to be first to win the spelldown twice in a row. I won on the last Friday in January, and I was determined to win when we took our places again on the first Friday in February. Half an hour later Frank and I were the only ones still on the floor; and Mrs. McKenny, firing word after word at us, was busy looking for harder ones.

Finally she gave the word "catarrh" to Frank. He hesitated, and my heart thumped at my ribs. I knew how to spell *that* one. But Frank kept trying it over and over under his breath, listening to the sound of it, and then his face lit up and he spelled it right. I went down on the next one, and we were even again. Well, I thought, we'd have at least two more Fridays—I still had a chance to make it two in a row.

The next Monday morning was so stinging cold that Poppie said little Presh couldn't go to school. The icy wind tore at the rest of us as we ran for the wagon, hanging onto our caps and scarves and trying to keep our skirts down. Andersons had put a spring seat on the floor of the wagonbox for the little girls, and covered them over, heads and all, with a thick quilt. Halbert lifted a corner of the quilt and popped our Nellie under it, into the seat with Nellie Shaulis, Ethel Matz, and his own little sister. Then Albert whipped up his team and we jolted over the frozen road, facing the wild cold wind.

Later, while we stood by the hot stove in the schoolroom, thawing the frost out of our faces, fingers and toes, I noticed that Renee Shaulis wasn't there. I asked her sister Nellie why she hadn't come, and the little girl said "Oh, she's sick today, so she stayed home."

That evening, when Poppie asked his usual question, I had to tell him about Renee.

"She's probably got the measles all right," he said. "But as long as she didn't come down in school, there's a chance you girls haven't been exposed yet, so I guess it'd be better if you didn't go any more."

So there went my last chance to beat Frank two in a row.

From then on the measles spread fast through all the

neighborhood. The cold deepened daily, and soon pneumonia added to the horror of the epidemic. And the horror reached its peak when, for four days in a row, the temperature stayed at twenty below zero and, by the end of the fourth day, three little children and old Mrs. Whaley had been buried at Walnut Grove.

Two of the children were from one family, where four little ones had been sick at the same time in a one-room soddy. The two in the bed in front of the door died a few hours apart, and two in the bed behind the door, out of the cold draft, got well. Simple, harmless "Big Jim" Whaley had wandered the countryside for years, visiting around among the neighbors and choring a little for his meals. Somewhere on his rounds he took the measles, and then went home to his mother. He got well, but poor old Mrs. Whaley took the measles from him and died.

Sally Waller, on the farm a quarter of a mile below us, was worried about the measles, too. "Dark people have thicker skins than light ones, and its harder for them to break out," she told Mama. "Jake and Mary Ann are light, but Bob is so black I'm afraid the measles'll kill him before he can get broke out." Sally was a Kentuckian and all her *a*'s were three times as broad as any I'd ever heard before.

Her three soon came down with measles, and had them hard. Mama did all she could to help her. Every day she sent Florry or me down with cooked food and extra medicines. But, minding her warning not to "expose" ourselves, we always left our offerings on the edge of the porch, then backed off to a safe distance when Sally came out to give us the latest report on her sick ones.

Then there came a morning when Sally, small, dark, and wispy anyway, looked as if a good breeze could carry her off without half trying. Her face, under the old shawl she had thrown over her head, was pinched and sharp with worry and loss of sleep. "I'm afraid I'm mighty near to playin' out," she told me, and I wish you'd ask your mama to let Florry come down and help me until my young ones get better. If Florry could give me a hand now, I'd keep her here and take care of her when she get th' measles, so she wouldn't be takin' 'em home to the rest of you."

But Mama, much as she wanted to help poor Sally, had to refuse. We needed Florry at home—for Mama had never regained her strength after little Heart was born, and her cough had been getting worse all winter —but the real reason was our fear of the measles. If Florry was to get them now, so late in February, she'd never be able to go to the Birdwood with us the first of March; and Poppie didn't see how he could hold things up to wait for her. Always, on the first of March, a good many farm families moved, and if one family couldn't vacate on time it held things up all along the line. It just wasn't done—except for something very, very serious.

So we kept Florry at home, and Poppie hired John Houk to help him get ready to move. Sally's three began to get better, the epidemic seemed to be slackening off a little, and the weather began to warm up a bit. It looked as if we'd get to move by the first of March after all.

Then, after supper on the last Saturday in February, Nellie said she didn't feel good. She was subject to little stomach upsets anyway, so when she began to throw up, Mama just gave her a dose of physic and hurried her upstairs to bed. When she was still feverish and upset the next morning, Mama gave her the usual treatment for colds and fever and kept her in the big rocker by the living-room stove.

Early that forenoon Aunt Bell drove her wagon up to our kitchen door. "Does anybody here have the measles?" she asked when Mama opened the door. Mama told her none of us did, that we hadn't even been off the place for three weeks for fear we would get them. "Nellie seems to have a little cold and stomach upset," she said, "but she has that every once in a while anyway."

So Aunt Bell dug her three young children out of the hay and quilts in the bottom of the wagon and spent the day with us. Uncle Earnest had gone back East to visit his folks, she said, and if she had found us sick with the measles she would have gone on to Grandma's. As it was, she would spend the day with us and stay all night at Grandma's. We didn't see Aunt Bell very often anymore, so we made the most of the day; even Nellie livened up and played a little.

Nellie was no better the next morning, so Poppie carried her down to the big chair by the heater again— and there, a few minutes later, she broke out all over with measles. We remembered then that Nellie had ridden to school under the quilt with Nellie Shaulis, that cold day, and that Renee had taken sick at home the night before.

"Well, I guess we're in for it now," Poppie said, "but if we can keep all of you from taking cold, along with your measles, we'll come out all right, along about next Fourth of July."

"We've exposed all Bell's children, too," Mama said.

"That's so," Poppie sounded like he'd just heard the crack of doom. "Well, all we can do now is send her word right away, so's she'll know what to expect."

Mr. Houk, John's father, came over later that day.

Just inside the door he stopped, wrinkled his nose and gave a couple of loud sniffs. "Whew," he said, "you've got measles here, I can smell 'em."

Poppie told him we sure had, and then he asked the old man if they'd mind keeping Dovey a while longer. Dovey had been visiting at Houk's since John came to help us, so Nellie hadn't exposed her. And since she'd had pneumonia the past two winters, and the measles would likely go harder with her than the rest of us, the folks thought she'd better not come home until we were all over them.

Florry was the next to come down, and right after her, Mama, Stell, and I all came down at once. When that happened, Poppie and John brought two beds and a cot down from upstairs and set them up in the front room, the warmest room in the house, and then he sent for Grandma.

Grandma had seen all of her own big family through measles and like ailments, so she knew a lot about sickness. But with all of us but Presh and Roy down at once, Poppie had to help her and they had to be on the job most of the time, day and night. The biggest chore they had was to keep enough vessels on hand for all of us to throw up in at once, and to get them to us in time—for one of us throwing up started all the rest off too.

At first Florry was the sickest. Her eyes swelled shut and her fever ran high for days, and then it was Mama. Dr. Fochtman came, looking worn and haggard from all the weeks he had spent taking care of measles, and said there was little more to be done for us than Poppie and Grandma were already doing. "Just don't let them up too soon, the backsets are usually worse than the measles," he warned.

Florry, Stell, and I began to get a little better about

the time Nellie was well enough to get up and dress. But Mama was still very bad, the baby was all broken out and crying most of the time, and Presh and Roy were beginning to run fevers. Poppie and Grandma shifted Stell and me to the little downstairs bedroom, where Nellie slept with us at night, and put the two little ones into our bed by the stove.

And by that time Poppie and Grandma were both about to give out from plain weariness, worry, and lack of sleep. There was still a case or two of measles in nearly every home in the community, so there was almost no help to be had. But at that point Mrs. Gus Matz and Mrs. Mary Pizer came over to help out a few days, the measles cases in their own homes being up and about again. After it was all over, Poppie said he didn't think he and Grandma would have lived through the measles either, if it hadn't been for those two good neighbors.

Presh and Roy had light cases and were up and dressed again after three or four days. Mama was still very sick, and Florry, Stell, and I were still in bed; but Poppie and Grandma, not wanting to impose on Mrs. Pizer and Mrs. Matz, took over the care of us again. They were managing all right, too, until Roy took sick again, the "backset" everybody feared and dreaded.

On the day that Poppie sent for the doctor the second time, Florry and I got up and dressed and tried to help a little.

The doctor came, and sat a while beside the bed where Poppie's and Mama's only son was burning with fever and fighting for breath. Finally he shook his head and said that only the best of nursing could save the little fellow now. So Poppie went as fast as he could to Cozad to bring Florence Savin, the only registered nurse we knew of.

For the next five days Florence hardly left Roy's bed-side for so much as a minute. If he had been her own she couldn't have tried any harder to pull him through, nor have been any happier when she finally did it.

By then the first of March was long past, and John, who had done the outside chores all the time Poppie was helping take care of us, had to leave to move his folks down to the Waller place below us, empty since Sally and her family had moved to Little Kentucky, weeks ago. And at sunup, three days later, a neighbor rode in with a note from Aunt Bell. Her three were down with measles, she wrote, and she needed help. Could we spare Grandma?

By the time Grandma had her things gathered up, Poppie had the buggy at the door. Poor Grandma turned to give us a last warning. "Now don't any of you leave this house for anything for a week yet. If you do, you'll probably take a backset too, and after all we've been through these past weeks you'd better do as I tell you," she told us.

They drove away, and the house, with Poppie and Grandma both out of it, seemed dreary and empty. Nellie and Presh were playing in the little bedroom where Roy, able to sit up in bed, could watch them. Mama, her white skin stretched tight over her bones, was still in bed in the front room. Florry, thin and bedraggled-looking, was washing the baby, and Stell was looking her scaling face over in a hand mirror. They all looked pretty tough, and I knew I did too. I felt as if I didn't have a body, as if I might only be a part of the air in the room.

I got up and floated to the south window and looked down the valley. The sun looked warm on the hills. Down the road at the Waller place the windmill wheel was spinning in the fresh spring breeze. Houks would be moving in there in a day or so, and Dovey would be with them. It seemed ages since we'd seen Dovey, and Mr. Houk said she had cried to come home and "have the measles with the rest of the kids."

I floated on to the kitchen and looked out the window there. Out by the stable old Love was prowling the barnyard and bawling to be milked. I had broken Love to milk and she thought a lot of me, tagging after me while I did my chores and rubbing her head against my shoulder while I milked the other cows. Poor Love, I thought, Poppie wouldn't be home for a long time yet, and somebody ought to be milking her. And all at once I had a body again, even if it was skinny and scaly, and I could hardly wait to get out of doors again.

I looked around. I was alone in the kitchen and no one was paying any attention to me. So I turned to the coat hooks behind the door, bundled into my wraps, and slipped out onto the little porch. After the long weeks, shut in with the sight and smell of measles, I had almost forgotten how wonderful wind and sunshine could feel. I stood there, breathing deep breaths of fresh, sweet air until I felt clean inside again.

Then old Love saw me and came trotting to the porch, bawling how glad she was to see me, and rubbing her head against me. I pulled her ears and petted her bony face awhile; then I reached inside the kitchen door, picked up a milk pail and sat down on the edge of the porch and began milking. The warm milk, foaming into the pail, smelled so good to me, and by the time I had finished milking the good old cow everything seemed right with me again. And I hadn't disobeyed Grandma either; for, since I was never clear off the porch, I hadn't actually left the house.

Chapter Twenty

MAMA was barely well enough to be out of bed when Mr. and Mrs. Clark, the people who had rented our place, pulled in with a wagonload of furniture. They had "put off" the family that had rented their place as long as they could, they said. But when that family had to move out of the house they had lived in, to make way for another family that had finally had to move out of the house they had lived in, Clarks couldn't do anything else but bring their things and move in with us.

Poppie said it wouldn't be worth while to move the beds back upstairs for the little while we would still be here, so Mama had the Clarks put part of their furniture up there, and the rest in the lean-to. They cooked on our stove and ate off our table—an unhandy arrangement all around, but the best we could manage—and Mama and Mrs. Clark were careful to keep from getting their pans and dishes mixed. Then, when Poppie took our cookstove and table on the first load of things he moved to the Birdwood, Clarks moved their furniture into the kitchen, after which we cooked on their stove and ate off their table.

Stell and Dovey went to the Birdwood with Poppie that first trip.

Poppie came back full of enthusiasm and in a great hurry to get moved. He had never seen such a country

for grass and water, he said, but he didn't seem to remember much about the house. It was pretty small, he
guessed, and not in very good shape; but spring rains
had started the grass early and the sooner we could get
our cattle up there the better off they'd be. Dovey and
Stell said the house was "kind of dinky and dirty," but
that the creek and the big trees were wonderful.

Mama, thin and worn and anxious, stood by on the
warm afternoon we loaded the last of our goods onto
the big wagon. During the last days of packing, I had
seen her take some of her things—the lovely transparent
Chelsea china cup and saucer that had come from England
as a part of her grandmother's wedding dishes, or her
"yards" of pansies and kittens—in her hands and pat
them gently, as if telling them good-bye. "They say
three moves are as bad as a fire on a body's furniture
and things," she said, "and this is our third move in
Nebraska."

Mama wasn't strong enough to go with us yet, so
now, watching us fit the furniture into the wagon, she
gave instructions and advice. She saw to it that we left
room for her canaries in the front, under the seat, and
told me to be sure to take them in of nights and to see
to their feed and water whenever we stopped. When
Poppie picked up her little sewing rocker, she told him
to load it where it wouldn't get scratched, or a rocker
broken off. "I've a feeling it'll never get there whole,
anyway," she said. So Poppie set the rocker down again
and left it till the last, then tied it on the very top of
the load, where nothing could crowd or scratch it.

We left Mama and the baby, with Florry to take care
of them, at Houks that afternoon and the rest of us
drove on to Grandma's for the night. Poppie and John
had already moved the cattle and chickens to Grandma's,

where Stell was to stay and look after them until Poppie could get back again.

After supper I asked Grandma to look at the middle finger on my right hand. It had been tender and sore for the last two or three days; now it was red, and swelled to twice its usual size. Grandma said it looked like I had a felon coming on it, and that a soap and sugar poultice would help it. But by the time I had tended the canaries and put Roy and Presh to bed, I was too tired to bother, so I went off to bed without the poultice.

We headed west at daylight. Poppie, Nellie, and Dovey rode in the big wagon, Roy and Presh in the buggy with me. The air felt balmy and springlike, and I would have enjoyed the ride, through country I had never seen before, if it hadn't been for the shooting pains in my sore finger that made me feel a little sick all over. Near noon we came out of the sandhills onto the river valley at the little town of Brady Island, and from there on I watched for cowboys. Instead, we saw nothing but trouble.

Spring rains and thawing ground frost had made the valley roads almost bottomless. We could barely crawl through the mud, and at the next little town, Maxwell, the wagon mired down to the hubs. The town seemed to be built in the middle of a big slough anyway, and we lost the better part of an hour there. We had to unload the furniture onto the soggy grass beside the oozing ruts of the road, pull onto firmer ground, and then carry the furniture ahead and reload it, with Mama's rocker tied on top of the load again. Poppie's horses had to lean hard into their collars to start the wagon, and the bottom of my buggy box scraped on the mud as my team waded through the bog.

All of us, and the horses too, were bone weary when we pulled off the road and made camp in a meadow that evening. We hadn't seen a cowboy all day, but by then I was too tired to care. Poppie and Nellie watered the teams as a nearby slough and staked them out to graze. Then we set up the tent and Dovey and I carried the birdcages inside and fixed supper. The valley here was wide and level, and while we ate a red glow spread above the hills, showing brighter as the sky darkened.

"Must be a bad prairie fire, off in the hills there," Poppie said.

We were on the road again by daylight, headed toward a gray smoke haze that hung above the hills where the glow had been. I started the day tired out, for the jumping pain in my swollen finger and the hardness of my bed had kept me awake most of the night. I had hoped to see North Platte that morning, but Poppie said we'd have to keep to the far north edge of the valley on account of the mud. So all I saw of that well-known cow town of Nebraska was the smudge of smoke above its railroad roundhouse.

We drove northwest all day, and ahead of us the smoke cloud grew steadily higher and blacker. And that afternoon the rope that held Mama's rocker on top of the load, worn through by the everlasting twisting and lurching of the wagon, fell apart and let the chair tumble off with a crash. Poppie and I stopped the teams and hurried to inspect the damage. "Oh, dear. What will Mama say?" I asked when I saw the broken rocker.

"Goodness knows." Poppie sighed. "But she'll say a plenty."

We tied the chair on again, tossed the piece of rocker into the wagon, and pulled on. After a while we left the valley and turned into a rough range of hills, north of a little town called Hershey. Shortly afterward the wind, blowing stronger now, brought the bitter smell of burning grass. And from then on we saw nothing but empty hills and the sky-climbing smoke cloud ahead.

Just at sundown we turned down a little swale and came out of the hills onto a level place beside the creek. At the same time the fire, fanned by the high wind, came roaring over the high hill directly across the creek. On the near side, tall, leafless cottonwoods stood like skeletons against the blazing sky. The rushing water of the Birdwood caught and reflected the firelight, and in the foreground, plain in the reddish glare, I could see a drab little frame house. Off to the left, a little shed stable and a ramshackle granary leaned against each other.

We unhitched while the fire licked its way down the steep hill and began to die in the wet grass on the far side of the stream. Then a sickening new odor came in on the wind. "What's that?" I asked. "It smells like burning wool."

"It is," Poppie told me. "A man named Heskett runs a lot of sheep in the hills over there. The fire must've caught some of them." Then he dug some matches out of his pocket and told me I'd find a lamp on the table. He went off toward the creek with the horses, and I climbed up on the wagon and handed the birdcages and some things we'd need down to Roy and the girls. As we started to the house a man came out of the red shadows and hurried after Poppie.

It was almost dark in the little kitchen. I lit the lamp and looked around me at the dirty, ugly room. Then I picked up the lamp and went through the rest of the house, with Roy and the girls almost stepping on my heels. The next room was small and dark, too, and a bed would have crowded both of the two tiny rooms beyond it. The whole place was grubby with smoke and fly-specks, and mouldy with filth and age. We trailed back to the kitchen. My tired, hungry, dirty little brother and sisters looked ready to break out howling any minute; and if they did I knew I'd join them.

Then Poppie came hurrying into the kitchen. "That was Cox, from up the creek a piece," he said. "He says the biggest share of the fire got away, farther north, and they need help to fight it. While you set me out a bite to eat, I'll slip down to the creek with my gun; a bunch of ducks flew in while I was watering the horses."

By the time I had some cold food on the table he was back again. He dropped five mallards by the door, pulled a box to the table, and sat down. "You'd better dress those ducks tonight, Gheet, before they spoil," he said between bites. Then he pulled his wallet from his pocket and got up to go. "Here, take good care of that. It's got our last forty dollars in it," he said, handing it to me and hurrying off into the night.

I hunted up a bucket and went to the creek for water, my four forlorn little shadows trotting at my heels. Across the stream clumps of tall dry weeds and grass still blazed up here and there, throwing flickering light against the trees on our side. The night wind was gusty and smoke stung our eyes and throats. It was lonesome and scary there, beside the dark, rushing water. I filled my pail and we hurried back to the house.

The girls and I made sandwiches, and we all sat on a quilt, spread down outside the door, to eat them. We made the sandwiches last as long as we could, to keep from going back in the house, and by then it was full dark, except off to the north where the fire burned orange-red against the night sky. I thought of Mama and Florry and the baby, and of Stella, all sleeping in nice clean houses that night. I thought of Poppie, off in the hills somewhere, fighting a wind-driven prairie fire.

And finally I thought of the beds to be made down in the dirty little shack behind us, and of the ducks by the kitchen door, waiting to be dressed.

We went in then and spread the tent canvas on the floor in the largest room, and made the beds down on top of it. The children wanted to go straight to bed, but I coaxed them back to the kitchen and lined them up at the table. Then I started on the ducks. They tried hard to stay awake, but it was no use. One by one, they dozed off and I had to put them to bed. All but Dovey. I kept her at the table with me and did my best to keep her awake until I finished the ducks. But, as the night wore on, her head bobbed lower and lower. Finally she slept, her cheek against the oilcloth-covered tabletop.

It seemed to me, then, that I had more to bear than I could stand. Here I was, miles from anywhere, in a strange, dirty house on a dark, windy night, responsible for my little sisters and brother, and for Poppie's last forty dollars. Every sound in the night made me jump. The wild, gamey smell of the ducks was making me sicker by the minute, and my sore finger kept getting in the way and being bumped. I was numb all over by the time I finally finished the ducks, shook Dovey awake, and dragged her off to bed with me. But I slept like the dead the rest of that night. I didn't even know when Poppie came back from the fire, near daylight, and went to bed.

Chapter Twenty-One

B<small>Y</small> DAYLIGHT the house looked even worse than it had the night before—all its dirt and grime and cheapness showed plainer. But we could see the Birdwood better, too, dancing down from the north to make a wide bend below the stable before it giggled away to the southwest. The tall old cottonwoods stood on the east bank, where the house was. On beyond, the low green hills spread away as far as we could see. But on the west side, where the fire had burned to the creek, the high, rough hills were charred and black under the bright blue sky.

Except for the tacky little buildings and the burned hills, it was so beautiful—and so empty and lonesome. The Cox place was north of us, a quarter mile or so, and Tom Heskett, a bachelor, lived about a mile down the creek; otherwise there were no neighbors anywhere near. But the road from the north country followed the creek to the river valley, ten miles below, and cowboys *might* come whooping down this valley anytime, headed for town and a lively time.

Poppie went right back to Dawson County to get the cattle and chickens. Presh and Roy went with him, but Dovey, Nellie, and I stayed on the Birdwood to clean up the house. There was nothing to be afraid of, Poppie told us, before he left; for in this country no one would

bother women and girls, and if we needed anything we
could call on Coxes.

So he left with the two little ones, and my sisters and
I were alone. All our lives we had been used to a big
family and a crowded household. Now, homesickness
moved in with us, making misery of the week we had to
live through until they came back again. We kept busy,
carrying water from the creek (easier than hoisting it
from the old dug well in the yard) and scrubbing on
the filthy little house. As much as I could, I kept a lookout on the road, hoping a cowboy would come along.
But no one at all passed through the winding valley, and
the trips to the creek were the only good things about
the long, lonesome days. Blackbirds perched on tall cattails there, their songs sounding like music floating up
through water. Neat wild ducks swam in the farther
bends of the stream, and snipes raced like little breezes
along the sandy banks.

One afternoon that week I saw a tall woman coming
around the upper bend of the creek. I figured she must
be Mrs. Cox, and I watched her drive a cow from behind a clump of chokecherry brush and then lift a newborn calf in her arms. Ever since I could remember we
had fetched and carried for our own frail little mother,
so it seemed natural to me to run out and offer to help
with the sixty-pound calf.

"Land, no." She laughed. "I can handle this little
fellow all right."

So I walked up the creek a little way with her. She
told me that her daughter Jennie would be home in a
few days. "She's about your age. She's been staying at
her sister's in town, going to school. She'll be glad to
know we've got some new neighbors on the old Sherman
place."

Just before I turned to go back, Mrs. Cox nodded toward the burned hills across the creek and asked, "How would you girls like to go with me to pull wool off Heskett's dead sheep? He told me to go ahead and get all I wanted. It'll come in handy for quilt padding next winter." I told her we didn't know anything about pulling wool, but that we'd be glad to go with her whenever she was ready.

That was a cold, drizzly day, and so was the next one, and that evening Poppie pulled in. Stell and the two little ones were with him, and John and Florry too. John had helped drive the cattle through and Florry had come to drive John's buggy. That left only Mama and the baby back in Dawson County.

The three-day trip had been a hard one, Poppie said. The big old bull had played out the first day on the road, and he had had to make arrangements with a farmer to keep him until he could go back to get him. The next day the weather had turned cold and wet, and that evening they stopped at a farmhouse on the lower end of the Birdwood Table. Poppie went up to the house to see if they could stay inside that night. A woman came to the door and he told her they had their own food and bedding, that all they wanted was a dry place to eat and sleep.

The woman said they had only two rooms, and that her husband was sick abed in one of them, but that they could use the other one. So Poppie and John carried the food and bedding into the little kitchen and then went out to take care of their stock. And all the time a herd of cattle, corralled beside the stable, bawled like they were in trouble. Back at the house again, Poppie went in to visit with the sick man. When he asked about the bawling cattle the farmer said they hadn't been fed since

he took sick, two days before, and he guessed they were
hungry. So Poppie told him he and John would feed
them, first thing the next morning.

"It was pretty late," Poppie said, "by the time we
got them fed and got our own outfit ready for the road.
Then I went up to the house to thank the woman for
taking us in. Just to be polite, I asked her if we owed
anything for the night's accommodation. And I'll be
blamed if she didn't charge me three dollars for letting
us sleep on her kitchen floor and feed her starving cattle."

A few days later Mrs. Cox came over, dressed for pulling wool. "It's dirty work," she told us. "You'd better
wear some of your papa's old clothes and button up good,
else you'll get cinders down your necks."

So Florry, Stell, and I, in sunbonnets and mittens, and
buttoned to the chins in some of Poppie's old overalls
and shirts, followed her across the creek and up the hill.
Puffs of fine, cindery dust flew up at every step, but
already blades of new grass showed green among the ashes.

At the top of the hill Mrs. Cox waved a mittened
hand at the black mounds dotting the slopes below us.
"There's our wool," she said.

A sickening smell came strong on the west wind and
we circled to the upwind side of a mound. Mrs. Cox
brushed at it briskly. The winter's growth of long, thick
wool had been so thick that the fire had burned only the
top quarter inch, and when she had brushed the burned
layer away the wool underneath showed white and smooth.
"This is all there is to it," she said, yanking a handful
of wool off the carcass and dropping it into the gunnysack she carried.

We scattered along the slope, took a sheep apiece,
brushed away the burnt layer, and began pulling wool.
The top sides finished, we turned the carcasses over and

pulled the wool on the undersides, where it was scarcely even singed; for the sheep had died of the smoke, or fright, and the fire had burned over them after they fell.

That was one of the worst jobs we ever got into. The April day was miserably hot and the dead-sheep stench was terrible. Our faces were soon as black as the sheep's top sides, and sweat ran down our foreheads into our eyes, burning like vinegar. The sifting, powdery ashes turned our clothes stiff, and the cinders inside our collars stung and scratched unmercifully. But the sacks filled fairly fast and we dragged them home, well before supper-time, and carried water from the creek for shampoos and baths.

Utterly worn out, we pulled off our clothes in our hot little rooms that night and tumbled into bed. Florry, Presh, and I shared a bed in one of the tiny bedrooms, Dovey, Stell, and Nellie slept in the other one. Poppie and John had the bed in the middle room, Roy slept on a cot beside it. Already the little house was crowded— and Mama and the baby weren't even here yet.

I was almost asleep by the time my head touched the pillow, but a minute later I had the horrible feeling that something was crawling all over me. I jumped up and felt for a match to light the lamp again. Florry had felt it, too, and was up almost as soon as I was.

Bedbugs, limbered up by the unseasonably warm day, were crawling and skittering over everything. From every crack in the old plaster, from every baseboard and window crevice they came, hordes of them. It was the same in the other little room. The place was alive with them.

"Oh, dear," Florry said, almost crying, "now we *are* in for it, but I'm glad they showed up before Mama got here."

Mama, afraid there would be bedbugs in any house

that belonged to Old Bill Sherman, had told us what to do before we left Dawson County. So every day we dragged all the ticks and bedding out into the sun and picked off every bug, and then we went over every crack and crevice in the walls and furniture with chicken feathers dipped in kerosene. Bedbugs can't stand that kind of treatment for long, and so we finally got rid of them.

On my seventeenth birthday I drove across the clean, green hills to meet the train bringing Mama and little Heart to the Birdwood. I had never been to Sutherland before, but Poppie told me I couldn't miss the way if I kept to the main-traveled road until I came to the bridge across the Platte River.

The past three weeks had been a backbreaking nightmare of dead sheep wool, bedbugs, and housecleaning. But the sun was bright and warm this morning, I was "dressed up" for the first time since we left Dawson County, and behind me the old house, scrubbed to the bare wood with main strength, elbow grease, and lye water, was clean again.

Sutherland was a little place, just a few business buildings strung out along the railroad tracks, and a scattering of homes under tall cottonwoods. There was a wagon or two on the street, the teams tied to hitchracks, but no saddle horses or cowboys. It seemed we hadn't moved far enough west, and I was beginning to feel cheated and disappointed.

Mama was not surprised when she saw how small and ugly the house was. "It won't be so bad, though, if Bill keeps his promise and builds on another room," was all she said. She loved the creek and the hills; they reminded her a little of Missouri, she said. And right away she planned to raise ducks. They'd be such a pretty sight, swimming in the creek, she told us.

After Mama came to the Birdwood we began having company. Mrs. Cox came over to spend an afternoon. Then Jennie, just home from school, and her brother Wynn came to bring us a pair of tiny orphan lambs. Wynn herded sheep for Tom Heskett, and Tom had told him to give us girls the lambs if we wanted to bother with them.

Jennie was a tall, quiet girl, fond of reading and studying. Wynn, a little older than Jennie, was a nice-looking young fellow, and right off he took a fancy to Stell, who had grown up and slimmed down in the last year. Her hair was black, like Mama's, her skin white and smooth, and she knew how to use her dimples.

And finally there came a Mrs. Duncan, riding side-saddle on a big, bony horse, with her three-year-old daughter bouncing along behind her. A tall, ungraceful woman, she hopped down, hauled the little girl off, and turned the horse loose to graze. "I'm Mrs. Duncan, Mrs. Jabe Duncan," she told us, "an' this here's my kid, Onie. Me an' Jabe work fer Tom Heskett. Tom's a bach, y' know, an' I do th' cookin' there."

Mama asked her to come in and lay off her bonnet. Onie stayed in the yard to play. Her mother hadn't bothered to put sleeves into the new little calico dress she wore, nor to hem any of its raw edges. A big safety pin held the dress together at the back of the little girl's neck. But from the pin down, it hung open—and she hadn't another stitch on under it. Gnats were bad on the Birdwood, swarming in clouds over every living thing, and poor little Onie had gnat bites all over her. Every few minutes she stopped her play to stoop over and scratch her legs, and whine "Darn them zeeties." And every time her mother yelled, "Straighten up, Onie, er ye'll sunburn yer back"; for the dress fell apart, all the way up to the pin, baring her naked, skinny little behind.

Mrs. Duncan was a high-powered talker. When she found out Mama wanted to buy duck and chicken eggs to set, she said, "Land, yes, I can let y' have all th' chicken eggs y' want but I ain't got no duck eggs. I know a woman as has, though." She told us where we could get the duck eggs, then she "lowed" she had better be getting home to get dinner for her menfolks.

That afternoon I helped Mama fix coops and nests, and that night we moved broody hens from the henhouse to the nests. The next afternoon I drove the buggy and a new buggy horse, Nancy, down the creek to Heskett's ranch, where Mrs. Duncan insisted that I come in and "set a spell" before we looked for eggs.

The house was a single big, unplastered, unfinished room. The windows had neither frames nor curtains, and a faded calico sheet divided the kitchen half from the bedroom half. But the whole barnlike place was as clean and tidy as could be. After a while, when I said I'd have to be starting home, Mrs. Duncan got up and took me out to the barns and sheepsheds after the eggs.

The nests were scattered around in feed boxes and mangers, and most had broody hens on them. "I've flang them hens off ever' day fer a month now," Mrs. Duncan complained, yanking them off again and picking the biggest and best-shaped eggs out of the nests for me.

Mama put the eggs under her setting hens that evening.

Mama had a way with all birds, but especially with setting hens. She liked to pet and visit with them while they brooded their eggs, and if a hen, halfway through setting, changed her mind about raising a family Mama could usually straighten her out and coax her into finish-

ing the job. But when she went to her coops the next
morning she got a jolt, for under one hen she found a
chick, still wet from the shell. Even the hen seemed upset.

Mama brought the chick to the house and asked me
where Mrs. Duncan got the eggs. I told her and she
said, "Hmfp, I thought so. Well, I'll have to raise this
little thing by hand, I suppose." She put it in a box and
gave it feed and water. But that evening, when she went
to the coops to slip it under a hen for the night, she
found it had a new-hatched brother—and for the next
three weeks a chick or two hatched every day.

Among her setters Mama had a good-natured old hen
she called "Mrs. Grundy." Mrs. Grundy had been mother-
ing puppies, kittens, doorknobs, and anything else she
could find to sit on for so long that all the feathers on
her breast were worn to stubs. So Mama divided Mrs.
Grundy's eggs among the other hens and gave her the
chicks as they hatched. Most hens won't have anything
to do with a family of all ages like that one, but Mrs.
Grundy was happy to claim and mother them all.

"But I can't help wondering about the eggs Mrs.
Duncan picks out of those nests to feed her family,"
Poppie said. "Some of 'em must be about ready to start
scratchin' when she fries 'em."

Mama set more than a hundred duck eggs, too, and
by the time she was through we hadn't enough laying
hens left to keep us in eggs. Then Poppie heard of a
woman, quite a ways down the creek, who had hens to
sell, and sent me there one afternoon to buy a dozen. I
found the place all right, a little soddy built against the
flank of a hill, back from the creek. Two dogs ran out,
barking at me, and a woman came to the door. "Tie
up your horse and come on in," she said when I told her

who I was and what I wanted. "We'll have to wait till dark to catch the hens."

I tied Nancy to a post in the yard and followed the woman into the darkest little house I had ever seen. Flies buzzed over everything, half a dozen hens pecked and scratched on the dirt floor, and another one blinked at me from the middle of the bed. The dogs followed us in and stretched out along the sod wall, a couple of half-grown pigs followed them in, rooted around in the clutter for a bit, and then laid down and went to sleep. The hen got up from the egg she had laid on the bed and left, cackling at the top of her voice.

After a while the woman got up and started supper. She said she might as well have it early, that her old man wouldn't be home for it, anyway. She tramped back and forth between her table and stove, stepping over and around the dogs, pigs, and chickens and scolding at them in a friendly fashion. When the meal was ready, she brushed the chicken feathers and dust off the table with the hem of her greasy apron, set the food and dishes on it, and told me to "set up."

The chickens began leaving the house to go to roost, so, as soon as I decently could, I laid down my knife and fork and said I thought I should be starting home, that it was quite a way to drive after dark. "You sure didn't eat much," she said, but she got up and went with me to catch the chickens.

Nancy was a fast trotter, and as soon as we had the hens sacked and loaded in the buggy I let her take a lively pace away from there.

The duck eggs hatched upwards of a hundred balls of fluffy yellow and grayish black. And once the ducklings found their way to the creek, where they spent most of the daylight hours, they were, indeed, the "pretty sight" Mama had said they'd be.

Before long, whenever she went into the yard and called—a special clear call she had just for the ducklings —the whole flock would come, waddling so fast they fell over their own and each other's feet. Then Mama would sit on the grass and let the gawky little things run into her lap. Those that couldn't climb onto her cuddled around her, all gabbling at once, and then Mama, half covered by the gray and yellow babies, made a pretty sight, too.

When, a little later, the ducklings began to disappear, a dozen or more at a time, Mama was almost as worried and upset as if some of the family had dropped out of sight. So she sat by the creek and watched, until she saw a big mud turtle float up and snare a helpless baby duck, and then she put all of us to work, setting frog-baited hooks in the bank as fast as we could.

By the time we had pulled the last of the hard-shelled thieves from the water, we had eaten enough turtle steak, turtle soup, and turtle hash to last us the rest of our lives. And by then the sixty ducklings that survived the turtle raids had shed their gray and yellow rompers and begun to go around in their grown-up clothes, some in snow-white Pekin robes, the rest in dark, dressy mallard coats.

Chapter Twenty-Two

JOHN stayed on with us on the Birdwood that summer, and on nice evenings and Sunday afternoons he and Florry walked along the creek or went buggy riding. By the end of June they had come to an "understanding."

But for Stell and me the summer was almost completely wasted. Nothing interesting or exciting ever seemed to happen, no parties, no neighborhood meetings of any kind. The long, empty Sundays were the worst. In Dawson County we had had church and Sunday school at Walnut Grove, and young folks stopping in in the afternoons, but here there was nothing. Wynn and Jennie, the only other young folks anywhere near us, weren't often free on Sunday. Wynn spent seven days a week with Heskett's sheep and Jennie and her folks usually spent Sundays at home.

I had asked Jennie about cowboys, and she had told me there were some in the hills to the north, and that they sometimes drove cattle down the Birdwood to the railroad. So far, not a single one had come along.

Even on the Fourth of July nothing happened, no picnic, no celebration. But a few days later Mrs. Duncan rode over to tell us she was "havin' a birthday party on Jabe nex' Sunday evenin'," and she wanted us to come. "Jennie 'n' Wynn'll be there, o'course, an' it'll be fine if 'y want t' bake a cake an' fetch it along. I'm bakin' some, too, an' makin' a freezer a ice cream. Tom puts up ice, y' know, an' we can have ice cream whenever we take a notion."

So Florry baked a cake, and she and John and Stell and I went to the party. Mrs. Duncan had pushed the partition curtain back to the wall and spread a pair of old lace curtains over the bed—giving a party-like look to the big, bare room. Mr. Duncan, a thin, dark little man, seemed pleased with the party his wife was having "on him," but Mrs. Duncan did most of the talking. Tom Heskett, she said, had gone back to Ohio to visit his girl. "An' 'twon't surprise me none if he don't come fetchin' a hi-falutin' bride back here one o' these days. Wonder what she'll say when she sees this here house?"

After a while she "lowed" it was time to eat, and Florry and I went with her to the kitchen end of the room. "I baked nine cakes t'day an' set 'em here in front a this winder t' cool, an' Tom's sheep dogs clumb up an' et 'em all," she told us, while she whacked Florry's nice cake into enough pieces to go around.

On the way home we decided that if she did bake nine cakes, and they all turned out like her ice cream, it was just as well that Tom's dogs ate them. For the uncooked ice cream, flavored with raw lemon juice, had been so sour and bitter that we could scarcely get it down.

On a sizzling morning a few days later, Poppie hitched Prince and Dolly to the wagon, put his bicycle behind the seat, and headed back to Dawson County to get the organ (stored at Grandma's) and the bull. Because of the awful heat he camped early, a little way east of North Platte. He staked Dolly near the wagon and turned Prince loose, knowing the big young horse wouldn't stray far from his mother. But when he got up at daylight

both horses were gone—Dolly had pulled her picket pin
—and the tracks led east.

So Poppie hauled his bicycle out of the wagon and
peddled after them. The sun was blazing down on the
steamy valley by the time he overtook them, still plugging right along back toward their old stable in Mc-
Carter Canyon, and it was noon by the time he had his
outfit on the road again.

At the sandhill farm where he had left the bull, the
farmer told him it was dead. "Died soon after you left,"
he said, "so we opened 'im up. He was full of the darn-
dest mess of old iron you ever saw, wire, nails, broken
clevises, hinges. No wonder he couldn't walk to speak of."

Poppie's face was gray and dripping sweat when he
pulled in home with the organ. He told me to put the
team away, that he had an awful pain in his side and
was going in and lie down awhile. By suppertime he had
gone to sleep and we didn't wake him. He was still sleeping when the rest of us went to bed.

All week, the little bedrooms under the low roof had
been like stewpots in the July heat. If it hadn't been
for the clouds of mosquitos along the creek we could
have moved our beds outside into the cooler air; as it
was we had to stay inside and steam all night.

Near midnight, that night, Mama called Florry and
me to come and help her. She was scared, and so were
we, when we saw Poppie, groaning with pain and holding his right side with both hands.

"You girls make some hot salt packs, quick," Mama
told us. "He thinks heat will help."

While I built up a hot chip fire in the range, Florry
set the big iron skillet on and emptied a small sack of
salt into it. We stirred the salt until it was piping hot,
poured it back into the sack and pressed it to Poppie's

swollen side. All the rest of that night we fired the range in the hot kitchen and changed the hot packs—but Poppie's pain never let up for a minute.

At daybreak Mama sent John to Hershey for the nearest doctor. "Get him on his way as quick as you can," she told him, "and then send Ma a telegram. Tell her Charlie's awful bad, and that we'll meet the train in Sutherland tomorrow morning."

The road to Hershey was a long one, a good eighteen miles by way of the Sutherland bridge—for there was no other way to cross the river—but John made good time going in. And gray-haired little Dr. Eaves came out as fast as he could, pushing his team hard through the terrible heat.

The doctor looked Poppie over, then told us he had "inflammation of the bowels, and a bad case at that." He left some medicine and said he'd be back the next day. So we knew Poppie was really bad; doctors didn't make such long trips every day unless the case was serious. Only a few years later, younger doctors were operating on patients like Poppie for appendicitis; but in those days they still called his symptoms "inflammation of the bowels," at least on the frontier.

I met the train in Sutherland the next morning. Grandma was on it. We hadn't doubted that she would be.

For the next two weeks we sweated out the worst heat wave western Nebraska had had in years. And all the time Poppie grew steadily worse. He couldn't keep a thing on his stomach and the terrible pain was wearing him out. "Doc," he whispered to the wilted little doctor one day, "I can't stand this any longer. Can't you get another doctor to come out with you and see if there's anything can be done for me?"

"I'll get McCabe up from the Platte and bring him out tomorrow," the doctor promised.

So Poppie lived through the rest of that day, and the long, terrible night. Too weak to speak, his eyes begging for relief, he waited while the two doctors held their consultation over him the next day. Then Dr. Mc-Cabe told him that Dr. Eaves was doing all that any doctor could do and that he couldn't suggest anything more. His words were a death sentence, and Poppie shut his eyes and accepted it.

The doctors left, and all that afternoon I sat by Poppie's bed, sponging his damp, gray face with cold water. I couldn't tell if it eased him or not, for he hadn't opened his eyes again and his breathing barely lifted his chest.

Toward four o'clock Mama went into one of the back bedrooms to lie down for a while. Grandma, Florry, and the younger children had gone to the garden to pick vegetables for supper, and I was alone with Poppie, trying to prepare myself to give him up. I didn't see how I could do it, how I could ever get along without him. Almost ever since I could remember I had been his "boy," and he had taught me so many things I needed to know. I thought of all the good times we had had, singing together, and of the times he had taken Florry and me to picnics and ball games. I even thought of the times he had been stern and cross to me, and now I could see the need, and be grateful for those times, too.

Then a knock at the kitchen door made me jump. Coxes, or Tom Heskett, come to ask about Poppie, I thought. But a stranger, a slim gray-eyed young man with black hair and mustache, stood at the door, his wide-brimmed cowboy hat in his hand.

"How do you do," he said. "My pardner and I are on the way to town with a little bunch of cattle. We stopped to water at Coxes and they told us about your father. We're campin' down the creek a ways and if there's anything we can do to help out, sit up tonight, or do the chores, we'd be glad to do it."

I thanked him and told him there wasn't, that we had plenty of help with the chores, and that we'd be sitting up with Poppie ourselves, tonight. So the cowboy put his hat back on his head, swung up on his tall gray horse, and rode on down the creek. I watched him go, the first cowboy I had ever seen, and so polite and friendly, too. He rode better than anyone I had ever observed on a horse, so easy and graceful, and it had been so good of him to stop to see if he could help us. If I hadn't been so worried about Poppie I might have thought of some thing to say to him to let him know he'd be welcome to come back to our house again. Now I might never see him any more, but it was already too late to think about that, so I hurried back to Poppie, afraid that he might have stopped breathing while I was gone.

But Poppie was still alive when morning came, and the morning after that, too. So weak that he didn't seem to suffer anymore, he was too far gone to know when the pain finally let up. As he had grown worse by slow degrees, so now he grew better, but for days we could hardly tell that he made any progress at all, only that he was still alive.

Grandma and Florry and Mr. and Mrs. Cox fanned and nursed him through the hot days, coaxing strength into him again, but I claimed the long night watches. I had been his right-hand help for so long that it seemed these hours belonged to me.

As soon as Dr. Eaves was sure that Poppie was going to get well, he said he wouldn't need to come out any more, that one of us could just as well drive to Hershey every few days for instructions and prescriptions. So I said I wanted to be the one to do that, too. I knew Mama wasn't able to make the long trip, and I thought I could do it better than any of the rest.

I went every week for a while, giving the doctor careful reports on Poppie. Hershey had no drugstore, so I had to drive clear back to Sutherland to have the prescriptions filled, and each round trip was a thirty-mile horror of heat and dust and gnats. The gnats were the worst. Clouds of the tiny, stinging pests followed me every mile of the way, and neither hat nor veil nor gloves could keep them off my face and wrists. I came home from every trip with my eyes swelled nearly shut and by head thumping with a sick headache.

Quite a while after the cowboy stopped at our door, the day Poppie was so low, I asked Jennie about him.

"Oh, that was Bert Snyder," she told me. "He's from Maxwell. He and Artie Plumer summer their cattle on Squaw Creek, north of here." So now I knew his name, and where he lived, and I wondered if I'd ever see him again.

The summer was nearly over when Poppie finally crawled out of bed and put his clothes on again. He was so thin he could wrap his shirt and pants twice around himself, but as soon as he could stand the trip he went to North Platte to pay his doctor bill. "I guess you don't remember me," he said to Dr. McCabe, "but I'm Charlie McCance, the fellow you and Doc Eaves came to the Birdwood to see, back in July."

The doctor stared at Poppie as if he had seen a ghost, then he jumped up and clapped him on the back. "Man!" he said, "I never expected to see *you* again. Maybe you don't know it, but you were sure teetering right on the ragged edge that day."

And about the same time, Old Bill Sherman, just back foom Pennsylvania, with train smoke still in his hair and whiskers, came to build on the room he had promised us. He moved into the old cellar cave, out back of the house, which he kept furnished with a bunk, a Topsy stove, a teakettle and a skillet. Bill's housekeeping was of the simplest. At mealtime he sat on the edge of his bed, which he never made, and ate out of his skillet. When, once in a long while, the skillet needed washing, he simply took it down to the creek, scoured it with a handful of sand and rinsed it in the stream. He borrowed our lantern to light his cave, and when it burned empty he brought it over and "borrowed" a filling of kerosene from our can.

But, after his hired carpenter had the new room under way, he spent most of his time tramping around the country and we weren't bothered much with him. Old Bill usually managed to drop in at some hay camp at mealtime. IIe liked tea but, this being a coffee-drinking community, he carried his own little tea sack with him. The water for a proper cup of tea shouldn't be too hot, he said, but "jist under bilin'," so, squatting beside some hay crew's campfire, he now and then stuck a dirty finger into the kettle of water heating there, to test its temperature for his tea. Though the camp cooks didn't like it, they put up with it, but Mama said, "Landlord or not, if he ever tries that in my kitchen he'll get his knuckles rapped with the stove poker."

The school on the upper Birdwood started in September. I knew I would be the biggest and oldest one there, and I didn't want to go, but Poppie wouldn't listen to me. Then it turned out that the school had no books for advanced pupils, and some had to be ordered for me. They hadn't come yet, late in the month, when we heard that the wild grapes were ripe up on East Creek. So Mama and I went graping, and Poppie, still almost too weak to walk to the stable and back, went along to drive for us.

At the forks of the Birdwood, a few miles north of our place, we turned up the east fork, where we found plenty of grapes on vines that climbed the steep sides of the deep, wild canyons. Poppie followed along the creek with the team and wagon, while Mama and I filled our buckets on the slopes above. By noon we had worked our way up the creek to its junction with little Squaw Creek. We ate our lunch there, in the shade of a rustling old cottonwood, and afterward I struck out for the upper slopes, leaving the grapes along the lower banks for Mama.

I stopped at a tangle of vines at the head of a steep draw and turned to look off across the hills to the south. Everything seemed to be all of one color that day, from the soft, pale gold of the bunchgrass to the deeper yellow of the cottonwoods and willows. The sun was warm and sweet and it was a day made for dreaming. While I stood there, a man on horseback turned a bend in the creek below and rode right out of my dream and up the hill toward me. His hair and mustache were black, he rode a good-looking big horse, and I knew his eyes were gray.

I turned and began picking grapes as fast as I could, pretending that I didn't hear his horse swishing through the tall grass behind me.

I was wearing an old outfit of Poppie's and I knew I looked a fright, but when he spoke to me I had to turn and face him. He asked me how my father was, and I told him he was fine, that he was down in the canyon with the wagon and would be glad to see him if he was riding that way. I couldn't think of any more to say, and I guess the cowboy couldn't either for, after a little, he said, well, he had just stopped to tell me the grapes were a lot better, farther up the creek, and that we'd be welcome to drive on up and help ourselves to all we wanted. I thanked him and he said good-bye, put his hat back on his head, and rode back down the hill.

From under the floppy rim of Poppie's old hat I watched him go. If I hadn't been dressed so awful, I could prob- ably have thought of something interesting to say to him —but this was the way things always happened to me.

A month later I was back in Dawson County.

Early in October Uncle John wrote that a typhoid epidemic had carried off Mr. Ericson, Poppie's renter, and that he would like to rent the place when the widow moved off. Poppie wrote back, inviting Uncle John and Aunt Irene to John and Florry's wedding on Sunday, October 19. They could talk about renting the place then, he said.

By the afternoon of the seventeenth, when Uncle John's drove in, everything was ready for the wedding. The new room, built across the south side of the old house, was all done, but like so many of our other front rooms, this one had to have a bed in it, too. It was a big, sunny room, though, and the double windows in its south wall faced the creek and the big trees. Florry's wedding dress, a lovely cream-colored brocade that Mama had made for her, hung, wrapped in a sheet, on the back of the front- room door.

John left for North Platte early on Saturday morning to get the marriage license, and Florry and I began baking and cooking for the next day's wedding dinner. In the afternoon Mama put little Heart down to play on a quilt spread on the ground on the south side of the house. The day was warm and still, and when she went out to bring her in she found a big rattlesnake coiled on a corner of the quilt, sunning himself almost within striking distance of the year-old baby.

I killed the snake while Mama, holding Heart tight in her arms, said she thought the snake came from the stony ridge above the road, that the bluff was probably full of snakes, and that we'd better get up there and clean them out before they bit somebody.

It turned out that we didn't have a wedding the next day, after all, for John came home just before daylight without the marriage license. The judge had been out of town all day, he said. He had waited until midnight for him, then he gave up and came on home. So, after dinner, John and Florry went off for their usual Sunday buggy ride—and Mama and I went up on the ridge and killed twenty-two rattlesnakes.

John and Florry were married in front of the double windows in the living room later that week, and afterward Nellie and I went back to Dawson County with Uncle John's. Grandma wanted Nellie, her favorite among the younger children, to stay with her that winter, and Uncle John and Aunt Irene wanted me to stay with them so little Irvie would have someone to go to school with. The schoolbooks, ordered for me weeks ago, still hadn't come, so Poppie said I could go.

John and Florry were staying on with the folks that winter and, for the first time since I was five years old, I wasn't needed at home.

At Uncle John's, for the first time in my life, I had a bedroom all by myself. It was the room that had been Grandma's, before she turned the main house over to Uncle John and his family. Across the entryway, in

BEND IN THE BIRDWOOD, DOWN THE CREEK TOWARD HESKETT'S RANCH

A narrow sheep bridge in the lower right corner

BILL SHERMAN AND HIS HOUSE ON THE BIRDWOOD

The young trees were planted after we lived there. Bill's cellar house is at the far right. The creek and the big trees below the house, at the right, are not shown.

the big room built on after Aunt Hester married, Grandma and Aunt Dicy petted and fussed over Nellie.

It was good to be back with my old friends again— Esther Shogren, Lillie Maline, the Holmes girls, and the rest. I was late getting started, of course, but I worked hard to catch up. The teacher, Sella Grunden, had a better education than most country schoolteachers, and the big Holmes boys (except Phillip, who had died in that summer's typhoid epidemic) came that winter to study algebra with her.

By the end of November Florry was back in Dawson County, too.

On the morning after Thanksgiving Grandpa Houk finished his breakfast and sat down in his rocker beside the kitchen stove. Then he said "oh," in a surprised sort of way, and died. Grandma ran out on the stoop and shouted up the road toward our old place. Mr. Clark was hitching up his team in the yard, and when he looked down the road where she was yelling and waving her apron he jumped in the wagon and came as fast as he could. But there was nothing he could do, except lay the old man on his bed and cover him with a sheet.

Grandpa Houk had been a Union soldier, so Grandma wanted Union soldiers for pallbearers. Old Bill Sherman was among those she asked to serve, and he and Poppie came down together from the Birdwood. In Cozad, Poppie made him clean up and buy a white shirt and a suit of clothes. The shirt, bought off a bargain counter, was an old-fashioned, stiff-bosomed affair. Old Bill couldn't be persuaded to buy collar and cuff buttons for it, so someone loaned him the necessary jewelry. Most of his old neighbors didn't know him when he showed up at the funeral, bathed, barbered, and decked out in his new outfit.

After the funeral John and Florry moved back to Grandma Houk's to look after her and the farm.

Toward the end of the year we had a fairly heavy snowstorm, and then a cold spell that turned the snow just right for sleighing. Sleighs weren't common in our section of Nebraska, partly because the snow cover was seldom good enough for their use, but on New Year's Eve I had my first and only sleigh ride when Fred Berg took me to the program and Watch Night service at Walnut Grove. That was to be my first Watch Night service, too. Fred had been my steady beau since I came back to Dawson County. He didn't look anything like the gray-eyed cowboy on the Birdwood, but he was lots of fun and he was *there*.

Fred had a good team and we drove over the hard snow at a lively clip, with the sleigh bells ringing out their music and the horses' breath smoking on the frosty air. At the church a good-natured argument was going on. Some of the folks said that not only a year but a century as well was to turn its back on the world that night; the rest declared the century had another year to go.

Then the program started, and while the singing and speaking were going on the wind came up and began to howl around the church. When the program was over some of the men went outside to have a look at the weather. They came in to report the temperature had dropped so far in the past hour that it would be too hard on the horses to keep them standing in the bitter wind until midnight. I felt awfully bad at missing the thrill of sitting up to watch the old year out, and everybody was grumbling a little about the cussedness of Nebraska weather, but we all bundled into our wraps and headed for our rigs.

While Fred and I, hanging onto the robes for dear life,

dashed for home that bitter New Year's Eve, I thought
of poor Charlotte and her ride in handsome Charlie's
sleigh. I didn't quite freeze to death, though, but I did
frost my feet so badly that I had a miserable time with
chilblains all the rest of the winter. Fred left me at my
door, and an hour later, while I shivered in my bed with
my icy feet wrapped in the tail of my long nightgown,
time, with a tick of the clock, turned the century up
from 1899 to 1900.

The weather played another mean trick on me a few
months later.

In March Uncle John moved to our old place in Roten
Valley, and we were no more than well settled in the
old house than Aunt Irene went into another flurry of
housecleaning. We had given the whole place a good
cleaning when we moved in, so I wondered why, a month
later, she needed to "do up" her clean curtains all over
again. But when her little girl, three-year-old Georgie,
began acting important and looking like she knew things
she wouldn't tell, I really began to sniff around for clues.

My suspicions jelled the evening Aunt Irene came out
of a brown study at the supper table to say she was afraid
her scarf had blown out of the wagon that afternoon.
"Maybe you left it at Florry's," Uncle John said, and
Aunt Irene gave him a look that wilted him.

My birthday was getting close, and if they had been at
Florry's while I was at school, and didn't want me to
know it, it was easy to guess they were planning a surprise party for me. I had never had a birthday party—
and I had wanted one for years.

On the evening of my birthday Aunt Irene began
clearing the supper table almost before we finished eating.
I wiped the dishes for her, pretending, as I had ever
since I came from school, that I hadn't noticed the Sun-

day spick and span look of the house, or that she had cut Uncle John's hair that day. And both of us pretended not to notice the ragged black clouds piling up above the hills.

By the time we finished, the first big drops were streaking Aunt Irene's clean windows, and fifteen minutes later it was pouring down. Then Aunt Irene brought out the pretty birthday cake she had baked and told me about the party she had planned for me. Florry was to bring the ice cream, she said; they'd been to see her about it the day she lost her scarf.

Uncle John grinned and said the whole thing had sure been hard on Georgie, that for two weeks the poor little tyke had been almost afraid to say a word for fear she'd give something away.

Chapter Twenty-Three

B Y THE first of May Nellie and I were back on the Birdwood. I was eighteen and my school days were over, or so I thought. But I couldn't see much ahead for me, except that the folks needed me and there was plenty to do, helping out there. Florry wouldn't be at home any more, and all the work she had done, and the responsibility she had carried, fell on me.

Mama wasn't so well either. Her cough was worse, on account of a late winter cold, but she already had several batches of new hatched chicks in the coops by the stable. She had given up raising ducks. The fall before a pair of coyotes and finished off more than half her full-grown flock in a single morning, and some town hunters had shot most of the rest on the creek a few weeks later.

But one thing on the Birdwood was better—this spring we had new neighbors. A family named Johnson had settled at the forks of the creek. Stell, with Wynn and Jennie, had gone to a housewarming party there, two or three weeks before I came home. She told me about the young folks there, Elma, Edna, and Ivan, and about Steve LaRue, a young homesteader on East Creek, who was already going steady with Elma. Tom Heskett was soon to be married, too. He had moved the Duncans down the creek to another place he owned, and a carpenter was at work, partitioning and finishing his house. He was

going back to Ohio for the wedding, and everybody on
the Birdwood was wondering what his bride would be
like. And I had found out from Jennie that Bert Snyder
had brought his cattle back to Squaw Creek that spring.

Old Bill Sherman, back again in the cellar behind our
house, was herding sheep for Heskett. He had rigged a
pitcher pump above the well in the yard, and every
morning at daylight he went there for a pail of water.
"Charlie, be ye dead?" he'd yell as he passed the house,
in a voice that roused us all. Old Bill had had a bad scare,
the first warm day that spring. He was herding on the
hill above the rattlesnake ridge when a bleating sheep
came running to him with blood dripping off its nose.
He rubbed the blood away and found the telltale double
puncture, then he stood up and rubbed his bloody hand
across his rusty bald head while he looked along the ridge
for the snake. He spotted it right away, crawling up
the slope. Not having anything else handy, he yanked
off a shoe and threw it at the snake. The rattler struck
at the shoe as it went by, then crawled inside it and
settled down, coiled and buzzing for business.

So Old Bill hustled to the ridge, grabbed an armful of
crumbly stones, and pelted the snake to death. Then,
without stopping for his shoe, he galloped down the slope
to the house, yelling at Mama to get him something for
snakebite, and stuck his head under the pump. Pumping with one hand, he scrubbed for dear life at the top
of his head with the other.

Mama came running with the soda box and asked him
how in the world he got bit on the top of his head. He
told her it was a sheep that had been bitten, but that
he had gotten some of the poison blood on his hand and
head. Mama told him she didn't think he needed to

worry, that the blood wouldn't hurt him any unless he had an open cut or scratch.

"Well, I got plenty gnat an' skeeter bites," he said. So Mama poured a batch of soda into his dirty paw and he smeared it over his dripping head, then limped back up the hill to his shoe and the sheep.

It seemed to me that Old Bill was almost always at our house for supper that spring. Without bothering to knock, he'd open the door, bow his "old bald pate" low and sing out, "The wild winds weep and the night's a-cold," or "Cold's the wind and wet's the rain," or even,

> Here shall 'e see
> No enemy
> But winter and rough weather.

He could always be sure of Poppie's "Pull up a chair and have a bite with us," but to Mama and us girls he was nothing but an old nuisance. But none of us—and I least of all—ever dreamed that he came to our house for any other reason than that he was hungry, and too stingy to buy his own groceries.

When Old Bill wasn't eating with us he hunted and fished for his meat, and his dirtiness was almost beyond description. One day he shot himself a mess of blackbirds from the flock that fed on the millet stack beside the stable. He stripped off their skins and feathers, then brought the skillet full of naked little things to the house and asked to borrow enough lard to fry them in. I dropped a spoonful of lard onto the unwashed, bloody little bodies. He hadn't drawn them and they looked like they had been rolled in coarse cornmeal. Then my stomach turned over when I realized that the "cornmeal" was millet, just as it had come from the birds' broken craws.

"What did Old Bill ever do with his new suit?" I asked when he was gone.

"Oh, he shucked it off and threw it on his bed when he got back from the funeral," Poppie said. "He's been sleeping with it all winter, but he'll probably never wear it again, anyway."

He was wrong. Old Bill wore it one more time.

Mama was sick, the next Sunday morning, and I made her stay in bed and let me wait on her. About the middle of the forenoon Stell went to the bedroom to curl her hair and primp for her beau. I was alone in the kitchen, washing a pan of prunes, when Old Bill croaked from the doorway,

> Tell me, where is fancy bred,
> Or in the heart or in the head?

"*I* wouldn't know," I said, keeping my back to the door, and wondering why the old coot had to keep bothering us all the time. He always ate more than all the rest of us put together, and no matter how much we cooked, when he was there there was never enough to go around.

"Grace," he croaked again, "will ye tie these cuffs shet fer me?"

I turned around. Old Bill was wearing his new shirt and pants. His cuffs gaped open on his skinny wrists and his new coat was wadded under one arm. I took the dirty piece of twine he held out to me and tied the cuffs "shet." Then he put on his sleazy coat and sat down to wait to be asked to dinner.

Old Bill often came to Sunday dinner, but this was the first time he had ever dressed up for it, and I couldn't help wondering why. The general effect, though, was spoiled by the wrinkles in his suit, and by the long fringe of dirty gray hair hanging down over his collar.

I finished washing the prunes and threw the water out.

"I didn't use t' wash my prunes afore I cooked 'em," Old Bill said, "an' then somebudy tole me I oughtta. So now I do, but I allus drink th' water. It's got too much good in it t' be throwed away."

After dinner Stell drove off with Wynn in his buggy, Dovey and the younger children went out to play, and I went to the front room to sit with Mama and little Heart. Poppie and Old Bill sat in the kitchen for a while, then put on their hats and left the house.

Late in the afternoon the children brought the cattle in, then waded off up the creek after minnows. Still later, when I noticed how far the shadows of the big cottonwoods stretched across the yard, I said it looked like the girls were going to stay away until the milking was done, so I'd better get at it. Down at the corral, I sat down to old Love and began squirting milk into the pail. I had always liked to milk, and never more so than on a quiet summer evening like this one. It was a time when I could think about myself, and about the gray-eyed cowboy, and wonder if I'd see him anymore.

Then Old Bill Sherman's squeaky voice came suddenly from behind me.

"Grace," he said, "ain't that yer cow yer milkin'?"

"No."

"Well, ye hev some cows, don't ye?" he asked, coming around beside me.

"Yes."

"Well, Grace, I been athinkin' that if we wuz t' get married an' keep yer cows right here on this place, we'd soon hev a good herd a cattle. What do ye' say t' that, huh?"

I kicked my milkstool out of the way and stood up. The squat old bachelor, all dressed up in his "good" clothes, was leering at me out of his sly, squinty old eyes. I was so mad I couldn't say anything at first, then I remembered that he was our landlord—so all I said was that I wasn't ever going to get married.

"Oh, goin' t' be an old maid, huh?"

"Yes," I snapped, and headed for the house, leaving Old Bill gazing wistfully at the cows.

I went tearing into Mama's room and told her what had happened, expecting her to feel just the way I did about it. When she laughed, I slammed back to the kitchen in a big huff and sat down at the table to sizzle awhile. After a little, Mama called me back to her bed.

"Never mind, Grace," she told me. "He's only a crazy old man and you mustn't pay any attention to him. Just stay in the house until some of the others come to help with the milking and he won't bother you any more. One of these days you can laugh about this, too."

"I don't see how I ever can," I said. "And anyway, I've had all I can stand of his 'Beauty is but a flower which wrinkles will devour,' and 'girls lose their bloom after they turn sixteen,' and all such stuff. I suppose he figures *I've* picked up so many wrinkles and lost so much bloom in the last two years that I'll have to listen to *him* if I ever want to get married!"

"No," Mama comforted, "he only wants your cows. It's their bloom he's after."

So I sat down and waited a while longer. Then old Love began to bawl in a mournful way.

"Oh, fiddlesticks," I told Mama. "I'm not going to wait any longer. I'm going down and finish the milking, and if Old Bill shows up again I'll ———"

But Bill was gone—he'd taken off for Pennsylvania,

Poppie told us next day—so I don't know what I would have done.

A few days after that, Missionary Scott, driving a single horse to an old buggy, turned in at our gate. Halt of speech, nearly blind, partly paralyzed, and bent almost double (all from an attack of spinal meningitis in his youth), the white-haired old man drove hundreds of miles every year, organizing Sunday schools in the lonely land above the forks of the Platte River. In slow, stuttering words, he told us he had come to organize a Sunday school on the Birdwood.

Poppie told him he was glad to hear it, that he could count on us to help, and then invited him to stay all night. At bedtime the old missionary asked permission to pray. It was hard for him to get on his knees, and up again, but his words came clear and plain while he talked with God.

The next morning he fumbled his way with his cane to the south windows and stood squinting at Mama's fuchsias and geraniums, blooming in the bright sun. Then he turned to her and jerked out, "Mrs. Mc-Cants, you—have—such—pre-tty—p'ants." Mama thanked him for the compliment to her flowers.

After breakfast we hitched up the horse and helped the good old man into his buggy. Bidding us good-bye, he shook the reins and jogged away, knowing his faithful old horse would turn in of its own accord at the next house on the road.

The next Sunday morning seemed like old times, with all of us except Mama and the baby rushing around getting ready for Sunday school. The biggest crowd I had seen on the Birdwood was gathered at the schoolhouse that morning. The Coxes were there, and the Ross boys and their sister, from away up on East Creek, and

Edna and Ivan Johnson, and Elma and her beau, Steve LaRue. Mrs. Duncan and Onie came, riding the same old bony horse, with poor little Onie scratching away at a new crop of "them darned zeetie bites."

Last of all came Star Ferbrache, her handsome red hair blowing in the breeze, and sand spurting from beneath her pony's flying hoofs. Fourteen-year-old Star, loving horses better than anything else on earth, had been riding almost from the day she learned to walk. Born in the Birdwood hills, and named for the glistening star-pointed, trumpet-shaped little white flowers that spread all across their slopes in late summer, Star was the only child of the Ferbraches, an elderly couple living below Tom Heskett's ranch.

There was no organ at the schoolhouse, so Poppie pitched the tunes and led the singing. At the organization meeting he was elected superintendent, then teachers were chosen and lesson material selected from the supply the gentle old missionary carried in the buggy with him. Afterward, everybody stayed around a while to visit. Star Ferbrache made her pony shake hands with Onie and my young brother and sisters. Jennie introduced me to Edna and Ivan Johnson; Stella Ross and her older brothers, Walter, Jim, and Millard; and to Elma Johnson and Steve LaRue. Then Ivan, a good-looking young fellow with snapping dark eyes, asked if it would be all right if he came to call on me, and I told him it would. Ivan wasn't a cowboy, but a farm boy at hand was better than two cowboys a long way up the creek.

That Sunday, for the first time, the Birdwood seemed like home to me.

Not long after that I saw North Platte for the first time. I went there with Ivan and his sister Edna, in a nice top buggy, to hear Teddy Roosevelt make a campaign speech.

I saw a sprawling town, mostly built around the locomotive roundhouse and the courthouse, and full of people and rigs by the time we got there. East and west of the long depot, a strip several blocks long was roped off against rigs and horses; so was all of the main street, from the depot to the courthouse. A big new pine platform, decked in flags and bunting, stood on the northeast corner of the courthouse square, and flags hung from every building in the town. More people than I had ever before seen in one place milled up and down inside the ropes, and bands blared and rigs of all descriptions drove up and down, stopping now and then to spill more people into the crowd.

We hadn't been long in town when a good-sized delegation of cowboys on horseback came flying by. They were a gay-looking bunch in their fancy Stetson hats and bright neckerchiefs and polished high-heeled boots, and they were whooping it up for sure. The gray-eyed leader rode a tall gray horse, and when he came against the rope barrier he simply sailed the horse over it and went on down the street. The rest of the cowboys followed, some jumping their horses over the rope, the rest detouring around it by way of a householder's lawn.

The day had started off cool and cloudy. Now the clouds thickened and it turned darker and colder. Edna, Ivan, and I walked up and down, waiting with the rest of the crowd for the Roosevelt special to pull in. At every turn we saw the frolicsome cowboys. One, a black-haired young Irishman, seemed to be having trouble. Though he was hanging onto his saddle horn with both hands, he was having a hard time staying on his horse.

I could see that Bert Snyder and some of the others were keeping an eye on him, and a good thing, too.

We had been in town nearly an hour when the long whistle of a train sounded across the town. The crowd began to heave and turn, drawing in toward the depot, and the cowboys came racing up to take their station in the front. The unsteady fellow had lost his hat by then, and was trying to cover his curly black head with a red bandana, but every time he came anywhere near his head with it he'd slip sideways in his saddle and have to grab the horn with both hands. Finally he missed the horn altogether and fell off in the street, plopping on the ground like a sack of soggy hay. Bert and another rider then jumped down and boosted him back into his saddle. Propping him up on each side, they headed him toward a wide building with a sign across the front that said it was the White Elephant Livery Stable.

Then the train pulled in and the bands began playing louder than ever. The crowd cheered like mad while the mayor and his committee of important Republicans pushed in around the car steps to welcome the stocky, mustached Roosevelt and escort him to an open carriage that was waiting to take him down the main street to the speaker's platform. The coal-black carriage team, a bystander told us, was the local undertaker's hearse team, the finest and handsomest pair in the whole country.

The crowd heaved itself around again and followed the carriage down the street, and the cowboys, without their hatless friend, came dashing back inside the ropes to overtake the procession. At the courthouse square, Roosevelt and his party mounted the platform and the cowboys lined up alongside it, removing their hats and quieting their horses. It was plain to see they admired this "roughrider" candidate for Vice-President.

By the time the preliminary speeches were over the storm was about to break. But Roosevelt began his speech anyway, his big voice booming out above the thunder and the rising wind. Five minutes later the clouds opened up in earnest, with a hard shower of icy rain. Roosevelt turned then to the cowboys and shouted, "Put on your hats, boys. No need to get your heads wet." Then the shower steadied to a downpour and he brought his speech to a quick close.

The driver brought the carriage to the steps and cramped the wheels. The crowd was already pushing up the street through the mud, and the cowboys had headed in a bunch toward the depot. From where we stood, waiting for the people in front of us to move out a little, we had a clear view of Roosevelt when he stepped into the carriage, and then stood looking out over the soaked crowd, waiting for the mayor to get in beside him.

Maybe the scene reminded him of the charge up San Juan Hill, or maybe he only wanted to have some fun with the important-acting little mayor. Anyway he gave a loud and mighty yell just before he sat down. The hearse team, scared half out of their handsome black hides, took right off on a dead run, setting the mayor down so fast that his feet went higher than his head. Within a block the runaway blacks and the bouncing carriage overtook the cowboys, and the whole outfit went tearing on up the street, flinging mud in all directions and giving the cowboys a tight time of it to keep ahead. The sopping crowd, livened up by the excitement, sloshed along to the depot to cheer the special out of town.

When the train had gone, Edna and I waited, soaked and shivering, in a doorway out of the wind while Ivan slogged off through the mud to bring the buggy. The last I saw of Bert Snyder and his friends, they were heading back toward the White Elephant, where their black-haired pal was probably seeing pink elephants by then.

HOME OF WILLIAM F. CODY IN NORTH PLATTE

The stuffed buffalo on the lawn is a memento of Buffalo Bill's hunting days

GRACE AND BERT SNYDER
Our wedding picture—October 23, 1903

Chapter Twenty-Four

IN JUNE Tom Heskett brought his wife to the Bird-wood. As it turned out, they were married in North Platte, and not in the bride's home in far-off Ohio.

Tom had come to Nebraska in the middle nineties and, in spite of the bad fire of '99, had done very well. By the time we moved to the Birdwood he had already proved up on his homestead quarter, west of the creek, and acquired a considerable herd of sheep. On his visit East, the winter before, he had agreed to be married in Ohio, but after he came home he learned that a married woman had no homestead rights. On the other hand, if his bride-to-be came west before her marriage, she could homestead a quarter section in her maiden name.

So Caroline Hayes gave up her wish to be married in her girlhood home and came alone to Nebraska to meet the man she loved. Wearing her handsome "going away" suit, she got off the train in North Platte and went with Tom to the courthouse to file on the land he wanted. They were married a few minutes later, and then drove straight to Tom's place on the Birdwood.

Stell and I wanted to go right down to see Tom's new wife, but Mama said we should give her a few days to get settled. So, before Mama thought it was time for us to call, she came walking up the creek to see us. We saw her coming through the big trees, a tall, fine-looking

woman, wearing a beautiful sunbonnet all covered with
crisp, starched little ruffles, and carrying a stout tree
limb in her hand.

Mama met her at the door, explaining why we hadn't
called first. Mrs. Heskett said it hadn't taken her long
to get settled in and that, with Tom away most of the
day with his sheep, she was lonesome and had too much
time on her hands. The limb, she explained, was for
protection from the cattle grazing along the creek. Used
to the tame, fenced fields of Ohio, she had been a little
afraid these free-ranging cows might not be friendly.

Our new neighbor was full of questions about the Birdwood and its people. She was glad to hear we had a Sunday school, for she had always gone to Sunday school
and church, back in Ohio, and in a new place she thought
it was a fine way to meet the neighbors. By the time she
tied on her bonnet to leave, it seemed like we had always
known her.

"Now come to see me, any time you can," she said.

"We will," Mama told her, "and you come back often."
She stood in the door, watching her until she was out
of sight. "Poor girl," she said then, "it's going to be lonesome for her here, so different from what she's used to."

But Caroline Heskett didn't intend to be lonesome.
She was in Sunday school the next Sunday, with her tall
young brother, Will Hayes. He had come out from
Ohio only the day before, she said, and was staying all
summer. And after Sunday school Poppie surprised us
with the announcement that there was to be a community
Fourth-of-July celebration in the Roberts grove at the
mouth of the Birdwood. Our district, he said, was to
furnish two patriotic songs for the program. Stella Ross,
the Johnson girls, Will Hayes, Stell and I volunteered

to sing with Poppie, and Caroline said she'd play the organ for us.

When Stell and I wondered what we'd do about new dresses for the Fourth, Poppie said we could take the butter and eggs to North Platte that week and trade them for dress goods. Jennie went with us and we spent a long time in Wilcoxe's department store, looking at a dozen bolts of pretty cloth. I finally picked a white dimity, polka-dotted in blue. On the way home we talked about patterns and styles. Stell, who knew a lot about style and very little about sewing, said she was going to "pucker her thing and put lace around it"—meaning she wanted to gather the blouse to a wide, lace-edged yoke. Jennie and I decided to make ours the same way.

Mama made Stell's dress but I made my own—the first Sunday dress I had ever made myself—and Mama said I did a good job of it.

The third of July was sultry and still, a "weather breeder," Poppie said. The Fourth was cool and cloudy, but we hurried through our chores, hoping the sky would clear by the time we were ready to start. But, if anything, it was colder and cloudier when Stell and I, shivering in our thin dimities, went out to the buggy.

"Maybe you'd better put on some wraps," Poppie said.

But Stell and I weren't going to cover up our pretty dresses with coats, *not on the Fourth of July!*

The big cottonwood grove at the Roberts place would have been a cool and pleasant place on a hot day. That Fourth it was dark and gloomy, with a cold, damp wind blowing through the trees. We went ahead with the program anyway, and then with the picnic dinner, even to finishing off the row of ice-cream freezers lined up at the back of the platform. Then the heavy clouds began to let down a cold drizzle that set the trees to dripping.

Somebody said maybe this was the "clearing up" shower, so we hurried around, putting the picnic things away and covering the organ. Then the few provident souls who had brought parasols and lap robes dug them out and shared them with the rest of us. And so we waited— for holidays on the Birdwood were all too few—and the best part of this one, the races and contests, was yet to come.

But it was no use. The rain came down harder and the wind blew colder, until, soaked and freezing, we all gave up and went home. When Stell and I climbed out of the buggy our dresses, so crisp and pretty that morning, hung on us like sorry rags and we were almost stiff as boards with the cold.

The sun was bright and warm again the next morning, so that afternoon I went down the creek to return Caroline Heskett's call. I could hardly believe the house was the same one that Mrs. Duncan had had her party in. There were bright rugs on the floors now, and lace curtains at the windows. The woodwork was painted in pretty colors and fancy doilies decorated the new furniture. It was by far the prettiest house on the Birdwood.

Before I left, Caroline took me into the bedroom and showed me the wedding gown she had never worn. It was a lovely thing, yards and yards of white shadow organdy and deep lace. Her cousin and her best friend had made the petticoat that went with it, she told me, and each of them had sewed a lock of her hair into the wide hem—a charm supposed to make sure they'd both be married within a year.

I walked back up the creek in the late afternoon. In spite of the twin plagues of gnats and mosquitos that lay over this upland country in the summer, it was pleasant here. In the evenings, when there was breeze enough to hold the mosquitos back, Jennie, Stell, and I often sat on the creek bank in the last glow of daylight. All around us the summer choir of crickets, frogs, and singing water carried on while we shared our thoughts, teased one another, and traded the gossip of our little world. Later on, now that Caroline and her brother and the other new neighbors had come to the Birdwood, we could probably have parties and literaries.

Then I rounded the bend below our house and saw Poppie, standing knee-deep in the creek, plastering mud on old Daisy's nose. The old mare's head was swelled up as big as a barrel and her legs trembled under her. A rattlesnake bite, Poppie said, and a big one.

Poor Daisy stood in the creek for days, her breath whistling through her throat so loud we could hear it up at the house. Every few hours we changed the packs of gluey mud on her nose, but day by day she grew thinner and her eyes duller. We all suffered right along with her, for like every other animal on the place, Daisy was a part of the family.

After a long time the terrible swelling began to go down and she came out of the creek and grazed a little. We knew then that she would live, but all that fall she looked more like a wrinkled bag of old bones than a horse. And, like most snake-bitten horses, she could never again hear a rattlesnake's buzz without panicking.

In September I was back in school. To my old argument that I was too old to go to school any more, Poppie said that I couldn't put in my time to any better advantage. "Even if you are eighteen, Gheet, you haven't gone to school as much as a fourteen-year-old should've," he said. "It wasn't your fault you had to miss so much, but now that you have the chance to go, I want you to make the most of it."

The teacher was Gertrude Jeffers, a young woman from North Platte. Miss Jeffers took a genuine interest in her school and enjoyed her work. I was her oldest pupil and she seemed especially concerned about me.

"Grace," she said, "you are a good student and I believe you'd make a good teacher. If you'll go as far as you can with me this winter, and then go to summer school and Teachers' Institute in the Platte next summer, I'm sure you can pass the county examinations in July and get a certificate to teach."

Her words opened a new door to me.

For a long time I had been worrying about what I was going to do with my life. Most of the girls I knew, unless they married early, went into other people's kitchens as hired girls, or became clerks or schoolteachers. A hired girl's job, at a $1.50 or $2.00 a week, was the last thing *I* wanted, and I didn't think I'd care for clerking. But teaching, now—some of the nicest people I had ever known, Florence Yoder, Aunt Bell and Aunt Hester, were schoolteachers.

Poppie was pleased when I told him Miss Jeffers' plan for me. "Learn all you can from her," he said, "and we'll see that you get to go to school next summer."

When the county superintendent, Miss Bertha Thoelecke, made her yearly visit to our school, Miss Jeffers told her she planned to make a teacher out of me. Miss Thoelecke said she was glad to hear it, that qualified teachers were always scarce in her county and that I could be sure of a school if I earned a certificate. So I dug into my books harder than ever, and began to watch my speech and grammar.

The school on the Birdwood was the smallest I had ever gone to, but it was never dull. For one thing there was politics. Miss Jeffers was a whole-souled Irish Democrat. Poppie was a good Republican, so naturally we McCances were Republicans, too. Star and the three Allens changed sides whenever they felt like it. Miss Jeffers and her side were for the silver-tongued Bryan, the rest of us for McKinley and Roosevelt. But our arguments had more heat than purpose, since none of us could vote; and after election day Miss Jeffers quieted all the way down and politics died a quick death.

And then there was Star Ferbrache. At noons and recesses, while Miss Jeffers worked with me at her desk, Star kept the rest of the school busy playing "horse," the only game she cared for. When they were all at it, bucking, pawing, prancing, snorting and kicking, our teacher must have wondered if she was in charge of a school or a stable.

Even on the cold winter day the plaster fell off the schoolroom ceiling, Star didn't forget to act like a horse. Some of the plaster chunks whacked us pretty hard on our heads, and the choking dust scattered us to the corners of the room. Star stood in her corner, pawing at her head and snorting and whinnying like a bronc in a sandstorm.

At a Thanksgiving party, that winter, I met Marie Johnson, the pretty Sutherland girl who was teaching the Ross school, up near the forks of the creek. Marie told me she had gone to the Teachers' Institute in North Platte the summer before, and I told her I planned to be a teacher, too, and that I'd be going to school and institute the coming summer.

Marie said she was glad to hear it, and that she would be going down to institute again, since every teacher in the county had to go, and that we could room together when she came. Then I told her I wished she'd go to summer school, too, that I dreaded going down there all alone

and not knowing a soul. She said she'd like to, but that
she had had the same work in high school and didn't
need to go.

Later that winter, John Houk filed on a quarter section just above us on the far side of the Birdwood, and
his mother, using her widow's homestead right, filed on
another next to it. Then Poppie rented that one from
her, and rented some more hayland down on the river
valley.

As soon as the frost had gone out of the ground,
Poppie and John built new sod houses on each of the
claims. Grandma was to live with John and Florry; we
were to move into her house. They finished John's house
first, so that he and Florry and Grandma could get settled.
But ours was not yet done when Earl Blaine, a frail wisp
of a baby, was born on the seventeenth of April.

After the birth of her ninth child, Mama could not
even sit up for weeks. "Of all my babies," she said, looking with despair at the tiny blue face beside her, "this
is the one that needs the best care, and I can't even feed
him."

Neither could Florry, with all her gentle coaxing, get
him to take a bottle.

After the sickly baby's coming, I said no more about
going to summer school. Because of all the extra work,
worry, and expense, I knew I must give it up.

"I know just how it is," Miss Jeffers said when I told
her. "I come from a bigger family than yours, and we've
always had to work like Trojans, too, and pinch pennies
all the way. But if I were you, I'd still go to school this
summer."

I think she must have talked to Poppie about it, too,
for on the last day of school she told me that she was
going back to school again that summer, and that she

would see me there in June. Good Miss Jeffers, how many times I have blessed her memory. Years later, I saw the tiny three-room house where the big Jeffers family lived. It was from that crowded little house that her young brother Bill hustled out and got a job as call boy for the Union Pacific in North Platte—and from there went on to become president of the road.

Late in May we moved across the creek into the new house. When we were settled there, Poppie said, "How much did Miss Jeffers say it would cost you to go to school this summer?"

I told him she had said that, if I was careful, thirty-five dollars would be enough for books and tuition and eight weeks' room and board. "But," I said, "I've given up going. With Mama and the baby so poorly and money so scarce, it's no use thinking about it."

"Gheet," Poppie told me, "I've been thinking how we can manage it. Florry will help look after Mommie and the baby, and I'll sign a note for you at the Sutherland bank so you can borrow the thirty-five dollars. You can pay it back out of your teacher's wages next winter."

We went to town the next day and borrowed the money, and a week later I was ready to go.

My few clothes hardly made a showing in the bottom of the little old family trunk, but the telescope Mama had bought for her first trip back to Missouri was far too shabby now to carry to town with me. On the way to Sutherland to the train, Poppie told me to inquire of Miss Thoelecke or Miss Jeffers for a clean, decent place to stay, to be careful what kind of friends I picked, to go to church every Sunday, and to write home the minute I was settled.

In all my life I had never felt so alone and lost as I did when I got off the train in North Platte that Monday morning. In the whole town I knew only Miss Thoelecke and Miss Jeffers, and I had no idea where to find them.

The main part of town was south of the tracks, toward the courthouse, so I headed that way. About a block from the courthouse I caught up with a gay little crowd of girls in pretty shirtwaists and slim-hipped, full-bottomed skirts. I walked along behind them, and when they went into a store I followed. They bought paper and pencils at the counter, so I stepped up and did the same. Then I tagged them out of the store and across the street. At the corner, where Roosevelt's platform had stood the summer before, they turned left and went into a big new brick building. I went in too, and felt better when I saw Miss Thoelecke at the desk in the front of the room. She was talking to a group of older people, probably the ones who would be our instructors, I thought.

I was far too shy to go up and speak to her, so I backed against a wall, lonesome and scared, and watched the room fill with girls and a few boys. Most of them seemed to know each other. They stood around in little groups, laughing and talking and having fun. Then Miss Jeffers came in, but before I could go over to speak to her, Miss Thoelecke stood up and tapped on the desk. The crowd began finding seats, so I slid into the one nearest me.

After her welcome to the summer school students of 1901, Miss Thoelecke said she hoped that, by the end of the session, none of us would still be filling rooms full of plaster. "You've no idea," she told us, "how many of my teachers have trouble with the plastering problems in our arithmetic books." Then she said that any students who didn't have rooms could see her in her office at noon and, after introducing the instructors, she left.

I signed up for bookkeeping, orthography, pedagogy, and language, all fine-sounding subjects, and bought my books. At noon Miss Thoelecke sent four other girls and me to a widow, who charged us fifteen dollars apiece for six weeks' room and board.

Our room, tucked under a low, slanting roof, was hot as an oven and smelled of mothballs. Our landlady cooked for her five children and five boarders on a coal range in a stifling, low-roofed little kitchen. Daytimes, we wondered that she didn't melt down entirely; night-times, in the hot, mothball flavored air of our room, we wondered that we didn't. And day and night I was homesick for the cool, new soddy on the Birdwood.

I was one of the very few in school that summer who had never gone to high school, so I found the work hard, especially bookkeeping. The instructor, a hot-tempered Mr. Jones, had no patience with anyone who didn't understand the subject. I had never studied bookkeeping, and when he found I was having trouble with it he paid no further attention to me; for it didn't seem to occur to him that he was there to help those who needed it. So, if it hadn't been for the help given me by four girls from the south part of the county, all high-school graduates who were studying teaching methods, I'm afraid I wouldn't have gotten far with that course.

These four, and my four roommates, all country girls like myself, made up my "crowd" at school. When the long, hot hours of classes and studying were over for the day, we ate supper and went out for the evening. Sometimes we sat on the courthouse lawn, listening to the town band until the mosquitos drove us home. Other evenings we watched the town girls, in middy blouses and full, black sateen bloomers, practicing basketball in the schoolyard. On still others, we walked to the west end of Church Street (now Fourth Street), crossed a little meadow and strolled past the big Cody town house and the tall, narrow Hershey house beyond it. Beyond the Hershey house there was nothing but more meadow and the river.

An old stuffed buffalo stood in the yard beside the Cody house. The snows and rains of many seasons had left ragged, hairless patches on his shaggy sides; time and the hot sun had faded his glass eyes to a sad, dusty color. Maggie Brogan, a girl in our crowd from the Clear Creek country west of Sutherland, said of him, "Myself, I'd have about as much use for a dead buffalo in *my* yard as a hog has for a sidesaddle." We all agreed with her.

On Sundays we went to church together. We belonged to almost as many different denominations as there were girls in our group, so we went to all the churches in turn. One Sunday they all went with me to a Christian church service in the Unitarian Hall; on another we all got up at five and went to Mass with Maggie in the big red-brick Catholic church on East Church Street—and so on down the line.

All the well-dressed girls at school pinned their wide-brimmed hats to their pompadours with fancy hatpins that summer. Some wore two, or even three of the long spikes in their hats, and I longed for one, just one, to wear in place of the plain little black-headed skewer I pinned mine on with. But I knew I shouldn't spend the money for one. I resisted temptation until just before the Fourth, when Marie Johnson wrote to invite me to spend the day with her in Sutherland. Then I went out and spent fifteen cents for a pin with a gay, dollar-sized bright-yellow head.

I pinned my hat on at a stylish angle the next morning and sailed off to school. At noon, when I took my hat from its usual hook in the hall, the pretty pin was gone. Why, I wondered, did these things always happen to me? There had been the Fourth when the fat, red-headed girl sat on my new parasol and broke the handle. Last year, the rain had spoiled my new dress. Now someone had swiped my pin, my one bit of new Fourth-of-July finery. Why, when I had so few new things, or good times, anyway?

I pinned my hat on with my old black pin, the next morning, and took the train to Sutherland. Marie and two young men, her beau and his friend, met me at the depot and we spent a pleasant day together at the town celebration. The train back to North Platte was due at eight that evening, and Marie and the young men took me to the depot.

"Your train's an hour late, lady," the ticket agent told me, so we walked back to the little park between the depot and the main street, where the fiddlers were tuning up for an open-air platform dance.

Poppie wouldn't let us girls go to dances. He and Mama used to dance, before they had a family, but the dances nowadays weren't like they used to be, he said, and he didn't want us girls to have anything to do with them. Marie didn't dance either, so we all sat on the benches at the edge of the platform and watched the sets form for the first quadrille.

At sundown the evening turned suddenly cold. The day had been so warm that Marie and I hadn't brought any wraps along, so the boys put their coats around us while we waited until time to go back to the depot.

"Sorry, your train's still an hour late," the agent said at nine.

Fourth-of-July dances always lasted till daylight, but by midnight it had turned so cold that more than half the dancers had given up and gone home. By two o'clock half the rest had gone, and at half-past four, when my train finally whistled for the station, only a few couples still whirled to the music, and the fiddlers were blowing on their fingers, between tunes, to take the numbness out. They had been paid for a night's fiddling and they were giving full value.

My friends and I, stiff with the cold of that July night, stumbled back across the tracks to the train. Half an hour later, as the sun came up on a winter-white town, I hurried, shivering, along the empty street to my boarding house. Roofs, fences, walks and trees were covered with thick, glistening frost. Garden plots and little sweet corn and potato patches in backyards along the street were frozen to the ground.

A good many new faces, some topped with gray hair, showed up in the schoolroom for the institute session. These were Lincoln County teachers, and it gave me a good feeling to know that I was almost one of them. I had passed all my summer-school examinations, even bookkeeping, and I would soon have my certificate.

Right then I wished I could see Poppie long enough to thank him for talking me into going back to school all those times I had been about to quit.

With Marie, I moved into a comfortable room at a Mrs. Hostetter's, where there was only one flaw in our pleasant surroundings. A boardwalk, from our back door to the customary little building at the rear, led directly past an open shallow pool into which the next-door kitchen sink drained. Clouds of flies picnicked all day at the pool and the summer sun kept the whole mess glowing. We held our noses, and traveled faster, every time we had to take the backhouse path.

I enjoyed Teachers' Institute, and by the end of the

two weeks I was so filled with enthusiasm that I could hardly wait to be in a schoolroom of my own. On the last day of the session I was awarded my third-grade certificate, licensing me to teach in the elementary schools of the state. Then Gertrude Jeffers came and took my hand. "Grace," she said, "I knew you could be a teacher if you wanted to, and I know you'll be a good one. Now you'd better go over to Miss Thoelecke's office and see what she has for you."

Miss Thoelecke had what she called "a rather unusual school" for me. Mr. and Mrs. Bernard Aufdengarten, ranchers in the far corner of McPherson County, fifty miles northwest of Sutherland, wanted a teacher, although they had neither a district nor a schoolhouse. According to state law, she explained, a community had to hold a six-months' term of school, at its own expense, before it could organize a district and draw state funds. The Aufdengartens were offering fifteen dollars a month and room and board to a qualified teacher.

"Most town girls won't even consider going so far away," she told me, "and even the country girls want to teach closer to town, but I hope you'll take this school, Miss McCance. The isolated places need good teachers, too, and there are only two pupils, so the work won't be hard."

I had hoped for a larger school and a real schoolhouse, but, on the other hand, I'd be going deep into the big ranch country. I wrote my letter of application before I went back to Mrs. Hostetter's to pack my trunk.

"Well, how'd you make out?" Poppie asked, when I got off the train in Sutherland.

"I have my certificate," I told him.

By the relief on his face, I could see how anxious he'd been about the outcome of my summer's venture.

Chapter Twenty-Five

BACK on the Birdwood, the family worries settled onto my shoulders again. Mama's hacking cough was worse and the tiny, spoon-fed baby's face had a pinched, old-man look. Mange had broken out in the range country to the north of us and was spreading toward the river. If our cattle got it we'd lose all we'd gained by coming to this country, Poppie said.

I began to wish I hadn't applied for the Aufdengarten school. If they hired me, I'd be so far from home. As soon as I could I went down the creek to see Caroline Heskett. It always did me good to talk to her. Before I left I asked her about the "charm," if it had worked.

"Oh, yes," she said. "My cousin was married in June. I sent my wedding dress back to Ohio for her to be married in." I was glad the beautiful dress had finally gowned a bride, but I would always be sorry it could not have been Caroline who wore it.

A few days later Jennie, Dovey, Nellie, and I rode up the creek a mile or so to pick chokecherries. We crossed over to the far side, tied our horses to some bushes, and began picking fruit in the thickets there. We had been out of sight of our horses for quite a while when I saw mine, old Daisy, grazing toward home on the far side of the creek, a piece of the broken bush dragging from the reins.

I pulled off my shoes and stockings, tucked my skirts up high, and waded across the creek to catch her. But when I reached for the reins the old mare snorted, threw up her head, and trotted away. Again I almost had her, and again she trotted off. Hopping barefooted through the stickery grass, I kept after her, grabbing at the reins every time I could get close enough.

The sun was boiling hot and I was getting madder by the minute—and of course that had to be the time for Bert Snyder to ride around the bend in front of me. I yanked my skirt down over my knees and stood there, feeling like my bare feet were all over the ground. The cowboy caught my horse and led her back to me. "Looks like you're having a little trouble." He grinned as he handed me the reins, then lifted his hat and rode on up the creek.

As soon as he was out of sight, I climbed on old Daisy, popped her a good one with the ends of the reins, and headed back to the cherry patch. It seemed that I just hadn't been born to charm cowboys.

The letter from Aufdengartens came the next day, accepting my application. But school, they wrote, wouldn't start before the middle of October, as they were building a new house and wouldn't have it finished before then.

On the sixth of October Stella and Walter Ross were married in North Platte, Stella in the pretty wedding dress I made for her. They went to live on the Diamond Bar, a ranch twenty miles north of us, where Walter worked. The next week Mrs. Aufdengarten wrote that school would begin on the twenty-ninth, and that I should come to the Lena post office with the Friday mail from Sutherland.

Mama and I drove down to Sutherland, a few days later, to get a few small things I would need to take with me. Mama hadn't been to town since Earl was born, six months before, and we were enjoying the lazy drive behind Nancy and Daisy, with Daisy's colt, too young to be left alone all day, jogging at his mother's doubletree. Just as we came to the top of the long hill overlooking the river valley, a rattlesnake buzzed on Daisy's side of the road.

Poor Daisy, remembering her snakebite, panicked on the spot; but this time her fear was for her colt. With a lunge that yanked the front wheel directly over the snake, she whirled in the tugs to look for the colt. The rattler coiled itself around the wheel rim, just as the mare lunged again and gave the wheel another half turn. The snake, a big fellow more than a yard long, rode the rim to the top and hung there, twisting and squirming only inches from my knee. I reached for the whip to knock the snake off the wheel before it fell into the buggy with us, but Daisy, past all control, made one more jump and got her nose on the colt. At the same time the snake slipped off the wheel and plopped to the ground. I handed the lines to Mama then, and jumped out to pound the snake's head into the ground with the butt of the whip.

Daisy, Mama, and I were all pretty shaky the rest of that trip.

I bought the things I needed. Then I used the last dollar of the money I had borrowed to go to school on to buy enough yard goods to piece a quilt top. I had been helping Mama piece quilts from scraps left over from our dressmaking, but this would be the first one I had ever made for myself, or from whole goods. I could hardly wait to get started on it—and I had no idea, that day, what a lifesaver it would be before the winter was over.

Shortly after sunup on Friday, Poppie and I were waiting beside the road when Mort Johnson, Marie's brother, came over the hill, his mules on a lope and the two-wheeled mail cart bouncing high. Poppie hauled the shabby old telescope out of our buggy and Mort stowed it under the cart seat, with the mail and some other bundles. I kissed Poppie good-bye and climbed into the cart. A minute later the mules were on the lope again, northbound on the long road to Lena.

Beyond the country drained by East and West creeks, the shape of the land began to change and flatten out. Every low flat hill seemed to billow into the next one, and they all looked alike. There were no fields or houses, nothing but hills and sky, and now and then a few cattle grazing on a slope. Every little hatful of wind that spilled over the edge of the prairie seemed to set the tall bunch-grass to running away across the hills, running on and on to the edge of the world.

Now and then Mort stopped to poke a newspaper or a letter into a homemade mailbox on a post beside the road. Sometimes he left a sack of tobacco or a little can of kerosene beside the post. Toward noon we passed up the west side of the Diamond Bar Lake. Instead of the wide, shining blue lake I had expected, it was nothing but a long slough, with the brown thumbs of tall cattails thick above the boggy swamp.

"It's generally low, this time of year," Mort said, then pointed out the roofs of the ranch buildings on the far side, where Stell and Walter lived.

We ate our lunches as we bounced along the crooked trail, and after that I began trying to find new ways to sit to ease my aching back. The sun began to slant well to the west, and still there was no change in the scenery.

I had never in my whole life seen so much of the same thing.

"It's always after sundown, this time of year, when I get to Lena," Mort said.

It was early dark when the tired mules loped over the last hill to Lena. Mort had told me about the place as we bounced along. It was only a ranch, with a little store and post office built onto the ranch house. The Reuter family owned the outfit, he said, and the big soddy was a handy stopping place for all travelers in this section of the hills.

I was cold, tired, and hungry, and the lamplight shining from the ranch house on the flat looked good to me. The mules stopped in front of the long soddy and I climbed out of the cart, so stiff I could hardly stand. There was another structure, almost as long as the soddy, in the nearby shadows, and I was astonished to see that it was built entirely of cow chips.

A man came around the corner of the house, said "Hi, Mort," and began to unhitch the mules. Mort fished his two mail sacks out from under the seat, pushed open a door in the end of the soddy, and stood back for me to enter. A big heating stove in the middle of the floor warmed the room. Behind a counter a middle-aged man and woman were putting up grocery orders.

All of the half-dozen people in the store turned to look as I came in. Then a neat, wiry little woman with a year-old child in her arms came toward me. Mort nodded to her and said, "Well, Mrs. Aufdengarten, here's your new teacher."

The woman looked me up and down, then she smiled and put out her hand.

I had been wondering, all fall, what the Aufdengartens would be like. And they, I realized now, had been just as anxious to know about the teacher they had hired, sight unseen. Mrs. Aufdengarten introduced me to the other people in the room, Mr. and Mrs. Reuter and three ranchmen, no longer young. Then she told me we still had an eight-mile drive ahead of us, and that we would eat supper here before we started.

"Go right on in," Mrs. Reuter called from the post office corner. "I'll be along as soon as I get this mail put out."

Mrs. Aufdengarten led me through a living room, past another busy heating stove, and on into the big kitchen where Maud Reuter, a serious, pretty girl about my own age, was taking up supper from her sizzling range. With three stoves to feed, I could see the reason for that enormous chip pile.

The big table in the Reuter kitchen was pretty well filled by the time everybody sat down. Besides Mr. and Mrs. Reuter and their three sons, and Mrs. Aufdengarten and myself, there were the three ranchmen, and Mort, who stayed overnight on his twice-a-week trips. After supper one of the Reuter boys brought Mrs. Aufdengarten's buckboard to the door and we headed out through the pitch-black night.

"Maud Reuter cooks a lot of extra meals in that kitchen," Mrs Aufdengarten told me as the Lena lights dropped behind us, "and she never takes a cent from anybody that eats there."

After a while the team slowed from a fast trot to a walk. "We must be coming to the first gate," Mrs. Aufdengarten said. "There's eight between Lena and our place."

"Then there must be several ranches along the road," I said.

"If you mean houses, there's only one. That's at Three

Mile ranch, one of Stewart and Haskell's places, where Brookings live."

The team stopped and I offered to open the gate. "No, I'll tend the gates," Mrs. Aufdengarten told me. "You can drive through, and watch Angie that she doesn't roll off the seat." And that, I learned, was to be the pattern of the months I spent with the bustling little lady. German by birth, the family had a high regard for the teaching profession; and any person, paid to teach, was not supposed to stoop to menial labor.

"Why is this country so fenced up, if no one lives in it?" I asked when she was back in the buckboard and we were on our way again.

"It's because nearly every valley through here is a hay meadow, with a lake in it. The cattlemen fence the meadows to keep the cattle out, and of course the roads follow the valleys, where it's leveler."

After what seemed a long, long time, I saw the lighted windows of a house. "We're almost home," Mrs. Aufdengarten said.

A man and two boys were waiting in the yard to take the team. The lady introduced them as her husband and sons, three different-sized shadows in the darkness, then led the way into a tidy kitchen.

"I'm sorry we didn't get these walls plastered before you came," she apologized, "but you have to wait for new sod to settle before you can plaster it."

"I know," I said. "I've lived in soddies half my life."

I followed her through an inner door, then stopped in surprise. The big room was one of the most attractive I had seen in a long while. On the far side, the curlicued top of a new organ almost touched the ceiling. Fine lace curtains, tied back at the wide windows, framed rows of blooming houseplants in bright cans on the deep sills.

Mrs. Aufdengarten pushed back a heavy curtain that hung across one corner of the room and put her sleeping baby down on a big bed behind it.

"What a pretty organ," I said, when she turned back to me.

"It oughtta be. It's the fanciest one in Montgomery Ward's catalog," a new voice chirped behind me.

"Now, Herman, don't bother Miss McCance. She's tired," Mrs. Aufdengarten said to the bright-eyed little boy sidling through the door behind me.

"This will be your room," she told me, opening the door to a room furnished with two double beds, a dresser and a table. "We only have three rooms, so the boys have to sleep in here, too. I hope you don't mind. You'll have to hold school in here, too. "It's the only room where you can be by yourselves and have it quiet." She went out and shut the door.

I sat down on my bed and put my head in my hands. The day had seemed a week long.

When I went into the kitchen the next morning, Mrs. Aufdengarten told me to go on outside and look around, if I liked, until breakfast was ready. I went out and looked up and down the valley. A dry valley, this one, rimmed all around by the pale, everlasting hills. A few yards away, a windmill pumped a thin stream of water into a little pond. There was no other dwelling in sight, and I had a lonesome feeling.

I went back to the kitchen and asked if we would be going to Sunday school or church tomorrow.

"Mercy, no!" Mrs. Aufdengarten said, and looked up from her stove in surprise. "There's no Sunday school within twenty miles, or church either."

School began at nine Monday morning—when Herman and Charlie and I carried three chairs from the kitchen to our bedroom and sat down at the table. At noon we carried the chairs back to the kitchen for dinner, and at one we took them back to the schoolroom. At four o'clock I dismissed school for the day.

Right away, I learned that ten-year-old Charlie, though a bright boy, cared little for books or study, and that, most of the time, there was a horse between him and the page he was supposed to be studying. Little Herman, on the other hand, learned so fast that it was a joy to teach him. "I want to get this schoolin' over with, so I can get at something else," he told me earnestly.

The days soon settled into a steady, monotonous pattern. Except for allowing me to dry the supper dishes, Mrs. Aufdengarten wouldn't let me help her in any way. So, from the time I left the schoolroom until bedtime, I had nothing to do except work on my pretty quilt and write a few letters. Before long I was living mostly for the days when Mr. Aufdengarten rode horseback to Lena for the mail. If it hadn't been for the letters from home, and from Jennie and the girls I had met at school, I would have curled up and died of homesickness long before Christmas.

Mrs. Aufdengarten was a good cook and "set a good table," but the ranch was in an out-of-the-way valley, and for days on end she was the only woman I saw. One Sunday a Mr. and Mrs. Drake, from Duck Lake, four miles south of us, came up to spend the day; and twice, Mrs. Aufdengarten drove to Lena on Saturday to get groceries. On the first trip I met Mrs. Cap Haskell, from Baldy Ranch, and on the second, a Mrs. Ed Huffman and her young daughter Mabel, from LaMunyon Flat, away off to the southeast. Friendly, pleasant people, all of them, but there were so many empty miles between their ranches and my boarding place.

Young cowboys seemed scarce, too. Eighteen-year-old Russell Brooking rode over from Three Mile once a week to give Mrs. Aufdengarten her music lesson on the new organ, and then stayed awhile to visit with me. But Russell, interested only in books and music, wasn't the cowboy type. I met only one other young man, a rancher who came to call on me one evening, but his dark, oily face and bold, black eyes smacked too much of the pictures I had seen of "slick" gamblers. So I refused his invitation to go for a ride and went to bed early, leaving him talking to the Aufdengartens. He did not come again.

I drew my two months' wages the day before I left to spend Christmas at home, and I was still five dollars short of enough to pay off my note at the bank.

Poppie was more discouraged than I had seen him in a long time. Our cows had the mange, and spent so much of their time rubbing their itching hides on trees and fence posts, and so little of it eating, he said, that he was afraid they'd be so thin by spring that they'd lose their calves.

But Stell and Walter and Florry and John came home for Christmas Day and we were all together again. That evening Roy, listening to the hubbub, grinned and said, "You girls sure have a ha-ha party when you get together, don't you?"

He was right! We sure did. And this one, I knew, would have to last me for a long time; for already I was dreading the day I'd have to go back to the sandhills. But I knew I had to, and in the end I was glad I went— for when I came shivering into the Lena store at the end of the long, cold drive, I saw an odd look of relief come over Mrs. Aufdengarten's face.

"Just about everybody up here said you wouldn't come

back," she told me, "but I said you would, that you weren't the quitting kind."

In a little while it was as if I had never been away. The days came up and died again, and each one was just like the one before it. In January a snowstorm blocked the roads for a little while—not that it mattered, for there was no place to go, anyway. There were no longer even Russell Brooking's weekly visits to look forward to; for Russell, lucky fellow, had left the hills and gone away to school again. If I hadn't had my quilt to work on, I'm afraid I would have gone out of my mind entirely.

Little Herman finished his first reader and started on another, but Charlie only glanced at his books often enough to keep his grades up to passing. I did everything I could think of to keep him interested, but he only said, "What's the use, when all the book learning a man needs is enough so he can count his cattle and the money they bring him?"

Then one day in March Mrs. Aufdengarten handed me a letter when I came from the schoolroom at four o'clock. The writing on the envelope was Poppie's. "Dear Grace," he wrote, "you will be sorry to hear Aunt Dicy is dead. She died at home and Ma would not let them embalm her. She thinks it is sinful and says the old way of sponging the corpse with salt water is best."

Out in the kitchen little Angie was getting a paddling —but Angie was paddled so many times a day that I didn't even look up from my letter.

"Mama and I went down to Walnut Grove for the funeral," I read on, "and afterward we went back to Ma's and she sat down in her rocker and folded her hands in her lap and said her work on earth was done and she was ready to go anytime."

I sat there, thinking of old Aunt Dicy, smiling her

happy, toothless smile, and singing "The Sailor's Bride" in her thin, cracked little voice, but it was harder to think of Grandma—*Grandma with time on her hands at last*. It was more than I could stand, and I went into my room and shut the door and cried out my grief and homesickness on my bed.

Then Charlie, hurrying into the room for something, saw me and backed out on tiptoe.

"Teacher's cryin'," I heard him tell his mother.

"What about?" she asked sharply, raising her voice above Angie's howling.

"I guess she feels bad because you spanked Angie."

Mrs. Aufdengarten marched straight into my room. "What's the matter?" she asked, ready to let me know that spanking Angie was *her* business.

In all the time I had been there I had never run up against the lady's sharp temper, and I was glad now that I had a good reason to give her. "I've just heard that my dear old aunt is dead," I told her.

"Oh, I'm sorry," she apologized, and backed out in a hurry.

That evening Mr. Aufdengarten asked me to come back the next year. "We'll organize a district this summer, and build a schoolhouse," he said, "and we can pay you more."

But I told him the folks needed me and that I planned to teach near home next year. The way I felt then, there wasn't enough money in McPherson County to hire me to come back to the sandhills.

Early in April Mr. Aufdengarten, commissioner for the west end of big McPherson County, rode down to Tryon, the county seat, to a commissioners' meeting. Tryon was forty miles southeast of Lena and the trip took three days, one to go down, one for the meeting, and one to return. He came home tired and "put out" at the unfairness of the "East Enders."

"There's more of them and they've got the votes to hold the county seat in their end of the county, but if they want to keep on collecting taxes from *this* end, they'd better let us move the courthouse to the middle of the county—or else we'll cut loose and make a county of our own," he threatened. Then he went on to say that, during the winter, Bert Snyder had bought the Patterson place, about eleven miles this side of Tryon. It was a good place, he said, with a big soddy in the middle of a nice wet valley. And while he was visiting with him, Bert had agreed that the county seat ought to be moved over to Nate Trego's valley, seventeen miles closer to Lena, which would be a lot fairer all around.

I was to hear a lot more about moving the county seat, quite a few years later, but just then I was wondering if Bert Snyder would come to the Birdwood any more.

A few days before I left the hills, Mrs. Aufdengarten had a birthday party for me. The weather was nice and all the young folks in the Lena hills were there, all five of them. A pretty girl, Gertie Thorpe, was visiting her aunt, Mrs. Cap Haskell at Baldy Ranch, and a young man, Gordon Jewett, a ranch hand for Stewart and Haskell, had moved in on Three Mile to feed out some hay there. Gertie and Gordon, with Maud Reuter and her two oldest brothers, were the five.

Mrs. Aufdengarten cooked one of her best company suppers; and afterward, to gay tunes from Montgomery Ward's fanciest organ, we enjoyed an evening of games and songs.

Perhaps Aufdengartens thought the party would make me change my mind, for after it was over they asked me again to come back in the fall. If I could have met these young folks sooner, back in the long, lonesome weeks of the winter, it might have been different. Now it was too late, and I couldn't get out of these hills soon enough.

Mrs. Aufdengarten took me back to Lena at dawn, the day after school was out. Mort Johnson was loading his mail sacks into the cart when we pulled into the yard, beside the far end of what was left of the chip pile, and a few minutes later we were flying down the valley behind the lively mules.

Mort pushed his team hard, and the lonesome prairie slid away behind us. I was so glad to be leaving the sandhills forever but, now that it was over, I wasn't sorry I had stayed with it. I had proved to myself that I could stand some pretty hard things; my lovely quilt top was finished; and I had earned ninety dollars. I still had every cent of it, too, except the thirty dollars I had paid on my note at Christmas time. Now I could finish off the note and go to summer school again, and still have a few dollars left for new clothes and a new bag to put them in.

Chapter Twenty-Six

AFFAIRS at home were in bad shape. The mangy cows were so thin they could hardly feed the calves that had lived through the spring storms, and Poppie hadn't had any cattle fit enough to sell for nearly a year. Mama, still thin and draggy, was worried about the frail baby, and about Grandma and Grandpa Blaine. Aunt Ollie had written that Grandpa was bedfast and Grandma was going blind.

"I wish I could go home and see them once more," Mama said.

I told her that maybe she could, this fall; for I would go to summer school again and work toward my second-grade certificate, and before I left I would apply for the home school. If I taught that one, I could stay at home and help out with my "board and room" money.

There had been changes on the Birdwood, too. Steve LaRue and Elma Johnson were married and living on his homestead, and Steve's brother Billie was going steady with Edna Johnson. A young couple, John and Daisy Weaver, had settled near the mouth of Squaw Creek, where we had picked grapes two years before. Another family, the Dikemans, had moved in south of us. The country was settling up fast now, and the free range was about gone. I could see why Bert Snyder had moved to the empty sandhills.

On my first Sunday at home Edna Johnson and Billie LaRue rode down the creek to see me. They tied their horses to the fence, down by the creek, and started up the slope to the house. On the way they met Charlie.

Charlie, a fine, big buck sheep, one of a batch of Heskett orphans from the year before, had handsome, curving horns and was the special pet of Roy and the girls. They drove him to their little wagon and he worked fine until he tired of the game; when he'd turn on them and butt them down until they turned him loose.

Now, streaking across the yard like a woolly bullet, Charlie hit Billie square behind the knees and folded him up like a jackknife. Edna screamed and Charlie backed up, waited for Billie to get up, then whammed him again. That time, Billie rolled over and grabbed Charlie by the horns. And that was the way we found them when we all ran out to see what the ruckus was. Poor Billie didn't dare let go of the bucking sheep's horns, and he couldn't get up unless he did.

Roy took Charlie away and the rest of us helped Billie brush the hay, dust, and chicken feathers off his Sunday suit. From then on, if we weren't around to stop him, Charlie butted every man that came on the place.

Before I got around to applying for the home school, a neighbor, whose children went to school there, heard about it and came over to warn me against it.

"I never heard of a teacher tryin' to teach her own brothers and sisters that didn't run into trouble," she said. "They're generally too easy on their own kin, and the rest don't like it."

Maybe she was right, I thought, so I applied for the school five miles south of us instead. The wages were thirty dollars a month, the director told me, and they would have my contract ready when I came home from summer school.

I went off to school wearing a stylish new skirt and shirtwaist that I had made myself, and carrying a new suitcase. This time, when I stepped off the train in North Platte, I knew where to go and what to do. On the way to the schoolhouse I met some of the girls I had known the summer before, and we went into the store together to buy paper and pencils.

Except that I roomed in a different house, and with a different group of girls, school was almost the same as it had been the year before. We studied hard, went to band concerts, watched the town girls play basketball, and went walking up Church Street, where the old buffalo, a trifle shabbier and dustier, still stood on the Cody lawn.

When I came home from school, I went right away to get my contract signed; but the district was having school-board trouble by then, and I ran into a hitch, first thing. The treasurer on the board was mad at the director, and the moderator, a new man elected in June, had failed to qualify for the post. The signatures of two members were enough to bind the contract, and the director signed it, but when the treasurer looked at it he swore he'd never put his name on the same paper with that so and so's.

"Never mind," Poppie said when I told him. "When it's time for school to start he'll have to sign it."

Poppie went with me when I went to see the treasurer again. I handed him the contract and told him I still had to have his signature before I could begin teaching. He stood beside the buggy a long time, studying the paper and glancing now and then at Poppie. Finally he took another look at Poppie, then walked behind the buggy and put his name to the contract.

On the way home, Poppie advised me to buy a new buggy to drive to school. "This old one would never make it through the winter," he said.

In Sutherland, a day or two later, he signed the sixty-dollar note I gave for the buggy, and on the way home I traded him one of my cows, a daughter of my bob-tailed Bess, for old Nancy. Again I was in debt for my first two months' wages, but I owned my own horse and buggy and I was mighty proud of my outfit.

I started school early in September, with sixteen pupils of all ages and sizes. The new family, the Dikemans, had spent three years on an isolated Canadian farm where there was no school, so Emory, almost as old as I was, and quite a bit taller, and his sisters, Jessie and Hattie, were all in the eighth reader together. By the end of the first day, I could see I'd have no time on my hands *that* winter.

Three weeks after school started Mama had another letter from Aunt Ollie, telling her that Grandpa Blaine was dead and Grandma, sick and totally blind, wanted her to come home as soon as she could. But Poppie was in debt at the bank and the mangy cattle were too thin to sell. There was only one way to get the money she needed for the trip.

"If you can wait until next week, you can have my first month's wages," I told her. The buggy dealer would just have to wait another month for his money.

Mama said she'd take my money if I'd take Daisy in exchange. Daisy was her only cow, the one Poppie had given her in place of Bunt, back in Dawson County, and I didn't want to take her, but Mama wouldn't have it any other way.

Mama decided to take Roy with her, since he wasn't old enough to need a ticket to ride on the train. Heart was to stay with Stell, who lived in North Platte now, where Walter was working on the railroad. Florry was to keep little Earl, and try to coax enough food into him to put some fat on his poor little bones.

"With the little ones all away, and Poppie down on the river with the cattle, you won't have so much to do," Mama told me.

Up until then our home school had been without a teacher; but that week Irene Miltonberger came to our place to ask for room and board. She was the new teacher for our district, she said, and the school board had sent her to us to see about accommodations.

Mama told her she could stay if she didn't mind sleeping three in a bed for the next week. So the new teacher moved in, sharing the front room bed with Dovey and me until Mama left for Missouri, and Poppie moved the cattle down on the river.

Irene, a tall, dark, pretty girl, the only daughter of a North Platte groceryman, had been halfway through the first month of her senior year in high school when she heard that the county, short of teachers as usual, was holding a special teachers' examination.

"I took the exam, just to see what I could do," she told us. "When I passed, and they gave me a certificate, I decided I'd better use it, and this is the school they sent me to."

Irene was like that, lively and impulsive, and she made herself right at home with us. Before she had been in the house an hour she was playing hymns on our old organ. When Poppie told her she certainly played well, she said, "I should. My mother was determined to raise me to be a lady, and almost ever since I can remember

I've been taking piano lessons from the best teachers she could find."

When Mama said it was nice that she had a piano, that she thought them better than organs, Irene said it was a perfectly whopping old grand piano, and that her grandfather Buchanan had brought it out from Iowa in an ox wagon years before. Then she asked if we'd mind if she brought some popular music back with her, the first time she went home.

"Why, no, you can play anything you like, I guess," Poppie told her, "only the old hymns are the best."

"Oh, I like them, too," Irene said, "but some of the new songs are so cute, only my mother won't let me play 'em. She won't let me play anything but hymns and classical music—she doesn't even know I can play any other kind."

To Irene, used to sharing the comforts of a big house with only one small brother, the daily hustle and bustle of our crowded little house was all fun. In fact, everything about our rugged country life interested and amused her, even the fleas.

Mama couldn't stand fleas, and their bites raised great welts on her tender body. There seemed to be millions of them in the yard and corrals, where we couldn't help picking them up and carrying them into the house in our clothes, and all through September we had been fighting the pests. Every night Mama made us spread newspapers on the floor in front of our beds and sprinkle them with a thick film of flea powder—the idea being that fleas jumping out of our clothes as we undressed would perish in the powder before they reached the beds.

But hardly a night passed that Mama didn't call Dovey and me out of a sound sleep to help her find and kill a flea in her own bed. Fleas didn't bother Irene, so she had a lot of fun out of our dead-of-night flea hunts.

After school was out, that fourth Friday, I drove down to my director's to get my wages. The district, being in debt, had to pay with warrants which had to be signed by all three board members and cashed at the courthouse in North Platte. The moderator, now in good standing, signed the warrant, too, and I drove on to the treasurer's house. He came out to the buggy and I handed him the warrant, but he looked at it so long that I began to be afraid he wasn't going to sign. Then he went behind the buggy, laid the paper on the buggy-box lid and wrote his name.

After supper I brought the warrant to the table, spread it out in the lamplight and looked it over. A line of small type at the bottom stated that it was not valid unless signed by all three board members *on its face*. But there were only *two* names on the front of the paper. I turned it over. The treasurer's name was on the *back*.

My heart hit bottom with a thump. We needed the money *now*, if Mama was to get to Missouri in time to see her mother alive, and I had planned to take her to North Platte the next day to cash the warrant.

"Look!" I handed the paper to Poppie. "That old reprobate did that on *purpose!* Why does he have to be so mean?"

"Never mind," Poppie said. "*I'll* go with you and Mommie in the morning, and we'll go by his place and get this signed *right*."

As before, when the treasurer saw that Poppie was with me, he signed the paper and handed it back.

Mama and Roy left for Missouri the next day. Then Poppie moved his sorry herd of cattle to the valley, where he had stacked hay for them that summer. So, for the rest of the winter, Irene, Dovey, Nellie, Presh, and I were alone in the soddy on the Birdwood.

The winter days, getting steadily shorter at both ends, were never long enough for all I had to do. I slid out of bed long before daylight and built the fire and routed the girls out to help me with breakfast and the chores. With a five-mile drive ahead of me, I had to be well on the way by the time the sun came up. Near sunset each afternoon I pulled the schoolhouse door shut behind me, buckled Nancy into the shafts, and trotted her home through the chilly evening. After supper I corrected papers and prepared lessons ahead, making sure I could pronounce every word and work every problem. Saturdays, we washed and ironed, cleaned the house, and baked enough bread to last another week.

Last winter's burden had been loneliness and too little to do. This winter's was too heavy a load of work and responsibility.

Poppie came up from the river every two weeks or so to bring us groceries and supplies. Between times, if we ran short, we sent to town by the neighbors for what we needed. Sometimes we were down to oatmeal and sauerkraut before the new supplies came in.

We kept the big sauerkraut barrel outside the door, with a washtub turned over it to keep the dust out. Irene and the girls came home one afternoon and caught one of the milk cows, old Daisy, eating out of the barrel. She hadn't eaten more than a gallon or two, they said, so they chased her away and skimmed off the top layer and threw it out. Then they jammed the tub on tight again.

The rest of that winter, whenever Irene thought of old Daisy, with long kraut whiskers hanging down her chin, it was enough to make her laugh till she cried.

When Poppie came up from the valley to spend Thanksgiving with us, he said Mama had written that Grandma was a little improved but still needed constant care. When Irene came back, after the holiday, she brought a little bundle of magazines with her. "I've been spending twenty-five cents a month for these for quite a while," she told us. "But Mama doesn't know it, so I have to keep 'em hid. Now I'll play you some of the latest pieces."

She sat down at the organ and played and sang, "Charming Billie," "The Little Mohee," "A Bird in a Gilded Cage," "Redwing," and a dozen more. Then she spun around on the stool and said, "My, that was fun, only don't ever let my mother find out about it."

Poppie came up again, about the middle of December. Old Bill Sherman, he said, had ridden out from town with him, to spend the rest of the winter on his place across the creek.

One evening, a few days before Christmas, I saw that we were practically down to sauerkraut and oatmeal again. I knew that Vedders were going to town the next day. The Vedders had moved in across the creek from us the fall before. I hurried a little faster, the next morning, so as to squeeze out the extra few minutes I'd need to go around by their place with a list. Zipping Nancy into her shafts, I hopped into the buggy and started her off with a good slap of the lines.

I was almost to the creek when, above the frosty screech of the buggy wheels, I heard Irene screaming at me. I looked back and saw her running down the hill, bareheaded and waving her arms. I pulled Nancy to a quick stop and yelled to ask her what had happened.

"Nothing," she yelled back, "I just forgot to tell you to give my love to Emory."

I could have cheerfully ducked her in the creek just

then—if only I'd had the time. For neither time, nor distance, nor anything else, let alone a few minutes more or less in the schoolroom, worried happy-go-lucky Irene.

I left my list at Vedders, told them I'd pick up the groceries that evening, and hurried on. Near dark, that cold, short December day, I stopped at Vedders again. With a fifty-pound sack of flour under the seat and the other packages on top of the lap robe beside me, I drove on to the creek.

The Birdwood, a wandering stream, seldom stayed in the same channel two days in succession. In the wider places, the water might flow at an even, shallow depth all across the creek bed, or it might suddenly cut a new, deep channel near one bank or the other. At Vedder's crossing the stream had covered its bed that morning; that night it flowed in a narrow channel on the far side.

Nancy crossed the sandy bed and stepped into the water, where she dropped almost out of sight. Startled, she plunged ahead to gain footing on the bank, and of course yanked the buggy into the hole. The icy water came up to my knees, and then to my waist. From the upstream side, water ran under the robe, lifting it up and floating sacks and bags into my lap. I grabbed at packages about to tumble into the creek and yelled at poor Nancy, who jumped ahead and jerked the buggy out on dry land. Water poured from the buggy on all sides, while Nancy shook herself, flinging an icy shower all over my upper half.

The quick ducking had scarcely dampened the groceries —even the sack of flour had only a thin wet layer on the outside—but by the time I reached home my skirts were frozen so stiff I could hardly get out of the buggy. By Saturday morning I was coming down with a heavy cold.

On Monday my throat was so raw I could scarcely speak above a whisper. The cold snap had deepened, too, and that morning there were ice ledges along both sides of the creek. The next morning, the Tuesday before Christmas, I could barely drag one foot after the other.

"Why don't you stay home and go to bed?" Irene asked.

But I knew my pupils would be at the schoolhouse, and as long as I was able to stay on my feet I didn't intend for them to make the trip through the cold for nothing.

The ice ledges along the banks of the creek were wider and thicker. Nancy stepped out cautiously on the nearer one. It held and we crossed it safely, but the farther ledge broke beneath her and she fell hard, smashing her mouth against the jagged ice and snapping a buggy shaft in two. She got up and stood shivering, with blood dripping from her mouth in little splashes on the ice.

An icy dawn wind whipped into my face and the black water rushed by below me. I just sat there in the buggy, feeling wooden all over and not caring if I never moved again. And at that moment Old Bill Sherman came over the rise on the other side of the creek, sized up the situation at a glance, and yelled gallantly, "Jist set where ye be, Grace, an' I'll wade in an' tote ye out."

"Oh, no, don't bother," I croaked, "I can get out just fine."

Moving fast, I leaned over the dashboard and unhooked the tugs, then crawled from the buggy onto Nancy's broad hips and unbuckled the holdback straps. Settling myself on her back, I grabbed the lines and hurried her back the way I had come, leaving the buggy in the creek and Old Bill, squat and round as a barrel in his winter layers, on the far side of it.

Later in the forenoon John Houk came by and helped me get the buggy home. We replaced the broken shafts with the tongue and I caught another horse, hitched him up with Nancy, and drove down to see my director. He took a look at me—and advised me to start my two weeks' Christmas vacation that day. So I went straight home and crawled into bed.

When Poppie came up for Christmas he moved us across the creek into the little one-room soddy on Walter Ross' homestead. From there, none of us would have to cross the creek to get to our schools.

The Saturday before school started again, I drove to North Platte. Stell, expecting her first baby soon, thought I'd better take little Heart home. Irene was riding back with me, too, and I spent the night in town with her. That evening she sat down at the grand piano in the fine parlor of her home and, with a wink at me, played the "ladylike" tunes that pleased her mother. It was all so pleasant and nice that I was sorry when bedtime came.

The next morning was cold and windy, sun dogs flanked the hazy sun, and there were dingy, threatening clouds in the northwest. I told Irene that we'd better not stay to go to church with her mother, as we'd planned, that I didn't like the looks of the weather and was afraid we might get caught in a storm before we reached home.

"Whatever you say," she agreed. She was still stuffing things into her suitcase when her mother, gowned and hatted for church, came in to tell her good-bye.

"Mercy, Irene, won't you ever learn to pack a bag right? Here, let me do it," Mrs. Miltonberger said. She finished the packing and told us good-bye, and I felt sorry for her. I knew she didn't like it because Irene had quit school, and I could see how hard it was for her to let her go so far out into the country, among people her family knew nothing about.

We were in the buggy and ready to leave when Irene remembered something she had forgotten to tell her mother. "I'm sorry, but I'll have to stop at the church and tell her," she said.

I drove to the handsome new Presbyterian church and let her out, then watched her going up the walk, trim and stylish in her pretty clothes. Irene could spend all her wages on herself; for clothes, the little music magazines she hid from her mother, or anything else she wanted. I couldn't figure her out. She had a beautiful home with high-ceilinged rooms, papered and carpeted in the latest fashion, furnished with matching pieces of furniture and lighted with electricity. Yet she was willing to leave it all for our crowded little soddy on the Birdwood.

When we were started again on the long cold drive against the wind, with little Heart tucked in between us, I asked her about it.

"Well," she said, "I'll tell you. I love my mother, but she is always housecleaning, and always at me to put things away and be careful. I'm just not a tidy person and it wears me out to try to be. At your house I can do as I please and have fun."

Well, maybe so. But if I had been in her place I didn't believe I would have figured it that way.

There were six of us in the one-room soddy the rest of that winter. We had taken only the furniture we had to have: beds, table, cupboard, stove and chairs, but Irene, except that she missed the organ, seemed to have more fun than ever. And she never seemed to run out of jokes to play on us. But there was *one* joke that didn't work out the way she had planned it.

One cold afternoon, before I got home from school, she cut a handful of horsehair up fine and sprinkled it into my side of the bed we shared. I always went to bed first, and that night, as I stretched out between the blankets, I felt a thousand miserable prickles.

I knew right away it was Irene's doing, so I eased over onto her side of the bed and pulled the blankets up to my chin. I hadn't said a word, and she pretended not to notice, but she sat a long long time at the table in gloomy silence. If all our extra bedding hadn't been in the other house, on the far side of the frozen creek, I *might* have suggested that we get up and change the blankets.

As it was, it was Irene who spent the night wriggling and scratching.

The high spots of that busy winter were the literaries, held every other Friday, and meeting by turns in my schoolhouse and in Winnifred Vedder's, over east in the Rosedale district. Literaries on the Birdwood were about like those in Dawson County, just different people and not nearly as many of them.

Poppie, and Winnifred's beau, Randolph Peterjohn, a young man from down on the river valley, came up for most of the meetings; and at almost every one Randolph, a fine singer with a deep burr in his voice, was asked to sing "The Ship That Never Returned."

> But for-r year-r-rs and year-r-rs ther-r-er-r
> wer-re sad hearts aching
> For-r-r the ship that never-r-r r-r-retur—r-ned.

Another favorite was "Every Nation Has a Flag but the Coon," a catchy song that came to the Birdwood by way of one of Irene's little magazines. Irene had a splendid voice, one that, in years to come, pleased the radio

listeners of three states, but there on the Birdwood she
had a thoroughly good time singing:

> The leader of the Blackville club arose last Labor Night
> And said, "While we were on parade today,
> I really felt so much ashamed, I wished I might turn white;
> For all the white folks marched with banners gay."

CHORUS

> Ireland has her harp and shamrock,
> England has her lion bold.
> Even China has her dragon,
> And Germany her eagle gold.
> Bonnie Scotland loves her thistle,
> Turkey has her crescent moon;
> And what won't those Yankees do
> For the old Red, White, and Blue?
> Every race has a flag but the coon.

> "Now I'll suggest a flag that ought to win the prize.
> Just take a flannel shirt and paint it red,
> And place upon it a chicken with two poker dice
>   for eyes,
> And have it waving razors round its head.
> To make it quaint, you'd have to paint
> A possum with a porkchop in its teeth.
> And be sure not to skip a policy slip,
> And have it marked 4—11—44.
> Then those Irish and Dutch,
> They can't guy us so much.
> We should have had this emblem long before."

CHORUS

At one meeting Poppie scored a big hit with the "poem"
he wrote after Irene fell in the creek.

Irene had to carry water from the creek for schoolroom use, and in the winter she had to cross the shelf
of ice to reach open water. In March, when the shelf
began to narrow and soften, she took to creeping out
upon it on her hands and knees to dip up her bucket of

water. But, in spite of her caution, the ice broke one morning and dumped her into the creek on all fours.

On the next Friday, when Poppie came up for Literary, Irene told him about her ducking. "Br-r-r, but that water was cold, and there I was, up to my elbows in the creek and yelling my head off," she said, laughing, "and little Heartie on the bank, yelling right along with me." (Four-year-old Heart went to school part of the time with me, and part of the time with Irene.)

"How did you get out of the creek?" Poppie asked her.

"Oh, I finally backed out."

"Yeah," Poppie said, "down on the river I see cows breaking through the ice every day, and getting out the same way."

That evening, at the meeting, he read his verses:

> A fair young schoolma'm, tall and slim,
>   Went to the creek for water.
> The ice was thin, she was afraid—
>   Her heart was in a flutter.
> She knelt down gently on the ice,
>   And reached out far asunder.
> There was a crack—an awful splash—
>   Her head went nearly under.
> The little fish swam to the Platte,
>   The muskrat sought the hills.
> The old bullfrog just winked his eye
>   And shivered with the chills.
> With all her might she screamed aloud,
>   "Save, Heartie, or I die."
> And little Heart did all she could,
>   By joining this wild cry.
> She reached the shore, she knew not how.
>   Ye fishes! What a row.
> Then she heard a sympathizer say,
>   "She backed out like a cow."

Every Literary had its "newspaper," read at every meeting, and made up of jokes and community news and gossip—a lot of it aimed at the girls and their beaux. A young man named Charlie —————— had been paying attention to me, and our turn came with this gem: "Question—How does Charlie show his religious devotion these days?" "Answer—By saying 'Grace' more than three times a day."

No one was "safe" at an old-time Literary.

Chapter Twenty-Seven

BY LATE winter cattle everywhere in the Birdwood country were in such bad shape that late storms and cold spring rains were sure to take a heavy toll of the mangy-hided herds. Poppie said the big outfits were planning to build dipping vats and dip their herds before turning them out on summer range; but the vats were costly to build and operate, so he supposed small owners like himself would have to take the losses.

Mama was still in Missouri, for Grandma, after lingering on all winter, had died and Mama was staying on a while longer to help Aunt Ollie sort and put away Grandpa's and Grandma's things.

March, as usual, was cold and blustery, and I was as busy as ever. One windy morning I told Nellie and Presh to go over to the other house, after school, and get a ham from the barrel there, so I could cook it that evening for lunches the rest of the week. When I pulled in home, late that afternoon, they were coming with the ham, their eyes red and their faces streaked with tears.

They told me how they had crossed the creek and started up the slope toward the dark, empty house; and then the strange notion had come to the poor lonesome little pair that, if they called to her, Mama might answer them. So they stood out there in the windy shadows and called and called. Finally, seeing how late it was,

they made a run for the door and pushed through it together.

The big meat barrel stood against the kitchen wall,
and hanging on a peg beside it was an old dress of Mama's
—so they just put their faces against it and cried out
their homesickness for her. Then, afraid of the ghosty,
creeping shadows, they hurried to fish a ham from the
cold brine and run as hard as they could for home.

The next morning was raw and cloudy, and the wind
was still howling down the creek when I started for school.
Before I was a mile along the road little bullets of sleet
began to pelt the buggy top. The sleet had changed to
heavy snow by the time I reached the schoolhouse and
unhitched Nancy on its sheltered side. By nine o'clock
the storm was a roaring blizzard.

All my pupils lived a good deal closer to the schoolhouse
than I did, and the storm had turned bad in time to keep
them from starting out. I wasn't worried about Irene
and the girls either, for the same reason, and I was warm
and safe in the schoolhouse. But poor Nancy, standing
out in the storm, concerned me. I was about to go out
and bring her inside with me when the door flew open
and one of my pupils, a big sixteen-year-old who lived
a quarter of a mile east of the schoolhouse, stumbled in,
looking like a snowman.

He said he had seen me go by and that he would help
me back to their place, where I could stay until the storm
blew itself out. I got back into my wraps and overshoes
and we went out into the storm. The snow was like a
white wall in front of our faces, but above the howling
wind I could hear Nancy, whinnying and whinnying.
We located her and got her into the shafts again, then
headed into the storm. Now and then the freezing wind
slacked off for a minute, thinning the snow enough for

us to glimpse the buildings ahead, and Nancy plodded toward them, her head tucked almost between her knees.

I was numb and out of breath by the time we stabled Nancy and plowed our way to the house, where we stopped in a lean-to to beat the snow off our clothes. In one corner, where the lean-to joined the main house, a long, tapering ridge of snow reached into the room from a hole low down in the sod wall. Three dogs, curled nose to tail, snuggled in a big cob pile in another corner. A double bed pretty well filled the rest of the space in the shelter.

"Darn dogs dug that hole so's they could get in here to sleep," the boy said.

Only the boy and his two sisters were at home. Their parents had left for town before daylight, a good two hours before the storm struck, and there was no possibility they would be home until the storm was over. But the one-room sod house was snug and warm, and Nancy was safe in the stable.

At bedtime the older girl, a fourteen-year-old, told me I was to sleep with her. She lit a lamp and led the way to the lean-to, where the flame danced and smoked in the icy draft from the hole. The snow ridge reached almost across the room now, and every few minutes a new gust of fine snow sprayed along its top.

"You dratted houn's, you," the girl scolded at the dogs bedded in the cob pile. "If you'd sleep in the barn where you belong, this place wouldn't be so freezin' cold."

Our fingers were numb and stiff by the time we pulled off our shoes, stockings, and dresses. My bedfellow didn't bother with a nightgown, and of course I didn't have one. The bedding was two featherbeds on top of a straw tick. In our long underwear and petticoats, we crawled between the featherbeds. The one above was almost weightless, but we sank deep into the one beneath us. Without blankets, or even sheets, the hard, icy feel of the rough ticking was almost more than I could bear.

My partner was soon asleep, but I lay awake a long time, curled in a tight, shivering ball and aching with the cold. The dogs snored in the cob pile and the wind howled through the hole in the corner, blowing snow into my face until I pulled the featherbed over my head.

I wakened hours later, wringing wet with sweat and almost smothered. But the wind had gone down and the storm was over.

The sun glittered on miles and miles of snow, that morning, as Nancy and I threaded our way through an ocean of high, wind-whipped drifts to the half-buried schoolhouse. At home that evening I found things about the way I had expected to; Irene and the girls had stayed home both days, popping corn and pulling taffy and having a high old time.

Ragged drifts of dirty snow still edged the ridges when my school closed on the third of April. The next day Poppie came up to help us move back to Grandma Houk's house across the creek.

Poppie was broke and in debt and completely discouraged. Calves up to three weeks old had died in the storm because their mothers were too poor and weak to feed them, he said, and some of the cows had died, too. Some of the rest, mangy and almost hairless, with bloody patches on their itching hides, had to be tailed up every morning.

I asked if there wasn't some way we could get them dipped. But he said there wasn't a vat within miles of us, and that it would cost more to build one than all the cattle on the creek were worth, that spring.

The weather stayed bleak and raw, raining one day

blowing a cold wind the next, punishing the poor cattle still more. I wrote to Mama to ask her to stay in Missouri until the weather settled. I couldn't bear to have her come home to things the way they were then.

On a morning near the end of April, the sky finally cleared and the sun shone warm and bright. It was the day I had been waiting for. Now we could set everything out in the yard and get the house cleaned and scrubbed and ready for Mama to come home.

We stripped the house to its skin in short order. Then the girls flew at the scrubbing while I took down the screen door to repair a piece of loose screen. In the middle of it all, Missionary Scott drove in to pay his annual call. We dropped the mops, brooms, and hammer, and carried chairs back into the house and sat down to visit with the feeble old man. When he was about ready to leave, he knelt beside his chair to pray. We knelt, too, and the gentle old missionary, his back to the open door, began his prayer.

Then a shadow fell across the floor and I looked up. Charlie, the big buck sheep, stood in the door, his cold yellow eyes on the old man.

"Oh, Lord, please don't let Charlie bunt that good old man into the middle of next week," I prayed.

And, for a wonder, all Charlie did was tiptoe across the floor and start chewing on the missionary's cuff. So the old man brought his prayer to an orderly close and, on the tail of the "amen," Nellie and Dovey grabbed Charlie and hauled him outside.

Poppie moved what were left of the cattle back to the Birdwood in May, and Mama and Roy came home soon afterward. Mama seemed as worn and thin as ever and her cough was no better. Florry brought Earl home, and Mama was disappointed to see that seven months of her loving care hadn't put so much as a pound of "new meat on his spindly bones."

Then Poppie asked Mama if she'd like to move back to Dawson County. Uncle John had moved to a farm west of Gothenberg, he said, and our place was vacant. He'd been told that cattle fed on cornstalks didn't have mange, he told us, and if he went home now and planted the place to corn, we could all move back in the fall, turn the cattle in the stalks, and maybe save what were left.

Mama said, "Then let's go back. Except for the creek, I've always liked it better in Roten Valley."

I knew the folks expected me to move back to Dawson County with them—and I didn't want to. Roten Valley no longer meant anything important to me, but I didn't feel that I could walk out on Poppie and Mama without a better reason than *that*. My director had offered me the school again, at higher wages, but when he came up the next week, bringing the contract for me to sign, I told him it looked like I'd be going back to Dawson County in the fall.

"Maybe you'll change your mind before then," he said. "Anyway, I'll hold the job open for you till August."

But, whatever happened in the fall, I intended to go to summer school again. One more term and I would have my second-grade certificate. I was twenty-one years old now, and it didn't look like I was ever going to be a cowboy's bride. So, if I was going to have to make teaching my life's work, I meant to make the most of it.

I met my good old Dawson County teacher, Mrs. Mc-Kenny, at school that summer. She had come back to brush up on new methods, she said, and she was so pleased to learn I was a teacher, too. She questioned me on the schools I had taught and the methods I used. Then she said, "Grace, I can see you're just like I am, you can't rest until you know every scholar in your school is learning all he can." No praise could have pleased me more.

Just after I came home with my second-grade certificate, at the end of July, Poppie came up to the Birdwood. Crops were good in Roten Valley, he said, and most of the district schools hadn't hired teachers yet.

"Now that you've got your new certificate," he told me, "you could have your pick, if you go back with me now and sign up for one."

"But maybe I could do better on wages if I waited until later in the summer, when teachers are scarcer," I said.

"Well, maybe so," he agreed. "I'll be coming up again in about a month. You can go back with me then. We'll have to clean up the house anyway, and you can see about your school at the same time."

So Poppie went back to Dawson County alone—and I had another month to make up my mind about what I would do.

Shortly after that, Daisy Weaver rode down from the forks to tell me Sam Marant was having a fish fry at his shack on East Creek the next week. Sam was a young rancher, getting a start in cattle on the Squaw Creek range, she said, and she and John, Elma and Steve LaRue, Edna and Ivan Johnson, and a few others were riding over to help with the fry.

"We'd like to have you go along," she told me. And then, as she was riding away, she said, "Oh, yes, Bert Snyder'll be there, too. He's helping Sam furnish the fish."

"Bert Snyder! Why, I thought he had a ranch in the sandhills now."

"Oh, he does, but he still runs cattle on Squaw Creek in summer." Daisy grinned.

I did up my best white shirtwaist that week, pressed my riding skirt, polished my high-topped Sunday shoes, and shampooed my hair. For once, I meant to look my best when I met Bert Snyder.

On the morning of the fish fry I crimped my bangs with the curling iron and put my hair up over the new round "rat" I had learned to wear at school that summer. I joined the rest of the crowd at Weavers, and we all rode together through the hills to Sam Marant's shack. Sam and Bert were sitting on the creek bank, pulling on their boots, when we rode up. There was a wet seine and a sizable pile of flopping, gasping fish on the grass beside them.

Sam brought some pans and buckets out to his wash bench on the creek bank and we all fell to cleaning fish.

"Whoever's going to fry fish better get started on 'em now," Bert said, after a while.

When no one offered to fry, he grinned and said, "Well, I guess I'll have to do it then. But with all these girls around, I sure thought I'd get out of cooking *one* meal, anyway."

He picked up a pan of fish and started for the shack. Then Daisy told me to go in and help him. "There's plenty of us to clean the rest of these fish," she said. Bert stopped to wait for me, so I went along and floured fish for him to fry on Sam's little stove. (And I suspected that day, and found out later it was so, that Bert had fixed it up with Daisy to make sure I'd be at the fish fry, and that I'd be helping him.)

After dinner the crowd scattered along the creek to pick late chokecherries. Bert picked with me, and when we were out of earshot of the others, he told me he'd like to bring an extra saddle horse, come Sunday, and take me riding. I said I'd be glad to go, and that he'd better come early enough to eat dinner with us, one meal he wouldn't have to cook himself.

He came on the tall gray that had sailed so easily over the rope barriers in North Platte, two years before. The led horse, a chunky bay, was wearing a good-looking sidesaddle. After dinner, when he brought the horses to the door and I went out, the gray horse shied at sight of me.

"Dewey is scared of women," Bert apologized, "but Midge here, is plumb gentle. I don't have a horse on the place gentle enough for a lady to ride, so I borrowed this outfit from Nate Trego's wife."

I remembered that Mr. Aufdengarten had mentioned Nate Trego, in the valley where the McPherson County courthouse should have been, and I thought how lucky Mrs. Trego was, having such a fine riding outfit.

We rode down the creek quite a ways, then crossed over and jogged back on the other side. A little way past Heskett's ranch I saw a baby's bottle in the grass beside the road.

"Oh, look," I said. "Mrs. Heskett was at our house yesterday with her baby, and she must have lost that on her way home. I'd better take it back to her."

Bert swung down and picked up the bottle, then he stood jiggling it in his hand a while before he handed it to me. Even then he didn't get back on his horse, but stood beside him, switching at the tall grass with the ends of his bridle reins, studying something over in his mind.

"Why not stop here a while?" he said finally. "This looks like a good place to talk."

So I got down from my horse and we sat on the grass by the side of the road and talked—and he asked me to marry him.

I had been hoping all day that he would, so all I said was "yes."

He looked surprised and then relieved, and then he let out a long breath. "Good!" he said. "I sure was afraid I'd have to put up a big talk before you'd say that."

We rode on home then, and a little later I watched him lope out of sight up the creek. But this time I knew he'd be coming back.

It was almost sundown, and in the west some little clouds with bright gold edges were drifting along the hilltops. I watched them, remembering the long days on the prairie, back in Roten Valley, when I had wondered what it would be like to sit in the sky and look down on the clouds, when I had first dreamed of riding away into the hills with my cowboy. Now, that dream was about to come true, even though the first one never could.

Chapter Twenty-Eight

BERT and I set our wedding date for October 25, less than two months away.

Bert said he had to freight his winter's supplies from North Platte to the ranch first, and move his cattle from Squaw Creek to the sandhills. I wanted to help Poppie get the Roten Valley house ready for the family, and then I'd have my wedding clothes to make.

I hadn't told anyone but Mama and Florry that I was soon to be married, but I still had Poppie to tell—and I wondered how I was going to break the news to him. I knew he'd be disappointed that I wasn't going to stay in Dawson County that winter, or use my new certificate, and I hated to tell him.

When he came up from Dawson County a few days later, I put off telling him until evening. Then, while I was washing up the supper dishes, he said, "Gheet, there's two good schools in Roten Valley that don't have teachers yet. I've talked to the school boards and you can have either one of 'em."

I picked up the dishpan and went outside to throw out the dishwater. I stood there in the summer night a little while, deciding what I'd say. But when I went in again he had his eyebrows hiked way up in his hair and his lips pursed out, the way he did when he studied something that had surprised him, so I knew Mama had told him. He didn't say anything more about schools for me to teach, and two days later we left for Roten Valley together.

I was sorry about Poppie having to give up his big plans to run cattle in open country. But he seemed cheerful enough, even happy to be back, as we drove past the fine Dawson County cornfields. I couldn't see it, though. Those fields reminded me only of hard work and long, sweaty hours behind a plodding three-horse team, fighting dust, gnats, and flies. All the land was under fence now, and there was no longer any need to herd cattle. Most of all, after nearly four years on the Birdwood, I missed the open range I had grown used to, but, then, I wasn't coming back to stay.

"It doesn't seem like it's been thirteen years since we first moved into this house," I told Poppie that evening.

The soddy had seemed so big and raw, that first night, and now it looked so little. I had been eight then, and there had been five of us girls. Presh and Roy had been born in the soddy, and it must have come near to flying apart, with all of us rollicking in it on stormy days. Heart and Earl had never lived here, but they'd be coming soon, and there'd still be six young McCances under the old roof. And Mama would still have to have a bed in her front room.

"You know," Poppie said, "if everything goes well and the cattle pick up down here like I think they will, I expect to be able to build a new house in three or four years."

"Maybe one with a parlor?"

"Yes, one with a parlor. Mommie would like that, wouldn't she?"

When we finished with it, the old house, all cleaned and papered and whitewashed, looked so nice that I wished I was going to be married in it. But I was afraid that the moving, and a wedding, too, would be too much for Mama, so we planned to be married in Bert's home, near Maxwell.

My wedding day was coming up fast, by the time the family was settled again in Roten Valley, and there were still my wedding clothes to make. But Mama helped me cut and fit my wedding dress, a lovely blue brilliantine, and she helped, too, with all the petticoats and under-things that went with it.

Everything was ready by October 23, the day Bert came for me, driving his father's good-looking buggy horse, Barney, to a nice top buggy.

The next morning, with Poppie's and Mama's wedding present—a glass table set, pitcher, tumblers, spoon holder, covered butter dish and sugar bowl—and my suitcase in the back of the buggy, we said good-bye and headed for Maxwell.

Bert told me more about himself on the way, how he had been "on his own" for half of his thirty-one years; how, at fifteen, he had earned a man's wages on a drive to northern Wyoming with a Paxton trail herd. Later, he had broken horses for Buffalo Bill Cody's Wild West Show, and had turned down a chance to go to England with the show.

"Bill offered me forty dollars a month for the year we'd be gone, but I could get that much at home and I thought I ought to have more for a trip like that. Now I wish I'd gone, just for the fun of it. But that was over ten years ago, and I didn't see it that way then."

After that he had worked for a big cattle outfit in Wyoming and Montana. Then, six years ago, he had filed on the Squaw Creek claim. He was next to the youngest in a family of nine. His father, Jeremiah Snyder, had been born in Ohio, his mother, Frances Miles, in New York, and they had met in Indiana. After their marriage in 1853 they had come west by degrees until, by the time they reached Maxwell in the early eighties, they were too old to go any farther. A little brother, William, had died somewhere along the family's westward trail. The rest were scattered from New York State to the West Coast. Two brothers and a sister, all married, lived near Maxwell; Pearl, the youngest, lived at home.

The sun was setting behind the purple hills across the river when, half a mile from Maxwell, Barney, of his own accord, turned from the main road and crossed the railroad tracks. Bert's home was just ahead, a low, sprawling white house beneath tall, bare cottonwoods.

Bert's father, a gentle little man with white hair hanging to his shoulders and a long white beard, looked like a prophet straight out of the Bible. His mother, thin and spare like my own, seemed worn to a sliver by all the hard years she had spent on the frontiers of her time. Pearl was small and plump and bustling. Big family photographs in heavy frames hung on the living-room walls. Among them was one of the little dead William, and another of a sister who had died on the West Coast. There was one of Bert, too, at sixteen, all dressed up in his first "boughten" suit and overcoat; clothes he'd bought with part of the money he had earned on the Paxton trail drive.

We were married in the living room at noon the next day, with the family, past and present, looking on. Bert's brothers, John and George, were there with their families, but his sister, Ann McCullough, would not be coming. Ann, Pearl told me in the privacy of her room, where she helped me put on my wedding dress, was expecting a baby right soon. Bert's best friend, Artie

Plumer, was the only guest outside the family at our wedding.

Late in the afternoon of that bright, warm October day, we started for the ranch. It wasn't quite according to my dream, for we went in Bert's covered wagon, with our wedding presents: the glass table set, half a bolt of lace curtain material, a parlor lamp with red roses painted on its big china globe, a dinner set of blue dishes, and the leather-bound Bible Bert's father gave us, all packed in the fresh hay that half filled the wagon box behind the seat.

Just before sundown, Bert swung the team off the road into a meadow, not far from the place where I had camped with Poppie and the children on the way to the Birdwood. He pulled in behind a haystack that hid the wagon from the road, and said he guessed this would be a good place to camp. Then he told me he figured Artie had "tipped off the boys" about our wedding, and that it wouldn't be safe to go on to a hotel in North Platte. "The boys are probably looking for me in town tonight," he finished, "so we'd better not show up there till morning. They'll all be gone to work then."

Bert, in the course of his rugged life, had camped out more nights than he'd spent inside, and long practice had made him a top hand at it. "This is my old roundup wagon anyway," he said, "so everything we need is right here."

While I unpacked the lunch his mother and Pearl had put up for us, Bert unharnessed and staked the team and rolled out his bedroll—outfitted with a pair of brand-new blankets—on the hay in the wagon box. Then we sat on the stubbly meadow grass beside the wagon and ate our wedding supper, while the warm autumn night settled down around us.

Shortly after sunup the next morning we forded the North Platte River, always low in the fall of the year, and drove on into town. We stopped to have our wedding pictures taken. Then Bert gave me some money and told me I'd better get some "curtain stuff" for the soddy's kitchen windows, while he picked up a few supplies for the ranch. That done, we headed on west to Florry's, where she and John were having a wedding dance for us that night.

Except for John and Florry, no one on the Birdwood had known Bert and I were getting married, and, since practically everybody not bedfast turned out for a neighborhood dance, the news of our wedding surprised the whole community. "No wonder we couldn't get you to sign up to teach our school," Mr. McNeel said when he shook hands with Bert and me.

The next forenoon we loaded the big box of things I had stored at Florry's, and the big rocking chair I had bought in the spring before Mama came home from Missouri. Then we put the pair of turkey hens Florry gave us with the other wedding presents in the back of the wagon and pulled out on the last leg of the trip to the ranch.

The sun was already slanting to the west when we stopped at Bert's claim on Squaw Creek to eat our lunch. We ate beside the spring in front of the little shack he'd lived in, those summers on the creek, and drank the cold, clear water that bubbled up inside the barrel he had sunk in the sand over the spring. Then we drove west again a little way, before we turned north for the long, steep pull up Squaw Creek hill.

"Sutherland is fifteen miles closer to the ranch than North Platte, but I do my freighting from the Platte on account of this hill," Bert told me. "It's too hard to pull with a loaded wagon."

From the top of the big hill he pointed out the ranch buildings, just barely to be seen five miles farther north. Then we drove on, down the long hill and over and around a lengthy stretch of smaller hills. A good many years ago there had been a few homesteaders in here, he told me, but some dry years had starved them out and now, except for Sod Camp, where a McNeel line rider stayed now and then, no one else lived in this section of the hills.

It was the shank of the afternoon before we drove through a gap in the hills and came into Bert's valley. He stopped the team to let me look across the oval meadow, rimmed all around by hills, with the ranch buildings looking a little lonesome in the middle. Seven or eight haystacks dotted the meadow; a black circle near the road a little way ahead was all that was left of another that had been struck by lightning.

Then Bert pointed to the right. "There," he said, "see that patch of light-colored grass over there. A settler tried to farm that strip once, and turned it into a blow-out. Took it a long time to grass over again. There's another patch like it on LaMunyon Flat, north of here, where Ed Huffman's ranch is now. Plow this land and it'll blow away every time. There ought to be a law against a man bringing a plow into this country."

I saw then how much he loved this sandhill country, and how strongly he felt toward anyone who damaged it.

We drove on to the buildings. The barn was first, a low shelter roofed and sided with woven wire and hay. There were corrals beside it, and a busy windmill that kept two big tanks filled with water. A little farther on, Bert stopped the wagon at our front door.

On the way to the ranch I had asked him about the house and he had told me it was "pretty fair-sized," and that there was a pump and sink in the kitchen. I had been glad to hear that. Usually the pump was out in the yard, and there was no sink at all.

The big soddy I saw from the wagon seat had a corrugated tin roof—no dirt top here, I was glad to see. Bunchgrass and prickly-pear cactus covered the unfenced yard, and north of the house a stunted cottonwood sapling seemed barely alive in the sand. "I've put out a good many cuttings since I moved here, but it's the only one that's lived, and it's the only tree for a good ways in any direction from here," Bert said of the sad little tree.

A couple of dozen speckled hens and a big Brahma rooster scratched in the sand near a bunchgrass-covered hump beyond the tree. The hump was his chicken house, Bert said. It had been the cellar until he put roosts in it, and nests for the hens to lay in. I could see that he was proud of his chicken layout, and even of the poor little tree. They made the ranch seem more like a real home, a place where he intended to settle down and stay a long time.

But it was the inside of the house I wanted to see.

It was fairly clean and mostly empty. In the big kitchen, beside the pitcher pump and wooden sink, there was a little four-holed cookstove, a table, four unpainted chairs, and a tall new cupboard. Bert told me he had used a stack of canned-goods boxes for a cupboard, up until he knew he was going to get married, and then he figured he'd better buy a real one. In the Platte, the day he went to see about it, he ran onto Nate Trego. Nate had been married for several years and knew about such things, so he took him along to help him pick it out. Later, he backed his wagon up to the store and loaded the cupboard and other supplies. But when he went in to pay for them, the storekeeper told him Trego had already paid for the cupboard. It had been his wedding present to us. So then Bert bought a nice set of dishes to put in it.

There was a big sunny southwest room, empty except for a little tin trash-burner stove and a naked old wire cot. The other three rooms were all in a row along the north side of the house. In the room off the kitchen, boxes of canned goods, hundred-pound sacks of flour and sugar, and cases of dried fruit were stacked along the walls and there was a little pile of coal in one corner. The middle room was empty. In the third one, our bedroom, an old iron bedstead was the only piece of furniture.

The house was floored and ceiled with wide pine boards, the walls were plastered and fairly clean, the deep windows were wide and double-sashed. There wasn't a curtain anywhere, and it seemed like there was an awful lot of bare space. But I liked it and I could hardly wait to get started fixing it up.

I was washing the breakfast dishes next morning and Bert was shaving at the mirror over the kitchen sink when a man rode into the yard. "That's Bob Robinson, from the next valley east," Bert said. "He's been riding over every day or so to feed the chickens."

He called "Come in," and a stocky young fellow pushed the door open, took a quick look around, then grinned and said, "Yep, when I saw that new cupboard and all those dishes, I figured you'd gone off to get married, Bert."

That forenoon I cut fancy scalloped edges on sheets of clean newspaper and lined the cupboard shelves. Then I put all our new dishes through a pan of hot soapsuds. And when I had them all in the cupboard: the glass set, the blue set, and the set Bert bought, they looked so pretty I could hardly bear to shut the doors.

Chapter Twenty-Nine

I HAD lived at the ranch a month before I left it for the first time, the Sunday before Thanksgiving, when we rode over to Tregos to get the mail.

Bert had spent the whole month picking cow chips from the winter bed-grounds around the meadow, and piling them up near the kitchen door. It was already late in the season for chip picking, he said, the evening we pulled in at the ranch. A heavy, wet snow might bury the chips on the prairie any time now, and the little pile of coal in the storeroom, freighted in across fifty miles of sandhills, had to be saved for really cold weather, or a long wet spell.

Except for mealtimes, I had been alone all day all that month. But I was busy, too, for I had my house to clean and "furnish."

All the time I was growing up, on the homestead and the other places we had lived, Mama had "made do" with the little or nothing she had on hand to fix up her homes. Now I found I could do the same. We didn't have a table for the living room, so I made one by driving two old broomsticks into the sod wall and laying a wide board across them. I covered the shelf with a pretty scarf and put the parlor lamp and the Bible on it and set my rocking chair beside it. With old blankets for padding and one of my quilts for a cover, I turned the old wire cot into a decent front-room couch.

For a spare bed in the empty middle room, I propped an old bedspring from the Squaw Creek shack on canned goods boxes, and covered the bed and boxes with the pretty quilt I had made that long, lonesome winter at Aufdengartens. There wasn't a closet or a chest of drawers in the whole big house, but I made out with stacks of boxes, covered with pretty calico curtains. And when I had hemmed and hung curtains at all the deep windows, the house really looked nice.

I hadn't actually been lonesome, that month, but sometimes, after Bert had driven away to pick another load of chips, I'd go out and stand in the yard, looking off across the hills and trying to "locate" the neighbors he had told me about. Except for Bob Robinson in the next valley east, there was no one else for ten miles in that direction. To the north only the "Rupp boys," a pair of middle-aged bachelors, lived between us and the Huffman ranch, up Lena way. An old couple named Skinner lived in the next valley to the west. They had two bachelor sons; the elder worked out to support his folks, the younger lived at home.

Tregos and Schicks were on west of Skinners. Nate Trego and Johnny Schick, old friends of Bert's, had married sisters and settled in the same big valley. South of us, fifteen miles away at the forks of the creek, our nearest neighbors were the Johnsons I had known on the Birdwood. Off to the southeast there was no one at all, not for miles and miles. Bert said this was a man's country, free range and lots of it, and he liked it that way.

So I was glad when Bert said we'd ride over to Tregos for the day and pick up our mail—which they picked up with theirs from a mailbox on the Sutherland-Lena

road, two miles farther west. I knew there'd be letters
from home, and I had been wanting to meet the Tregos
ever since I came to the ranch.

I'll never forget the ride across the hills that crisp,
sunny November morning when I, a rancher's wife, went
to pay my first call on another rancher's wife. Bert
always had good horses, and that day he rode Mage, a
long-legged, powerful bay, and I rode the big gray,
Dewey. Bert said Dewey was the smartest and best horse
on the ranch. He was fast and quick, and it hadn't taken
long to gentle him to my long riding skirts.

In the first valley west of ours we passed the Skinner
soddy, lonesome-looking against the hills a half mile north
of the trail. Then there were only empty hills until, at
the end of our six-mile ride, we came out into the Trego
valley, a long, wide flat with an old, bare, dry lake bed
in the middle. The Schick soddy squatted on the north
bank of the old lake, and Tregos' house, half log, half
frame, was located under a high, dark hill half a mile
farther on. I was surprised to see a log house in these
treeless hills, but Bert explained that it had been built
on the Dismal River, away to the north, where trees
grew. Years later it had been moved down here, then
Nate Trego bought the ranch, got married, and set up
housekeeping in it. Later, he had added two more rooms.

Nate Trego was tall and thin. He had kind eyes and
a warm, friendly smile. His wife was plump and quick,
with dark, laughing Irish eyes. She told me she was sorry
she hadn't been over to see me yet but, since she was
"expecting" in another month, she wasn't making any
trips away from home now. They already had three
children, Harriet, six; Helen, four; and little Bill, two.

Mrs. Trego (we have been good friends for nearly
sixty years now, but we still call each other "Mrs. Trego"

and "Mrs. Snyder") was a fine cook—but she had milk and cream and butter to cook with. "I've been trying to get Bert to break a cow to milk," I told her. "But he says you can't break a range cow, and if you could she wouldn't give enough milk to keep a cat."

"I know," she said, laughing. "You'll find out it takes quite a while to break a cowboy to milk cows and plow a garden."

At dinner they talked about Mike David, and the big Thanksgiving dance he was giving to celebrate the opening of his store in Tryon. Mike, a young Syrian, had come to Tryon five or six years back, a peddler's pack on his back. For a year or two he had tramped the hills with his wares. Then he bought a horse and buggy to carry his goods and covered a wider scope of country. After that it didn't take long to put up a real store, Tryon's first, and the opening was to be Thanksgiving Day, and the big dance that night.

Tryon dances were held in the courthouse, and usually on Friday nights. They lasted all night, and folks coming from a distance took care of any county business they might have before they left for home on Saturday morning. "In a county as dang big as this one a man has to make a trip to the county seat count for all he can," Bert said.

"It's too bad the county seat has to be so far down in one end of the county," I said, remembering Mr. Aufdengarten's long rides to commissioners' meetings.

"You're darn right it's too bad," Bert said. "This county's seventy-two miles long and the county seat's only twelve miles from the east end. It ought to be in the middle, somewhere around Nate's place here, but with three quarters of the people living in the east end, we'll never be able to move it by vote."

Bert and I rode down to Tryon for the big Thanks-giving dance.

It was early dusk when we topped the last long hill and looked down on Tryon, the only town in all of big McPherson County. There was yellow lamplight in the windows of the courthouse, the new store, and the town's three houses. Back of one house, the only two-story build-ing in the county, a few cottonwoods showed against the skyline. They were the only trees in town. Beside the courthouse and the houses, windmills turned in the fresh-ening night wind.

We tied our horses to the hitchrack and followed a sandy path through a turnstile in the barbed-wire fence that kept the settlers' cattle from rubbing the corners off the sod courthouse. Mike David shook hands with Bert at the door and bowed to me. The tall, dark, good-looking storepeeker was in his early twenties. He had a neat little mustache and flashing white teeth; his words were quick and clipped-sounding, and he was the politest man I had ever met.

In the middle of the room two fiddlers and a guitar player, perched on chairs on top of the big commissioners' table, were playing a lively tune, and the dance was already in full swing. At midnight, when the musicians laid down their instruments and hopped off the table, Mike invited everybody to step across the street to see his new store.

The "street" was a half-acre patch of loose sand, and the little one-room sod store was so new it still smelled of damp sod and pine boards. By the light of a hanging kerosene lamp we filed through it, appreciating the good stock of hardware, groceries, shoes, overshoes, and over-alls piled on the unpainted shelves. There were even a few "notions" and bolts of cotton cloth for the womenfolk. Small and rough as it was, the store had a solid look about it and Mike was tremendously proud of it.

Back at the courthouse, we ate Mike's bologna sandwiches and ginger snaps and drank his strong black coffee, and then the dance went on. Around two in the morning a few couples began digging sleeping children out of the sardine pack under the big table. The dance was still going strong when, at four, Bert said we'd better be going, that he had arranged to meet a fellow at the Diamond Bar that day to work some cattle. I had had a good time and met a lot of friendly people, but when we fell into bed a little before daylight, that November morning, it seemed to me I had never in my life been so tired.

An hour later Bert called me to fix his breakfast while he did the chores and fed and saddled his horse. The sun was just coming up when he rode west a little later. I watched him halfway across the meadow, then washed up the breakfast things and tidied the kitchen and went back to bed.

The sun, shining square into my face through the west bedroom window, woke me. Still groggy with sleep, I stumbled to the front door and looked out; and there was Bert, riding home across the meadow with the sun going down behind him.

Early in December, Bert shut his crop of calves up in the big corral to wean them. It was a noisy business. The calves lined up inside the fence and bawled for three or four days and nights, and the mothers lined up on the outside and bawled for the same length of time.

I coaxed at Bert to milk one of the bawling cows. Even if she didn't give much, I said, I could do a lot with just a *little* milk and cream for cooking. "It won't work," he said, but he got on his horse and roped and hauled two of the long-legged, balky mothers into the little corral. A week later, when they still tried to kick the place to pieces every time we went near them with a milk bucket, I had to admit the idea was no good.

That fall, too, I learned another fact that most ranch wives learn, sooner or later—that, to a true ranchman, *cows* come first. On a ranch the seasons are marked only by calving, branding, haying, and shipping. In the spring the rancher can't leave his cows until their calves are all on hand and wearing his brand. In summer he has to put up enough hay to last them through the winter. The first frosts have come by the time shipping is finished, and after that he must be around in case of a prairie fire or a blizzard, twin threats that hang over the herd until the hay is all fed in the spring—and by then it's calving time again.

I had planned all fall to go down home at Christmas time, and bring Nancy and my buggy back to the ranch, and I had hoped that Bert would go with me. But he said he couldn't leave the ranch that long in winter. So he took me down to Florry's and I went on to Roten Valley with her and John. And Pearl, who had been wanting to come up to the ranch, was to come back with me in the buggy.

I stayed on with the folks for a week after Christmas, enjoying the bustle and fun of my big family again. The crops had been good in the valley, the cattle were doing well again, and Poppie didn't look worried any more. On New Year's Day we went to Aunt Hester's, where I saw Grandma McCance for the last time. After Aunt Dicy's death she had gone to live with Aunt Hester. Now, looking more than ever like an old piece of good whitleather, she still helped with the housework and the care of her little granddaughter. Her mouth was firm and her shoulders straight and she meant to keep busy and do her full duty to the last, the Lord willing, and more could hardly be expected of a body while passing through this vale of tears. When we left she gave me a big box of carpet rags. "I've sewed up more'n Hester'll ever get made up, so you might as well have these," she said.

The next day I left for the ranch with Nancy and the buggy. But that night at Maxwell I found Pearl sick abed with a bad sore throat, so I had to make the long trip back to the hills alone after all.

Bert had butchered a beef while I was gone, and on a bright, cold January day we drove over to Skinners with a front quarter in the back of the buggy. Skinners had no cattle, and to Bert a winter without beef was unthinkable, so he had been taking the old folks a quarter each winter he'd been in the hills. They were a lonely pair, this old couple, marooned for the last years of their lives in the north end of a sandhill valley. They made the most of our visit, chattering like friendly magpies, and when we left they followed us out to the buggy.

"I see you've been able to get lilacs to grow in your valley," I said of the row of leafless little bushes beside the soddy, the first I had seen in the sandhills.

"Oh, you oughta see my posies in the spring." The old lady sparkled. "And wait till you've seen the wild roses in bloom on these hills. That hill, back of the barn there, is covered with 'em, come June, and it's the prettiest sight in all creation."

Winter closed down on us soon after that, and I wasn't off the ranch again until spring. Nate Trego came by once, on his way to commissioners' meeting in Tryon, and brought our mail. Their baby, little Mose, was born on New Year's Day, he said. Bob Robinson stopped in a time or two, so did the Rupp boys and one or two other lone horsebackers, but that was all.

I came near having time on my hands again that winter. But Grandma had told me, long ago, that if she ever ran out of anything else to do she could always sew carpet rags. So I brought out the rags she had given me, put Bert's wornout shirts and old cowboy blankets with them, and started in to sew enough rags to make a carpet for the living room.

The winter was nearly over when Bert began to run a fever one evening. Three days later, with the fever scorching him to a crisp, he decided the cows could look after themselves for a day or two and let me put him to bed on the couch by the living-room stove. I wanted to go for help then, but he said no, that he'd be all right if he stayed in bed a day or so. But two days later, when he was finally willing for me to go, he was so sick that I was afraid to leave him. This was the one thing I had been afraid of, so far out in the hills, and now I didn't know what to do.

And then, a little after dark, Nate stopped in. He had gone through the south end of the valley early that morning, on his way to commissioners' meeting, he said, but figured he'd have more time to stop on the way back. As soon as he saw how sick Bert was, he said it looked like he'd better hit the road for Sutherland at daylight and see old Doc Gordon. "You'd better take my Mage horse then," Bert said. "He'll get you there and back in a day, and come in pullin' on the bit besides.

Nate took Mage and went on home, and I sat up with Bert again that night. By morning he was so weak and sunken-eyed that I was afraid help would come too late after all. I hadn't had my clothes off for two days and I was ready to drop in my tracks from weariness, worry, and lack of sleep. I didn't see how I could possibly get through that day alone—and then Johnny Schick came riding in to see what he could do to help. Bert asked him to see that the cattle were fed, and then dozed in a half-delirious sleep.

Nate came just after dark, bringing medicines and instructions from the doctor. They sent me to bed and told me not to worry, that they would sit up with Bert that night and have him on his feet by morning.

I was pulling off my clothes in the bedroom when I heard Nate tell Bert, "That Mage horse of yours is sure a dandy. I rode him more than seventy miles today, and, like you said, the nearer home he got the faster he traveled."

Nate was right about Bert. He was on his feet by morning, and ready for breakfast. Two days later he was out looking after the cattle.

In March I set half a dozen hens in little coops behind the barn. One afternoon, after I had tended them, I stopped to watch the cattle drifting in to water at the tank in the big corral. One cow had a new calf with her, and I went up to the fence for a better look at the little fellow. The other cows looked walleyed at me, then backed away and headed for the open, but the calf's mother just stood and chewed her cud. Then I noticed her bag. Most range cows have skimpy bags, but this one was full and deep, like a good milk cow's.

I stood looking at her for a long time, thinking how good a drink of fresh milk would taste, and of all the things I could do with milk and cream and butter; of the cakes and cream pies and custards I could bake to take the place of the stewed prunes, dried apples, and canned peaches of which I was so tired.

I brought a throw rope from the barn and tossed the

loop over the cow's head. When she didn't seem to mind that, I pulled the loop tight and tied her to a snubbing post in the middle of the corral. Then I brought a pail and walked up to her, talking to her the way I used to talk to old Pearlie and Love, and then I went ahead and milked her.

At supper, when Bert asked where all the milk came from, I told him about the cow.

"Oh, yeah, *that* cow. She's one of a bunch I brought up from Maxwell last spring. Her mother's a milk cow and she was a skimmer calf, that's why she was so tame," he said.

So Bert kept the cow in, and we broke the calf to drink milk from a bucket. And from then on we had plenty of milk, cream, and butter. Now, if I only had a garden.

But when I asked Bert about *that*, just a little fenced-in patch by the tank, where I could water it, he said, "You can't raise a garden in the sandhills. Everybody knows that."

Chapter Thirty

GRASS came early that first spring I was on the ranch, and Bert said he would have to hurry to get the cattle dipped and moved down on the Squaw Creek range.

After the big mange outbreak, Ed Huffman had built a dipping vat at his ranch. He dipped for all the ranchers round about, at so much a head, and Bert had dipped there the past three springs. I went along, the day Bert drove his cattle up there, and when I saw the vat I understood why Poppie and the other little cattlemen hadn't been able to afford one.

It was a watertight tank, almost as big as a railroad freight car. A big, open fire, kept going under its steel bottom, warmed the foul-smelling dip, and corrals, chutes, and ramps led into and out of it. A crew of men on horseback, yelling and swinging their ropes, crowded the cattle up a chute to the vat and pushed them off the ramp into the thick, brown dip. They went all the way under and came up swimming, headed for the slope at the far end of the vat, where they scrambled out onto another ramp and down a chute to the holding pen. Dipping was rough and dirty, and now and then a critter drowned in the vat, but in a few years' time it rid the range of mange.

Bert caught a bad cold the day of the dipping, and the cold turned into quinsy, an ailment he'd had twice

before, he said. The first time he had been where he could
go to a doctor and have the abscess lanced. The second
time, two years back, Nate had come along just in time
to keep him from choking to death. "He whetted his
knife good and sharp and flamed it with a match, then
he reached down in my throat and cut the gathering,
and that was the end of it," he told me.

But this time we had to tough it out by ourselves, for
Nate was away and there was no one else Bert wanted poking around in his throat with a sharp knife. He couldn't
eat, or talk, and by the end of a week of walking the
floor in torment it looked like he might starve to death
before he choked. Finally, he took one of my long hat
pins and held the point in a match flame. Then he handed
it to me, making signs for me to stick it down his
throat and puncture the abscess.

I tried, but I was too much afraid of poking the point
through his windpipe, or his jugular vein, to dare to stick
it through anything at all, so we had to give that up.
At daylight, next morning, he made signs that he wanted
to try to drink some milk. I gave him the glass and he
took a mouthful. He tried twice to swallow it. On the
third try, it went down. Then an awful expression came
over his face and he *yelled*, "My gosh! Why would you
give a man *rotten* milk when he's sick anyway?" He
ran outside, spitting and sputtering.

I was so surprised to hear him talk, and at what he
said, that I couldn't move for a minute. Then I ran
out after him. He was standing in the yard, looking
sheepish. "I guess that gathering broke when I tried to
swallow," he said. "It was that pus squirtin' into my
throat that tasted bitter as gall."

June came, scattering drifts of wild rose blossoms over
the hills, and old Mrs. Skinner was right—there was

nothing in creation quite like the Junetime glory of the sandhills. Near the end of the month, Pearl came up to spend a week with us.

Bert was too busy getting ready for haying to take his sister home at the end of her visit, so I took her back to Maxwell in my buggy. While I was there I made myself a new dress on her sewing machine, a dress trimmed with dozens of rows of fine tucks.

I went back to the ranch by way of Florry's and stayed there long enough to make her a dress like mine, with all the rows of little tucks. When I left I took Grandma Houk along for a visit at the ranch.

The Squaw Creek roads, always rough and rutted, were the worst I had ever seen them, and by the time we pulled in at the ranch that evening I had a terrible backache. A few days later our first baby, too soon by many weeks, was stillborn. I blamed myself; I shouldn't have made the long, hard buggy trip in the first place, and I shouldn't have treadled a sewing machine all those hours, making those little tucks. But I had always done such things, and it hadn't occurred to me that it could hurt me now, or the baby.

Bert made a coffin from a stout little ammunition box, and I told kind old Grandma Houk where to look in my box cupboard for a lovely little featherstitched silk doll quilt that Aunt Ollie had given me years before. They wrapped the baby in the little quilt and laid her in the box. And while Bert nailed the lid gently down above her, some lines, learned long ago, came into my mind:

> You are quiet,
> and forever.
> Though for us the silence is so loud with tears.

Bert buried the tiny coffin in the yard at the foot of the little cottonwood tree. As soon as I was able, I went out and put a frame of narrow boards around the little grave.

I was up and about again by the day of the big hailstorm, one of the worst ever to strike our section of the sandhills. The only reason it didn't cause more destruction was because there were so few homes and gardens to be damaged.

Bert had finished haying and Grandma Houk had gone home, and I was alone that day, except for Towser, the Shepherd puppie Bert had brought up from the creek across his saddle a few weeks before. The day was hot and sultry, even at sunup, when Bert left for the creek. By noon even the soddy, with the doors shut and the blinds pulled, was terribly warm. Towser, who usually waited on top of the old manure pile south of the corrals for Bert to come home, left his post and dug in on the north side of the house where there was still a scrap of shade.

In the middle of the afternoon purple clouds suddenly rushed out of the northwest. I hurried outside to hustle a batch of half-grown chickens into their coops and to get a tub of dry chips. But the storm came on so fast that I was still at the chip pile when lightning and thunder began to rock the valley. I ran for the house with the chips, at the same time that Towser came flying around the corner, his tail between his legs, and dived into the deep recess of the kitchen doorway. He crouched there, shivering and whining, and I stepped over him to set the tub down in the kitchen. And then the sky seemed to break wide open. Rain and hail poured out, crashing on the tin roof with the most unearthly roar I ever heard.

The sickly green blaze of the lightning was a steady

THE SOD COURTHOUSE IN TRYON, AS IT LOOKED WHEN I FIRST SAW IT IN 1903

Nate Trego is the center horseman in the picture

THE McCANCES, 1905

Front row: Esther, Poppie, Earl, Mama, Roy. *Back row:* Nellie, Florry, Ethel, Grace, Stella, Elsie

glare; the hail made so much noise on the roof that I could no longer hear the thunder. I ran from one window to another, but I couldn't see a thing for the sheets of rain and hail. I was glad that I didn't have a garden out there, getting the living daylights pounded out of it, but I wondered about my young chickens; their coops sat flat on the ground. The valley must be a running flood by now.

The passing of time is all comparative, fast or slow, depending on what one waits for. Five minutes would probably seem like a short time if you were going to be shot dead at the end of it, but the minutes were endless while I waited for the terrible fury of the hailstorm to let up. Then it stopped as suddenly as it started, and I flung on my wraps, pulled on a pair of Bert's old boots, and ran outside. A strong wind was blowing and it was cold, colder by at least seventy degrees than it had been fifteen minutes before. All across the valley hail and water rushed by in a foot-deep flood, and deep white drifts of hail had lodged against the north sides of the buildings and corrals.

I sloshed to my chicken coops, and icy water splashed over my knee-high boot tops every time I stepped into a low place or slipped off a slippery clump of bunchgrass. Most of the poor chickens were floating on top of the water in their coops. A few were still on their feet but so cold and wet that, by the time I had them all gathered into a tub, they were stretched out flat, too, as dead-looking as the others.

I rushed twenty-two of them to the house and built up a quick, hot chip fire. Then I spread all the stiff, blue carcasses on the oven door and on chairs and boxes around the stove. In a little while twenty of them were on their feet again, chirping drearily and picking at the feathers plastered to their skins. They reminded me of embarrassed ladies trying to pull their petticoats down around their bare legs.

By the time I had revived the chickens the sun was shining again, Towser had gone back to his knoll to watch for Bert, and a big, bright rainbow arched across the valley. The water had mostly all run off, leaving the yard beaten as bare as the floor, and the little cotton-wood hadn't a leaf left.

Late in the afternoon Bert came jogging up across the meadow, splashing through pools of water and drifts of ice. Where he had been, over on West Creek, the sun had blazed all afternoon, he said, but on the way home he saw there had been a big rain on Squaw Creek. South of the big hill drifts of hail, carried down the creek on the high water, had lodged in the bends, and on the north side the hail had mowed the grass clean. The farther north he rode the worse the damage the storm had left behind it.

Little Jake Rupp rode down from Shinbone Valley the next day. He and Chris hadn't finished haying yet, "But ve qvit now. Der isn't a t'ing lef' to cut," the little Dutchman told us. Not a standing spear of grass in all of big Shinbone Valley, or any of the valleys to the north.

We ate Christmas dinner that year at Tregos, and when I came into her kitchen Mrs. Trego was setting the table for fifteen. "Oh, Nate ran onto a shack full of half-starved homesteaders down on East Creek the other day," she told me. "They looked like they hadn't had a square meal in a coon's age, especially the kids, so he told 'em to come up and have Christmas dinner with us."

May Trego was used to "extras" at her table anyway, for their ranch, so near the main road from Lena to the

Platte Valley, was a natural stopping place for north- and south-bound travelers, and the family seldom sat down to a meal alone. For years Mrs. Trego baked big batches of bread every other day, or oftener. "I wouldn't be surprised," she told me once, "but what, when Gabriel blows his horn for me I'll have to tell him to wait while I take my bread out of the oven."

Grass was as late, that second spring, as it had been early the year before; and because of it I came to own a good steer calf.

Artie Plumer and Bert's brother John brought a bunch of thin, weak cows up from Maxwell to the Squaw Creek range for Bert to look after. They could hardly have done a worse thing, for the first new grass came on in the soft, boggy bends of the creek: death traps for the weak, hungry cattle. Bert rode to the creek every day that May, and almost every trip he pulled bogged cows out of the marshy bends.

One evening he roped a played-out cow and drug her from a bog. The next day he found her dead, with a newborn calf bawling over her. "It was too far to carry the poor little fella home on my horse," he told me when he got home, "but if you want to drive down tomorrow and get him, you can have 'im."

Early the next morning I hitched Nancy to the buggy and went after the calf. I found him beside his dead mother, glassy-eyed and too weak to bawl any more. I brought him home and hand-fed him for a couple of weeks. Then we put him on a range cow that had lost her calf—but I didn't forget that he was mine.

That spring, too, I made up my mind I was going to have a garden.

A package of Kinkaid garden seeds had come in the mail, in March, and I didn't intend to let them go to waste. Moses P. Kinkaid, the Nebraska congressman who campaigned with the free garden seeds, had gotten a new homestead law passed in Washington the year before. Under the new law, a homesteader could file on a full section of *sandhill* land, instead of only the one quarter allowed in other parts of the state. The shabby family we had met at Tregos Christmas Day were the first "Kinkaiders" to come into our section of the hills.

This time, when I asked Bert to fence off a garden patch in the corner of the big corral by the tank, I promised him that, if I couldn't raise all we could eat on it, I would never say another word about a garden.

"I tell you, you can't raise a garden in the sandhills," he told me again. But he went ahead and fenced off the little patch I wanted. The soil was soft and rich and I planted my seeds in close, straight rows. Two weeks later, the garden was green with fine, thrifty vegetables. Another week and we'd have all the radishes and lettuce we could eat.

Then a man from Tryon came riding through the hills, looking for a horse he had turned on the open range in the fall. He found it, running with some others near our place, and brought the whole bunch into our corral. Bert roped the horse for him, but when the loop tightened on its neck it bawled and snorted and jumped the high, tight new fence and landed, upside down, in my garden. He wallowed down half the garden getting on his feet again. And by the time the men had dragged the fighting bronc out through the narrow gate in the corner, they had plowed up the rest of it.

The horse's owner looked at what they'd done and said, "My gosh! What will your missus say?" Then he left, before he had a chance to find out.

After a while Bert came to the house and told me I'd

better come out and look at my garden. "I told you you couldn't raise a garden in the sandhills," he said sadly.

Near the end of May Mrs. Johnny Schick brought her six-month-old twins and came over to spend an afternoon with me. She said she had come on purpose to bring me a warning. "You never can tell about a baby. I've had six and I know. If I were you, I wouldn't put that trip off much longer now. If you do you're likely to get caught right here in these hills."

I hadn't planned to go down to Florry's for another three weeks yet, but she might be right, and I couldn't afford to take a chance—not after what had happened a year ago. So I packed my suitcase and headed south a day or two later. Bright buffalo pea blossoms covered the green hills and the season was coming fast toward its rose-crowned peak, but I hoped to be home again before the roses faded, or at any rate in plenty of time to cook for Bert's hay crew.

At Florry's I learned of Grandma McCance's death. She had died of a heart attack the week before, in less than twelve hours after she felt the first pain, and they had buried her beside Aunt Dicy in Walnut Grove. So Grandma had gone the way she wanted to, busy right up to the last, with no time on her hands to worry about.

I had been at Florry's a month when Nellie Irene was born on the twentieth of June. For most of the month it had rained hard every afternoon, and when Bert came down to see the baby he brought old Daisy, a work mare, for me to drive home with Nancy. "This is the wettest summer we've had in years," he said, "and the Squaw Creek road is washed so bad you'll need two horses to get the buggy home."

Stell and her little boy went home with me, and we left for the ranch the day the baby was two weeks old.

The July sun was hot and the road was only a twisting, lopsided washout that got rougher by the mile. On Squaw Creek a wheel dropped into a hole with a jerk that broke the doubletree in two.

"Well," I told Stell, "I guess this is as far as the buggy goes."

We unhitched the team and Stell took little Merle with her on Daisy, and I took the baby with me on Nancy and we went on to the ranch, leaving the buggy half tipped over in the ruts behind us.

Later, when the hay was up and the hay men gone, Stell and I went down to Roten Valley. Bert took us as far as North Platte, where he loaded up a load of winter supplies and pulled right out for the ranch. I hadn't been to town since I had taken Pearl home, more than a year before, and I needed some things from the stores. It was early September, but the afternoon was frightfully hot, and the baby was too heavy to carry while we shopped. I was about to give it up when I saw a sign above a little shop, advertising baby buggies for hire. I went in and rented the only one there, an enormous, high-wheeled thing with a faded silk umbrella askew above it.

That night we stayed in North Platte's best hotel. Our second-floor room was clean and cool and we washed ourselves in a big washbowl on a commode, with water from a tall stoneware pitcher. But for the rest of our toilet we had to travel down a long hall to a back door, then across a high, narrow, railed bridge that spanned a dreary patch of ash piles, tin cans and garbage, to a slim, narrow two-story affair that was labelled "Ladies" on one side and "Gentlemen" on the other.

Poppie and Roy met us in Cozad the next afternoon with a new two-seated carriage, the kind we used to admire so much in the Fourth-of-July parades. In the two years since I had been home Poppie had built the new house—and Mama finally had her parlor. She brought the key from its "hidey hole" in her keepsake box in the top drawer of the old bureau and unlocked the door to show it to me. But she had told us so often about the parlor in her old home in Missouri that my first glimpse of this one was like looking into a room I had seen before.

Mama crossed to the window and ran up a fringed green linen blind, letting the sunshine in through the stiff lace curtains. And there was the Brussels carpet, with its big red roses and green leaves, and the red velvet love seat against one wall, the organ against the opposite one, and a big unframed seascape on a white and gold easel in the far corner. Two high-backed rocking chairs flanked the clawfooted center table, and the big family pictures in their wide frames hung on the flowered walls.

I looked at Mama, so frail and wispy, standing there in the middle of her parlor, and suddenly I understood what that room meant to her. It was her symbol of prosperity; it meant that she had won out over all the hard years when she had had to have a bed in her front room.

Chapter Thirty-One

Tregos spent Christmas of 1905 with us, and at dinner Nate said in his quiet way, "Bert, it looks to me like we're about to see the last of the free range in this country."

"Why? You don't think those Kinkaiders are going to bother us any here, do you?" Bert asked.

"I'm afraid so. Several took homesteads south and east of Tryon last fall, and I look for more to come in the spring."

Bert didn't see it that way. A man couldn't raise enough cattle on a lone section of land to make a living, he said, and if he plowed it up it would all blow away on the first hard wind. "The ones that are trying it down there'll soon find *that* out, and that'll be the end of it."

"I hope you're right, but I'm thinking we'll soon have a Kinkaider on every section in these hills," Nate said.

Well, Bert said, he wasn't going to worry about it.

But on the first day of May, 1906, a little old man, bent and ragged and dirty, drove a rickety covered wagon into our yard. One of the horses he drove was a pretty fair animal but the other was a sad-looking rack of old bones. The old man said his name was Ed Matthews and that he had filed on a section of land in this valley the fall before; and what was more, according to the "locator" who had shown him around, our buildings were on *his* land and what were we going to do about it?

Bert told him that couldn't be, that he had *seen* the section corners when he bought this place, so he knew he had the right location. "Why didn't you and your locator ask me? I could've showed you that section line."

"You wasn't home," the old man said.

The trick, we learned later, was a common one with some "locators." They picked a time when the owners were gone to point out choice valleys to their prospects, then furnished them a false set of section corner numbers and convinced them that the man who owned the buildings already on the land was only a squatter. They collected fat fees for their work, and by the time the poor settlers found out that they had actually filed on stretches of dry hills *next to the good valleys,* the locators were long gone from the place.

But Bert fed the team and brought the old man in to dinner. He had come from Missouri, he told us between knifefuls, and one of his horses had played out in the bogs on the Platte Valley. It had "gone down" for the last time on the Birdwood and Ferbraches had loaned him another (the better one of the two) to finish the trip. Now, as soon as he "got sot" on his claim, he was going to take the horse back and get a job of work for the summer.

After dinner Bert showed the crusty old man the numbered section corner stake, set by surveyors years before, near the south end of our valley. He had to give in then, that his claim covered only the narrow south edge of the meadow and the rough sandy hills to the south of it. So he drove his outfit just over the boundary line and set up his camp at the west edge of the old plow scar. Bert offered to help him "get sot," but he said he didn't need any help from anybody, then went ahead to scrape out a shallow hole in the ground, set the covered bows of his old wagon over it and move his bunk and stove inside. That done, he came up to tell us he was going to turn his horse loose in the meadow and go back to the Birdwood.

"Sure, turn 'im loose anywhere. He can water with my stock and I'll keep an eye on him," Bert told him.

But the poor old horse, starved too long, grew thinner and thinner. He stopped one day on a knoll a hundred rods north of our house, too tired to take another step. Bert carried water and hay and a little grain from our chicken feed to him—but rest and care had come too late and in June he lay down on the knoll and died. The carcass was out of sight of the house and there was too little meat left on its bones to make much of a smell anyway, so Bert left it where it lay.

Not long after old Matthews moved into our valley I drove down to Tryon with a buggy load of butter and eggs to trade at Mike's store. The town, a hustling, bustling place this spring, had more than doubled in size since the summer before. A new false-fronted frame store, a pool hall, dance hall, and a livery stable had gone up along two crooked, sandy streets and three or four half-built new houses were scattered on the flat. A dozen teams switched flies at the hitchracks, and most of the people I saw in the stores were strangers to me.

In August old man Matthews came hoofing it up across the meadow. He was just back from the Birdwood, he said, and he wanted his horse. Bert took him up to the knoll and showed him what was left of it. He offered to loan him a horse if he needed one, but the old man said he guessed he'd get along, and stomped off to his little dugout.

Before long the story got back to us that the horse had died because Bert had knocked its teeth out so it couldn't eat the grass off his range, and that our roosters crowed so loud and so early that the old man couldn't get a good night's sleep. Worse still, our cattle bothered around his house all the time, and some of them had run off with his broom and eaten it up.

In September Artie Plumer came up to see about shipping some cattle he and Bert owned in partnership. "Bert," he said, "you'd better hurry up and file on the best land next to your place here. You've already got a neighbor in this valley, and by spring there'll be a lot less unclaimed land around here. You'll be plenty short on hay and grass if you don't look out."

But Bert still refused to get excited about homesteaders.

Our son, Miles William, was born the last day of September. I had gone down home for his birth, and Bert came hurrying for a quick look at him as soon as he got the word. He had to hurry back, he said, for the hills were dry as tinder and the danger of prairie fires was bad. So, when I was ready to come home, I'd better take the train to Sutherland and he would meet me there. Then he told me that his sister, Ann McCullough, was moving into Brady from the ranch to put the children in school and he wished I would stop off and visit her on the way. I told him I'd try.

Miles was two weeks old and I was just up and around again, the night I stood in the doorway at Poppie's and watched a bright glow in the sky in the far northwest. Only a big prairie fire could light up the night like that, and if it was within fifty miles of our place I knew Bert was out fighting it. The glow was still there the next night, and I would have given almost anything to have had news of that fire. But the next afternoon it set in

to drizzle for thirty-six hours and the first hard freeze
of the season followed the clearing weather, and by then
the night sky was calm and dark again.

The day the baby was three weeks old Poppie and
Mama took us over to Uncle John's place, a few miles
east of Brady. We stayed all night, and the next afternoon Uncle John and Aunt Irene took us on to Brady.
We stopped first at the little depot and I went in and
bought my ticket and asked when my train was due.

"Two o'clock in the morning," the agent said, and he
slammed his stamp against my ticket in a mean way.
Then I asked if he could tell me where Jim McCullough
lived and he snapped back, "I've no idea. I'm just the
relief agent here and I don't know the burg."

So I went to a store across the street, where I was told
that Ann hadn't moved to town yet. There'd been some
delay, the friendly storekeeper said, and they wouldn't
be moving in for a week or two yet.

I asked Uncle John, then, to take me to the hotel. But
when we pulled up in front of the shabby little place,
two blocks from the depot, he took one look at it and
said, "I sure hate to leave you here."

I didn't like the looks of it any better than he did,
but there was no help for it now. Bert was to meet me
in Sutherland the next morning and I had to go on. So
Uncle John helped me carry my children and luggage
across the broken-down porch into the smoky little office,
where I told him a forlorn good-bye.

I paid a sad-looking woman for a night's lodging and
followed her to a cold, dark, smelly little room. The
only furniture was a sagging bed and a battered old
dresser, and when I turned back the dirty blankets I
uncovered gray, wrinkled sheets—with a mess of hair-
pins, gum wrappers and lint between them—and a pair

of filthy pillows. In the end, I put Miles and Nellie to bed between their own little blankets and pulled the cleanest of the bed blankets over them. Then I turned the wick low in the foul, smoky little lamp, put my coat on, and lay down across the bed. But I got up again in a hurry; for as soon as it was dark and quiet, hordes of bedbugs came crawling from every crack and crevice in the room.

I turned the wick up again and sat on the bed beside my sleeping babies. At midnight, when I couldn't stand the horrible room another minute, I took my suitcases and hurried through the dark, empty street to the depot. The waiting room was empty, except for the night agent at his counter on the other side of the ticket window, and I pushed my bags inside the door and hurried away. Back at the hotel, I took a sleeping baby in each arm, blew out the light, and got out as fast as I could.

When I came into the waiting room again the agent pushed his green eye shade up on his head and took a long look at me. He seemed about to say something, then he pulled the shade down again and turned back to his clacking telegraph key. I sat down on the hard bench in the dim little room, both babies in my lap, and began to wait for two o'clock.

An hour and a half later, when the minute hand on the waiting-room clock pointed to five minutes of two, the agent still sat at his counter. There must not be any mail or freight to go out on this train, I thought, since he wasn't doing anything about getting it to the tracks. At two sharp the rails began to sing and the train whistled for the station, but still the agent didn't move. Why, I wondered, with a scared feeling in the pit of my stomach, why wasn't he getting up to put me on the train.

The train roared on by without even slowing down, and Miles and Nellie woke up, screaming at all the noise. And then I got up and went to the ticket window to ask why the train hadn't stopped.

"That train never stops here," the agent told me. "It runs in two sections and that was the first one. The second one stops, but it's not due till five o'clock."

"But the day agent sold me a ticket for the two o'clock train."

"He should've known better, and I'm sure sorry. When you came in, right after midnight, I had a notion to ask you why you were so early."

I sat down again, wondering if I could possibly hold out till five o'clock. But the agent brought an armful of canvas mail sacks and folded them down on the bench to make a bed for the baby, so I only had Nellie to hold in my arms the rest of the night.

If there is a drearier place in the world than a small-town depot waiting room on a winter night between midnight and five o'clock in the morning, I never want to see it. The only furniture in the room, not counting the spittoon box of old ashes, was the wooden bench and a tall, potbellied rusty stove. The floor was gritty with crusted tobacco juice and coal dust. Everything smelled of stale tobacco and old, old train smoke, and the only light came from a smeary, sputtery little wall lamp.

The second section was late, of course, but it came at last, and at daylight we pulled into North Platte. Little skifts of dirty snow lay along the tracks there, and at Sutherland it was hoof-deep on Bert's team.

On the way home Bert told me about the big fire. It had burned off a wide sweep of hills southeast of the ranch, he said, and the whole country had turned out to fight it. After a day and a night they had had it almost whipped, and then the wind changed and sent it roaring on again. A day later they wiped it out, down in the big bend of the Birdwood. A settler had been caught and burned to death in a head fire that swept a stretch of hills southwest of Tryon in the Rosedale district and a good many haystacks had gone up in smoke, but the fire had not touched our range.

When the fire was over, Nate had taken Bert and Wallace Baskins, a rancher from the head of the Loup River, twenty-five miles east of Tryon, and a wagonload of Huffman men home with him. Most of them had hardly eaten, or slept at all, since the first day of the fire. Nate was "batching," since Mrs. Trego had moved to Sutherland with the children when school started, but he "rustled up grub for the whole bunch," Bert said, and while they were eating, the drizzle that would have helped so much, two or three days ago, set in. So the whole tired bunch of them had bunked down at Tregos, so worn out they slept until noon the next day, and by then the rain had turned to snow and they all had to ride home through a bad storm.

Bert hadn't any more than got back to the ranch in time to check the cattle than he had to start out again to meet the train—but at that he had slept since I had.

Our own trip home that day was long and cold. Heavy snow slowed the team to a walk, and on Squaw Creek frozen drifts across the road forced us to travel on the steep hillsides and ridges, where the snow was not so deep. By the time we came in sight of the soddy in the middle of our frozen valley, I was so tired and cold that I was numb all over. And there were still fires to build in the cold house, and supper to get and the babies to feed and put to bed, before I could think of rest and sleep for myself.

Chapter Thirty-Two

Hardly a soul passed through our valley that winter of the deep snows. There was, as yet, no north and south travel past our place; and the east-west road, broken out only once or twice all winter, soon drifted full again. Even old man Matthews had locked up his dugout and gone to the Birdwood for the winter.

Late in February Nate Trego slogged through the drifts to commissioners' meeting. On his way home the next day he stopped in. "Bert," he said, "this country's going to be full of Kinkaiders in the spring. I just filed on a section joining my place, and Ed Huffman and his boys, and the rest of the fellows up that way, are filing on their best meadows and haylands. It sure looks to me like you'd better hustle down and file on your meadow and a piece of your best rangeland."

Bert agreed that it was time to act.

Since he had filed on the Squaw Creek claim, several years ago, he could claim only three more quarters now, so he filed on the north half of the meadow and the half section of range next to it.

May had come before the last of the big October drifts melted into the spongy ground, and it was surprising how the winter's snow, added to the heavy rains of the past two summers, had changed the face of the sandhills.

Good-sized lakes now stood in most of the "dry" val-

NORTH END OF TRYON, AS IT LOOKED IN 1908 WITH A KINKAID PICNIC CROWD GATHERING FOR A CELEBRATION

THESE PICTURES WERE TAKEN IN THE SUMMER OF 1912
Bert and I are sitting in the car. Billie is the baby. Nellie and Miles stand on the
running board. Unless the weather was really bad, Bert always drove with the top
back and the windshield turned down.

leys. The old lake bed in Trego's valley was half full again, and there were two ponds in our meadow, a small, deep one near the north end and a large, shallow one just west of the house. An old stack bottom, rising with the water in the big one, floated along the west bank until a hard wind brought it across to the east side, where it lay all summer, like a big, gray old badger only a few rods from the house. Ducks, geese, cranes, and even a few pelicans stopped to feed and rest at the new lakes, and curlews and sandpipers came to stay on their shores. The cactus disappeared from the yard and short green grass replaced the bunchgrass. When our lone cotton-wood began to shoot up and look like a tree, Bert was encouraged to set out scores of new little cuttings in rows around the yard.

On the heels of the melting drifts, I took Miles and Nellie with me in the buggy and started for Tryon with butter and eggs, my first trip off the ranch in almost six months. In the south end of the old Robinson Valley, empty since Bob had left the hills a couple of years before, I was surprised to see a tent pitched on the prairie, beside the knee-high walls of a new sod house. Out on the flat two men followed a team and a breaking plow; at the tent a dog barked and a large, plump woman came out.

I drove up and stopped, and the friendly newcomer told me her name was Katie Kirts. The men with the plow were her husband, George, and his brother John. They were from Missouri, she said, and I was the first person they had seen since they pitched their tent a few days back.

I drove on toward Tryon, wondering how long it would be before there'd be soddies in every valley along this road. Bert still thought homesteading was a flurry

that wouldn't last long and that it would be over before it did the country much harm. But I wasn't so
sure. Anyway, a few more people in these hills wouldn't
hurt anything, and when there were enough there would
surely be schools. I didn't want to have to move to town
when Miles and Nellie were ready for school, as Mrs.
Trego and Mrs. Schick had to do, and leave Bert to batch
on the ranch.

Tryon was bigger, and more sprawling than ever.
There were a new blacksmith shop and a candy store. A
sign above another little building read "Tryon Graphic
—Printing." A couple of two-story buildings were going
up. One was the new hotel, the other the Odd Fellows
hall. A four-horse team, pulling a load of lumber through
the deep, loose sand in the street, was straining at the
tugs. Mike David's little sod store looked old and shabby
among all the new frame buildings, but Mike and his
clerk seemed to have all the business they could handle.

When Bert moved the cattle down on Squaw Creek
that same week, he found a new soddy in the bend where
the road crossed the creek. A big family named Bussard
had filed a claim there. On a hot, still spring afternoon
a few days later a young man and two women in a big
wagon stopped to ask if they could pick a load of cow
chips off our range. They had come from Happy Hollow, they said, a new settlement eight or ten miles to
the southeast, and they had been told they would find
plenty of chips on Bert Snyder's range.

Bert sent them to his winter feed ground, where the
chips were thickest, and they came back with a full load.
They stopped in for a drink before pulling on, and I
set chairs for them and brought glasses and a pitcher of
cold water. The women's faces were sweat-streaked and
sunburned, their skirts and stockings were full of sand-

burrs. The young man's name was Reuel Conroy; one
of the women was his sister Margaret, the other a neighbor, Mrs. Mattie Lou Miller.

Mrs. Miller, a small, graceful, pretty woman, dropped
onto her chair with a long sigh and pulled off her cotton flannel gloves and her bonnet. Then she looked sadly
at her slender, dirty hands and wailed, "Oh, dear, I'm
ruined, I'm just ruined, that's all there is to it."

"Oh, we'll live through it," Margaret Conroy said.
"And I'm so thankful to have all those nice chips." She
took off her bonnet, too, and fanned her round, plump
face with it.

The Conroys, old Tom and his eldest son Mike, had
taken claims in the settlement the fall before and had
put up several stacks of hay before going back to their
old home in Dawson County for the winter. When they
came back in the spring their hay was all gone, burned
in the big October prairie fire. Margaret had taught
school for several years. Now, she said, she planned to
live on her homestead in the summers and teach in the
winters.

Mrs. Miller had always lived in town and her husband was a railroad man. The chance to own a section
of land, just for living on it for five years, had been a
bait he couldn't resist, she said. But when their sod house
was built he had had to go back to his railroad job, and
she and their two little boys were "holding down the
claim."

It was an ordinary arrangement. The Kinkaid law re-
quired a claimant to build a set of "improvements" on
his homestead within six months of his filing date. Most
Kinkaiders were out of cash by the time they had put
up a sod house and barn and plowed up a patch of prairie
for a cornfield, so they either went back to old jobs or

found new ones, leaving "the wife and kids" to hold down the claim.

All that summer of 1907 homesteaders trickled into big McPherson County, more than doubling the 1900 population which, according to the *Tryon Graphic*, had been 517. Now, with a count of over 1,000, there was enough to hold a celebration, the first of the big Kinkaider picnics. It was held in Tryon in September and lasted three days. The entertainment was all homemade: bronc riding, steer roping and horse racing in the daytimes, and dancing all night in a big "bowery" the committee built in an empty space between two new stores. Ranchers and settlers from fifty miles around came to the big doings. The town and all the flat around it was filled with tents and rigs and covered wagons. Ed Huffman, Jim Haney, the Whitewater ranch and other big outfits, brought their hayfield cook and bunk wagons along for their men. They also furnished most of the saddle horses and wild stock for the races and contests. Bert and I camped with the Huffmans and Baskins, sharing their tent and campfire.

Margaret Conroy and her tiny Irish mother were among the picnickers. So were Mattie Lou Miller and her handsome little boys, Glenn and Dean. But most of the big crowd were strangers to me, and it seemed odd to see so many women and children—in what I had come to think of as a man's country.

The afternoon shows we had at the big picnics would be called "rodeos" now, but in those days we had never heard of the word. They were held in a wide swale west of the courthouse, and the people sat or stood around the edges to watch. There were neither corrals nor chutes. Men on horseback kept the wild stock bunched for the ropers and riders, and it was a lively show all the way.

Most of the horses had to be blindfolded and "eared" down to be saddled, and the riders, once they got on and somebody yanked the blindfold off, were on their own. There were no "pick-up" men. A man rode until he was thrown or the horse quit pitching.

The races and contests were open to all comers. There were all kinds of horse races: relay races, potato races, men's and ladies' straight races. The whole show was free; but if a performer got hurt, bad enough to need a doctor, they took up a collection to pay his bill.

A friend of Bert's offered me his high-lifed little bay for the ladies' race. The horse, excited by the crowd and the noise, began to rear and fight the bit as soon as I got on him. But we came in a close second anyway, even though he was headed the other way when the starting gun went off.

That evening scores of cooking fires blazed on the big flat. Children ran back and forth between the camps, babies cried, and men and women called to each other. Then the twang of fiddles tuning up called everybody to the big bowery in the middle of the town.

Hours later, we sorted Miles and Nellie from the other played-out, sleeping children in a corner of the dance floor and headed for the tents beside our own campfire. The grass was wet with a heavy dew and a cold little wind blew across the valley, setting us all to shivering. By sunrise the dew had turned to glittering frost—and all the picnickers knew they would go home to gardens frosted black.

That afternoon Ira Huffman challenged Bert to a steer roping and tying contest. Bert drew first chance to rope. The hazers cut a big three-year-old from the bunch and headed him across the flat. Bert, on Dewey, caught him in two jumps. Bert had trained the tall gray horse himself and it was something to see them work together. The instant the throw rope loop left Bert's hand Dewey stopped and leaned back, braced for the throw. But the galloping steer hit the end of the rope with something like the force of a runaway boxcar, and snapped it off at the saddle horn. The steer kept on going.

Bert had jumped off as soon as he made his throw, and was already running toward the steer when the rope broke. He saw then that he'd lost his chance for a tie-down, but he didn't intend to lose his rope, too. So he jumped back on Dewey and caught up to the steer in less time than it takes to tell it. He reached down and caught the steer's tail and yanked the tail over his shoulder, then he spurred ahead and threw the big critter flat on the prairie. Before it could get up again, he jumped down and jerked his rope off its neck. Then, waving his hat to indicate he was through with his part of the show, he stepped up onto Dewey and rode back to the arena.

Throwing a steer by its tail was an old trick to Bert, one he had learned on the Wyoming range, but it was new to most of the picnic crowd and they cheered and hollered like everything at the unexpected and exciting bit of horseplay.

Ira made his try next, and caught his steer in good time. His rope held and the steer went down, but he was a big, heavy man and when he jumped down for the tie he sprained his ankle and had to give it up, too. So they shook hands and called it a draw.

On the way home from that picnic we topped a hill and saw a herd of antelope on the next hill ahead of us. Antelope had been a common enough sight when I first came to the ranch but they had been getting scarcer every year. This herd seemed to stand on tiptoe for a minute, watching us, then they poured away over the rim and out of sight. We didn't know it then, but their going was a sign of the change that had come to the country; for that was the last herd of antelope we were ever to see in the sandhills.

Chapter Thirty-Three

DURING the first four years I was married I was without a sewing machine; while Skinners, over in the next valley, had three of them. Mrs. Skinner had brought hers to the hills with her; Mr. Skinner had inherited his when his sister, the widow Lombard, had died on her claim over northwest of Tregos; and George, the eldest bachelor son, had won his at a raffle up at the Lena store. I had tried to buy one of them; but Mrs. Skinner didn't want to sell hers because she had had it so long; Mr. Skinner didn't want to sell his because it had been his dead sister's; and George didn't want to sell his because he thought he might get married someday and need it.

But I needed a machine the worst way, so in the fall of 1907 I spent the orphan calf I had brought home from Squaw Creek for one. He had grown by then into a fine two-year-old steer and he paid for a good cabinet-style sewing machine. I ordered it from the Montgomery Ward catalog when we made out our regular yearly order.

Every summer, in August, we sent off a big order for a year's supply of groceries, dry goods, tools, and whatever else we needed to run the ranch. In those days the mail-order company listed several pages of "premiums," furniture, linens, jewelry, and the like, and the bigger the order the better the premium. Our orders usually rated pretty good ones, and the first year I was on the ranch I picked out a nice dresser to take the place of the goods boxes I had used until then.

The freight came to North Platte some time in September and Bert hauled it home from there. Those trips were long and hard. He'd leave well before daylight with the big wagon and a four-horse team, and it would be dark by the time he pulled in on the fourth day at the end of the hundred-mile round trip. He made three or four trips every fall, sleeping out two nights and in town one. There was ever a feeling of the need to hurry with the trips and to get the freighting done, for the sandy roads were hard enough to haul heavy loads over; a snowstorm could stop the trips altogether and we were always afraid winter would catch us with part of the freight still in town.

The year I ordered my sewing machine, the freight trips were shortened by thirty miles and one day, for that summer a bridge was built across the North Platte River north of Hershey and Bert could freight from there. The road to Hershey went east of Squaw Creek hill, down a string of valleys that led through Happy Hollow, where the Conroys and Millers lived.

Bert made several extra trips that fall. The six months allowed for building "improvements" on his Kinkaid claim were about up, so, besides the big Montgomery Ward order and flour and sugar and coal, he hauled enough lumber to build a new frame house and barn. When he left on the first trip I told him to be sure and bring my sewing machine on that load, no matter what else he had to leave behind. And while he was gone I cut and basted a pile of little clothes for Miles and Nellie.

It was full dark when the heavy wagon pulled into the yard at the end of the third day. As soon as Bert had taken care of the tired teams, I helped him unload the crated sewing machine and drag it into the kitchen. I could hardly wait to get it open—and I've seldom been so disappointed. For it was nothing but a beautiful sewing machine *cabinet*. The head, shipped in a separate crate, was still in the Hershey depot thirty-five miles away, and I had to wait until Bert made another trip before I could sew a stitch.

As near as Bert could tell by sighting across the meadow from the corner survey stake, the boundary line between his deeded land and the homestead ran about forty feet north of the soddy we lived in. So he located the new house just north of the imaginary line and a little west of the cottonwood tree that now stood tall above the baby's grave. He hired a Kinkaider to build the house, two good-sized rooms with full-length porches on both sides, north and south. (A new survey line, run a few years later, went right through the middle of the south porch.)

The new house was nearly done when I took Miles and Nellie and went down home for Christmas, leaving Bert and his carpenter to batch for the week or so I planned to be gone. John and Florry and Walter and Stell went home for Christmas every year, but I hadn't been there since the first Christmas after I was married. Of course we didn't know it then, but that was the last time we were all to be together.

Ethel and Nellie were grown young ladies, and Elsie, at fifteen, was going to parties with neighbor boys Poppie approved of. Esther was a plump nine-year-old and Roy, thirteen and husky, was Poppie's right-hand man, filling the place I had held so long and been so proud of. Stell had two boys but Florry, already married nine years, was still childless.

Ethel and Nellie had taken over the cooking and cleaning some three years back and Mama, freed from house-work and new babies, had time at last to fuss all she liked over her youngest, spindle-shanked, frail seven-year-old little Earl. She had kept him in shoulder-length curls, and in blouses with wide, ruffled collars, until he was past five. "The rest of you grew up so fast," she told me once, "but I'm going to keep my last one a baby as long as I can."

She had all the time she wanted, too, for her birds. The deep windows in the dining room were full of canary cages. Billie, a bright gold bird, was a roller she had ordered from Germany a year ago. He was trained to sing in a soundproof room where all he ever heard was soft violin music, she told me, and that was why his songs were so low and sweet. His young sons, trained by their foreign-born and educated father, sold well in the community and Mama had made enough money on them to help pay for Polly, her young parrot.

Polly could exactly imitate the voice of every mem-ber of the family. When she called the dogs, Tige and Daisy, they could never be sure it *wasn't* Esther, call-ing them to a meal of table scraps. So they always came. Then, when she'd yell "Sic 'em, sic 'em," and nearly fall off her perch laughing, they'd slink away with their tails between their legs, shamed at being fooled again. At milking time Roy, with a "Soo-o calf, soo-o calf," called the skimmer calves to the yard gate to their buckets of separated milk; but Polly called them a dozen times a day, and kept them bawling at the gate for hours. Mimicking Ethel or Nellie, she yelled "Supper, Poppie" every time she heard, or smelled, meat frying in the kit-chen. Sounding just like Esther, she gave Earl a good scolding almost every time he came in the room where she was. "Esther scolds and bosses Earl around a lot now," Mama told me, "and Polly's just helping her out." The rest of the time she whistled, sang, laughed or cried —until someone pinned an apron over her cage to shut her up.

Poppie still set an early deadline for the girls when they went out with their beaux; but he had grown deaf in one ear and if he was asleep with his good ear to the pillow he seldom heard them when they came in. So they had been getting away with a little time-limit stretching—until the nights turned cold and they began stopping at the dining-room heater to warm their feet. While they took off their shoes and perched their feet on the heater's footrail, they whispered and giggled, very low so as not to wake Poppie. But Polly soon learned to whisper and giggle too. She'd begin as soon as the girls settled down at the heater, and keep it up after they had gone to bed, getting louder and louder until she wakened Poppie. He soon caught on, and, if the hour was late, the girls were in for a good scolding next morning. So, to keep Polly quiet, they had been slinking off to bed with cold feet—and the three of them hadn't spoken one pleasant word to the gabby parrot in weeks.

Florry and John, and Stell and her family, went home the day after Christmas. The next day I started making a new black dress for Mama, and as I worked on the fine black cloth it came to me that, as far back as I could remember, I had never seen my mother in anything but black. I wondered if that was why, although she was only forty-seven now and her hair was still crow's-wing black, she had *never* seemed young to me.

"Mama, why don't you let me make you a dress in some other color, blue or green, or a pretty buff?" I asked her.

"Oh, my, no! I wouldn't feel comfortable in anything but black," she said, and I knew there was no use saying any more about it.

While I sewed, Polly, bobbing, ducking, and chinning herself on her perch, would now and then leave off humming like a sewing machine and scream "Pretty Polly, pretty Polly," until Mama handed her a scrap of the black cloth. Draping it around her neck, Polly'd pull and pat it until she had it crossed just right on her bright breast. Then she'd set both feet on her perch, say "There" in a satisfied tone, and sit like a statue for half an hour, steeped in her own vanity.

I hadn't quite finished the dress when we began coming down with bad colds. I was still miserable with mine when Miles took sick.

Miles was the plump, healthy kind that such sickness went hard with. He sickened fast, and we sent for Doctor Fochtman on New Year's Day. The good doctor shook his head over the feverish baby and told me what I already knew—that we "had a mighty sick little boy on our hands." Pneumonia, he said, and I had never been so scared. So many babies died of pneumonia.

Miles was a bottle baby. Since he was a tiny thing he had seemed to think more of his bottle than anything else, and now he hung onto it as if his life depended on it. "He's too sick to take milk now," the doctor told me that first day. "Just keep warm water and a few drops of cream in the bottle, and let him have it as much as he wants it." Day and night, he held it in his hot little hands, and now and then he took a tiny sip. Once, when I went to take it from him to put in fresh water and cream, he held it tight and tried to cry out. But the cry hurt him, twisting him with pain, and after that I filled the fresh bottle first and offered it in exchange for the fever-hot one he held, and then he willingly gave it up.

After three long weeks, there came a day when the baby was too weak and sick even to sip from his bottle; a day when the doctor listened to his feeble heartbeat and shook his head and didn't say a word.

Aunt Irene had stayed with us most of the time, doing what she could to help, and Mrs. Frank Woodside, from the old Holmes place on the far side of the schoolhouse, came over to help at night. But it was Poppie who was my main help and stay. When everyone else had given up, he kept telling me that "God and Doc Fochtman" would pull my baby through. And when even the doctor didn't think it could be done, Poppie still said we'd save him.

And that's the way it was. The baby finally began to get better, but the way back was slow. We never left him alone for a minute, and for two weeks after the crisis the doctor came every day to direct us in the delicate care he needed. One thing he cautioned us about was to keep the air dry. "Don't even hang any wet clothes in the house," he said. Nowadays we are told to keep the air moist, and when anyone gets a sniffle we start the vaporizer the first thing.

Late in February I took the children home, and even the trip back to the ranch was a part of the long nightmare. We went as far as Maxwell on the train and stayed all night with Bert's folks, where I had left the team and buggy on the way down, two months before. The sun was barely shining when we left the next morning, and by noon the day had turned cloudy, cold, and raw.

I hurried the team along, for Miles was still thin and weak and I was afraid he'd get chilled and be sick again. Even so, it was getting dark by the time I drove down the steep hill to the forks of the creek, across from the Johnson place. I planned to stay all night there, and lamplight shining from a soddy window never looked so good before. Then, at the edge of the creek, I had more trouble.

Nancy remembered her years on the Birdwood and was willing to take the crossing, but her teammate, a little mare from the ranch, would not put a foot into the water. I tried again and again to get her into the creek, but all she would do was rear up and lunge backward. When Nellie began to howl with fright, I got out and unhitched the team. Then I took the children across the creek on Nancy, and on to the house, where I turned them over to Mrs. Johnson.

Mrs. Johnson was alone in the house at the forks that night, so I had to go back and get the buggy across by myself. I managed it by riding back across the creek and looping the other mare's bridle reins over my arm and coaxing at her until I got her to follow Nancy across the stream. When she found out it wasn't going to hurt her to get her feet wet, I led her back and hitched her up again with Nancy and drove the buggy across.

We went on home the next day. The carpenter had finished and gone, weeks ago, and Bert had moved into the unplastered new house. The plaster was stored in the old soddy, but he hadn't been able to find anyone who knew how to put it on. Even so, the house didn't look bad, for the inside finish, a new "patent lath," was a solid sheathing of neat, grooved boards.

Chapter Thirty-Four

IN THE spring of 1908 homesteaders' wagons rolled into the hills in a steady wave. Among the first to come our way were Ed Price and his wife and six children. Their section joined us on the north. Right behind them came old man Brandt, a short, round Dutchman who filed on the next section east. The Moorhead family took a claim in the hills just west of our valley and lived all summer in a little oilcloth and canvas shelter. Young Bob Harrison took a section cornering us on the northeast. Bob Kirts, brother to George and John, filed on a hilly patch north and east of old man Matthews'. A friend of theirs, an old man named Van Dyke, settled on a section next to John's.

One warm day that spring, a neat, plump woman carrying a fat baby came to our door. "I'm Mrs. Charlie Harris," she introduced herself. They had taken a homestead just southwest of Moorheads, she said, and her husband wanted to see Bert about something and had asked her to ride along. "Mr. Harris was ready to go before he asked me," she told me, apologetically, "and he didn't want to wait for me to put on another petticoat. I only have on two, and it's the first time I ever went away from home without at least three." They were building a three-room frame house on their place, she said—and

I could see she was proud that they wouldn't have to live in a soddy.

Up in the Huffman and Shinbone valleys, too, sod houses were sprouting out of the sand like mushrooms after a rain. Charlie Daly, a young Tryonite, had located in the north end of Shinbone ahead of the rush. Fred Schell, a family man, and his sister Agnes, and George Van Meter, Miss Eva Wagner, and the Foster brothers, Frank and Charlie, with their families, had all taken claims in the big Huffman Valley.

Miss Schell, a clerk from a North Platte store, and Miss Wagner, a schoolteacher, hired Dana Lombard, son of the dead Widow Lombard, to build each of them a little ten-by-twelve frame house. George Van Meter, a bachelor, kept count of the sods that it took to build his house—1,875, he said.

Many of the first Kinkaid homes were hardly more than molehills, put up in a hurry and with very little cash outlay. Some, built by settlers who came to the hills with more cash in their jeans, were good-sized, well finished soddies, or even small frame houses. Water was not a problem. Almost anywhere in the valleys a settler could drive a short piece of sand-pointed pipe into the ground and screw a pitcher pump to its top end and pump water.

In some sections of the range country the ranchmen and the settlers came to blows over ownership of the land. But in our part of the sandhills the ranchers took a surer and more peaceful way. The old-timers knew that the Kinkaiders could not make a living on sandhill land without outside help. A single section was not sufficient to keep enough cattle to support a family, and not many of them could ever expect to own more. Most of them had no cattle anyway, and the sandhills area was not a farming country. "Proving up" took five years, and any settler who gave up in less time lost title to the land and left it open for reentry—and in that case the whole thing had to be done again by somebody else. So, the ranchmen figured, the quickest way to get their range back was to help the original settlers stay on it until they proved up, and then buy it from them.

They hired the homesteaders and their sons to help with ranch work, lent them horses and machinery, and now and then gave the more needy ones a quarter of beef. Certainly they saw to it that no settler's family, or his livestock, went hungry if they knew it. In the end, only a few of all the men and women who came so hopefully into the hills stayed on to become a permanent part of the community; but for a few years there were neighbors aplenty.

Northeast of us, we could see the smoke from Bob Harrison's stovepipe, curling above the low hill that hid his house. South of us, old man Matthews hitched his chunky little new horse, Socks, to a rickety plow and broke out the old field again. Down at Tryon, a church and more new houses were abuilding, and Mike David had just come back from Syria with a bride.

That spring we found a Kinkaider to plaster our house, and as soon as the frost went out of the ground we set out the bundle of lilac, honey locust, and Bouncing Betty sprouts that Grandpa Snyder had sent up from Maxwell. All through the sandhills settlers were planting cottonwood cuttings around their shacks and soddies and breaking out level patches of prairie for gardens and cornfields.

Most of the Kinkaiders came to the hills in narrow-tired wagons—horse killers in a land were the narrow rims sank deep into the sandy trails. So, at one time or another, most of our new neighbors came to borrow

Bert's wide-tired freight wagon to haul lumber for roofing their soddies. When old Mr. Van Dyke, with the help of the Kirts brothers, had the walls of his soddy laid up, they all came over to borrow the wagon.

At sunup four days later George Kirts came pelting to our door on a bony little horse. On the way home with the lumber the night before, he said, old man Van Dyke had bounced off the load and the wide tire of the loaded wagon had run over one of his legs between the knee and the ankle. They had taken him on to their house and put him to bed, and waited until morning to see what to do.

"But now it's swole up so bad we can't tell if it's broke or not, so we'd like for you to come over and take a look at it," George said.

During his cowboy days out west Bert had had experience with "setfasts" on horses and with cowboys' bruises and broken bones, so he saddled up and went back with George to see what he could do. After he looked at the leg, he told Mrs. Kirts to heat a pail of vinegar as hot as she could bear her hand in, and then throw in a double handful of salt and put the old man's foot in it. While George and his wife dipped the hot mixture over the black, swollen leg, Bert cut some pieces of new board from the load on the wagon and whittled them into shape for splints. When the hot vinegar had taken the swelling down some, he strapped the splints tight to the broken leg and came on home.

The old man lay around at the Kirts' place most of the summer, then discarded the splints and walked without a limp. That winter, while he was back in Missouri on a visit, he had the leg X-rayed. When he came home he told us the clean-knit lines of the break showed that the leg had been broken straight across in two places, and the section between "split clean in two lengthwise."

So the summer went along until an evening late in August when another terrible hailstorm roared across the hills. It pulverized my garden (for the third time in five years) and shredded all our young trees and bushes and riddled the gravelled tar-paper roof on the new house. The heavy rain that came with the hail poured in through the ruined roof and down the walls, and by morning the plaster was peeling off in soggy chunks and strips. I knew then how Mama had felt after the big storm that ruined her first nice living room.

The Kinkaiders suffered, too. Their gardens and corn-fields were mowed flat, the sod was washed from their roofs and their homes soaked inside and out. Matthews' old canvas shelter completely dissolved in the storm, and he was all but washed out of his dugout.

Our "big tree," the tall cottonwood by the baby's grave, soon covered its nakedness with new pale green leaves, but the little trees and bushes never recovered from the beating they had taken. Bert hauled new cedar shingles out from Hershey, and a new "plasterboard" that came in sheets we could nail to the walls ourselves. Old man Matthews, turning down all offers of help, built a new little soddy beside what was left of his old dugout.

When the house was clean and tight again, I took the children and went down to Florry's for a quick visit. The trip was longer now, for John and Florry had moved to a new house south of Sutherland, so I started early. In what had been the long, empty stretch between Squaw Creek and the forks, I saw quite a few new soddies, and the smoke from the stovepipe chimneys of others. At the forks there was a new post office in the Johnson house. It was called simply, "Forks, Nebraska."

It was three days after Thanksgiving, and John and Florry had just come home from Grandma Houk's funeral. "I hadn't had time to write you about it yet," Florry said. She took me into the old lady's room to show me where she had died in her rocking chair on Thanksgiving evening—just nine years to the day from the Thanksgiving morning when Grandpa Houk had died in his rocking chair in McCarter Canyon.

"She always put on her gown and nightcap and sat here to smoke her pipe before she went to bed," Florry said of the old lady, who had come long ago from a section of the South where the women smoked clay pipes, "and I found her like that the next morning. She had been dead all night."

Florry was proud of her new little four-room frame house, and happier than I had ever seen her. After ten years of marriage her child was to be born in the spring. That short visit was the sweetest I ever had with Florry.

By spring fences, like seams on the backside of a patchwork quilt, were beginning to stitch the open range. But cattle could still stray far from home, and Bert heard that several head carrying his brand had been seen on the Dismal River, twenty miles north. He left early on the morning of May 7, 1909, to pick them up.

Toward two o'clock that afternoon I saw a team and buggy coming up across the meadow on a fast trot. A good many travelers passed through our valley now, so I thought nothing of it; not even when it turned into our yard, for most rigs stopped in on their way by. But I was a little surprised when I saw Ben and Amos Ross, Stell's young brothers-in-law, getting out of the buggy. I could see, by the looks of the team, that they had driven hard all the way from the Birdwood—and suddenly I knew something was wrong.

The boys came in, bad news plain on their sunburned faces. Amos, the older one, held his cap in his clenched fist and stepped around on the kitchen floor as if he was trying to find firmer footing. He tried twice to speak before any words came, and then he blurted out, "Florry died last night." The words seemed to hit me like a blow on the side of my head, setting up a pounding throb that made it hard for me to think.

"*No!* Florry *can't* be dead," I said.

They went on tell me she had died at Stell's, leaving a two-day-old baby girl, and they had been sent to bring me back to Hershey so I could catch the train to North Platte, where Stell and Walter lived. I still did not believe them. I knew there had been some mistake, but the thing to do was to hurry and get started. I could catch the train at Hershey if I could only think what to do, but Bert was gone and I'd have to take Miles and Nellie with me. But it was Friday and most of their underwear was dirty. Of course I could pack their dirty clothes and wash them out tomorrow, but if I took time to get the children ready I'd never make the train in time. So I rushed around, trying to think what to do, trying to get ready, and all the time I kept saying to myself, "Florry's only unconscious. She'll be coming to by the time I get there."

I wasn't making much headway with anything—and then I saw old man Matthews, riding on the seat of a two-wheeled cart behind Socks, drive into the yard. I had never dreamed the cantankerous old man could be the answer to prayer, but there he was, and I ran out to ask him if he'd stay with the children until Bert came home. He said he would, that he'd only stopped on his way home from Tryon to give them a package of gum, and he wasn't in any hurry anyway. Small children seemed to be the old man's one soft spot, and I was thankful for it as we drove away, leaving the three of them in the yard admiring Socks and peeling sticks of gum.

The boys pushed their tired team hard on the way back, and I sat stiff and tense, pushing my feet against the upslope of the buggy floor as if I could make the rig go a little faster. And every minute of the way, my head hurt and pounded where the words "Florry died last night" had hit me so hard.

Along the way little prairie lilies glistened in the new grass, and wild penstemons were just opening their blue bells. The sun was warm on the slopes where meadowlarks called their cheery invitations to "come and sl-e-e-p with me." Florry and I had loved to listen to them, long ago, and to call back "someday I w-i-l-l." I knew Florry couldn't have died just at the beginning of the spring season she had aways enjoyed so much, just when the baby she had longed for all the years of her marriage had been given to her.

At the old Ross place on the Birdwood we stopped long enough to exchange the played-out team for a fresh one, then we raced on toward town. When we topped the last hill above the valley, where we could see the border of trees that hid the river, we observed the streak of black smoke that marked the train's rush down the valley to the little depot.

Amos put his team to a hard run and we flew down the hill, across the long bridge and on toward town, where the train was already stopping at the depot. Amos jumped to his feet then and brought his whip down across the tired horses' sweaty backs. They gave us their last burst of speed—but it wasn't enough. The train was pulling away from the depot when I jumped out of the buggy. And, after all the hours and hours I had waited on trains, this one wouldn't wait even a minute on me, not even when I ran down the track after it, waving my handbag to try to stop it.

So Ben and Amos took me around to the livery stable, where I hired a rig and team and hurried on to North Platte. Even when we stopped in front of Stell's house, I still believed the message was a mistake, that somehow Florry would be all right when I went in. I paid the driver, grabbed my suitcase, and ran up on the porch. Poppie met me at the door and I could barely manage to ask, "Poppie, has she come to yet?"

"No, Grace, she's gone," he said. And then I knew there was no hope.

He took me into the living room, where Florry lay in her coffin. She looked sweet and peaceful, and I smoothed her quiet forehead and her soft brown hair. Then a baby's thin cry sounded in the next room, and I thought of what Florry and her daughter would have meant to each other, and how no one can ever measure the loss to a newborn baby of a mother's love. Some lines I'd read once came back to me:

> There is no loss, except the loss of heaven,
> Like that which fills a wife and mother's shroud.

I stooped then and kissed Florry good-bye before I went in to see the baby; a wee, lovely thing with a tiny puckered face and a fuzz of brown-gold hair.

They told me that Florry had known, soon after the baby came, that she could not live, and that she had named her little girl Margie Mae and given her to Stell. For Stell was the only one of us who lived in town, and Florry wanted her child to have the advantages of good schools and music lessons, an easier, better life than she had ever had.

We left for Cozad the next morning, taking the four-day-old baby with us. Roy was waiting at the depot with the family carriage, and the town hearse was there beside him. Mama had the cool, dim parlor unlocked and ready for Florry; and I remembered how she had used to worry lest we have a funeral in the family before we had a proper parlor for the corpse.

In spite of the embalming, or maybe because of it, a faint, unpleasant odor had spread all through the house by the time dinner was over, so we opened all the windows and doors to the fresh air. Aunt Irene and Uncle John were the first to arrive, and then the neighbors began to come in. Some of them stayed to sit up that night, and when someone asked if we were sure the screens were all good and tight, so there wouldn't be any chance a cat could get in and bother the body, Elsie turned white and got up and hurried outside.

And all the time that Florry lay a corpse in the parlor Polly, sighing just a little, stayed in her cage and bothered nobody.

We buried Florry from Walnut Grove church on Sunday, and laid her to rest in the pretty cemetery across the road. Poppie had helped set out a young cedar hedge around the burying ground a few years back, and it was surprising how tall it had grown already.

Stell took the baby back to the Platte with her, and Ethel and I went on home with John to help put Florry's things away. Among them I found enough pieces, cut and laid in neat little piles, for a "Wild-goose Chase" quilt. I told John I'd take them home with me, and when the baby grew up I'd make them up into a quilt for her.

Chapter Thirty-Five

BY THE fall of 1909 the circle of homesteaders around us was without a gap. A Miller family had settled on a narrow strip of land east of old man Brandt, and Dave Wickard had taken the section between Moorheads and Pierces, where he built a little dugout and moved his family in. In the next circle beyond, on the far side of the Wickard place, a Mr. James Lovall built a good two-room soddy for his family. Frank and Oscar Cather, bachelor cousins of future novelist Willa Cather, filed claims in Shinbone Valley, near Jake Rupp's ranch. Two big families, Kemmerers and Les Skinners, had settled in the Trego Valley, and a Mr. Duncan had filed on a part of a section northwest of Bob Harrison. The old man, a one-armed veteran of the Civil War, used to complain that he was "old and infernal and had only one wing."

All through the hills the settlers had already held meetings to organize school districts and build sod schoolhouses. The Schell school was in the Huffman Valley, near Fred Schell's soddy. The Happy Hollow school was near Miller's, and there was another southwest of us, just south of Trego Valley. Eva Wagner taught the Schell school that first year, and Mattie Lou Miller the one in Happy Hollow. All of the schools were five miles, or more, from us, but I wasn't too worried yet. Miles and

Nellie weren't quite old enough for school, and by the time they were, we would probably have one.

I was more concerned that fall with going to Cozad to see Poppie and Mama and Ethel off to California. Mama's health had failed fast, after Florry's death. Her cough was worse, too, and Poppie was afraid she wouldn't live through another winter in Nebraska.

I was all packed to go when Pierces stopped at the ranch. They were on the way home from a visit down in eastern Dawson County, and they said a mysterious sickness had stricken a lot of children down that way, killing some and crippling others. That same week I had a letter from Poppie, telling of the deaths of two little boys near Cozad. They had died of some strange disease, and one of them was Aunt Anna's little boy.

Bert didn't think I should take the children where so many youngsters were sick and dying. I agreed—until the next week when I had another letter from home. It said the sickness seemed to have run its course and there hadn't been any new cases since the first hard frost, more than three weeks back. But Bert was still afraid to have me take Miles and Nellie down on the valley, and I couldn't go and leave them with him either, for he was shipping cattle that week and wouldn't be at home. So Mama, Poppie and Ethel left for California, and I was not there to see them off.

Poppie didn't stay long, but Mama and Ethel spent the winter in Fresno. In February I had an interesting card from Mama, picturing a boxlike little airplane, with some printed lines beneath that read: "Paulhan breaking the altitude record, 4600 feet." Mama wrote on the card, "I saw this airship fly a race with an auto. It was quite a sight and I looked every minute for one of them to get killed."

That flyer had been up almost a mile, and from that high up one could look down on a cloud. The frail, clumsy little airship didn't look like a very safe perch from which to do it, but I envied the shipman—*he* had seen a cloud from the topside.

We didn't have much snow that winter. By March the prairie was brown and dry and the ranchers were worried. There had been several small fires all through the country, but no bad ones since the big October fire four years ago. But that March we had dry grass, high winds, and settlers thick as prairie chickens. Nothing happened until Saturday the twenty-sixth, the day before Easter, 1910. The morning was fair and quiet until about ten o'clock, when the wind came up suddenly. Toward noon, Bert noticed an odd cloudy streak just above the far southeast hills, and by then one could hardly stand against the force of the wind. An hour later we could smell smoke, and see the first bits of charred grass flying by. Bert saddled his horse then, to ride and hunt the fire—and that was when we discovered that Miles and Towser were gone.

None of us had seen Miles since dinner. He wasn't in the old soddy, where a little drift of grassy ashes was piling up against the south door, or in the granary, the barn, the corrals, or the chicken house.

Miles and Nellie had walked down to visit old man Matthews once or twice, and they had gone to Bob Harrison's with Bert, when he and Bob had fenced a horse pasture between the two places. They liked old Mr. Matthews, and they were crazy about Bob and his bell-horned Edison "talking machine." It could be that Miles had taken off to visit one place or the other by himself, so Bert jumped on his horse and headed for Bob's on a high lope.

I took Nellie by the hand and went up to look behind
the hill where Ed Matthews' old horse had died, but there
was nothing there but the sun-dried bones. We hurried
back and looked again in all the places we had looked
before, and we called and called, but the howling wind
drowned our voices and I knew it was no use. In the
barn we stopped to catch our breath. Nellie's face was
freckled with specks of soot, and bits of gray ash were
caught in her hair. While we stood there, I saw Bert
riding past the garden toward Matthews', so I knew he
hadn't found Miles at Bob's.

The barn was low and narrow and I could see it all
at a glance, but I looked in the mangers again. Then
I saw a piece of old rope, with a clumsy loop in one end,
against the wall by the barn door. I picked it up and
hung it on a nail, for it was one of Miles's favorite play-
things. He had practiced roping with it all winter, so
he would "be a good hand when he got to Wyazona."
Bert had talked a good deal the past year about moving
on to Wyoming or Arizona, where the range was still
open. Miles had put the two together and made his plans
to be a "cowboy in Wyazona."

Then Bert came riding out of the haze again, alone,
so I ran out and climbed the corral fence for the third
or fourth time and looked across the rocking valley. I
couldn't see far because of the smoke, but I saw Miles,
plugging across the flat toward home with Towser trotting at his heels.

He said he'd gone up to see Bob, but there was nobody
home so he had started right back. Then he saw a skunk
in a trap Bert had set for coyotes by a cow carcass in
the bottom of a blowout by the trail. Of course he
stopped to get a better look at it, and while Bert was
riding across the pasture and back, close to the blowout

both times, Miles and Towser were squatting below its rim watching the skunk.

Bert rode away to find and help fight the fire, and in a little while it was dark. We could see the light of the fire then, off to the southeast, but we couldn't tell how far away it was or how near. Bert came home sometime the next morning, but we didn't know until later how the fire started, or the damage it had done.

That Saturday morning, down near the south boundary line of McPherson County, two carpenters by the name of Fisher had driven across the hills to work on a neighbor's new house. Southwest, across a few more hills, another settler, one Kemp, was trying to break up a patch of prairie for a garden. But the sod, matted with a long, heavy growth of old grass, had resisted the plow and, after half a dozen rounds, Kemp had decided to make it easier by burning off the mat of dead plants.

The blaze would have burned out in a few minutes, except for the freakish little "dust devil" that danced straight into the middle of the burning patch. The fierce little whirlwind had sucked up bits of the burning grass and flung them across the plowed strip onto the dry, open prairie. The wind that came up so suddenly that morning probably began to blow about then—and so the big fire got its start. Less than half a mile away the carpenters, plagued by the high wind, gave up trying to hang onto their lumber and started home, not even knowing that a prairie fire was on the loose.

At Conroys, seven or eight miles north of Kemp's place, young Reuel had eaten an early dinner and left for Tryon on horseback to meet the daily mail from North Platte. Conroys had gotten a new post office, Brighton, established at their place, nine miles southwest of Tryon, and

Reuel had been appointed its postmaster. His post office supplies were to come in that day on the Tryon mail.

About the same time that we were hunting for Miles, Reuel rode into town through the smoky haze. Tryon was full of worried settlers who had come in to do their regular Saturday trading and visiting. Caught there by the fire, they didn't know what to do next. For the terrible wind held the smoke so low to the ground, and spread it so far over the hills, that it was impossible to tell where the fire was. It might be twenty miles away, or just over the next rise.

At four o'clock the mail came in on schedule and the crowd hurried to ask the carrier about the fire. He had traveled the last half of his thirty-five-mile route through the smoke, he said, but he didn't know any more about the fire's location than they did. So the uneasy settlers still didn't know what to do. Those who lived to the south were afraid to start home lest they run into the fire, and those who lived in other directions were afraid to go looking for the fire lest they miss it in the thick haze and be cut off from their homes.

Reuel decided to chance going home. His supplies, postage stamps, a record book and a cancelling stamp, had come in a locked mail sack with the key tied to the outside, so he took the sack and started off into the face of the big wind. About three miles out he came to a smoking strip of burned prairie, though he still couldn't see the fire. He crossed the strip, and then a fireguard that had just been plowed around a settler's buildings. At the house, the settler told him that he and his boys had plowed the fireguard early in the afternoon, and the head fire had reached the guard about an hour before he came along. The fire had split and burned on north on either side, but they hadn't been able to

whip out either blaze and the fire had joined again and
burned on north.

Reuel reached home a little after dark. His father
and his brother Michael were hitching a team to a wagon
they had already loaded with wet sacks and kegs of
water. A short-grazed pasture directly south of their
homesteads had split the fire and saved their places, but
the head fires had gotten away from them, too. That
was the trouble all along: everybody was afraid to leave
home before the fire came along, so there were never
enough people at any one place to whip it out.

The three Conroy men drove across the hills until they
caught up with an arm of the fire; and by then men
were coming from every direction, for as soon as it got
dark they could locate the fire by its light against the
sky. All night the men plowed fireguards and flailed the
edges of the fire with wet sacks. They had managed to
turn it to the east and narrow its front line considerably by dawn, when their fireguard met other tongues
of flame that moved in at an angle, some three or four
miles east of our valley, the nearest the big fire came
to the rangelands of the northwest lake country. The
fire fighters went home to bed then, too worn out to
remember that it was Easter Sunday.

The Big Easter prairie fire behaved all along in a fashion
new to the sandhills. Other big fires had advanced behind a fairly solid front, but this one was split by the
settlers' plowed fields and short-grazed pastures into a
good many different fires. Some of the head fires had
starved out against fields and fireguards, but most of
them kept going over stretches of grassy hills. The high
wind made a difference, too. In places it seemed to hold
back the fire, almost smothering it in its own smoke, or
keep it to a narrow strip that barely managed to work

sideways along a field until it reached open prairie again. So, in spite of all the fighter crews could do, some of the many head fires reached Tryon that night.

At six o'clock the county treasurer, young Clarence Cline, left the courthouse and started afoot for his home, half a mile to the south. And even then, because of the thick haze of smoke and blowing sand, the fire couldn't be seen from the town. But a bare quarter mile from the courthouse, at the head of a little swale, the poor man walked right into the fire. It roared over the rim of the hill and caught him before he knew what had happened, so he took the only way out—straight through the strip of fire. With his clothes and high-topped boots blazing, he ran across the quarter-mile strip of plowed field that had saved the Cline buildings from the fire and jumped into the stock tank by the barn. His mother was watching from the kitchen window. When she saw him coming, a living, staggering firebrand, she ran out. She helped him out of the tank and led him to the house, and then went for help. When they cut his charred boots off his feet that night the skin, all the way to the boot tops, came off with the blistered leather.

Two or three other head fires came down on Tryon that evening, but the fields, fireguards, and fire fighters turned them east or west and saved the town. Two or three miles on northeast, old Judge Seeley and his wife were caught in the path of a strip of fire. The two old folks beat the blaze back with buckets of water and wet sacks and saved their buildings, then they drug themselves off to their bed. They never got up again, for a week later they died, only a few hours apart.

At the Nelson place, six miles farther on, there was a big frame barn, the finest in the county, and a dozen head of the best draft stock in the hills. Just before dark the men there tied the horses in the barn and sat up to watch for the fire. It was past midnight when it came, and somehow they failed to fight it off, so the screaming horses died in the burning barn.

In another little valley, directly in the path of still another strip of fire, an old lady, a Mrs. Sawyer, had spent that Saturday alone in her dirt-roofed soddy. Her two grown sons had gone to North Platte that morning, and when they came home that night the narrow board-walk from the gate to the soddy's door was nothing but a strip of ashes. But their mother was safe inside her little earth house, and the fire had burned past so fast that she hadn't even been uncomfortably warm while it was going by.

The fire burned on to the Dismal River, far to the north. Day and night, men fought the tricky blaze, turning it, if they could, from haystacks and good pastures. Several times they had the stubborn fire whipped to a thin strip but they could never put it out entirely. So they held it to the narrowest possible front and hoped they could finally drown it in the little, twisting river. But, almost on the high bank of the narrow stream, the south wind swung suddenly to the west. For another thirty miles, then, it out-stripped the weary fighter crews until, just short of the little town of Dunning, the driving wind died at last and the men got the upper hand.

Hay and cattle losses in the big fire were heavy. Dewey Wisner, a rancher north of Tryon, found fifty head of his steers in a fence corner, roasted to death in a pile. Up toward the Dismal, Jim Haney had helped his brothers fight the fire past their ranches. Then he rode south to see about some cattle he had in a pasture near Tryon. Some were dead; others, badly burned, blind, and bawling with pain and thirst, had to be knocked in the head. But a few, in spite of singed hides, seemed to be in fair shape, and he drove them across the burned hills to the home ranch. A few days later their hides began to shrivel and crack, like old shoes left too near a hot fire, and most of them had to be killed.

It had been easy for most of the Kinkaiders to drive the few head of livestock they owned to the little plowed fields near their buildings and keep them safe while the fire passed. South of Tryon a boy, Jon Dahlin, and his sisters held the family milk cows in the middle of a field while their parents and older brothers fought the fire— and Jon had been far more afraid of a cranky cow in the bunch than of the fire. In the middle of another little field in Happy Hollow, Mattie Lou Miller and her two little boys had likewise waited while the fire burned around them.

Every spring and fall since the country began to settle up, smaller prairie fires had burned off good sandhill rangeland. But now, with Judge Seeley and his wife in their graves and Clarence Cline teetering on the edge of his, the county officials and the big ranchers decided it was time to put an end to the burnouts. They suspected carelessness on the part of certain homesteaders who had little to lose, and suspicion this time settled first on the Fishers, the carpenters who had been working where the fire might have started.

The county accused the pair of carelessness with matches and charged them with setting the fire. Fishers denied the whole thing, and said they hadn't even known there was a fire at the time they quit work and went home. But the county went ahead and tried them.

According to law, a recorded value of property lost in the fire had to be determined before there could be a conviction. So the county called twenty-five men to the stand and asked each of them to set a value on the grass or other property he had lost. To a man, they refused to name a figure; for by then there was considerable doubt that the Fishers had set the fire. A further investigation had shown that the path of the burn seemed to lead a little farther back—to a garden patch where some straggling furrows were fringed with burnt grass.

Mr. Kemp wasn't there, though. Before anyone could get around to ask him any embarassing questions, he had loaded up his few possessions and left the country. So the trial fizzled out and the case was dismissed, but there were no more big prairie fires during Kinkaider times.

Clarence Cline, after months of agony, was finally able to go back to his work in the courthouse; but for the rest of his life he carried the scars of his terrible run through the fire.

Chapter Thirty-Six

NOW that there were more people in the country, there was more going on. Some of the things that happened were good, or funny, but more were hard and sad; for the sandhills was a tough country on women and children, and sometimes on the men, too. Doctors were miles away and home remedies were simple and scarce. Living conditions were rough for most, and the weather was often harsh.

When the little Wickard girl got pneumonia, there wasn't much they could do for her. She wasn't sick long, anyway. Mrs. Pierce and Mrs. Lovall and I took turns helping nurse her. In my turn, I put a bottle of fresh chicken broth in my pocket and rode Dewey up to sit up all night with the baby.

Dave Wickard worked down on the river valley most of the time, and came home once a month or so to bring groceries to his family. While he was home in April, the second spring they lived in the hills, the family set out a windbreak of cottonwoods north of their home site. Dave plowed the furrows and his wife and the older children set the cuttings, while the eighteen-months-old baby toddled after them. A cold rain set in before they finished and they all got soaking wet, and that was how the little girl came to get sick.

George Van Meter made her little coffin and read her

burial service from an Episcopal prayer book. We all sang a hymn or two, and then buried her in a little grave on the hillside above the dugout. Before he went down on the valley again, her father put up a little square of barbed-wire fence to keep straying cattle off her grave.

During the Kinkaid years, there came to be quite a few graves in the hills, each with a bit of barbed-wire fence around it. Wickards moved their baby down on the valley when they left the hills, but most of the lonesome graves are still there.

That same year, in haying, when Eva Wagoner was thrown off her rake and had her ankle twisted pretty bad, George Van Meter took her to the doctor in North Platte, sixty miles away. That must have been a long, hard ride for her in the jolting buggy, but it had a happy ending; for George and Eva were married the next year. By putting their two homesteads and their two little bunches of cattle together they had a good start, and so stayed on in the hills to build a good-sized ranch and raise a daughter.

Two family men in our neighborhood met violent deaths during those early Kinkaid days. One lived over west of Skinners. He was hauling a load of coal for a ranchman to the north when the wagon upset on a sidling road and he was buried under the coal. He was dead when someone came along and found him. The other, a man named Thrasher, lived a mile or so south of Matthews' place. He was freighting lumber from Sutherland for Tom Heskett when his wagon upset, too, down on the Birdwood, and broke his neck. Both men left poor widows and little children.

Dave Wickard came near being another dead man, the winter after he came to the hills. He was shucking corn near Hershey and bad weather had kept him from

making his regular trip home. The snow was still deep
in the hills when he finally started out, and it looked
like a new storm was building up in the northwest, but
he knew supplies at home were low so he pushed right
along. He might have made it before the new storm
struck if one of his horses hadn't got sick on the road
and slowed him up. But he kept going until, out on
the Birdwood Table, the poor horse lay down in the trail
and died. It was snowing by then, and getting colder
by the minute, so he unhitched the other horse, put a
gunnysack of groceries across its withers and got on and
headed on into the storm.

Dave Wickard was a thin little man and it was a
wonder he didn't freeze to death before he got to the
Bussard place on Squaw Creek. As it was, he was frozen
to his horse, and so cold he couldn't even talk, and Bus-
sards had to cut his pants off him before they could get
him off the horse. When he was thawed out and able
to travel again, they loaned him a horse to take back
down the trail to hitch in with his own to pull his load
on home.

One forenoon during that same stretch of bad weather,
we didn't see any smoke coming from the stovepipe in
the south end of our valley. So Bert took a loaf of fresh
bread and a sack of coal and rode down to see what was
wrong. There weren't any tracks in the fresh snow at
the soddy door, and old Socks was standing forlornly
beside the pitcher pump in the yard. Bert pushed the
door open and went in. Old man Matthews was huddled
deep in his musty bed and it was icy cold in the smelly
little room.

When Bert asked him if he was sick, the old man said,
"No, I ain't sick, but I used up the last of my fuel
yesterd'y an' the snow's too deep to go after any."

Bert told him to stay in bed until he got a fire going and got the place warmed up a little. He picked up the lid lifter, to take the lid off the old stove. But the old man yelled at him to put it down, and then began to scramble out of his ragged blankets. "I'll build my own fire," he said. "You might break my stove."

Bert put the lifter down and said he'd go out and pump some water for the thirsty horse. But Matthews yelped at him to leave the pump alone. "It'll be froze," he said, "and you'll prob'ly bust it all to pieces."

When there didn't seem to be anything he could do, Bert left the coal and bread and came on home, leaving the old man wrapping his feet in some gunnysacks he used for overshoes.

I went down home twice that year of 1910. The first time I went for Decoration Day, to go to Florry's grave with the rest of the family. The second time was in October, when Ethel was married.

While I was there in May, our old world passed through the tail of Halley's comet. All that spring we had been watching the bright comet sail through the sky at night, and there had been a good deal in the papers about it. It was one of the big comets, they said, and it only came around about once every seventy-six years. There was quite a lot of concern over what might happen when the earth passed through its tail. Strong, gaseous smells, a rain of shooting stars, earthquakes and tornadoes were some of the things predicted.

On the night the comet came the closest, it was a beautiful bright star with a long streak of sparks behind it. We watched it quite awhile before we went to bed, but we were all sound asleep when, sometime after midnight, a big noise woke us up. The first thing we noticed then was a terrible smell, and next we realized that the racket was the dogs barking and tearing around. Then Roy clattered down the stairs from his room and yelled, "Yep, I guess that's comet gas all right." But by then we were awake enough to know that it was just plain old skunk gas.

That evening I had helped Mama poison an egg and hide it in the chicken yard for the skunk that had been digging in to get her chickens. The strychnine had made him sick almost as soon as he ate it, and he had put out the gas while the dogs were finishing him off.

The comet was directly overhead, but it wasn't making any disturbance of any kind. From then on it was dimmer every night, until it finally disappeared.

The wedding was at six o'clock on October 24, when Ethel and Audie Wofford were married in Mama's parlor. Audie was the tall, good-looking forest ranger Ethel had met in California the winter before. It was a pretty wedding, and the only one I ever got to see in the parlor. Nellie had been married there more than a year before, but I didn't get to go to her wedding.

The wedding day was bitter cold, with a strong wind blowing out of the north. John Houk, who had come from Sutherland a day or two before in his new Buick runabout, drove into Cozad that afternoon to meet the train Jennie Cox and her mother were coming in on. While he was in town, he picked up two gallons of fresh oysters that had been ordered for the wedding supper.

Like most cars of its day, John's didn't have a windshield, and splitting the sharp wind at fifteen miles an hour had all but frozen the marrow in Jennie's and Mrs. Cox's bones by the time they got to Poppie's.

By six o'clock the parlor was full of the relatives and neighbors invited to the wedding. The big wedding supper after the ceremony went off fine, too, except for the oysters. We had set them outside the kitchen door to keep cool, and then forgotten all about them until after the wedding—and by then they had frozen solid and bursted the cans.

The winter that was setting in by the time I got back to the ranch was the one that almost finished Dave Wickard. Because of its deep snows and extreme cold, the children and I didn't once get away from home again until late the next March, when we all drove down to Conroys one forenoon to get the mail and spend the day.

Old Tom Conroy and his wispy little wife, both as Irish as Paddy's pig, welcomed us as though we'd been a bit of old Ireland itself. Mrs. Conroy hurried to put a few more "praties" in the kettle she was boiling for Tom and "the bys," Mike, Abe and Reuel, all grown men; and then she was ready to visit, too.

We hadn't had the mail since Christmas, when Bert had gone after it horseback, but the big news at Conroys that day was the railroad. *It was coming through at last.*

As far back as 1890, when plans were laid and money raised to build a branch of the Union Pacific from Kearney, Nebraska, to the Black Hills of South Dakota, sandhillers had been looking for the railroad. There weren't many people in the hills then, but every man of them had been terribly disappointed when the tracks petered out at little Callaway, in the middle of Custer County. After that there had been talk, now and then, that the railroad was about to start building again and come on through, but it had never amounted to anything. But, *this time*, according to the latest newspapers, picks and hammers were already swinging at the Callaway end of the line and the railroad was *really* on the way.

"You won't know Tryon, next time you see it," Reuel

told us. "A lot of new buildings 've been staked out, and as soon as the snow goes off a little more, so they can put freight outfits on the road, they'll start hauling lumber. Tryon's going to be ready for that railroad when it comes."

But no one seemed to know just where it would come through, the Conroys said. It might go through within a mile of our place; or south of us, around the head of Squaw Creek; or north, up through the Huffman valley. But it didn't matter too much, just so it came through the hills somewhere.

As we drove home that afternoon, stopping every mile or so to open and shut a gate in a barbed-wire fence, I could see that Bert was studying pretty hard over something. Finally he said, "You know, this might be a good time for us to sell out. I guess I'll ride up and see Gordon Jewett. He's been talking of selling for the last year or two."

The first Kinkaider that came into the hills with a plow tied to his wagon had foretold the sure and speedy end of the open range. And, after all the years the ranchmen had been used to miles and miles of unfenced prairies, it was a bitter pill for them to take. The big operators paid their hired hands to take claims on their home range and nail down enough land to carry on with, but the little ranchmen couldn't do that, so Bert and Gordon, feeling smothered between the fences, had been talking of following the open range on west to Wyoming or Arizona, or north to Canada.

As soon as the roads opened up, the last batch of locators flocked into the hills, collecting good fees from the Kinkaiders they settled on the last poor, scattered scraps of free land. That spring, with the railroad build-ing northwest at a fast pace and every section of the sandhills "homesteaded," things began to boom. Some of the earliest Kinkaiders intended to sell out, just as soon as the railroad came on into the hills and upped the price of land enough. But most were getting ready to put better "improvements" on their land. Frame houses in place of soddies, windmills above their pumps, bigger groves and cornfields on land that hadn't blown much—yet.

Bert and Gordon left for Cheyenne in May. Even with the coming of the railroad they had waited so long for, the sandhills didn't look good to them any more. There were just too many people.

They were home again in time to get ready for haying. Gordon liked a layout he had seen near Big Piney, Wyoming, but Bert hadn't found anything that suited him. We'd go ahead and sell out anyway, he said, and then he'd look around some more.

Chapter Thirty-Seven

HAYING was probably the *hardest* long job on the ranch. Feeding lasted longer, all winter, but it hardly ever took all day and it was a quieter, more humdrum sort of job. Calving was often more disagreeable because so much of it was in cold, bad weather, but there were lots of nice days, too, when everything went fine, but haying was a bad job for most of the month or six weeks that it lasted. It was bad because of the horses we used to do it with.

Most of the forty odd head Bert owned were tough, wiry little animals—with just enough mustang blood in them to keep them broncs all their lives. The sweep and rake and stacker teams worked every afternoon, but the mower teams worked only on alternate forenoons. Pulling the heavy mowers through the long thick grass was a killing job, so a fresh team was hooked to each mower every other morning. It was the mustang blood that made the whole bunch able to work those hard half days in the hayfields on nothing but sandhill bunch-grass. The rest of the year they ran wild—on quite a piece of open range before the Kinkaid days, in a big pasture of their own afterward. So every summer they had to be broken to work again.

Bert raised a few colts, too, and it always took a week or so to get the colts and the rest of the herd ready to travel in double harness. And every summer the wild bunch, biting, kicking, bucking and striking, put up a hard fight against the sight and smell and feel of harness leather.

When Bert first brought the bunch in, they came on a high run, all fat and slick and pretty. But Bert had worked with horses all his life, and for quite a few years with broncs like these, and he knew how to handle them. Some of his ways seemed pretty hard, but in the end they saved him, and the broncs, a lot of trouble. The first thing he did was to shut the worst of the wild bunch in the little corral for two days and nights, without food or water. Hot as it usually was at that time of year, it was hard on the horses, but it took enough of the fight out of them to make it possible to harness and hitch them to the breaking cart without smashing things up too much.

The breaking cart was a strong wooden box bolted between the heavy iron wheels of an old mowing machine. The tongue was a tree he had found somewhere, thick and heavy and hard to break. Bert hitched the broncs to the cart, one at a time, with old Bally. Bally was a big, heavyset sorrel mare, one of the few really gentle horses we ever had on the ranch. She simply would not run away, so a bronc, anchored to her, didn't have much chance to run either. She didn't have any use for a horse that "sulled," or balked, and when that happened she just reached across the tongue and bit him until he changed his mind and went along with her. Good old Bally helped Bert break a lot of colts and broncs, but she took a world of punishment doing it. They bucked and kicked and banged the tongue against her knees; they reared up and came down across her back; and they jerked her all over the place before she and Bert finally had them going well enough to hitch to a mower and head for the hayfield.

We had so many runaways those summers we put up the hay with the wild bunch. There was never a summer without smashed mowers or rakes or sweeps, and we had to be on the lookout every minute or there would have been more. Newcomers to the hills would ask Bert why he didn't get rid of his broncs and get some big gentle horses from down on the river valley. "You'd only need half as many, and you wouldn't have all these runaways and smashups," they'd tell him. And Bert would explain that the big valley horses couldn't even *live*, let alone work, in this country without year-round grain feeding; and there was no grain, except what was hauled in over forty miles of sandhill trails. But the tough little mustangs could rustle their own living in the bunchgrass hills while they worked in the hayfields, and then live through the long winters without any attention whatever.

Once put to work, most of the broncs tamed down enough to be fairly dependable as long as no one gave them a chance to start anything—but a few never did get over trying to be killers. Molly was one of these— and more about her later.

Looking back on them now, some of our runaways were funny. But during the years they were happening I was always afraid. From the day Bert brought the wild bunch in until the day he turned them out again, I was afraid the men, or the horses, or the machinery would be smashed up before night. Usually it was only the machinery. We were pretty lucky with the men and the horses.

Any little thing, or maybe nothing at all, could start a runaway. One night during haying a sudden thunderstorm came up and lightning struck the telephone line in the meadow, two poles west of the yard fence, and burned the wire in two. The next morning, on the way to the hayfield with his mower, Bert drove square into one of the down wires in the tall grass. The loose wire twisted around the team's feet and scared the wits out of them. Of course they started to run. Bert sat back on the lines and tried to hold them. They were bucking and lunging like everything, but he kept them from running until one of the lines broke and he fell backward off the seat. He still had the other line, though, and he leaned back on it with all his weight and circled the running team around and around him. But one line wasn't enough to hold them and they finally jerked it away and tore out across the meadow with the mower bouncing behind them.

I heard the commotion and ran out in the yard in time to see Bert fall off the mower. After the team jerked loose, I saw him put one hand against his side, and then he went on walking around in a circle, with his head bent down. I was sure he was hurt and I ran as hard as I could to see. But when I asked him, he grumped back, "I'm not hurt. I just lost my blamed pipe when I fell off that mower." So I helped him find his pipe, and he went off to get the team and see how much the mower was damaged.

The hired hands had some funny runaways, too. One old fellow we called Pat mowed into a bumblebee nest one day, and the bees came boiling up in a hurry. They stung the poor fellow through the holes in the mower seat and dive-bombed his team. The horses took right out, as hard as they could go, but Pat managed to stay with the outfit until they outran the bees and he could circle the runaways to a stop. By then Bert had caught up to him with his own mower, and Pat jumped off his and began fanning his scorching rear with his hat.

"I tell you," he told Bert, "Hell ain't half a mile from here right now."

Another hand, Mike Conroy, had a runaway with the rake. His started near the south end of the meadow, and the first good bump bounced Mike off in front of the rake, where he rolled over and over inside the curved teeth with the hay. The team headed for the barn, across a stretch of meadow that was already cut and stacked. Bert saw the runaway, but before he could get there to head it off, the horses caught a rake wheel on a corner post of the garden fence and jerked themselves to a stop.

Mike crawled out in front of the teeth and felt himself to see if he was hurt. Except for being scratched by the hay stubble he'd rolled through, he didn't seem to be damaged otherwise, but he *was* upset because he'd swallowed his "chaw" and lost the rest of his tobacco plug out of his pocket besides.

But, for most of the years we lived on the ranch, I did the raking. I liked to rake, and Bert always said I could rake more hay in an afternoon, and do a better job of it, than any man we ever had. It saved hiring one extra man, and I would rather run the rake than cook and wash for the extra hand anyway.

Nellie was only two years old when I took over the raking. She was too young to be left alone, so Bert fastened a stout little prune box to the rake frame by my feet and I took her along in the box. Later on, Miles rode in the box and Nellie played in the old buggy that we took to the hayfield and parked beside the stacker. Still later, when they were old enough, they drove the

stacker team and looked after their two little sisters at
the stack.

I always had the gentlest team of the bunch on my
rake and I never had a runaway, but I came near it twice.
My team was a pair of little mares, May and Daisy.
May would run if she had a chance but Daisy wouldn't.
When anything went wrong *she* went straight into a
sulk and balked in her tracks, and that was all that saved
me what might have been some bad runaways.

One day the neckyoke ring bolt broke and let the
tongue drop. That was all May needed for a starter
and she lunged ahead to run. But the tongue had banged
Daisy on the knee as it went down, and that made *her*
mad. So she stuck her nose under the neckyoke and set
her feet and went into a big sulk. May tried hard, but
she couldn't run and drag the whole outfit by herself,
so nothing happened. It was the same the time I raked
through a bumblebee nest the mower had missed. The
bees that stung May made her try to run, but the bees
that stung Daisy balked her on the spot. The bees that
stung me, through the holes in the rake seat and several
other places, made me feel the same way Pat did.

Now, to get back to Molly. She was a slim, dark bay
that came to the ranch in a bunch of unbroke mares
Bert traded the Squaw Creek claim for. He broke her
right after he and Gordon got back from Wyoming,
and she stayed mean and unreliable to the last. By the
Fourth of July that summer the rest of the wild bunch
was as ready for the hayfield as they'd ever be. But of
Molly he said, "She has to be watched every minute. She's
looking all the time for a chance to strike a man in the
head, or to kick things to pieces and run away."

On the morning of the Fourth, Bert hitched Molly
and a somewhat gentler horse to the wagon and said

we'd drive over to Tregos to spend the day. The mowers were ready to start in the meadow the next morning, and a twelve-mile drive on a hot day would take a little of the ginger out of Molly, he thought.

We drove at a good clip across the meadow and up the high west hill, and on past the Moorhead and Harris places. In the Skinner valley we rattled past the little frame shack Lawrence had built on the section he homesteaded south of his folks' place. He had gone on living with the old folks, except for the night or two a year he spent in the shack to hold his claim rights; and cattle had stood around the empty building, scratching their itchy hides on its corners until they had tramped out the grass and started a blowout. The sand kept on blowing until the blowout was four or five feet deep around the shack, and Bert laughed that day and said it looked like Lawrence would need a ladder to get to his door, and that he'd better move the shack off its pinnacle before it tipped off.

I hadn't wanted to take the children on that drive with Molly, but Bert was so sure she'd be all right—and, anyway, we didn't get to go visiting very often. We did fine, though, as far as Trego Valley, and I was just beginning to think we'd make it all the way without any trouble when I realized the horses were running away. We had traveled at a fast trot nearly all the way, and the team had gone from that into a *run* without the least warning. A runaway team is traveling *fast*, and it is a frightful thing to experience.

As soon as he felt the team break its pace and start to run, Bert had jumped to his feet and thrown all his weight back on the lines. The wagon was bouncing and swinging until I could hardly stay in the seat, and I hoped he could keep his balance and not be pitched out; but mostly I was thinking of Miles and Nellie in the back.

I somehow managed to scramble over the back of the seat and get to them without being thrown out. I sat flat on the floor and grabbed them both and pushed their heads down in my lap. Then I bent over them and held them there, hoping that, if the wagon did go over, the steel-shod rim of the box might not come down on their little necks.

The seat bounced loose and came down in the wagon and danced a wild jig on the floor behind me, and the rattle and bang of the wagon were terrific. Bert was still on his feet and pulling on the lines as hard as he could, but he didn't seem to be slowing the runaways down any. They stopped suddenly, when they came against Tregos' yard fence, and the racket we made, coming across the flat, had brought the whole family running to see what was happening.

As soon as we stopped, I straightened up and looked around. Bert had lost his hat, and his shirttail was whipping in the breeze. My scarf had come off and all the pins and combs had bounced out of my hair. My hands were so numb I could hardly let go of the children; I had been holding onto them so hard it was a wonder I hadn't strangled them myself. The horses were covered with lather, and foam dripped from their open mouths and their breath whistled in their throats. Molly had been running with her inside front leg over the tongue, and had rubbed almost all the hide and flesh off the inner side of it.

Before we left that afternoon, Bert tied a jerk line to Molly's good foreleg. If she started anything on the way home, he could stand her on her head before she got going, he said. But Molly didn't try to start anything. Her leg was stiff and sore and caked with dried blood, and she limped home like a tame old horse.

Bob and Charlie Harrison helped us put up the hay that summer. They were both good hands with the broncs, but Bert never let them work Molly. After her leg healed, he put her on his own mower and worked her hard there, but she seemed to get meaner and more savage every day.

Nothing too bad happened, though, until the August afternoon we finished haying, when Bert drove his mower into the yard to cut the summer-long growth of grass there. He had Molly on the mower, but after the long weeks of hard work she had put in in the hayfield, he figured she was safe enough for that last job. She wasn't, though, for on the last round a cottontail skittered out of the grass at the edge of the garden and she exploded into a wild run, taking her ever-willing mate along with her.

Bert threw all his weight on the lines and jerked back on the team as hard as he could. There wasn't enough room in the yard for the runaways to get a good start and he might have stopped them before much damage was done, except that the end of the sickle smashed into a pile of posts out by the chip pile, and the jolt pitched him backward off the seat.

The team jerked away from him then and seemed to go completely crazy. Dodging fences and buildings and the big tree, they flung the mower in all directions. The sickle was screaming against the cutter bar, and gear wheels and pieces of iron were flying all over the place. The team finally cornered themselves in the angle where the yard fence joined the corral, but by then there was nothing left of the mower but the tongue they still dragged.

"That mare's going to kill somebody yet," Bert said, "and there's no use taking any more chances with her." He led her out into the hills the next day and shot her.

Chapter Thirty-Eight

ON THE nineteenth of August, 1911, Buffalo Bill Cody brought his Wild West Show and Congress of Rough Riders to North Platte for the fifth, and last, time. The famous old scout had put the world's first real wild West show on in North Platte on the Fourth of July, 1882, when Bert was ten years old. He had seen that first show and the other three, too, including the one in 1898 that I missed when Esther picked that day to be born, and now he planned to see this one.

We drove down to Hershey in the big wagon on the eighteenth, for Bert never made the long trip to the road without bringing home a load of freight. We stayed all night at the hotel there, and went across to the depot the next morning to take the train to North Platte. A big crowd was already waiting, and more people were coming all the time, afoot and in rigs.

Of course the train was late, and after an hour or so in the August heat the dressed-up crowd began to look pretty droopy around the edges. It was smothering in the little depot, and even hotter on the gritty platform outside. Children cried for drinks, and then had to be hurried "out back," and nearly all of them complained that their feet hurt.

When the train finally pulled in, it was already loaded to the eaves, but the sweating conductor managed somehow to get the rest of us in, too. "Watch out for children," he kept yelling. "Hold 'em up so they won't get stepped on, and keep movin'."

The people standing in the aisles squeezed closer together and the people coming up the steps pushed a little harder and we all got in. Bert set Nellie on the back of a seat and I put Miles on another. The conductor finally jammed the platform gate shut and the train whistled and groaned out of town. The windows were wide open and smoke, dust, and cinders sifted through the hot air and settled on everybody, but nobody complained—we all felt lucky just to be on that train.

North Platte was almost as crowded as the train had been. There were forty thousand people there that day, we heard, and it seemed like it—acres of people, horses and rigs, and even a few smelly "gasoline buggies"; and at the show that afternoon the walls of the enormous tent had to be extended some two hundred feet to accommodate the crowd.

There wasn't a foot of empty space left in the tent by show time, when the cowboy band began to play. Then Buffalo Bill, dressed all in satiny white buckskins, rode into the arena on his proud white horse and all the forty thousand people stood up and waved and cheered and cheered. Again and again Cody circled the arena, doffing his big white hat to right and left, and his long white hair shown in the sun. He stopped beside a tub and stepped down from his horse. He was past sixty-five then, with only six more years to live, but he moved as easily and quickly as a young man. He scooped up a hatful of water and offered it to his horse, and when the horse finished drinking he dipped up another hatful of water and drank it himself. Then he swung back into his saddle and led the grand entry into the arena. We

saw the finest riders in the world that afternoon, cowboys, cowgirls, Arabs, Indians, and Cossacks riding, roping,
shooting and singing. Cody himself rode at full speed
around the open-topped arena, shooting and breaking
dozens of glass balls high above us.

The show was pretty well over when I discovered Miles
was gone from his seat beside me. Our seats were near
the bottom of a tier, and people on the ground in front
of us kept standing up to see better, and then, of course,
we couldn't see. Miles had been complaining about it
but I hadn't thought he'd leave, in a crowd like that,
and I didn't even know just how long he'd been gone.

We told Nellie not to move from her seat, no matter
what happened, and Bert went one way along the bottom
row of seats and I went the other. I had to push my
way through the packed crowd and it was slow going.
I stumbled over people and they gave me ugly looks,
but I kept on. I knew our only chance was to find Miles
before all those people got up to leave. But I was so
afraid, and I was looking so hard, that all the people
seemed to run together into a blur. I had the awful feeling that I might be looking right at him, in his little
checkered shirt, and never see him at all.

I was almost a quarter of the way around the enormous
tent when I heard someone calling, "Mrs. Snyder, Mrs.
Snyder." Half a dozen rows above me, Margaret Conroy was waving her parasol and calling, "Here he is! I
have him!"

My knees went weak with relief and I almost sat
down in a stranger's lap.

"I saw him hiking along down there, so I called him
up here where I could hang onto him," Margaret told
me. And Miles said, "Mom, I was just tryin' to find a
place where I could see good."

All that summer and into the fall, the railroad was still the big news. Mile by mile, it crawled through Custer County and into Logan County, east of McPherson County, but it hardly ever went where the settlers and ranchers expected it to. It even seemed to go out of its way to miss established little inland towns—and then build new ones close by. In Logan County it built directly through the old community of Logan and then, as if the old settlement wasn't there, it built a new town of the same name, complete with depot, three miles away. A railroad town without a depot didn't have much chance, so old Logan died, and it began to be said that the railroad built new towns wherever the fastest-talking promoters, with land to sell, wanted them.

Gandy, the twenty-five-year-old county seat of Logan County was likewise almost directly in the railroad's path. It was an up and coming town and never dreamed the road would miss it; and when it did, by snaking through the hills a mile and a half to the north, the Gandyites' wrathy howls curdled the air for miles around. And then, when the road fizzled to a stop a little later, barely three and a half miles west of Gandy and only yards from Wallace Baskin's ranch house, all of us McPherson County folks joined in Gandy's bitter howl.

The Union Pacific went ahead and built a depot behind Baskin's barn, and laid a Y track for its daily branch-line train to turn around on. And there didn't seem to be a thing we could do about it, except to go on hoping that the road would build on in the spring—some spring, anyway.

Overnight, a new town, Stapleton, popped full grown out of the prairie at the end of the railroad. Poor old Gandy, left high and dry, soon lost her two banks and her drugstore to the upstart new town. But when Stapleton began to talk of taking her courthouse, too, it was too much. So Gandy made sure it had enough votes to keep the county seat, and then it went ahead and got even with the Union Pacific for passing it by.

According to state law, a railroad had to locate a siding and a depot *within the limits of any corporate county-seat town* it passed through. So Gandy incorporated a strip of land sixty-six feet wide that reached from the north side of the courthouse to the railroad tracks, a mile and a half away. Then, of course, the Union Pacific had to build a depot and side track at the track end of the strip. The little depot looked kind of funny, sitting there on the prairie, clear out of sight of the town. And for the next twenty years Gandy, the town sixty-six feet wide and a mile and a half long, fought with Stapleton at every election to keep the courthouse.

But I was more concerned that summer about a school than I was the railroad. Nellie was six and Miles five, and I knew they should be in school, but most of the homesteads in the circle around us were owned by bachelors, and there weren't enough children in our section of the hills to let us form a district. Bert said not to worry, that we'd be sold out and gone before another winter; so I added a blackboard and primer to the Montgomery Ward order and taught them myself, that winter.

We hadn't sold yet by the first of March, but Bert was sure we would as soon as things opened up in the spring. He was so sure that he had me pack all our household things before I went down home to wait for the birth of our third child. He'd haul the things to the road as soon as he sold out, he said, and then he'd go on west and find us a new ranch.

So, just before I left, the neighbors brought a big basket dinner and came in to give us a farewell send-off.

The old neighbors were there, Huffmans and Quinns and Pinkertons, and quite a few of the new ones, Schells, Fosters, Lovalls, Pierces, and Van Meters, and they were all still trying to talk Bert out of leaving. They told him he was making a mistake, that the sandhills' best times were just ahead. Everybody will have telephones before long, they said, and the railroad will come on through and we'll see high times and good years from now on. But Bert said we'd be leaving as soon as he could sell the place.

Billie Lee (she was supposed to be a boy) was born on April 12, and when Bert came down in May to take us home he wasn't so sure of selling. It didn't look like the railroad was coming any farther this year, he said, and the sandhill boom had petered out. Anyway, in two years or less, a lot of the Kinkaiders would be proving up and selling out, and we could buy several sections around us then, and start spreading out again.

He didn't seem too disappointed, and I was glad we weren't leaving, but I reminded him there were some things to think about if we stayed, such as a school, and building onto the house. He said we'd build before winter, and that the school business would work out someway.

Back at the ranch, I unpacked our things and planted a bigger garden and caught up on the news. Henry Downing, the young Whitewater foreman, was going steady with Lottie Lovall, the oldest of the three pretty Lovall girls. Harrises had a new baby, and Lawrence Skinner hadn't had to bother to move his little shack. A high March wind had done it for him, rolling it clear over and setting it right-side up again on level ground. Frank Cather, over in Shinbone Valley, had bought a new Ford, and was getting around through the hills pretty good with it.

Bert hired young Bill Lovall to help him haul lumber for the addition to our house, and Moorhead, from the claim west of us, to build it. The new house, built across the west end of the old one, had a front room and a bedroom downstairs, and two bedrooms upstairs, one for Miles and one for Nellie. The living room had a big double window in the south wall, for my houseplants, and an open stairway to the rooms above. I had always wanted a house with an open stairway.

Other sandhillers were building that summer, too. Dave Wickard built a sixteen-foot-square frame house and moved his family out of the dugout. Lovall's built a long frame room across the end of their soddy, and Johnny Schicks put up a tall, two-story house on high ground, north of the old soddy that was gradually settling into the slough as old Dry Lake filled again. Lottie Lovall had homesteaded a piece of land in Pinkerton Valley, near Whitewater, when she turned twenty-one, and her father built a tight little soddy there for her. Lottie was to teach the Pinkerton school, and she would live in her own house that winter.

As soon as haying was over, Bert and Bill put up a new barn beside the little corral where the broncs did time every summer to take the fight out of them. They built the barn tall and wide and solid, with a big hay-mow above and a garage on one side—for we had bought a car.

By August Frank Cather had decided the Ford wasn't his caliber and that he was really a big-car man. So he came down to our place, doing close to twenty-five miles across our level meadow, and offered to sell us the Ford. He was a good salesman, for on the fourth try he sold Bert the car.

The third time he came he told Bert he'd take the

whole family anywhere we wanted to go. So Bert said
he guessed a trial run to Hershey and back would be
good enough, and that he'd make up his mind then.
Frank waited several days, until a good rain had firmed
up the sandhill trails, and then he took us to Hershey.

Bert sat in front with Frank, and the children and I
rode in the back seat. The Ford putted right along and
we only had to "take low" on a few of the longer hills,
so we rattled into Hershey just a little past noon. Frank
took us to dinner in a fly-plagued little restaurant, and
then we got back in the car and drove home.

We had left old Towser dancing a jig on the little
rise where he always watched for Bert to come home,
barking and fussing at the noisy, smelly critter that was
running away with his family. When we rattled into
the yard again and got out, he jumped all over the children and whined and licked their faces. It was easy to
tell he had never expected to see them alive again.

The trip convinced Bert. We had been to Hershey
and back, seventy-two miles, all in the same day, and
it wasn't even dark yet. He bought the car for five
hundred dollars.

Frank took Bert back to Hershey a few days later to
make out the transfer papers. When that was done he
went on to North Platte to order his big car, something
with eight or twelve cylinders, and left Bert to bring
the Ford home.

Bert was still sweating when he drove into Conroys'
three hours later. "If I could 've had my choice," he said,
"between starting out alone in that darned car or riding
over again the meanest horse I ever tackled, I'd 've taken
the horse."

Chapter Thirty-Nine

OUR new car had a black wooden body and a carriage top that could be raised and hitched to the brass-bound windshield, or folded back flat, out of the way. There was a tall metal box of tools and tire-patching equipment fastened to one running board, and a long cylinder of gas for the Presto headlights fastened to the other. The gas tank was tucked handily under the front seat. One had only to get out of the car, lift out the seat cushion and unscrew the tank cap to put in gas. If we wanted to check on how much gas was in the tank we used the wooden foot rule that was carried on top of the tank. One inch of gas on the rule equalled one gallon of gas in the tank.

From the day Bert drove it home, we learned a lot about Fords. We learned about "Bat." and "Mag." and about ignition, compression, chokes, coils, axles, carburetors, commutators, and spark and gas. Frank had shown us a few things, like how to set the spark and gas levers on the steering wheel before we "cranked 'er up." It was important, he said, to set the spark just right, otherwise the engine might "kick back" and break the cranker's arm. But we learned most of what we came to know by experience, and by studying the greasy instruction book that came with the car. When the differential or the transmission or some other part broke, we took it apart and put in the new pieces and put it together again, all by the diagrams and directions in the book.

The first month, except for having to push the Ford over the bad hill between our place and Lovalls, or the worse one between our valley and Harrises, we got along fine on the first short drives we made. Our car had doors to the back seat but none in front, and that was a good thing. A person in the front seat could get out quicker to push when we came to the bad places. I'd sit on the edge of my side of the seat while Bert advanced the gas and started up a hill. As soon as we began to lose headway in the sliding sand he'd "take low," and if I saw that "low" wasn't going to get us over the hill I'd jump out and grab a fender and push as hard as I could. If that didn't do it, we backed down and changed places and I drove while Bert pushed.

After the hills settled up, September came to be the month for fairs. The first fair, the year we bought the car, was held at the new town of Flats, eleven miles west of us. Flats was nothing but a sod building, where a Mr. Haynes lived and kept a store and the new Flats post office; but anyplace that had a store and a post office was called a town.

We made the trip to Flats in a little over an hour. Nothing happened on the way except, near the end of the trip, when Bert had to honk two or three rigs out of the road so we could get by. To do that he squeezed a big rubber ball near his elbow on the left side of the seat. The honk that sounded like a sick calf bawling, came out of a big brass horn up front beside the engine.

Light buggies didn't make much noise spinning along the road, and they usually pulled over in a hurry, but a big wagon made so much racket the driver sometimes couldn't hear our first honk. Bert would have to **pump** hard on the bulb then, to build up enough noise so the outfit could tell we were coming. Bert always drove at slow speed past the rigs, ready to stop and jump out to help the driver quiet his team and keep him from having a smashup or a runaway. And we weren't being "stuck up" when we honked for the right of way for our automobile. It was simply that the rigs could get out of the deep trails, and we couldn't.

Our Ford was the only car parked among the rigs on the flat in front of the store, and there was as big a crowd around it all day as there was at the regular exhibits. A long, open-front canvas shelter had been set up beside the store for the exhibits. I entered the things I brought and then looked over the other exhibits. It was a big display, and a good one for a country that had been settled such a short time. To this day I have never seen pumpkins as big and pretty as the ones Mr. Lovall brought to that first Flats fair.

It was almost dark when we climbed into the Ford to go home. Most of the folks who were staying for the dance came to watch while Bert opened the gas jets and lit the burners in the big brass head lamps. Several were of the opinion that it would be kind of risky, driving through the hills with no more light than *that*, and *we* weren't so sure but what it might be. For a car couldn't *see* to follow the road the way horses did.

But, after we got started, it seemed that we could see as much of the twisting road ahead as we needed to, even though it was a dark night. We had just decided that there wasn't much to night driving after all when the lights went out. Frank must have done more of it than we thought, for the tank on the running board was empty. Bert walked on to Tregos, half a mile ahead of us, and borrowed a lantern to hang on the radiator cap; and so we made it on home.

Later in the month, when Stapleton celebrated its first anniversary with a big fair, we took that in, too. It was forty miles to Stapleton, the longest trip we had made, but we started early and pulled into town a little before noon.

Stapleton was so new that it still smelled of raw pine boards and pitch. Most of its buildings hadn't even been painted yet, but there was a real merry-go-round at the fair, and hawkers with balloons and Cracker Jack. In the afternoon the "local" came in. It consisted of only two cars, pulled by a gasoline motor instead of a steam engine, but the Logan countyites were mighty proud of that little train. It turned around on the Y and stopped in front of the depot for a while before it tooted its shrill little whistle and pulled out.

It was hard to believe that, only a year ago, Baskin's ranch had had all this prairie to itself.

Counting ours, there were three cars in Stapleton that day, and each had quite a crowd around it most of the time. Along in the afternoon, young Bill Baskin asked to drive ours. He had driven a car once or twice before, and Bert told him to go ahead. While he was gone, on a little spin up the valley, a sudden hard shower came up. When we were ready to start home, an hour or so after he got back, Bert couldn't get a sputter out of the engine.

Men and boys stood six deep around the car while Bert tinkered with the balky engine. Two or three of the watchers had driven cars, and quite a few had ridden in them, but everybody offered advice. Bert tried about everything they suggested, except building a fire under the Ford. He even fished the jack out from under the back seat and jacked up a hind wheel, and then cranked some more. Nothing did any good, so we finally gave up and stayed all night at Baskins.

The engine took off at the first spin of the crank the next morning. A little while after that, we found out that every little shower (even a heavy dew, Bert said) gave a Ford "damp coils." When that happened, nothing on earth would start the engine until they dried out again.

When the fairs were over, Bert took the top off the car and hung it up in the garage for the winter. He said we wouldn't need it for shade until next summer, and that we'd make better time and more miles to the gallon without it. He liked to drive with the top half of the windshield folded down, too, the cold wind whipping our faces in winter and the bugs peppering us in summer.

In December Bert's brother George invited us to a family dinner at his home on Christmas Day. I hadn't been away from the ranch at Christmas time since the winter Miles had pneumonia, and Bert never had, to stay all night. But now that we had the car, and if the weather held good, he thought we might leave the cattle long enough to go.

We started at daylight on the twenty-fourth. The weather was clear, but a cold south wind made the trip a misery for me. In the back, Miles and Nellie sat on the floor between the seats, wrapped in heavy quilts, but in front the wind whistled over the windshield and up through the floorboards, and kept me grabbing at the quilt I tried to keep around the baby and myself.

We stayed with Bert's parents that night, and by morning the wind had swung to the north and it was even colder than the day before. But it was less than two miles on over to George's, so the drive wasn't too bad.

A clipping from the *Maxwell Telepost*, sent to us later

by Pearl, gives a good account of that gathering: "The family of Mr. and Mrs. Jeremiah Snyder, with the exception of a daughter in Oregon and one in New York, were all together at the Christmas board for the first time in many years. After the finest dinner imaginable, such as only Mrs. George Snyder can cook, some time was spent in visiting and then Mr. Swancutt, the Brady photographer, came out and photographed the group— twenty-eight in all. Those present, beside the hosts, Mr. and Mrs. George Snyder and sons, were Mr. and Mrs. Jeremiah Snyder; Mr. and Mrs. John Snyder and family; Mr. and Mrs. Charles Sullivan (Pearl) and daughter, all of Maxwell; Mr. and Mrs. A. B. Snyder and family of Brighton, who motored down on Tuesday for the occasion; and Mr. and Mrs. James McCullough and family of Brady."

We spent Christmas night at John's, and the next morning the temperature was well below zero and the north wind blowing harder. John tried to talk Bert into staying over until it warmed up a little, but Bert said it looked like a storm was building up and he'd have to get back to the cattle.

I sat in the back with the children that trip and tried to keep the quilts tucked in around us all. But I'd hardly get one flapping corner fastened down before another one came loose and whipped around our ears. Two miles out from John's a cloud of steam suddenly plumed above the radiator cap. It was the first time *that* had happened to us, but we knew what it meant—the "radiator was froze up."

Bert jumped out and hauled one of our quilts up front and tucked it around the engine. While we sat there on that cold, bare meadow road, waiting for the radiator to thaw out, I tried to anchor the quilts we had left so they'd stay down when we started on. But as soon as we got up speed again it was the same old thing, and the quilt on the radiator kept whipping loose, too, or else the engine would begin to boil. In either case we'd have to stop while Bert got out and fastened the quilt down again, or lifted it a bit to give the engine a little more air.

We had the side curtains along, under the back seat, but without the top on the car there wasn't anything to fasten them to. Bert was so used to being out in all kinds of weather that it didn't bother him much, facing that freezing wind for seventy long miles, but I was more dead than alive when we pulled in at the ranch that evening; and I had wondered a hundred times that day why in the name of common sense he hadn't put the top on before we started.

After the first of the year we had to buy a license for the Ford. The state didn't start making metal license plates until 1915, so Bert made our first tag by painting the number on a foot-long piece of siding board left over from the new house.

There were several cars in the hills that spring. Jim Haney had a Model T, and so did Conroys and another Happy Hollow family, the Dolphins. Charley Daly, the county clerk, drove his Ford past our place every Monday morning on his way to Tryon, and back to his ranch again on Saturday evening. Down at Tryon Jack Chrisp fastened a box on the rear of his little "runabout" and advertised it for hire as a livery car. Fred Roberson, the blacksmith, had added a "garage and repair service" to his shop, and Mike David had taken to keeping half a dozen barrels of gasoline on hand beside his store.

Bert bought a barrel of the gas and stored it in the cellar—and then forgot to put some in the Ford. Sister Nellie and her little boy were visiting us at the time,

and Preacher Ware was holding Sunday services at the
Schell schoolhouse. We started for the schoolhouse that
morning, but up in Shinbone Valley, half a mile from
Jake Rupp's soddy, we ran out of gas. Bert walked on
up to Jake's and borrowed a horse to ride home after a
gallon of fuel. While he was gone it began to rain. We
dug the side curtains out from under the back seat and
hustled them on, but it took quite a while to button
all the buttons down. By the time we were done it had
quit raining and we were all wet.

It was nearly noon when Bert got back. I drove the
car on up to Jake's then, and Bert followed on the horse.
Of course the friendly little old bachelor came right out
and asked us to come in. I had a good idea what it would
be like in Jake's house, but it would have been the height
of bad manners to refuse him, so we stopped.

The little unplastered soddy smelled of mould, stale
grease, and saddle leather. The legs of the chairs settled
into the damp, slick dirt floor when we sat down, and
flies by the hundreds seemed at home everywhere. Of
course kind little Dutch Jake started in to get dinner
for all of us. I tried to stop him, but he went right
ahead and built up a hot chip fire in his grease-coated
old stove and put the coffee on. Bachelors seldom made
light bread, but I thought sure he'd go ahead and mix
up a batch of biscuits with his cracked, horny old hands.
He didn't, though. Instead, he opened a box of soda
crackers and heated some canned goods, then he swiped
off his oilcloth table cover with a greasy dishrag and
set the meal on. By the time Bert came in everything
was ready, and Jake was so happy to have us there that
we had to eat with him.

Later that summer we made a trip to Stapleton after
mowing machine repairs. We left the ranch in the cool

of the morning, but by the time we started back in the
afternoon the day had turned hot, the first real sizzler
of the season. Before we'd gone far the engine began to
boil. We hadn't thought to bring a jug of water along,
and there weren't any houses in sight along the road, so
we had to stop every mile or two to let the engine cool
off. At the little Ringgold store, halfway back to Tryon,
we filled the radiator with cold water and started on.
Two miles farther on the car stopped. The engine was
still running all right but the wheels wouldn't turn, even
when Bert advanced the gas and "took low."

We shut off the motor and got out the instruction
book. As near as we could tell, after we had studied it
a while, we had a broken axle. Any way we looked at
it, we were in a bad fix.

Bert always wore high-heeled boots, since he didn't
even own any other kind of footgear, and a two-mile
walk on a hot day would turn his feet into solid blisters.
But there was no telling how long it might be before
someone came along, so there didn't seem to be any other
way out. Then, just as he started off, a wagon rattled
over the hill from the east.

The driver said he was going to Tryon and that he'd
pull us on in, only he didn't have anything to tie us
on with. Neither did we. He offered to take us all to
town with him, but the only seat on the wagon was
the narrow board he was sitting on. It was probably
a hundred or more in the shade by then, and there'd be
no shade for us in the wagon. I said I'd stay in the car
with the children, and Bert rode off in the wagon.

The afternoon seemed to get hotter by the minute.
The children began to fret for a drink, and Miles and
Nellie yelped every time they moved and touched the
hot metal rods that held up the car top. The faint smell

of sun-scorched weeds that came by on the dry wind began to make me sick at my stomach. Even when the sun finally dipped down toward the hilltops, it didn't seem any cooler.

Just before sundown Jack Chrisp rattled up in his runabout. Bert had sent him, he said, and he crowded us all into the little car and took us back to Tryon. Bert was waiting for us in front of the restaurant. He'd bought a new axle at the garage, he told me, and we'd go back after the car the next day and pull it home with a team and wagon. Now, as soon as we ate, Jack would take us on home. But I had such a pounding sick headache by then that I didn't want a bite, so I stayed in the car with the baby and he took the others to the restaurant. It was already after eight o'clock, and Miles and Nellie had been hollow with starvation for quite a while. It was also Saturday, "ice-cream day" in Tryon, and they topped off their suppers with a dishful apiece.

On the ride out to the ranch, Bert and Miles sat in the box on the back and Jack and I and the baby sat in the seat, and Nellie curled up on the floor boards by our feet. The night was close and sultry and hot, and gassy exhaust fumes boiled up around us. I got sicker by the minute, and by the time we pulled into the home yard Miles and Nellie were sick too, and throwing up all over everything.

After the first year or so, cattle and horses seldom stampeded at sight of a car bouncing along a sandhill trail; but a team and a car, meeting unexpectedly at the top of a hill, was another story. It happened to us one day. The hill was long and steep and we barely made it up our side. A four-horse team, pulling a heavy load, was straining up the other side at the same time. The lead team and the Ford met face to face at the top. The four horses stood on their hind legs and tried to go in all directions at once; for a minute or two it looked like the lead team might get right into the Ford with us.

Every once in a while we made a trip in the Ford when nothing went wrong or broke, but the times when we had trouble are the ones we remember. Compared to the cars we have now, those early machines were simple affairs. Even so, there was no end to the things that could go wrong with them a long way from home.

Once, halfway home from North Platte, we had trouble out in the middle of the big Rosedale pasture. The Ford was running fine until, part way up a little hill, the engine began to miss. Before we got to the top it died altogether. We backed down, cranked the engine, and tried again. That time, when the engine began to sputter, I jumped out and pushed. But it died again and we had to back down. We traded places and tried once more. When we still couldn't make it, we backed down and on across the little swale at the foot of the hill and part way up the hill on the other side, then we took a good run at the hill ahead. But that didn't work either. That was a four-cylinder hill, and for some reason we had only three. So we got out the book and tried to find out what made the engine miss every time we lost headway on the slope.

We adjusted the coil points and tried to make it up the hill. Then we looked under the hood and adjusted a few things there and tried again. We were just about to give up when we found the trouble, a loose sparkplug wire. Each time we had trouble, and found the remedy, we knew what to look for the next time.

But another time, on the way home from a trip to the Platte, the Ford quit us completely some twelve or fifteen miles south of Tryon, and we couldn't find the trouble. We tried for an hour but we couldn't get a spark out of that engine. And that time we had more than the balky Ford to worry about, for off to the northwest the smoke of a prairie fire had been showing up for two hours or more.

We were still tinkering on the engine when a settler on his way to Tryon came along in a little two-wheeled cart. By then the smoke was darker and thicker, back of a long hill on our left, so Bert gave up on the car and rode to Tryon with the settler to get help. Before he left he pulled a handful of matches out of his pocket and gave them to me. "If the fire comes over that hill," he said, "get the kids out on the flat and set a backfire. Never mind the car—just look out for yourself and the kids."

For nearly three hours we waited there, watching the smoke build up above the hills. No one else came along. I couldn't tell how near the fire was, but I picked out the spot where I'd start my backfire if I had to. As soon as it burned on east and left a strip wide enough, I'd get the children onto it and the main fire would burn around us. We'd lose the car, but we'd be safe enough.

When it began to get dark I could see the glow of the fire beyond the hills. It didn't look too big, or too close, but I couldn't be sure. And then I saw the headlights of a car come bobbing over the hill ahead, the prettiest sight I'd seen in a long while. They belonged to Fred Roberson's little car, and it didn't take the old garageman long to find our Ford's trouble, some small thing, and fix it so we could go on home.

Bert told me afterward that just after he got to the garage Mrs. Roberson came in to tell Fred supper was ready, and that Fred told her it would have to wait, that he couldn't leave that poor woman and her children sitting out there in the hills while he stopped to eat.

Chapter Forty

THE first day of March, 1913, a Mr. Frazier, from Missouri, filed on a rough little piece of land just east of the Kirts's valley. The Fraziers, Mr. and Mrs. and three sets of twins, set up a tent on the land that same day and moved in.

The twelfth of March was a mild, springlike day, so warm that Miles and Nellie played outside without their wraps and Bert worked all day in his shirt-sleeves. But late that afternoon a dark, ugly haze began to spread across the northwest sky.

Bert had turned the cattle into the south end of the meadow to clean up stack bottoms, and toward sundown most of them came to stand in an uneasy line along the west yard fence. One was a shaggy old Longhorn cow with a four-foot spread of heavy horns, the only one of her kind left in our herd of blockier solid colors and "whitefaces." The long-legged old cow looked across the fence for a long time, a sadness in her big eyes. Afterward, I wondered if she had known, somehow, what lay ahead.

By dark the sky was overcast and a fine mist was falling. Soon after we went to bed, a light mournful wind began blowing across the valley from the south. Sometime in the night it swung to the northwest and came roaring back across the hills. By morning the worst blizzard since 1888 was going full blast.

A true blizzard is a terrible thing, especially to a ranchman. In a few hours it can wipe out all that he has worked years to accumulate. To Bert, this one was a nightmare. The milk cows were shut in the old barn, the work team and Silver, the Kentucky Whip stallion, were in the new one. Everything else was out in the storm.

Because the blizzard struck after midnight, it didn't catch anyone in the hills out on the road, but it was bound to be hard on the people living in Kinkaid shacks. Even in our tight, plastered house, the cold wind seeped in and kept the rooms chilly around the edges. We had to keep the fires roaring to hold the cold back, and soon after breakfast the bucket of coal we kept on the enclosed north porch for emergencies was gone. The rest of our little winter coal pile was out in the cellar, less than a hundred feet northwest of the house.

Bert bundled up in overshoes, two coats, and his heavy Scotch cap to go after a new supply. I tied a long wool scarf around his neck and face, just below his eyes, and he took two pails and the scoop shovel and went out into the storm. I watched at the kitchen window but I couldn't see a thing; the blizzard was like a thick white curtain on the other side of the glass.

A half hour went by and Bert hadn't come back. In the big blizzard of '88, people had been lost and frozen to death between their houses and outbuildings, and I knew it could happen to him in this one. Then I heard something hit the porch wall and I ran out and opened the door. The wind jerked it away from me and flung it back against the wall so hard it splintered the boards, but Bert stumbled through the doorway with his two pails of coal. The part of his face that showed between the scarf and cap was a solid sheet of ice.

He staggered on into the kitchen and I unwound the frozen scarf from his head and broke the layers of ice off his eyes. He had had a terrible time, he said. His eyes were frozen shut before he'd gone half a dozen steps, and the snow was so fine and thick that he could hardly breathe. He had run into a high drift between the house and the cellar, and it had taken a long time to work around the west end of it so he could go on. He'd been lucky to find the cellar, but he'd had a hard time getting its sloping door open against the wind. Coming back, he had quartered west again, toward the end of the big drift, but, fearful of going too far and missing the house, he hadn't gone far enough and had fallen off the face of it and spilled the coal in the snow. The drift broke the force of the wind a little, though, and he'd managed to pick up most of the coal. He hadn't even known he was back to the house until he bumped into the porch.

He looked at me then, misery in his eyes. "Mom," he said, "I don't see how the cattle can ever live through this."

To make the fuel last as long as possible, we moved what we'd need for the rest of the day into the living room and shut off the kitchen and let the fire go out there. The storm seemed to get worse as the day wore on, and I kept thinking about the folks in those little frame shacks scattered through the hills. Wickards and Moorheads, and that tent over in the next valley. A tent couldn't even stand in such a wind.

By evening the house fairly shook and shivered in the roaring wind. I made up the settee in the front room for Miles and Nellie to sleep on that night, and moved my plants away from the frost-white window. Bert banked the fire on the last of the coal and we went to bed, but neither of us did much sleeping.

We were up again at daylight. The storm had blown itself out, toward morning, and the day was bitter cold. Bert stirred up the fire and dressed and went out without waiting for breakfast.

A narrow space around the house had been kept free of snow by the whipping winds, but just beyond it the drifts were eave-high on the north, east, and south. Bert climbed the sloping face of the north drift and hurried to the barn, where he had to shovel through a long drift to get to the door. He saddled Silver and rode off west on top of the deep, frozen snow. The children and I watched him from the west window, the only one not shut in by the big drifts.

"Looky," Miles said, "Dad can ride right over the tops of the fences this morning."

Before Bert reached the far side of the meadow, a few cattle came over a hill from the northwest and drifted down toward the snow-covered lake at that end. He headed them toward a half-buried haystack beside the lake, and then rode on out of sight. At least the cattle weren't *all* dead.

I fixed the children some breakfast before I wrapped up and went out to see what I could do for the milk cows and chickens. From the top of the big drift at the back door, about all I could see was snow. The corrals were *full* of it; the cellar and the chip pile were under the drifts, and there wasn't a fence post in sight anywhere. I could hear the cows bawling in the old barn and a rooster crowing in the chicken house. At the south end of the valley a faint streak of smoke showed that old Matthews had come through the storm alive.

The bitter wind made my eyes sting with tears while

I shoveled through the packed snow to the chicken house door. The poor chickens were a sorry-looking bunch, huddled in misery on the one little corner of their roost that wasn't under snow. Drifts even *hung* from the roof above them, where the powdery snow had built down from cracks in the shingled roof until they almost joined the drifts below.

From the chicken house I slipped and slid on over the hard drifts to see about the cows. The long, low-roofed old barn was completely covered by the biggest drift I had ever seen. It started more than a hundred yards behind the barn and built up and up until it hung over the front in a curling, frozen wave, six feet high. Inside, the cows stood bunched at one end. As the snow blew in through the cracked old walls they had trampled it underfoot for thirty hours, until their backs came against the underside of the roof. The rest of the barn was filled solid with snow. So was the granary beside it, and the icy stuff was packed so hard that I could hardly hack it away to get at the little pile of corn on the floor. The water tank, too, was under a deep drift. It took me most of the forenoon to shovel things out so I could feed and water the poor chickens and cows and do the milking.

Bert rode for days, looking for cattle. He found some, smothered or frozen, against the fences where they had drifted early in the blizzard. Others, the ones that survived the storm until the fences drifted under, were scattered all through the hills. Some, down but still alive, he shoveled out of the drifts and hauled home on sleds. A few of them lived, but most died later in the miserable slush that covered everything as the great drifts melted.

All through the hills Kinkaiders made good money that spring, skinning dead cattle. Clayton Bussard and one

of his Squaw Creek neighbors skinned ours—and old man
Matthews waited, his skillet in his hand, while they took
the hide off a heifer that had died against the fence not
far from his door. By the time the snow was gone, he
had the carcass cut down to the horns and hoofs and a
few bones.

While the skinners worked on the cattle he'd already
found, Bert kept on riding the hills and draws, looking
for others. By the end of April he had accounted for all
but one of our herd: the half that had died in the blizzard and the half, poor storm-beaten things, that still
lived. Only the old Longhorn was still missing.

On his rides through the hills, Bert saw the neighbors
and heard their stories of the blizzard. Fraziers had had
it the toughest. Their tent had gone down about daylight and Mr. Frazier had crawled outside to see what
was going on. He had never known such a storm as
that one, and he knew they were in trouble. The tent
stakes still held the flapping canvas down, so he crawled
back inside and told his family to dress in a hurry and
they'd try to get to the Kirtses. The tent popped and
cracked over their heads while they pulled on clothes and
wraps, but the stakes still held. When one of the youngest twins couldn't find his cap, his mother tied the table-
cloth over his head and they were ready.

Mr. Frazier took Sadie and Sylvester, nine years old,
by the hands and led the way. Millie and Sylvie, twelve,
held hands and came next, and Mrs. Frazier, with Donnie
and Johnnie, seven, followed them. The double ruts of
the wagon road that led past their tent were worn deep
across the half-mile-wide flat to Kirtses, and Mr. Frazier
kept his bearings by walking with his left foot in the
right-hand rut. The others followed close behind, and
somehow they kept in line and kept going.

They knew they had almost made it when they bumped into the barbed-wire corral fence north of Kirtses' house. But the worst of the trip was still ahead, for the storm was a solid wall of white by then and they'd have nothing to guide them after they left the corner of the fence. The soddy was no more than one hundred feet away, but it was such a little target in that storm. It would be so easy to miss it and go stumbling off into the empty hills beyond.

They left the fence and headed toward where the soddy should be, and, by chance, for all he knew, Mr. Frazier held to the right direction and bumped square into the house. If they had started that awful trip even an hour later, after the ruts began to drift full and freeze, they probably wouldn't have made it.

Mrs. Wickard was home alone with her children during the blizzard. Whenever the weather looked threatening she put up a rope from the corner of her house to the pump and on to the barn. Twice, the day of the storm, she followed her rope to the barn to feed and milk her cow and take care of her calf and pig. On the first trip she found one of her little hen pigeons with her head covered with an almost solid ball of ice. She broke the ice away and took the little hen to the house with her, and later in the day she flew up on top of the cupboard and laid an egg.

The hill behind the Wickard buildings broke the force of the storm considerably. Had the buildings been out on a flat, as most people's were, the guide rope would have drifted under, along with everything else.

Up in the Pinkerton Valley, Lottie Lovall was keeping her two sisters with her for the school term. Lottie's little soddy was one of those built on an open flat, and when the girls got up that morning to get ready for school, their door was already blocked by a drift as high as the house. The weather had been so warm the day before that they, like almost everybody in the hills, were caught with almost no fuel in the house. Their little pile of coal and chips was outside so, when their fire went out, they went back to bed.

New and tight as the little soddy was, snow soon began sifting into the room, piling up on the cold stove and festooning down from the open rafters. When it began to sift down on their bed, the girls put an umbrella up over their heads. When they got hungry they hopped out of bed long enough to fix cold sandwiches. To them the blizzard was an exciting adventure and they had no idea how awful it had been until the next morning, when Henry Downing rode down from Whitewater and tunneled through the big drift to their door.

Their fuel was under six feet of frozen snow and they couldn't stay on in the cold house any longer. So Henry led his horse and went ahead, breaking the bitter wind for them across the mile-long stretch of meadow to Pinkertons. The only living thing they saw was a big three-year-old Whitewater steer, his head and eyes covered with a thick coat of solid ice, standing on the flat with his tail to the icy wind. They could see then that the blizzard had been a killer.

No human lives were lost in our section of the hills, but livestock losses were enormous. Nearly all the big ranches lost heavily from their range herds. For Whitewater it was all of the yearlings and hundreds of cows. Two hundred head of O'Brian cattle died in Brown Lake; all but one of Harry Pinkerton's weaned calves drifted into the lake in his valley and died there. It was the same at Jewetts and Aufdengartens.

Gordon Jewett's neighbor, Jack Palmer, and his hired

hand, Dana Lombard, rode across Palmer's meadow the morning after the storm. Dana said, "Jack, it looks like your lake's full of cattle." Jack squinted at the humps in the snow on the lake and said, "Naw, those're just muskrat houses." But they weren't, not many of them. They were Jack's dead cattle.

A few were lucky, like Nate Trego. His cattle, on their winter feed ground under the high, dark hill, had protection enough to weather the storm; but poor Johnny Schicks, out on the flat where there was nothing to break the sweep of the blizzard across the valley, lost more than half his herd.

For us, the story of the blizzard had a strange end.

In May, when only a few soggy snowdrifts still showed on the north sides of the hills or in the deep hollows, Hebe Haney, a seventy-year-old bachelor, proved up on his claim and held a public auction of his few belongings. Mr. Haney's place was southeast of the Frazier claim, and the day after the sale Charley Harris picked him up and took him down to Tryon to bank his money. On the way back to the old man's place they overtook a fellow walking along the road.

The man, a neighbor of Mr. Haney's was a strange sort. Slim and dark, he walked like an Indian, so soft and easy that one didn't hear him coming. Charlie knew that there had been a little bad blood between the two, an argument or disagreement over money a year or two before, but he thought the trouble had been settled and that it would be all right to ask the man to ride along with them.

The fellow got in the buckboard, behind Charlie and Mr. Haney, and they drove on. A few minutes later he struck the old man on the head with a heavy iron bolt wrapped in a handkerchief. The testimony Charlie

gave at the inquest the next day, tells the story best:
"All at once I heard a lick struck. I looked around and
saw S——— trying to pull Haney out of the seat. I
told him to let go but he wouldn't so I knocked him
down with the butt of my whip. When he got up he
pulled a gun and said 'I want some money.' Mr. Haney
said, 'Charles, he has a gun.' I asked S——— why he
wanted to kill us and he did not say anything. I whipped
up then and we drove off. S——— was still standing
in the road. I didn't think the old man was hurt much
until we got near his place and he began to talk with a
thick tongue. He was still sitting up in the seat when
we got to his place but when I helped him out of the
buckboard he couldn't stand up alone. He said he was
sick, so I took him over to Boldman's place."

When the old man died that night, before a doctor
from North Platte could get to him, Charlie said, "If I'd
known he was hurt that bad I'd of hit S——— a lot
harder."

S——— had gone on home after his attack on the
old man. When he heard that Mr. Haney was dead and
the sheriff was looking for the murderer, he took to the
hills afoot, with his gun. By morning posses were riding
the hills, looking for him.

Bert rode with the posses, part of the time by day,
part of the time at night. On the nights he was at home
he padlocked Silver in the barn and slept with his revolver under his pillow. On the nights he was gone I
wedged chairs under the knobs of the outside doors,
since we didn't even have keys to any of our house doors.

They never found the murderer, but on the fourteenth
day of May, while he was still looking for him, Bert
found the old Longhorn. She lay in the bottom of a

deep blowout west of the meadow. He had ridden by that snow-filled hollow several times since the blizzard, but not until two months after the storm did the snow melt enough to let a patch of her spotted hide show through.

Chapter Forty-One

ALONG with the excitement stirred up by poor Mr. Haney's murder, the county seat ruckus flared again that spring. The East Enders were campaigning for a new and bigger courthouse in Tryon, but the West Enders said they'd vote it down, unless the county seat was moved to the middle of the county. The East Enders said they'd never consent to *that,* so the West Enders said all right then, they'd secede and organize a new county of their own.

For us, a county seat at Flats wouldn't be any closer than it was at Tryon, but Bert was on the side of the West End people. They had had to travel the whole length of the county long enough, he said. But he didn't want to see the county split in two, either, as that would mean higher taxes and bigger expenses for everybody. So he tried to stop the split by proposing to some of the West Enders—Trego, Schicks, the Rupp boys and a few others—that they ride down to Tryon some dark night and swipe the courthouse and records and move them to Flats before Tryon woke up in the morning.

Of course they couldn't move a sod building, but Bert said the roof would do. They could haul it to Flats and set it up on posts, and call it a courthouse until the county could build a new one. Once they had the roof and records located there, he was sure there'd be votes enough to hold it. Deals like that had worked in other Nebraska counties. It might have worked in ours, too, but when Bert put his plan to Mr. Huffman, the good old man said, "Why, Bert! *You* wouldn't steal a courthouse, would you?" So they didn't do any more about it, and in June the county divided in the middle.

The west half became Arthur County, the ninety-third and last of Nebraska's counties. There was already a little town of Arthur, up near Aufdengartens, and the new county set up a tent there for a courthouse. Later, when they could afford it, they built a 28 x 24-foot frame courthouse in the middle of an acre of sand and bunchgrass. The little building later became famous as the smallest courthouse in the United States.

The dividing line between the two counties was on the west side of Flats, and Bert and the other ranchmen, left in what was now the new west end of McPherson County, were more than ever against the big rise in taxes that would be needed to build a courthouse in Tryon. So they voted it down again.

By 1914, the exodus that had started the year before was general all through the hills. Moorhead sold out to Charlie Daly; Bert bought the Wickard place and the Bryant and Harrison sections. Old man Matthews wanted to leave, too, but he wouldn't sell to Bert and no one else made him a good offer, so he stayed.

A few other poor souls left, too, but they had to take a harder way out. Mrs. Charlie Harris was one, and a homesteader's wife from over on the west side of Shinbone Valley was another.

Mrs. Harris took sick the summer after the big blizzard. By November she was bedfast with dropsy. Mrs. Pierce, Mrs. Lovall, Mrs. Frazier, and the widow Thrasher and I took turns doing the family washing, taking in cooked food, and doing anything else we could. Two weeks before Christmas, Charlie's sister, good Aunt Jessie Stoddard, came down from her home in Baldy Valley to help care for the dying woman.

The snow was deep in the hills when she passed away at daylight on December 23, leaving four young children. Shortly after sunup Charlie drove into our place with the children. He wanted to leave the girls with us, he said, while he and the twelve-year-old boy, Albert, drove on to Tryon to get a coffin and rough box, and to phone his sister Matt in the Platte. We urged him to bring the boy and Aunt Jessie and come back that night, too, but only Aunt Jessie came.

Charlie had bought a nice coffin and shroud, she said, and she and the widow Thrasher had "laid out" the dead woman, but Charlie would not leave her. The funeral was set for Christmas morning, as early as the neighbors could gather. They were taking her to the Eclipse grave-yard, up on the Dismal, and the funeral had to be early to give them time for the long drive there.

The government had started its new parcel-post serv-ice the March before, and we had ordered Christmas presents for our three from Montgomey Ward. The pack-ages had come to Brighton post office, weeks back, and I had put them away for Santa Claus to see to. But there was no sign of Christmas at our house that Christmas Eve when, out of the snow and the cold and the dark, instead of Santa in his sled, Charlie's sister and a hired driver in a Hupmobile came to our door, bringing pack-ages and bundles.

They had been fourteen hours on the road from the Platte, shoveling through snow and sand, and they were almost too tired and cold to eat the hot supper I hurried to set out for them.

"I bought these things after Charlie called me yester-day," Aunt Matt said of her bundles, "and I planned to get here in time to give them to the children today. Now, late as it is, I guess we'd better wait until after the funeral."

I bedded them all down that cold night, the two aunts, the three little girls, and the hired driver, and I was thankful for my store of warm quilts, most of them pieced during the long, snowbound winters I had spent on the ranch.

That Christmas Day was one of the coldest days of the whole winter. Even wrapped in quilts and robes, the Ford and Hupmobile radiators would have frozen solid before we could cross the meadow, so Bert hitched up a team and filled the wagon box with hay. I cut all the blooms from my geraniums and fuchsias and wrapped them in a thick roll of newspapers, and all of us climbed into the wagon. The aunts and the children and I dug down into the hay and turned our backs to the cutting wind and pulled the robes over our heads. Even then we ached with cold at the end of the two-mile trip.

A few neighbors and the minister, a gray-headed little homesteader from the south end of the Skinner Valley, were there ahead of us. I gave my flowers to Aunt Jessie and she went into the bedroom with Charlie and Aunt Matt and shut the door. After a while they came out, weeping, and the year-old baby, Mary, began to cry and reach for her father.

The rest of us went into the icy bedroom where the coffin was. They had put one of my apple blossom geraniums in the dead woman's hand, and the rest of the little bouquet on top of the plain gray coffin.

"I wonder where Mama got that pretty dress. I never

saw it before," twelve-year-old Letty said of her mother's pink shroud.

We stood in the kitchen while the preacher read from his Bible. Charlie had put the baby on the edge of the table and dropped into a chair beside her. At the end of the service he put his head in her lap and sobbed.

The other men closed the coffin and carried it out to the rough box in the wagon, and Charlie gave the baby to Aunt Matt and went out and climbed up on the seat in front of it, beside a neighbor who was driving. Young Albert, Aunt Jessie and her husband, and one or two others got into another wagon and the two rigs pulled out on the freezing seventeen-mile drive to Eclipse, where a new grave had been hacked out of the frozen sand.

Aunt Matt and the girls went home with us again, and that afternoon we opened the Christmas presents.

A year or so later Charlie married the widow Thrasher, and then both families had a full set of parents again.

Over in Shinbone Valley, the other woman's trouble started with a lump under her arm.

Soon after the hills settled up, the women, from our place on northwest, had organized a Guild. We met once a month, when weather and roads permitted, and when we found a family in need or trouble we did what we could to help. That Shinbone family, always hard up, always teetering on the edge of next to nothing, had eleven children and was one of our neediest cases.

The lump had become a running sore by the time we first heard about it. We outfitted the woman with clothes and arranged for her to go to a clinic in Missouri. But even then she had to wait a little longer—until her twelfth child was born.

On a rainy night, in the already crowded two-room

soddy, the new baby kept his appointment with life, and two weeks later the poor mother left for the clinic. She was gone only a week or so, and as soon as she came home, Mrs. Charlie Foster, Mrs. Lovall, and I went to see her and find out what the doctors had told her.

"They said I should 've come sooner," she said. Then her face crumpled. "Those doctors, they read me my death warrant right there," she sobbed.

After that, all we could do was stand by. By the next spring she was no longer able to leave her bed. From then on, through May and a long, hot June, I rode horseback to take my weekly turn in the little soddy, tending the poor thin body on the hot bed for a day. The awful smell of the rotting cancer had seeped into everything in the house, the beds, the children's clothes, even the bare sod walls. I always rode away in the evening with a sick headache and a churning stomach.

Death released the suffering woman on a hot day in early July. The Guild ladies washed and dressed her for burial and held the funeral out in the yard, under a blazing sun, the next morning. She was buried on a slope back of the scabby little house. At only a little past forty, she was done with a life that had been full of trouble and hardship.

A family from another part of the county adopted the baby, and some relatives showed up to take the smaller children. A few weeks later the father loaded the rest of the family into his old wagon and pulled out for some spot beyond the sandhills. The empty soddy soon fell down, and cattle grazed in the yard where the barefooted children had played. For a while a sagging barbedwire fence protected the weedy grave, until the cattle pushed it down and grazed there, too, trampling the unmarked mound until no trace of it remained.

The next January we lost another of our nearest neighbors when old Mrs. Skinner died of pneumonia. It was cold, the day of the funeral, but I remembered how dearly the old lady had loved "posies," and I wanted to take her a bouquet of blossoms from my houseplants. We started out in the Ford, but halfway across the meadow an axle broke and left us sitting there.

"Well, I guess Grandma Skinner won't have any posies at her funeral after all," I said. But Bert said he'd saddle up and ride over with them, so we drained the radiator and walked back to the house and I wrapped the flowers in a newspaper cone for him to carry to the funeral.

Old man Matthews froze his feet one bitter night, that same January, in the new, unlined little frame shack he had built the summer before when his old soddy was about to fall in on him.

The old man had never quit blaming Bert for owning the meadow he had thought he was filing on. So, when he wouldn't let us help him when he needed help, Charlie Harris had taken over the job. It was Charlie who found him with his feet numb and turning black, and had the county commissioners take him to North Platte to have his toes amputated. They sent the poor old fellow to an institution in the eastern part of the state, after that, and we were alone in our valley again.

Chapter Forty-Two

A SHORT-LIVED new boom stirred the sandhill country again in the summer of 1915. The *Tryon Graphic* printed reports that the Burlington Railroad Company was planning to build a railroad from Kearney to Bridgeport, a little town in northwest Nebraska, and that the Burlington's interest in the sandhills had stirred the Union Pacific to the point where it was certain to build on from Stapleton the next spring.

"For the present, ONE railroad will serve our town and county very well," Editor Dunn wrote in the *Graphic*, "and when it comes we understand we will have to move our printing office off the right-of-way through the middle of town."

The boom came too late to help many of the Kinkaiders. Some had already sold, at prices ranging from $3.50 to $5.00 an acre; others had left their claims to the mortgage holders and pulled out. Down at Tryon, though, everybody was excited. Fourteen four-horse wagonloads of lumber for Mike David's new store pulled into town in one afternoon, and there was talk about the good prospects for a new courthouse, and even a high school.

But before the new store was done, or ballots printed to vote on the courthouse and high school, all hopes for a railroad through the county had gone glimmering again. The United States was loaning all its money and selling all its steel to France and England to fight a war. So the boom died and Mike's big new store was about all there was to show for it. That, and our new schoolhouse, which probably didn't have anything to do with the railroad boom.

Miles was nine then, and Nellie ten, and until that fall they had had only four months of public school. That had been two years before, when Margaret Conroy taught the school five miles southwest of us. We had furnished her free board and room, and a team to drive to her buggy, in exchange for her taking our two to school with her.

Margaret, a good teacher, had her hands full that year. Where, only five years before, there had been nothing but cattle, coyotes, jackrabbits and prairie chickens, six Kemmerers, five Skinners, Albert and Letty Harris, two little Moorheads and two or three other youngsters followed half a dozen trails across the prairie to the little sod schoolhouse.

The school yard hadn't been fenced, and cattle had rubbed against the soddy until some sods had tumbled out of one corner, leaving a long, ragged hole. That hole worried Margaret. "I'm afraid a snake will crawl in some night and get in one of the desks," she said. But the weather stayed warm and no one bothered to fix the hole—until the October morning when one of the Skinner boys met her when she drove up. "He was in the schoolhouse, Teacher," he said of the big bull snake he was swinging by the tail.

"It might be a rattlesnake next time," Margaret said. She had the big boys stuff the hole with sand and grass before she called school that day.

After Christmas, when the days were short and the weather bad, Margaret moved to a boarding place near her school and I went back to teaching our two myself. It was a job that was harder and harder for me to find time for, especially after our fourth, Flora Alberta, was born at the ranch in May, 1914.

Ours was an odd situation. When the other districts organized all around us, in the early Kinkaid days, they had left a big chunk of country in the middle where nearly all the settlers were bachelors. When Fraziers moved in, less than two miles from us, I had high hopes that we would get a district and a schoolhouse that summer. But, in the aftermath of the big blizzard, the Haney murder and the county split, no one got around to doing anything about it, and the Frazier twins went off to the Happy Hollow school that fall.

Six to eight miles northeast of us, in the unorganized area, there were three families with small children, Steve Clifford, Howard Pinkerton, and the Powells, but most of the taxpayers didn't want to go to the expense of organizing a district and building a schoolhouse until the other children were old enough to go to school.

So Miles was nine and Nellie ten before we had a school of our own. It was a nice little plastered frame schoolhouse, but it stood in the middle of the big district, five miles from us. Pretty Florence Hatch, the daughter of a ranchman on the Dismal, was the first teacher. Because most of the children had quite a long way to go, afoot like the Frazier twins, or horseback like our two and the Powells and Pinkertons, the board set a seven-months' term of school, September through December, and March through May, leaving out the two worst winter months. Even that short term was never finished, for the pretty teacher died at her boarding place of acute appendicitis before the end of school.

The Christmas program at the new schoolhouse was the

first one most of the children had ever been in, and they
enjoyed it so much that most of them went ahead and
learned all the other parts, as well as their own. By
Christmas week there was a heavy covering of snow on
the ground and Bert put the wagon box on sled runners
for the trip to the schoolhouse. Then, near dark on the
big evening, when the weather turned bad and a new
storm blew up, Bert said we'd better not try to go. But
Miles and Nellie begged so hard that he finally changed
his mind.

It was snowing when we started for the schoolhouse
and the night wind was cold, but the wagon box was
full of hay and we had plenty of quilts and robes. So
the only mishap of the trip happened when three-year-
old Billie tasted the thick frost on the steel rim of the
wagon box. When she jerked her tongue away, she left
quite a patch of its tender hide pasted there.

Howard Pinkerton and his family and the Frazier
twins were at the schoolhouse ahead of us. We waited
a while but no one else showed up, not even the teacher.
When they were sure the storm had scared all the rest
out of coming, Clarence and Doris Pinkerton, Miles and
Nellie, and the twins went ahead with the program. They
sang *all* the songs, spoke *all* the pieces, and acted out *all*
the dialogs. It was quite a program after all.

We had a seven-months' term of school again the next
year. By the year after that the world was at war and
teachers in the sandhills were almost as scarce as Cadillacs.
So we had no school that year.

A few years later, when Miles and Nellie had finished
the first eight grades and Billie and Bertie were halfway
through them, the school was closed again. Fraziers and
Powells had sold out and left the country. Steve Clifford had been elected county clerk and had moved his

family to Tryon. The younger Pinkertons went east to another school that was no farther from them than ours had been, and our two rode west five miles to a schoolhouse at the edge of Trego Valley.

So, one way or another, we managed to get them educated, even though the last two went through high school nearly two thousand miles from the sandhill valley where they grew up.

Chapter Forty-Three

BY 1917 most of the Kinkaiders were gone from the hills. Lovalls had sold out to Lottie and Henry Downing and moved to Colorado to put the two younger girls in high school. Pierces sold to Bert and moved to Washington. Old man Matthews had died in the institution, and Bert had bought his place from the relative who showed up to claim his estate.

The country was settling down again in a new shape. Schools were smaller, or discontinued altogether; dozens of little post offices, no longer needed, had disappeared. Ranches were bigger, and so were the blowouts left behind by the settlers' breaking plows. Most of them left little else but those plowed fields, where the blow sand drifted for years, and the young cottonwood groves that shaded the crumbling walls of their soddies. A few more years and there would be nothing but some worn-out, rusted machinery, or a broken stove or a twisted iron bedstead, half buried in sand under the cottonwoods, to mark where the homes had been.

A few of the vanished homesteaders had been the tumbleweed kind—blown here and there across the land by the winds of hard luck, or just plain shiftlessness, but most of them had been good people, hardworking, home-loving folks. All of them had followed the lure of free land into the hills, and many of them had paid dearly for it in the end. They had paid with hardship and loss. They had paid with five years of their lives, and some of them with life itself. A few, like Conroys and Van Meters, had come to stay, and the hills would never again be as empty as when I first went into them.

During the years when the Kinkaiders were leaving the hills they held little public auctions to dispose of the things they didn't want to take with them. The sales were social affairs as much as anything else, for everybody from miles around came for a day of visiting and for the free lunch at noon. We went to quite a few of the little sales, usually in our car—it was easier, that way, for Bert to bring home the batch of old, unmatched dishes and kitchen odds and ends he always bought for a dime or a quarter.

One sale that will be remembered a long time by a lot of people was Frank Foster's, up in the Huffman Valley. Frank had come to the hills with more money and possessions than most of the Kinkaiders, so his was a fairly big sale. He held it early in the spring, too, after a winter of deep snows, and people came from thirty miles around. Fosters hadn't expected anywhere near such a big crowd and, even though they sliced the free lunch bread and bologna thin as a scared whisper, they still ran away short on sandwiches and ginger snaps.

Early that afternoon the hungry crowd began sorting out children and cranking cars or hitching up teams. Almost before the sale was over, cars and rigs were fanning out in all directions, headed for home and an early supper. We were among the first to leave, the throttle pulled down an extra notch and chugging right along. We passed two or three wagons, on the way out of the valley, before we started up the first long hill. Then, halfway to the top, we heard a familiar pop and whistle.

We all climbed out, and Bert hauled his latest old boiler full of scarred pans and dishes out from between the seats so he could fish the tire irons and the jack and pump from under the back-seat cushion. While he scraped and patched the punctured tube, the wagons *passed us* and went on out of sight. We finally loaded up and started on again, the throttle pulled down another notch and hitting the bumps a little harder. There weren't going to be many old dishes to sort and put away this time.

Along with the other changes that came to the hills at that time was the reorganizing of the old Guild into the Helping Hand Club. The Guild had been organized as an Episcopal ladies' society in the early settlement years, when Preacher Ware, an Episcopalian minister, traveled the hills holding services in homes, schoolhouses, or even on the open prairie. When the minister was recalled from the sandhill field, about 1916, and no other sent to take his place, there was no longer anything to hold the Guild together. So the members met in October, 1916, to reorganize and draw up a new constitution and set of bylaws.

Our constitution was tailored to fit our special needs and circumstances, and so was somewhat different from those governing most women's groups. ARTICLE 2 read, "The object of this club shall be the upbuilding of the community socially, intellectually, and morally, and the helping of the needy wherever found." ARTICLE 4, "All meetings shall be opened and closed with prayer." ARTICLE 5, "Three shall constitute a quorum to do business."

Though our club sometimes had as many as two dozen members, it covered a territory a full thirty miles across, from our place on the south edge of the circle to ranches up above the Dismal on the north. Sandhill weather and

roads being what they were, sometimes no more than
three members could make it to a meeting.

ARTICLE 6 read, "Roll call shall be answered by a scripture verse or some lines of prose or poetry written for
the elevation of the soul." ARTICLE 7, "Meetings shall
be held on the first Wednesday of the month at the
homes of the members, as they be taken in alphabetical
order." ARTICLE 8, that the meeting time be used for
"club work, fancy work, music or literature." ARTICLE
10, that the hostess serve "not more than one meat, two
vegetables, one salad and one dessert, and a twenty-five
cent fine be imposed on anyone violating this rule."

Since the club, in a way, took the place of the church
services we no longer had, and because the meetings were
also the main social affairs of the community, the members' families went too. Also, considering the usual state
of the roads, it was a good thing to have a man along to
get the car through the bad places. The meetings were
all-day affairs because, no matter where we met, some of
us always had a long road to travel. I lived on the south
rim of the big circle and there was no one to come by
and pick me up, so when the meetings were not too far
away, and the roads were bad and Bert too busy to go
with me, I went horseback.

Every woman in the community, the hired man's wife
as well as the rancher's, was welcome to join the club
if she wanted to. And in time our membership came
to be so large that, if the day was nice and the roads not
too bad, there might be anywhere from fifty to seventy
men, women, and children at a meeting. At that point
we changed the last article in our constitution to read
that the hostess "furnish only the meat, drink, bread
and potatoes." Each member attending then brought a
covered dish, and that way, even though only three or

four members "made it to club," there would still be a
good dinner. When practically everybody came, a club
dinner was a banquet, a picnic, and a ten-course dinner
all in one.

One or two years, due to storms, bad roads, epidemics
and the like, not more than three meetings were held in
a twelvemonth; and it was not until 1924 that, for the
first time in its history, the club held a meeting every
month of the year. Very few of the charter members
are alive now but, after almost fifty years, the club is
still meeting and working, and the rules set then are
the ones that guide it still; as the daughters and granddaughters carry on, meeting the needs of the community
as they arise.

One of the early-day members put it well when she
wrote these lines for one of our programs:

> Each month we get together,
> Though our homes are far between.
> And sometimes it's quite an effort,
> As our roads are rough and mean.
> But our club is what we make it
> And it's up to us to do
> The things of most importance
> And to see they're carried through.

After we got into the war, the Helping Hand ladies
exchanged their quilting needles for knitting needles and
began turning out sweaters, socks, and wash cloths by
the bale. The club held a good many Red Cross benefit
dances and suppers, too, during the war years. One of
those affairs was a big barn dance and oyster feed at Tom
Quinn's barn on the Dismal, on the far north rim of
the club circle.

People from three counties came, and the Red Cross
benefitted by $181.55. Those who didn't hold with danc-

ing came early and ate all the soup they could hold, so that, in one way or another, everybody did his bit. When the fiddlers tuned up, the babies and small children were bedded down on a hay pile in a corner of the big hay-mow and the dance was on. Around midnight, Tom cleared the dance floor for his mother. The tiny, wrinkled, old lady was famous in the sandhills for her fast Irish jigs, and that night she picked up her long skirts and kicked up her heels like a two-year-old for the boys in khaki.

Grandma Quinn had come from Ireland when she was a girl of seventeen. Back in 1884 she married John Quinn in the "Church of the Wildwood" in Red Oak, Iowa, and came with him to his homestead on the Dismal. She was the first white woman in all that section of the sand-hills and, for a long time, the only one. Tom, her oldest son, was born beside the wagon when she and her hus-band were on the way home from a timbered spot on the river with a load of wood. She had been a widow for a long time now, but she was still as lively and merry as a girl, and she never missed a church service, a dance, or a gathering of any kind, even if she had to walk to get there.

A few weeks later, there was another big benefit dance and box supper, this time at Flats on a Saturday night. Two weeks before this dance, Bert and I rode horseback to one of the last of the Kinkaider sales, down on Squaw Creek. In the crowd that day there was a little girl with a bright red rash on her face. I heard someone ask the mother if she didn't think it dangerous to take the child out when she had measles, and the woman said no, that she only had the "Liberty" measles, and wasn't very sick, anyway.

During the war, it was so unpatriotic to have German (three-day) measles, that everybody had "Liberty" measles instead.

We had invited a pretty teacher from a neighboring school to go to the Flats dance with us. She came on Friday and stayed all night with us. Saturday morning I got up with a scratchy throat. I was too busy, baking and cooking for the boxes I had to fill for the supper, to pay much attention to it at first. But by five o'clock that afternoon I knew it wasn't any use—I wouldn't be going anywhere that evening.

"You go ahead and take Miss Lewis to the dance," I told Bert. "I'm going to bed."

So Bert and the pretty teacher bounced away in the Ford and I crawled into bed, shaking with a bad chill. When I could quit shivering, I asked Nellie to bring the lamp and my hand mirror to the bed. I wasn't surprised when I saw that my face and neck were broken out with "Liberty" measles—I had been *smelling* them for the last hour.

Chapter Forty-Four

DURING all the years Preacher Ware served the sand-hills he had dreamed of a church on the banks of the Dismal, beside the little Eclipse burying ground. Even after he was recalled from the field, he continued to work for a church building there, and by the spring of 1917 there was money enough in the till to make his dream come true.

The United States declared war on Germany on April 6, and right afterward the weather went on a late spring rampage that blocked all roads in the hills. The day the storm started, the preacher was on his way from North Platte to Eclipse to stake out the site for the new church. He managed to get on to Tryon before all travel stalled in the drifts.

For the next three days neither an automobile nor a wagon turned a wheel on the sandhill roads. On the fourth morning, a good-sized force of Tryonites turned out to open the road from Tryon to Lena. All along the way ranchers joined the snow shovelers to help get the mail and the minister through, and by Saturday night the mail was in Lena and the preacher at Placer Tucker's ranch on the Dismal, just over the hill from the cemetery.

On Sunday morning two or three ranch families broke through the drifts to Tuckers, and after church services at the ranch the men went along to help Preacher Ware set stakes in the snow to mark the location of the new church. By the time the snow was gone men and teams were on the road, freighting lumber and supplies for the church building.

The heavy runoff from that big storm raised the lakes in our meadow and filled a new pond in a low place at the south end of my garden. Water squished under our feet in the yard all spring, and little frogs croaked at night in the wet grass outside our bedroom windows. The water level was high in every meadow in the sandhills that summer, and the mosquitoes were a plague to man and beast. There was a day, just after we finished haying, when I thought they'd eat me alive, shoes and all.

Not long after he came to the sandhills, Oscar Cather had married Myra Lombard, the daughter of old Mr. Skinner's widowed sister. That summer of the mosquitoes, Myra was near death from tuberculosis, and the Helping Hand ladies were taking turns sitting up with her at night.

We were in the middle of an August heat wave the afternoon I rode up to spend the night with the sick woman, and I didn't hurry my horse. I had never been to the Cather place, up beyond big Shinbone Valley, and when the road finally faded out in a tangle of meandering cattle trails, all I could do was keep to a northwesterly direction. After a while I came to a fenced meadow. Beyond it, back of a low range of hills, I could see the top half of the tall, narrow frame house I had been told to watch for. I followed the fence to a gate and let myself through, then I headed across the uncut meadow toward the house.

The hot, damp grass was stirrup high and the mosquitoes came out of it in buzzing clouds. They settled on my face and neck and arms and ankles and dug in with a thousand stingers. They stung my poor horse, too, until he danced and snorted and tossed his head in misery. I slapped the little beasts with both hands, but for every handful I mashed, a whole hatful buzzed up to take their places. By the time I reached the tall house in the hills on the other side of that meadow I was a solid welt.

Myra was very bad that afternoon. Oscar said she had been "out of her head and talking wild" most of the day, and that she kept trying to get up and they had to hold her in bed until she quieted down. Poor thing, she wasn't hard to hold, for her strength came in little spurts that soon ebbed away, but someone had to be with her all the time.

Poor Myra, not yet out of her twenties, had had a hard life. While she was still a little girl, her father had disappeared, team and wagon and all. The family had lived down on the river valley at the time, where every once in a while a man, traveling some lonely road, never showed up at the end of it. Sometimes the team and wagon were recognized by chance in some faraway community and could be traced back to the man who had done murder to get them, but Myra's father and his outfit were among those never heard of again. When the sandhills were opened to settlement, the widow and her family had homesteaded northwest of her brother's place, where the poor woman died a few years later.

Myra's sickness had taken hold of her not long after her marriage. She was already pretty far gone when her youngest brother, Henry Lombard, went off to war. After that she had worsened fast. Oscar hired a girl then, to do the housework and look after their little boy. But more help was needed, and that was when the Helping Hand Club stepped in to do what could be done.

That evening, after his chores were done, Oscar came

and sat a while in the hot little sickroom. He was a short, chunky little man with a tired, beaten look in his face and the droop of his shoulders. "I meant to take Myra down to Kearney to the TB hospital, as soon as I got straightened around this summer," he told me, "but Henry left for the war and she took this bad spell before I could get to it. As soon as she gets strong enough to stand the trip, I'll take her anyway. I guess it's too late to do her much good, but they're fixed to take better care of her than I can. It's a queer thing, but she keeps saying she's going to see Henry again."

Poor thing, I thought, she'll never live to get to the hospital, let alone to see Henry again.

On the way home the next day, I kept to the hills that skirted the mosquito-ridden meadow, and at the top of one I came suddenly onto five coyote puppies, rolling and tumbling in play in the draw below. I pulled up short to watch them. I couldn't help enjoying their baby play, even though I knew every one of them would, if he had the chance, grow up to be a cruel hunter. I had seen too many turkeys and chickens and ducks killed for fun, and little calves half eaten and still living, not to know the damage these five would do if they lived to grow up.

When the puppies saw me and streaked for their den, I jumped off my horse and ran down the slope, hoping I might be quick enough to club one or two of them with the butt end of my quirt as they dived into the hole. I might as well have saved my breath, for the sly little fellows scattered in five directions and popped into other holes under the edge of the hill. In two seconds the draw was empty and still; but I had a good idea that the smart old mother had watched the whole thing from somewhere on the ridge, where her tawny fur matched the bunchgrass so well that I could not see her. I could see why, though every man's hand was against them, we always had coyotes.

Every day, the next week, I expected to hear of poor Myra's death. And I could hardly believe it when we heard, instead, that she was getting better. And then that Oscar had taken her to the state hospital at Kearney, where she still said she was going to live until Henry got home. But Henry was somewhere in France and no one knew when he'd be home, and Myra had only a little piece of a lung left.

By the end of the summer the new church at Eclipse was finished, a pretty white frame building beside the peaceful, grassy graves on the banks of the Dismal. Before the day of its dedication in September, the funerals of two little girls had already been held in the church, and from that time on it has been used mainly for funerals. It has never had a resident minister, or even regular Sunday services, but again and again it has been the scene of last, sad good-byes. There has been only one wedding in the pretty church in the near half century it has stood on the lonesome prairie. And that was one February, when such a bad snowstorm came on the night before that many of the guests and most of the wedding party, except for the bride and groom, couldn't even get to the church.

Also, 1917 was the year that I became a postmaster and that, just before the ground froze too hard to dig postholes, the telephone line finally reached the ranch.

Back in 1906 or 1907, when the telephone line first headed north into the hills from Sutherland, we had bought a share in the company. The line reached Tregos and Schicks that first summer, and we had expected it to come on over our way the next year. Instead, it went

north little by little, up through Shinbone Valley to
Huffmans, then finally curved back as far as Lovalls,
where the money gave out.

Now, from Schicks to Harrises to us, the line crow-
hopped across the hills, part of the way on little poles
of its own, most of the way on two-by-four sticks nailed
to fence posts. The day the lineman installed our box
telephone was one we had waited for for a long time.
It was to be almost another ten years before the line
went on to Tryon, and until it did we had to phone by
a long, roundabout route to reach North Platte and
points east. Even so, it was good to be linked by something more than a sandy, crooked trail to town and doctors, and to our neighbors on the north and west.

I made the first call on our new phone to Lottie Downing. After supper Charlie Harris called Bert, and for a
little while they yelled at each other as though there
wasn't any phone line across the two miles of hills between them. When Bert used the phone, he always raised
his voice according to the distance. If he talked to Nate
Trego, six miles away, he yelled about three times louder
than he did at Charlie.

There were a dozen or more phones on our line, and
each had its own ring, a short and a long, or two shorts
and a long and a short, and so on. A "general ring" was
one long, long ring. "Central," or anyone else on the
line, rang that one in case of emergency, or to broadcast
news or information of general interest. I wrote all the
"rings" on a card that I fastened to the wall beside the
phone. After that, except when the flimsy little line
went down in a storm, we were as close to our neighbors
as the west wall of our living room. It was a good feeling.

There were some people on our line who "listened in"
every time the phone rang; but most of us only did it

when the whole country was stormed in, or when we were keeping track of a serious illness in a neighbor's family, or when we were interested in the progress of a neighborhood courtship. The first to take down a receiver could hear the click, click, click of all the others coming down, and it was a sure thing that no one ever said anything on the party line that he didn't want the whole country to know about.

A lot of the party-line talk, the first two years we had the phone, was about the war.

The first we had heard of the trouble in Europe was in the summer of 1914, while we were still haying. It had all seemed so far away, then, but it had soon come closer, when so many on our side of the ocean said they didn't see how we could keep out of it.

Grandma McCance's brothers had fought in the Civil War, and two of them had almost starved to death in a Southern prison camp, but that had been a long time ago. The Spanish-American War had hardly touched us, for I hadn't known anyone who fought in it. So it was hard for me to think of the United States at war, or of what it would mean for Roy, just turned twenty-one, or Johnny Pierce, Dewitt Foster, Reuel Conroy, and Bill Lovall.

And then there was our local "pro-German." His parents were German but he had been born in the United States and the country had been good to him. Yet he declared that he hoped "Germany kicked the face off the whole kit and kaboodle, the United States too, if it mixed into the war." His neighbors said he'd better be careful how he shot off his mouth, or he'd get some sense kicked into *his* head. There were hard feelings, of course, and they got worse after we went into the war. Then the German sympathizer stopped the mail car and took

THE TEN BAR RANCH HOUSE, WASHHOUSE, AND BARN, AS SEEN FROM THE WEST

EPISCOPAL CHURCH ON THE DISMAL RIVER

the United States flag off its radiator and "stomped" it into the sand, and ordered the mail carrier "not to let him see him carrying that rag there any more."

There was a law against mail carriers fighting while carrying the United States mail—and the pro-German was a big man besides—so the mail carrier kept still until he got back to town, where he reported the whole affair. The German sympathizer was arrested and given a hearing, and then turned loose under bond until the next term of court. Of course there was a lot more ugly talk, and a good deal of it was over the telephone.

The "post office" came to us on a cold November day in 1917—and stayed at the ranch for the next twenty years. Its name was "Lilac" and it began back in the 1890's, in a settler's soddy some twenty miles north of Sutherland. It was named for the single, stunted little lilac bush that was trying to grow in front of the soddy, and it lost its first home when the settler abandoned his claim and moved away, a year or so later.

For the next year or two, Lilac was a covered tin box between the bleaching ribs of a cow carcass on a hilltop beside the mail road. The mail carrier exchanged mail addressed to "Lilac" for outgoing mail or messages left in the "post office," and usually left tins of tobacco or a few groceries, ordered by the ranchmen who occasionally showed up to sort out their mail or provisions.

In time, Pophams rescued the government orphan and gave it a home at their place on the head of West Creek. After that it went to one of the Fowles ranches near the Diamond Bar, and still later to Tregos for a little while. It had several homes during the Kinkaider years and, by 1916, when it landed at Archie Stoddard's soddy in Shinbone Valley, it had traveled over most of the western half of McPherson County. The next year, when

Archie sold out, he asked us to take it in. If we didn't, he said, it would probably be "discontinued." We thought we might as well. We had been following it around after our mail for the last two or three years anyway, ever since Brighton had been "discontinued."

There wasn't much to the post office, just a cracker box divided into eight pigeonholes, a record book and some report blanks, a tin tobacco box with some postage stamps in it, and a cancelling stamp and the mail-sack keys. I put the cracker box on a table in the storeroom, with the record book and the box of stamps on top of it and the keys in one of the pigeonholes. The four families who picked up their mail at Lilac had a pigeonhole apiece, and we kept small tools and odds and ends in the other three.

The mail came twice a week, Tuesdays and Saturdays. The first few months we had the post office, the carrier made the trips on horseback from our place to Forks, sixteen miles south, and back again. The mail carrier was paid a small salary. My pay was the "cancellation" on the few letters and packages mailed at Lilac.

After Forks post office was discontinued the next spring, Henry Coker, an old cowboy friend of Bert's bid in the sixty-mile route from Sutherland to Lilac and back. Henry carried the mail in a long succession of Fords, beginning with a runabout with a homemade box on the back end. He usually made it to our place by noon and ate dinner with the family while I put up the mail.

When the weather was dry and the roads full of loose blow sand, he might be hours late; and in winter, when the snow was deep in the hills, he carried the mail on a sled behind a single horse. The trip, one way, took all day, and he stayed all night with us and made the return trip the next day. When the Ford broke down somewhere on the road, as it did every once in a while, Henry borrowed a horse or a rig and took the mail on through. When he was late, any of Lilac's patrons who happened to be waiting for mail ate dinner with us, too.

Henry carried just about everything used by sand-hill people on that sled, or in the box on the Ford, and ran a shopping service for most of the families on his route besides. He picked up full cream cans, left beside the mailboxes along the road with a "want list" tied to the handle, and left the "empties" and the groceries on the next trip back. He carried puppies and young pigs, crates of chickens and turkeys, car and mowing-machine repairs, feed and seed, medicine, cans of gasoline and coal oil, and saddles and horse collars. Even the tall cabinet-style Silvertone phonograph we ordered from Sears Roe-buck came up on the sled one cold, snowy winter day.

Roy went overseas in early June, that last year of the war, with a shipment of replacements for the hard-pressed Rainbow Division. Every mail day after that I snatched the long, long "casualty lists" out of the mail sack and turned to the Mc's, first under "dead," then under "missing," and then under "wounded." Those lists, put out every day by the War Department for newspapers and post offices, came in bales on our twice-a-week mail and it seemed like they made up most of my reading for the 108 days Roy was in the front-line trenches. When, early in October, what was left of his riddled outfit was pulled back to the rear for a rest, I could quit searching the lists for his name.

He wrote to me then, from "somewhere in France," to say he hadn't had a scratch but that he'd had enough of war and wished he were home, helping Poppie and Earl shuck out the corn. He had tried to enlist twice, the first year of the war, and had been rejected both times because he was a fraction of an inch too short. Then, in April, 1918, he was drafted and Poppie wrote to ask if I could come home for a family reunion before he left for camp.

I wanted to go, oh, how I wanted to go. But the weather had turned cold and stormy and Bert didn't see how I could get away. He couldn't leave the cattle in such weather, he said, with little calves coming every day, and he was afraid to have me take the car and try to go alone. So Ethel came home from California for the reunion, and Roy went off to camp, and then to Europe. I put a small, gold-framed service star in the front-room window and wrote to him every week.

But when I read his letter that October I thought he might be home before the corn was out at that. For the Allies had crossed the Hindenburg Line, and the Germans were running so fast toward the Fatherland that the Yanks could hardly keep up with them.

Then came the eleventh of November. That morning in the sandhills was so warm and sunny that Bert rode off to his work in one of the pastures without a jacket. A little later Mrs. Lovall phoned. She had spent the past month with Lottie, who was "expecting," and she was calling to tell me her new grandson had arrived just before midnight. She had been up all night, she said, and needed a helping hand.

I told her I'd be right up, and hurried out to the barn to saddle a horse. Just as I led him out, Nellie came flying from the house. "The war's over, the war's over, THE WAR'S OVER!" she was screaming at the top of her voice. "Central just gave a general ring and said the war's over!"

I rode away, thinking that the hills had never looked so peaceful and pretty as they did that morning, the day that was to be the beginning of lasting worldwide peace. I watched a flock of wild ducks, flying high over the hills, and thought of the way men were flying now. They had been doing it for the last ten years, and two or three of the little planes had even flown across the sandhills. The roar of their engines had brought every man, woman, and child running to watch them, and had stampeded cattle and horses clear out of their pastures. I wondered again if I'd ever look down on these hills from an airplane—and I knew I would if so much as half a chance came my way.

At Downings, we were so happy for little Jimmy that day, because he could grow up in a world made safe from war by the terrible one just ended. Maybe it was a good thing we couldn't see ahead to the day when Jimmie, too, would go hurrying off to Europe in a soldier's uniform.

Roy didn't get home in time to shuck corn after all. Instead, he spent the winter and spring in the Army of Occupation in Germany. But Henry Lombard came home with an early shipload of soldiers, and went straight to Kearney to spend his short furlough with Myra. And two hours after the train that carried him back to camp pulled out of the station, Myra died.

As for the sandhills' pro-German, his lawyers had managed to delay his trial until the end of the war, and after that the people were so busy stocking up on white flour and sugar that they didn't care any more. So nothing ever came of the charges against him.

Chapter Forty-Five

THE FLU did not reach us, back in the sandhills, the winter of 1918-19, when it was so bad in the towns and cities and army camps. The accounts we read of it, in the papers and in letters from friends and relatives, made us afraid to leave the ranch all winter. Most other sand-hillers stayed away from town, too, and that is probably why it missed us the first winter.

Everywhere, the papers said, schools and churches and movies were closed. People sickened faster than the doctors could get to them, and gravediggers could not bury the dead as fast as they died. Out in Canon City, Colorado, Mr. Lovall was a flu victim and his coffin, stacked with others in the cemetery, was unburied for days.

The flu worried me most on Mama's account. She had had several hard sick spells the past few winters, and I was afraid she'd never live through this if she got it. But Poppie and the girls wrote me that they were staying home, too, and using every care not to bring it home to her. Then, early in February, Mama's good friend, Ida Byler, spent a Sunday with her. A day or two later they were both sick abed.

"Be sure and tell Ida I've got the flu," Mama told the girls. From then on, until she got too weak to talk, she kept asking if Ida had called yet to see how she was.

"Not yet," the girls said, not daring to tell her that her dear old friend was already dead and buried.

But somehow Mama pulled through again, and when Roy finally came home from the war she was there to meet him at the door.

Because of the flu, we didn't send Nellie away to high school that fall. But the epidemic tapered off in the spring, and then seemed to die out, and in the fall of 1919 we sent her down to John's, at Maxwell, to go to school with her cousins. And that winter the flu came to the sandhills. It didn't seem to be quite so deadly, for few people in the hills died of it, but it was bad enough —and it struck fast. Tregos were the first in our community to get it.

In January, young Bill Trego drove down to Sutherland for a wagonload of supplies for the ranch. He stayed all night in town and headed back to the ranch the next morning. That evening, when the team pulled in at the ranch, Nate found him unconscious on the load. The rest of the family had it then, and Downings had it next.

Bert was the first in our family to take sick. I gave him bromo-quinine tablets and put him to bed on the settee by the front-room fire. All night and all the next day, his bones ached so hard he could scarcely stand it. The only thing that seemed to relieve him at all was his old-time Grippe remedy—two tablespoons of straight whiskey in a glass of hot water every two hours.

I helped Miles haul hay to the cattle for two days. The weather was cold, zero and below, and frozen snow on the ground made it hard to get around. But I managed well enough until near the end of the second day, when my feet began to feel so heavy that I could hardly drag one after the other. Back at the barn, I unharnessed the work team while Miles filled their manger with hay, and never in my life had a harness felt as heavy as that one did when I tried to hang it on the peg. By the time I got to the house I was so tired, and ached so hard all over, that I wondered if I could even get to bed. Bert was still too sick to help me any, so I took the last of the bromo-quinines, pulled off my clothes, and fell into bed.

Miles came in the next morning to see how I felt, and I told him he'd have to build up the fires and look after the girls, for I was too sick to get up. Then Bertie came downstairs, crying because she "hurt so bad all over," and I took her into bed with me. Billie came in then, and said she'd get breakfast while Miles did the chores. She was only seven, and it made her feel pretty important, helping out that way.

But Bertie and I were too sick to eat and Bert said he didn't feel like it either, so I told her just to fix something for herself and Miles. She boiled nine eggs, hard. Then Miles came in for breakfast and told her he didn't care for hard-boiled eggs. So he boiled five more, soft; and Billie was so offended that she sat right down and ate *six* of her hard ones.

When Miles finished his eggs, Bert told him to call Charlie Harris and ask him to come over to help with the feeding. "Tell him he won't need to come in the house," he said, for Harrises hadn't had the flu yet.

Charlie said he'd be right over, and Miles went out to hook up to the hayrack. Then Bert came staggering into my room with a glass of whiskey and hot water. "Drink this," he said, and I did. But if it eased the pounding in my bones any, I was too sick to know it.

Two or three hours later he brought me another glass of the whiskey and hot water. "I can't drink any more of *that*," I told him. "I'm not used to it and I can't stand it." Sick as I was, I knew that.

But Bert insisted that I drink it. "It's all we've got for medicine, and you have to have *something*," he said. I was too miserable to argue with him, so I drank it.

A few minutes later the room began to whirl, and then the bed, and I seemed to be sinking fast into some deep, dark place. I screamed for Bert. But when he came he was whirling, too, and I couldn't keep track of him. "Hurry, call a doctor, I'm dying," I told him.

He must have thought I was, for he rushed to the phone and called the Sutherland doctor.

The doctor, bucking frozen snow drifts, was a long time getting to the ranch. And by the time he got there, I was sober again. Bert's second glass of medicine had made me a little drunk and, sick as I was anyway, it had been a near thing.

Old Dr. Gordon, who had looked after sandhill folks for a good many years, would have left us a six-months' supply of pills, sympathy, and good advice. But the old doctor had gone to California to rest his tired bones in the sun, and the young doctor who answered our call seemed more concerned about getting started back in time to get over the worst of the roads before dark. He left a few pills for Bertie and me, told us we'd be all right in a day or two, and snapped his bag shut and hurried away.

Half an hour later, Billie began to cry with the ache in her bones. Bert put her to bed on the settee and gave her a pill from the little bottle the doctor had left.

At sundown Miles stumbled in. "I guess I can't finish the chores," he said. He seemed sorry to have let us down this way.

"Sit down, son, and get warm," Bert told him. Then he came into the bedroom to say that he thought he'd better call Nate and see if one of the boys could come over right away. For there wasn't enough fuel in the house to last through the night and, since Tregos had all had the flu, it would be safe for one of them to come in and help us.

So he called Nate and shouted our troubles across the hills, and Nate said he'd send Mose over as soon as he finished his supper.

Then Miles came to the bedroom door. His face was flushed and feverish and he carried a little pail of water and a tin cup. "I guess I'll go on up to bed," he told me.

"Get covered up as quick as you can," I said. "I'll send Mose up to see how you are, as soon as he gets here."

Bert gave him the last of the pills, and he dragged up the stairs, going alone to his cold, dark room. I wondered if he'd ever walk down again, and I wanted, more than anything in the world, to get up and make him a bed by the fire, but I was too sick to raise my head off the pillow.

The evening dragged along. We knew it would take Mose quite a while to get to our place; slippery as the roads were, but when he hadn't come by nine o'clock we began to worry. Bert got out of bed and emptied the last of the coal into the living-room stove. I heard him open the front door and shut it again. Then he came to my door and said, "It's black as a stack of black cats tonight. I'm afraid Mose is having trouble finding his way over here, so I guess I'd better leave the light burning to guide him across the meadow."

He went back to bed and the hours went by. The lamp burned dry and went out, and the fire died and the house grew cold. I stared into the dark, trying to locate the windows in my room, but the walls might as well have been solid. As far back as I could remember, I had never before known a whole night so dark that I could not tell where the windows were. I worried about Miles—and Mose, too. Miles might be delirious, and uncovered in the cold. Mose's horse could have slipped on the frozen snow and fallen with him, and he might be freezing to death in the hills somewhere.

I was never so glad to see daylight as I was that morning. And with the dawn, Nate and May Trego came bouncing over the frozen ruts in their car, bringing help and comfort and a fat, dressed hen.

Mose had started out, they said, but had lost his way in the black night. His horse had finally brought him home again, but they hadn't called us because it was so late, and they didn't want to make anyone get out of a sickbed to answer the phone.

By noon, the smell of rich chicken broth had us all hungry. Miles got up and came downstairs. Bert and Billie got up and dressed, and Bertie and I moved out onto the settee for the rest of the day.

There was a short stretch of good weather after that, and Miles and the girls started back to school. Then winter closed down again, and all through March and April storms beat across the hills. Freezing temperatures held for days on end and we seldom saw the sun.

In April the little calves began to come. Morning after morning Bert brought in near-frozen newborns to be rubbed back to life by the kitchen stove. Then my setting hens began to hatch, and as the chicks pecked their way out of the shells into the killing cold, I gathered them up and brought them in to dry off on the oven door. Next, Bert's fine bird dog, Fannie, gave in to the endless wet, freezing weather and came down with pneumonia. We brought her in, too, and made her a bed behind the kitchen stove and doctored her the best we could.

Bert was blue and cross when we lost a calf. Bertie

mourned over every baby chick that died, especially the three that Mr. Truby sat on. Mr. Truby was the nice young man who taught the Huffman school and boarded at Downings. He came to meet the mail every Saturday, and that morning Bertie had wrapped three cold, sick baby chicks in a piece of old blanket and put them on a chair by the oven door. Mr. Truby mistook the bundle for a cushion and sat down by the stove to warm his stinging hands and feet.

And all of us grieved on the sleety day that pretty Fannie died, and the girls wept while we buried her in the frosty ground beside old Towser.

In the middle of all that, Nellie wrote us a homesick letter. I wrote right back, "Nellie, you may be homesick down there at Maxwell, but if you were here you'd be sick of home."

Chapter Forty-Six

B Y THE spring of 1920 the Ford was twelve years old, a ripe old age for a car in the sandhills, where the roads were nothing but crooked, sandy trails and every mile dealt it a thousand bumps and twists and jerks. Everything considered, that car had given us a lot of service, and a lot of experience, too.

There was the March, back in 1915, when Nate stopped in on his way home from commissioners' meeting to ask us to come on over and go to the St. Patrick's Day dance with them in their new Dort. The dance was only two days away, and our Ford had a cracked differential. But we had the repairs on hand and Bert told him we'd be over if he could get the car fixed in time.

Until then, we had never gone anywhere together without the children, but when it looked like Bert would have the car done in time, we sent Miles over to Fraziers on horseback to bring Silvie back to stay all night with them.

Bert tightened the last nuts and bolts on the Ford's rear end just before suppertime. After supper, we left Nellie and Silvie doing the dishes and went out to the car. Bert cranked it and we got in. He switched from battery to magneto, retarded the spark, advanced the gas, released the hand lever and let up on the foot pedal— and we took out *backward* at a fast clip. He braked to

a stop and tried again, and for the next fifteen minutes
we backed all over the yard.

"I must 've put something in backwards," he said finally.

It was too late to do anything about the car, but Bert
said we could still make it on horseback. He saddled a
couple of horses while I changed into my riding skirt
and rolled my dress skirt into a flour sack to take along,
and Tregos were still waiting for us when we loped into
their yard.

There were a good many cars among the rigs and saddle
horses around the Flats store at that St. Patrick's dance.
Ira and Florence Huffman were there from Swan Lake
in their Hupmobile, and Bird Huffman and his new bride,
Ruby, had driven down from the old home ranch in
their Ford. Lottie and Henry Downing, Conroys, and
Charlie Daly and his family had all "motored" to the
dance. At midnight, when the dancing stopped for lunch,
we sat together while we ate sandwiches and cake.

As horses, good and bad, had been the favorite peg on
which to hang the conversation of an earlier day, so
now, wherever people got together, automobiles were sure
to get a good overhauling. In any gathering in our country there were likely to be as many owners of Fords as
of all other makes put together; and everybody, their
owners included, poked fun at the old "wooden Sallys"
and the new "tin Lizzies." But it was the kind of fun
you keep for something you're fond of.

Ira Huffman, who had the county Hupmobile agency,
had a good deal to say about the Hup's extra horsepower.
Some of the others said they didn't believe extra horse-
power helped much in sand, that it just dug a stuck car
in all the deeper, and anyway a Hup was too low. It
was apt to high-center on a cow chip. Dorts and Reos
came in for a share of the talk, and then someone told

how the Happy Hollow Dolphins carried spare axles and a lot of other repairs in the space under the back seat of their Ford, so they'd have what they needed when they had a breakdown. Charlie Daly laughed and said there was no need of that, that when anything went wrong with a Ford you could always fix it with a hairpin and a wad of chewing gum.

Nate had already told them about our "backward" Ford and they'd had a good laugh about it. Now Bert agreed with Charlie. "That's right," he said, "and the darned things don't even have to be all there to keep running. A while back, we drove ours several miles before we discovered one of the wheels was missing, and then we had to go back after it."

"I can remember several times when we've had to go back after all four of them," I reminded him.

One of those times was in January, 1918. We had no more than pulled the car home with the team and wagon, one morning, than Pearl called to tell Bert that Grandma Snyder was very low. Within an hour he was on his way, on horseback, and he pulled in at the old home place at Maxwell in time to see his mother before she died.

When Pearl phoned again, five months later, with the message that Grandpa had passed away in the night, the car was in running order but Bert had a "kink" in his back and could not drive. He couldn't help crank the the Ford either, and Miles and I had a hard time getting it started. Bert could hardly move at all, or even sit up, but we managed to get him dressed and into the car, and I did the driving.

That was the first time we ever left the children home alone, overnight, and it seemed to me they were pretty young—Nellie wasn't quite thirteen and Bertie was barely four—but there wasn't time to do anything else.

After the funeral, we went home with John's for the night, and all that evening we watched a heavy bank of low, threatening clouds, off in the northwest. The weather was nice where we were, but it looked bad in the vicinity of those clouds. If a big storm broke anywhere near the ranch the kids might be in trouble, especially with Billie and Bertie so deathly afraid of thunder and lightning.

Bert's back was better by morning and we started home early. In Tryon we stopped to fill up with gas from the new pump Mike had put up in front of his store. A third of the buildings in town stood empty, and there were hardly any rigs or cars in the sandy streets any more. But Mike looked cheerful and prosperous, and while he cranked gas into our car he said he'd heard there had been quite a hailstorm, on north and west, the night before.

We hurried on, and in the Kirts's valley we saw the first signs of the storm. The road there was wet and packed and the grass flattened by hail. At the ranch, the cottonwoods were completely stripped of their new leaves, and my big garden, all green and thrifty when we left, was just a smooth bare patch of ground.

The storm had struck about chore time, but while the ugly clouds were piling up in the northwest, Miles and Nellie had carried all the hens with little chickens from their coops to the haymow. It was a good thing they did, they said, for hail and water had run a foot deep through the yard before the storm was over.

They had had their worst trouble with the two little girls, scared almost out of their wits by the crashing thunder and roaring hail, but they had still managed to milk the cows and finish up the chores in good shape. We couldn't have done much better if we had been there.

One of our worst breakdowns happened the fall Miles

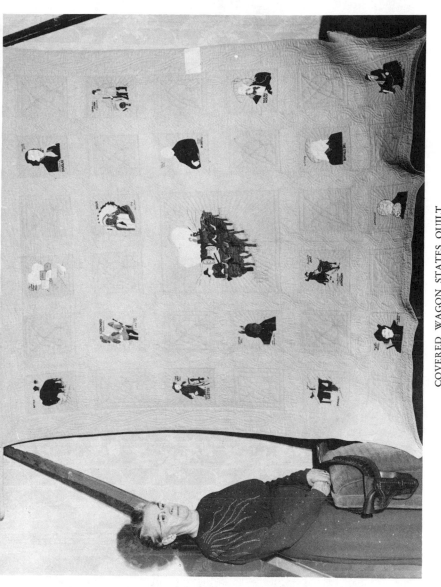

COVERED WAGON STATES QUILT

Because the family called this one "Dad's quilt," the reporter who wrote a story on it asked to have Bert's revolver and holster in the picture.

GRACE SNYDER
This photograph was taken soon after she moved to North Platte from the ranch
in the sandhills.

was eleven. Bert and the girls and I had gone down to
Hershey one morning, expecting to be back to the ranch
before sundown. But on the way home the Ford quit us
cold as we were passing Earnest Moore's place, twelve miles
north of town.

Always before, we had managed to get home the same
day we broke down, but this time it took us two days.
We put up at Moores—Earnest was one of the "regulars"
who came to the ranch for two or three days every fall
to hunt ducks and prairie chickens—and by dark he and
Bert had the Ford taken apart and strung out in the yard.

I didn't sleep much that night for worrying about
Miles. He was the one in our family that things always
happened to. The summer he was eight, a colt he was
riding had run away with him and jumped a fence and
fallen on him, and the past winter he had slipped off a
high load of hay and landed on his head on a patch of
ice. He was knocked unconscious both times, and I could
think of all kinds of things that could happen to him,
all alone on the ranch that night. He might have been
hurt while he was trying to do the chores, or he might
have set himself and the house afire, trying to fix his
supper.

Earnest took Bert back to Hershey the next morning
after repairs, and by the middle of the afternoon they
had the Ford going again. It was almost dark when we
pulled in at the ranch; the house was still standing, and
Miles was coming out of it to see what had kept us away
so long.

Everything had been fine with him, he said. He just
came home from school and brought in the milk cows
and milked and took care of the other chores. Then he
filled up on bread and milk and plum butter for supper
and went to bed. He did the chores again in the morn-

ing, and ate bread and milk and plum butter for breakfast. Then he filled his dinner pail with plum butter
sandwiches and went on to school. That evening he had
done the chores again, and when we came home he was
just ready to sit down to bread and milk and plum butter
for supper.

So, when the Ford broke down again, on Squaw Creek
in the spring of 1920, Bert didn't even bother to bring
it home. Instead, he bought a new one from the Tryon
Ford dealer. That Ford had a tin body, electric lights,
a self-starter, and three doors. The fourth, on the driver's
side in front, *looked* like a door but it didn't open. The
men simply stepped over the side of those 1920 Ford
"touring cars" to get under the wheel, but women drivers
in long skirts had to get in from the other side and slide
through.

Just after we bought the new car we went down to
Maxwell to bring Nellie home from school. Since Bert
had some business to see to at the land office in Broken
Bow, fifty miles east of Stapleton, we went around that
way on the way down. We parked in front of the courthouse and went in. When we came out, all the cars on
that block had been moved to the next one and a grader
was pushing dirt and gravel around in front of the courthouse. We walked on down the street and climbed into
the first new Ford we came to—and Bert had the engine
going before we discovered it wasn't ours. (In those
days, no one ever bothered to take the ignition key out
of a car in our part of the country.) We climbed out
in a hurry and looked around to see if anybody had seen
us, and then we saw that there were four new Fords, all
as exactly alike as blackbirds on a fence, parked in that
block.

We went on to Maxwell, coming into town through

the hills from the north instead of by way of North
Platte. As usual, spring rains had made a loblolly of the
river valley roads, and when we started home the next
morning, Bert said we'd make time if we missed the
Platte again by heading straight into the hills north of
Maxwell and cutting across, northwest, toward Tryon.

Bert was never happier than when he could take a
shortcut somewhere. A sensible idea for a man on horseback in open country, but one that didn't work so well
with a car in fenced farming lands. And that is what
those hills had become in the years since he had last ridden through them.

There was no main road, just wandering wagon tracks.
Bert tried to keep to a general northwesterly direction,
but fences and new-listed fields got in his way and kept
him zigzagging until he had no idea where we were. The
day got hotter and hotter, and we meandered on and on,
over dim trails and through empty pastures. We got
stuck several times and had a bad time getting out.
Finally we ran out of a road altogether. But Bert kept
on, until we high-centered on a sandy ridge. It took us
quite a while to dig ourselves off the high spot, and to
backtrack to the last wagon road we had seen. And
when we finally came out on a main road—the well
traveled stretch from Stapleton to Tryon—it was nearly
sundown and we were still east of Ringgold and more
than twenty-five miles from home.

Chapter Forty-Seven

ALTHOUGH she weighed less than one hundred pounds, Dr. Harriet McGraw was all grit, from the top of her snow-white head to the soles of her number 3 shoes. She came to Tryon in 1919 or 1920 by a long, roundabout road.

Born Harriet Gudmunsonur, in Iceland, and orphaned while a very small girl, she was sent alone, with a "shipping tag" sewed to her coat, to an aunt in Canada. While still in her teens she came to the United States and earned her way through school, nurse's training, and medical college. She started practicing in Lincoln, Nebraska, but the years of hard work and study had injured her health and she was having a hard time of it.

Then she heard, by chance, about big McPherson County, where there was a fine, healthy climate but no electricity, no roads, and *no doctor*. So she and her one-armed husband, big Joe McGraw, moved to Tryon.

For the next twenty years she fought sandhill roads and weather to look after McPherson and Arthur County people. It wasn't unusual for her to travel forty miles through the hills to answer a call, and if she couldn't take care of the patient in his own home she loaded him into her car and took him to hers, where she could give him the treatment he needed. Every now and then she raced the stork, or the death angel, or both, over sandhill trails, and *she* was usually the winner. The fact that some people never paid her a cent for all the times she answered their calls, did not keep her from hurrying back the next time they sent for her.

Besides being the county's only doctor, she was its Official Physician and Health Officer and its Registrar of Births and Deaths. Her husband, a lawyer, soon became County Attorney and County Coroner. He was also his wife's driver, for the tiny doctor never tried to drive a car over our sandhill roads.

The doctor had been in Tryon a year or two before we had to call on her.

Bert was riding a big young horse he called Antelope on the east side of the big pasture one January morning when the bridle broke. The falling headstall struck the horse on the knees, scaring him into a blind runaway. Bert stayed with him, hoping he'd run himself down and stop. But when Antelope headed at top speed for the line fence between our place and Kirtses, he figured there was going to be a smashup, so he jumped. He lit on his left shoulder on the frozen ground, knocking the joint clear out of its socket.

He managed to walk on to Kirtses, where the brothers, John, George, and Charlie, put him in their car and brought him home. We put him to bed, and then I phoned Tryon (by way of Sutherland, North Platte, and Stapleton) and asked the doctor to come out as fast as she could.

She did, and whisked into our kitchen like a stiff breeze an hour later. She made a quick examination of Bert's shoulder, all swelled up and purple by then, and told us to put him on the floor in the middle of the living room, where she could get at him. The Kirts boys, who had stayed to see if they could be of any more help, carried him out and put him where she said.

The doctor showed me how to give the chloroform, then she knelt down beside him. When he was unconscious, she lifted his arm above his head and tried to force the joint back into its socket, all the while talking to herself, ". . . terrible swelling . . . tough job . . . could 've got to him sooner . . . the poor darlin' anyway."

Finally she whirled on the Kirts boys and snapped, "Listen, you! This isn't going to work, so I'm going to try to *pull* that joint in, and I want you fellows to hold him still. Don't let him move an inch. Do you hear me? Not one inch."

The three men got down on their knees and hung onto Bert for dear life.

The doctor sat flat on the floor and put her foot into his armpit and took a tight hold on his arm. Then she set her teeth and pulled with all her might. When the shoulder didn't give, she eased up and took a full breath and tried again. The cords in her slender neck stood out like little ropes, but she couldn't pull the joint in place. "Oh, for a man, a good, strong *man* on this side," she said, almost crying.

All this time, Joe was standing by, offering advice and criticism. "If you'd try. . . . Why don't you? . . . It looks to me like. . . ." Until the doctor snatched some aspirin out of her satchel and handed them to him.

"Here, take these for *my* headache and get out of here," she ordered.

Joe took the pills and marched out in a big huff.

"As my husband, he can tell me how to do other things, but he can't tell me how to take care of my patients," Dr. McGraw declared.

In the end she had to give up. "We'll have to take

him to North Platte to a doctor that's man enough to do the job," she said bitterly.

The Kirts boys helped us put him in the McGraw car and they drove away.

Somewhere on the other side of Tryon Bert's head cleared and he wanted to know what was going on. When the doctor explained the situation to him, he said, "Pshaw, if I'd been awake I'd have had you put the wire stretchers on me. You could 've pulled it into place easy, then."

"Man, now you're talking," the little doctor moaned. "Why didn't *I* think of that?"

In North Platte, after the shoulder was set and taped in place, the three of them went to a restaurant for supper.

"After all the chloroform you've had today, you'd better take it easy and stick to soup for supper," the doctor advised Bert.

"Not on your life," he said. "I didn't have any dinner today and I'm hungry. I'm going to have steak and eat every bite of it."

The doctor and big Joe had missed their dinners, too, so they all had steaks and ate every bite.

. It was long after dark by the time they got back to Tryon again, so Bert stayed all night with McGraw's. At three o'clock that morning a loud knock on the door woke them all.

A knock on the doctor's door at that hour was not unusual, but this time the call was for the doctor's husband. The sheriff was at the door, with a message that had just come in. There was a body out at old man Embrey's place, over in the southwest corner of the county, he said. And Embrey, who was already on his way in to give himself up, wanted the coroner to go over and have a look at it.

"Somebody's pulling your leg," Joe told the sheriff. "Embrey wouldn't kill anybody."

"Just the same," Bert called from his room, "if Embrey sent word there's a dead man at his house, you'd better go out there after a dead man."

Old man Embrey was an ex-prospector who had made more than one trip to California by oxteam in his younger days. In the early Kinkaid times he had lived a few miles south of us, where Bert had come to know and like him.

On the way across the county, Joe stopped to let Bert off at the ranch, and then went on to Embrey's place, where he found a dead man in the house.

It seemed that a few neighbors had dropped in at Embrey's the evening before and, due to some bootleg "hootch" someone brought along, the party had got a little rough. When one of the men grabbed a hatchet and started playing ring-around-a-rosy with one of the other guests, Embrey, a "peaceable" man, thought the fun had gone far enough. He got his gun and ordered the hatchet man to settle down. Instead, the fellow turned on him. Embrey warned him not to come any closer, but he kept on coming, and so met "an accidental death due to a gunshot wound in the neck."

The county, after rendering the "accidental death" verdict, washed its hands of the case. According to his neighbors, the dead man had been an "ornery trouble-maker" anyway, and neither his widow nor anyone else would claim the body. For a while it looked, as Bert said, "like old man Embrey would have to winter the corpse," but a sister finally came and took it off his hands.

That was the winter, too, that Miles built a one-tube, battery-operated radio set with parts he ordered from Montgomery Ward. It was one of the first sets in our part of the hills and the neighbors came in to listen on it. You really listened "on" it, rather than to it, for it had no loudspeaker. Instead, there were two sets of headphones, but one earpiece could be unfastened from each set, so that four people could listen at the same time. The first time one of Trego's little granddaughters clamped a set to her head, she waited anxiously while Miles twiddled the dials and knobs. When a thin howl finally came through, her face lit up. "Oh goody," she cried, "I hear a coyote." There was always plenty of static, those first years of radio.

There were few broadcasting stations within range of our little set. One of the best was Henry Field's powerful KMMJ in Iowa. Between advertisements for incubators, baby chicks, and garden seeds, Henry put on some fine programs: old fiddler contests, harpists, orchestras, singers, and hog callers. Another station I liked was WOW, at Omaha, for it brought me in touch again with my old friend, Irene Miltonberger Lowell.

Irene's husband and teen-age twin sons were musicians too, and the family, then living in Omaha, was on radio several times a year. On Sundays, too, the station broadcast Preacher R. R. Brown's entire church service from his Omaha Tabernacle, where Irene was often his soloist. When conditions were right, her warm, rich voice, traveling across three hundred miles of Nebraska land, sounded almost the same as it used to in the little house on the Birdwood.

But, so often, conditions weren't right. Stormy weather made the static howl so loud we couldn't hear anything else, and the battery was always going "dead" in the middle of a program. Usually a very special one, that we had looked forward to for a long time. In winter, when the roads were blocked with snow; or in haying, when all hands were busy from dawn to dark, it was sometimes days, even weeks, before we could get the battery to town to have it charged. But, in spite of all its drawbacks, that first little radio was a big help. When it worked, it brought us the finest entertainment, the latest news, and even weather forecasts. Bert did a better job of predicting the weather, by watching the sun go down and smelling the wind, than the radio weatherman did, but the forecasts were interesting anyway.

In the fall of 1924 that poor perennial, the Sandhill Railroad Boom, budded again. The *Tryon Graphic*, the *Arthur Enterprise*, and the *Bridgeport News* quoted each other to the effect that the railroad would build on to Medicine Bow, Wyoming, the next spring. The *Tryon Graphic* stated that several new business concerns were ready to locate in Tryon the minute the first rail was laid beyond the Y in Stapleton.

But the spring of high promise came and passed again, and the railroad failed to move one foot farther west. And with that failure the boom—and the long, long dream—died for good. But a new dream was already taking its place, a dream of automobile highways up and down and across the hills. For, by then, nearly every family in the sandhills owned an automobile or a truck, or both, and the machines themselves had made the roads more impassable year by year. For one thing, their narrow wheels wore the ruts deeper; for another, every driver "took a run" at each hill as he came to it. When the front wheels struck the base of the upslope, they always twisted a little in the loose sand, making a "crook" in the road at the bottom of the hill. Every car over the road made the crook a little worse, and every wind that blew deepened the sand a little more. When a piece of road finally got *too* bad, a new road was started beside the old one or, in some cases, the county commissioners or the landowner spread hay or barnyard manure over the bad places. But wind and shifting sand soon wiped out such "repairs," and the life of an automobile in the sandhills continued to be a hard one.

By 1925 nearly every sandhill home had a telephone and a radio, and some even had furnaces and electric or carbide light plants. Only the roads still belonged to the horse and buggy days. But McPherson County made a start on its dream highway that same summer by putting a caterpillar tractor to work throwing up a low grade south of Tryon on the North Platte road. The tractor made pretty good progress—what time it wasn't pulling stuck cars out of the sand on the detour alongside the new grade—and by fall a three-mile stretch was done. A follow-up crew spread hay over the packed-sand grade, and McPherson County had its first strip of "paving."

That summer, too, the county finally got its new courthouse.

Back in 1916 there had been a special election, to vote the bonds for the four thousand dollars needed to put up the building the county commissioners had in mind. But too many voters in the west end of the bobtailed county still smarted over the East Enders' stubbornness in the matter of moving the county seat, and the bonds failed to carry. Before anything more could be done about it we had gone to war; and after the war there had been a while when money was "tight."

Quite a few years earlier, the old sod walls had been enclosed with a frame shell, but that, too, had become so weak and weather-rotted that the county officers who worked in the building declared that nothing but the wallpaper and the paint held the old walls up and kept the roof from falling down on their heads. So, early in the spring of the last railroad boom, when the voters were in good spirits, the commissioners said something would *have* to be done about the courthouse.

The bonds carried, that time, and the new brick building, the finest in the whole county, was built at a cost of twenty thousand dollars.

Chapter Forty-Eight

POPPIE sold the Roten Valley place during the war, and bought another farm in the valley south of Cozad. The house was a big one, eight rooms, and the summer I first saw it I thought what a blessing all those rooms would have been to Mama, years ago, when all of us were growing up around her in crowded little houses. Now only Earl and Esther were still at home, since Elsie had married a young Platte Valley neighbor, Cecil Ristine, the son of a pioneer Dawson County family.

Mama had moved her parlor from the old house to the new one without getting a single thing out of place, and she had hung a gourd nest on her front porch, under an old honeysuckle vine, and made friends with the wren family that moved right in. But most of all, she gloried in the big old trees around the house, and the blooming rosebushes in the yard.

"How queer life is," she said. "No matter how hard I tried, I couldn't get a tree or a rosebush to grow in Roten Valley, and here they come up everywhere and we have to keep hoeing them up."

Poppie had taken me down to the big timber lot on the back of the place. "I always wanted to burn wood in Nebrasky, like we used to in Missoury," he said, "and here we can."

He showed me his fine alfalfa fields, too. Years before,

shortly after we came to Nebraska, Poppie had been interested in alfalfa. They called it "Lucerne" then, and
it was new to that part of the country. He said at the
time that it was a good crop plant and the country would
be full of it someday. Most people had laughed at his
prediction, so I knew how pleased he was, now that it
was one of the main valley crops, worth hundreds of
thousands of dollars to the community.

After only seven years on the valley farm, they sold
it and moved to California. Mama was still having hard
sick spells every winter, and Poppie said it was time they
went to a place where there was no winter. Most of
the rest of the family were out there anyway. Nellie
and Stella had gone before the war, Roy had gone after
he got out of the army, and Earl had followed him. Esther
had married a young minister and gone to live in the East.

In less than a year they brought Poppie home again.
A swerving car had struck him down, on a curb only
a block from the Long Beach apartment where he and
Mama lived. There wasn't a mark on him that showed,
and he looked so natural in his coffin. Even the little
lift to his eyebrow was there, as if he was surprised at
what had happened. I smoothed the thin white hair back
from his forehead, remembering the May evening when
he stood in the door of Stella's house and said, "No, Grace,
she's really gone."

We buried him beside Florry, in the blue winter shadow
of the tall cedar hedge he had helped set out so long ago.

A year later we were headed for the West Coast ourselves.

Bert had said, several years before, that when the two
younger girls were ready for high school we would move
where there was one. Now the time had come, and we
were moving to a high school two thousand miles away,

in Salem, Oregon. His sister Alice lived out there, and he thought it would be as good a place as any to spend the four years we'd have to be away from the ranch. I was glad to go there, too, for I thought I'd soon get to go on down to California to see Mama. I didn't realize then, that though I'd be on the same coast with her, I would still be almost as far from her as I was on the ranch.

We leased the ranch, the post office included, to another ranchman and made the trip West in two cars. One was the old 1920 Ford, bobbed off behind the front seat and remodeled into a "mess wagon" with a cupboard on the back, like the wagons Bert had known on the roundup in his younger days. The other was a new Ford, exactly like the old one except that all four doors opened. Miles drove the mess wagon Ford and Bert and I spelled each other driving the new one.

We stopped on the way for three weeks in Yellowstone Park, where we camped at all the best fishing spots. At Yellowstone Lake, Bert filled his old cow-camp Dutch oven with dry beans and water, put the lid on, and buried the whole thing in the ground. While he built a fire on top of it, he told us there was no better way to cook beans, slow like, with all the flavor and richness sealed in.

He dug the pot up the next day and sampled the beans. They hadn't cooked a bit, so he buried them again and piled more fuel on the fire. At the end of four days of baking, when the beans were still as hard as bullets, he said he guessed it was the "altitude," and threw the souring mess out.

In August we dropped down into the beautiful Willamette Valley, where we bought a home near Bert's sister's, five miles north of Salem. Our house faced the Salem-Portland highway, and just across the pavement from our front porch there was a big stand of grand, towering pines. Trees that had been big, they told us, when white men first saw the Willamette Valley.

Before school started, we drove on to the coast to have a look at the Pacific Ocean. Except that its color was different, and its waves never still, it might have been the sandhills, rolling on and on to the skyline.

Bert liked the Oregon climate, and the fishing, and visiting with the copper-skinned boys from the Chemawa Indian school up the road. Otherwise, he was a lonesome stray, on a range far from home, for nobody there spoke, or understood, cow talk.

But I had never had it so good. Bert's sister, Alice, right away invited me to join her busy neighborhood quilting club; and there was nothing out there to keep us from getting together to quilt whenever we liked.

In the old Hayesville community where we lived the land was divided into "ranches" of a few acres apiece and the houses were close together. It seldom snowed, even enough to whiten the ground, and the roads were graded and graveled, where they weren't paved.

Nellie, married and living in Maxwell, saved the letters I wrote her during those years in Oregon. When I read them over now, thirty years later, I see what a lot of my time I spent on quilts. In one letter, I wrote, "I have finished a Saw Tooth quilt in red, green and white, and have started a pretty new one called the Double Wedding Ring. The rings are made of little print pieces and I'm exchanging prints with the quilting club ladies. I want as many different pieces as I can get."

And in another, "I have made twenty-two blocks for my Log Cabin quilt. The pieces you sent me were just what I needed to finish the Wedding Ring. Alice and I have quilted two quilts for her and one for Mrs. Brown.

We are to help Mrs. Liphart with a quilt, and then all of them will help me quilt one next week. I am starting on a Necktie quilt now, cut out forty blocks for it this afternoon while Alice and I visited."

Just before our third Christmas in Oregon, I wrote that I was having some of the ladies in to help me quilt the Saw Tooth, and that it looked like we might soon have a new car. "Anyway we are going out in a Chrysler tomorrow and a Chevrolet Sunday, and then we'll try a Buick. Daddy likes the Chevvie best. The rest of us want one of the others, but I expect a Chevrolet is what it will be."

The girls and I had been talking new cars to Bert for the past six months. But he said he didn't see any need of buying a new one as long as the old one still ran all right.

In addition to crossing the mountains and desert on our long trip West, the old Ford had made at least two trips into Salem and back, almost every day, getting the girls to school. The miles had counted up, and they all showed. And besides, the old car looked so "dated," the girls said, on the road with the new cars that had stationary tops and glass all around. But that was another thing Bert didn't like—you couldn't fold that kind of a top back in winter, or take it off altogether, and all that glass would be mighty dangerous if you had a wreck. And besides that, he didn't like the new cars on account of the gearshift that had taken the place of the old planetary clutch, and anyway, he said, none of us knew how to drive the new kind.

He was wrong there. Billie knew how. She and her boy friend were driving to Portland one Sunday in a Chrysler when a wandering bee had stung the boy friend between the eyes. She had had to take over then, and learn how to drive the Chrysler so they could finish the trip. After that she had visited a Salem Buick dealer. When she told him her folks were thinking about buying a new Buick, and that she would like to learn how to drive one, he had been glad to oblige with some free lessons.

But even after Billie told Bert she was pretty "smooth" on the new gearshifts, he kept putting us off. So we were still driving the old open Ford when the rainy season came on. We dug the shabby old side curtains out and buttoned them on, but most of the "isinglass" was cracked and broken and they didn't do much good.

And then, on his way out from town one day, something in a field on his right caught Bert's attention. He looked away from the road to see what was going on— and took down a whole row of mailboxes before he got stopped. Fortunately, the old side curtains were torn beyond repair, though not much else about the car was damaged.

It was right after that that we began riding out in the Chryslers, Buicks, and Chevrolets. As I had expected, we bought the Chevvie.

"You folks 'll have to do all the driving from now on," Bert told the girls and me, when the dealer delivered the new sedan. "I'm not going to fool with the darn thing."

We spent that summer in Arizona and California. Bert wanted to visit some old friends in Arizona, and take in the Indian snake dances. I wanted to see Mama, for the girls had written that she was failing fast.

She was such a little thing that summer, just a wisp of gristle and bone, though her hair was still crow's-wing black in spite of her seventy years. I offered to make her some new dresses; for the sheer black voiles and chiffons she wore could not be bought ready-made in the stores. But she said no, that she had all she'd ever need and she'd rather visit.

She seldom left her apartment any more, but, the few times she felt up to it, I took her down on the beach and sat with her in the warm sun, watching the everlasting breakers falling to pieces on the wide, flat curve of sand. We talked of the things that interested her most; of her twenty grandchildren, of Merle and Nellie, the married ones, and of Margie, teaching school in Nebraska. "Margie is such a pretty girl," she said. "When she was here with me last summer, I could see so many of Florry's ways about her." But mostly she talked of Poppie, and of the long-ago days on the homestead and the old place in Roten Valley.

"Everything seemed so hard then," she said. "I hardly ever saw a well day, and there was always so much to do and so little to do with. But I know, now, that those were the happiest days of my life. Poppie was there, and all of you children, and when night came you were all in your beds and safe. Except for Ethel and Earl, you were always a healthy bunch. I guess I had lots to be thankful for."

She remembered the summer Poppie went hunting on the Dismal and shot an antelope, and used the hide to make a breast protector for the catcher on his baseball team. And the summer we bought the new riding cultivator. "Remember, Grace, how he let you ride the new one and he walked behind the old one? You and Florry and Stell went to Cozad with Sally Waller that Fourth of July, and Poppie was going to ride the new cultivator while you were gone. And then it broke down just before quitting time the night before, and he had to walk all day behind the old one after all."

We talked of Polly, too, and Mama laughed about the

time the new Walnut Grove minister made his first call on them and heard Polly mumbling to herself in the kitchen. "He was too polite to say anything then, but for quite a while he thought we had a feeble-minded child in our family. Poor Polly. I took her with me when we moved to the valley farm, and when I came down to the dining room one morning, she was all hunkered down on her perch. I asked her if she was sick and she said 'uh huh' in such a sorry way. She died before sundown, and Margie and I buried her under the rosebushes in the yard."

In Arizona, Bert and his friends drove a long way across the desert to see the snake dances—the Indian rain prayer—and had a bad time getting home through the downpour. At the end of the summer we went back to Salem for the girls' last year in school.

After we settled in Salem, Miles joined the army and spent three years in the Philippine Islands. By the spring the girls graduated, he was due to sail for home, and on May 23, 1931, I wrote Nellie:

Your letter was here when I came home from quilting today. We have a new tent and trailer and our things are all packed, ready to start in one more week, as soon as the girls graduate.

Miles is on the ocean now and I will be so glad when he is on this side again. We are going over to Alice's one day this week. I want to help her get her Bear Paw quilt started. I helped quilt one like it at the church last week and she wants me to show her how. I'm going to miss the church and club, but I'm anxious to get started home.

When we left Salem a week later, Alice said through her tears, "You'll be back. Everybody that lives here a while always comes back." But Bert and I never went back, although we left a part of ourselves in the lovely valley. In its clear fishing streams, in the church and the quilting club, and in a grave on a high mountainside, where our dearest friend of the Oregon years buried her fine young son on a sweet spring day.

Perhaps it was an unseen mercy that called young Jack to his early sleep on the green mountain. Ten years later, his grave might well have been a shell-torn hole on some far Pacific shore, where his mother could not go when the rhododendrons bloomed.

Chapter Forty-Nine

THERE had been changes in the hills while we were away. Henry and Lottie Downing had moved to Colorado, Kirtses and Harrises were gone, too, and Eva Van Meter was dead. At long last, Stapleton had won the county-seat fight, over in Logan County, and poor old Gandy was practically a ghost town. But the roads were the same, crooked and sandy and almost impassable. Except for the short strip of old "highway" between Tryon and North Platte, where gravel had replaced the hay, the sandhills' good-roads system was still a dream in the sandhillers' heads.

Earl and Roy brought Mama home, that first winter we were back in Nebraska, and we laid her to rest between Florry and Poppie. After the funeral, my brothers and sisters and I drove out to the old home in Roten Valley. All the buildings we remembered were gone and new ones stood in their places. Only the bare hills and crooked old Stump Ditch reminded us of the home we had known there. Then we drove on to the farm south of the river. There nothing had changed since Mama and Poppie had walked out the door, seven years ago. Even to the wrens nesting in the old gourd under the honeysuckle, it all looked the same.

The girls did not go back to the ranch with us, so I set up my quilting frames in the sunny upstairs room that had been theirs and went on with my quilting. I finished the quilt I had made for Margie from the old-fashioned print pieces her mother had cut before the girl was born, and then I pieced and quilted a lovely new one, all white and yellow. The morning I finished that one began a day we will never forget in the sandhills, May 22, 1933.

All through the Midwest the winter and spring had been dry. Fierce dust storms were plaguing Kansas and Colorado and Oklahoma, but we hadn't experienced the terrible "black blizzards" of the thirties until that day.

In North Platte, the day before, Bert had bought a pretty bay saddle horse. I left him there, to ride the horse home the next day, and took Bertie back to the ranch to spend a week with me.

The next morning, while I finished my quilt, Miles left for Huffmans with a batch of petitions for the *daily* mail route that he and the neighbors were trying to put through. And all forenoon the south wind, that had started as a breeze at sunup, grew stronger. By noon it was howling up the valley, and a thick haze of *red* dust had dimmed the sun.

Early in the afternoon the haze turned to a queer greenish gloom that soon hid the sun. At three o'clock it began to get dark. I told Bertie to turn on the carbide lights in the kitchen, while I ran out to see about my little turkeys.

Just outside the door Lupas, Miles' big collie dog, looked up at me with scared, worried eyes. I held the door open for him and he scooted inside, his tail between his legs. I started for my turkey coop, only a few yards from the house, and the wind was so strong that I had to bend over and push to make headway against it. The chickens, I saw, had already gone to roost. I found my

504   NO TIME ON MY HANDS

turkey hen hovering her poults just outside her coop. Like all turkeys, she hadn't had sense enough to take her family the rest of the way to safety. I pushed her on into the coop and began to gather up the week-old babies, counting them as I poked them in after her. And even before I could gather them all, the last of the dim light was sucked up by the terrible wind.

In thick darkness I fumbled in the grass a little longer, then I gave up and started for the house. Near as it was, I couldn't see it, and the wind was a screaming banshee. I began to run, and the wind slammed me against the porch wall. I felt my way along until I found the door, and then I pushed it open far enough to get inside.

In the kitchen, Bertie was standing under the hanging carbide lamp, her face a sickly white in the dim light it cast in the dusty gloom. "Look!" she said. "Look at Lupas, and *feel* the floor, it's *breathing!*"

Lupas was flat on the kitchen floor, his head stretched out and his eyes glassy. And the floor *was* breathing, slow, regular, up-and-down waves of motion. Bertie and I stood where we were and waited. There was no place to go; the old cellar had long ago filled with water and caved in. It was hard to breathe, and the air seemed to be *stretched tight*. We both sensed it, a feeling that the walls were about to burst, *outward*.

A few minutes later the floor steadied and the tension eased. Lupas stood up, wagging his tail and looking ashamed of himself.

Within an hour, the wind began to go down and we could see the sun through the thinning haze. I went out to look for the rest of my little turkeys. The chickens, upset by the short night, were coming off the roost and wandering around, swiveling their heads and clucking at each other. The hen and little turkeys in the coop were all right, but I never did find the others.

"I'm afraid that wind did some damage somewhere," I told Bertie. But there was no way to find out. The telephone line was dead and Miles and Bert didn't come home that night.

Miles pulled in first, the next morning, and Bert rode in a few minutes later.

Miles said he and Bird had been so busy checking petitions that they hadn't paid much attention to the storm. When the early darkness came on, Bird had turned on the Kohler electric light above the table and they had gone on with the checking. They hadn't even noticed when Ruby took the children and went to the cellar. It was evening when they finished their lists, so Bird said Miles had just as well stay all night and they'd go together the next morning to talk with the Flats postmaster about the new mail route. Miles hadn't worried when he couldn't call home, for he thought Bert was back by then.

Bert had started early, intending to ride the new horse all the way home that day. He was well up toward the Birdwood by the time the wind became bad, and at noon he stopped at Tom Hoatson's. Tom and his hired man had listed corn, until the whipping wind drove them from the field an hour before noon. They all sat around after dinner, waiting for the wind to go down. Around three o'clock, when it showed no sign of letting up, Bert started on.

A little later the greenish haze closed in, and before he knew it he was lost in the howling duster. If he had been riding a horse from the ranch, he would have given it its head and let it take him home. But this horse had never seen the ranch, so he was no help—if anything, he was apt to turn and try to go back to his former home.

So Bert kept him headed away from the wind and rode on. After a while he saw a light, a dim glow that didn't seem to get any nearer or any brighter, though he rode toward it for what seemed a long time. Then it began to rain, big, wind-driven drops of mud that stung like bullets. Then the horse stopped, suddenly, and wouldn't go any farther. Bert figured he had come to a fence. He swung down from the saddle to see—and slammed right into a man, who must have been standing almost at his stirrup. Dark as it was, and the wind roaring so, neither of them had known the other was there.

Bert said he almost yelled out loud when he bumped into the other man. With it getting dark in the middle of the afternoon, and the stinging rain and the howling wind and the spooky light that came no nearer, he was feeling pretty jumpy anyway.

The horse had stopped at the gate to Ivan Johnson's backyard, and the fellow Bert bumped into was Ivan's hired man. They put the horse in the barn and went to the house, where Ivan's wife had supper almost ready. It wasn't four o'clock yet, but when they lit the lamp everybody began to get hungry, so she started supper.

An hour or so later, when the sun began to shine again, Bert rode on to the O'Brian ranch, only nine miles from home, where he put up for the night.

That afternoon, after the broken telephone line was spliced, we heard about the tornado. Along with the dustbowl williwaw, it had ripped across the Tryon hills the afternoon before while Bertie and I were standing on the heaving floor in our own kitchen.

A true tornado had never been known in the sandhills before. The funnel winds do their damage on the river valley, now and then, but there is something about the rolling hills that breaks them up, so they say, and destroys their power to hurt.

But that day half a dozen farmsteads, just north and west of Tryon, were hit hard. At one place six people, three of them little children, were killed outright. At another, two old-maid sisters died. At the June club meeting, we worked on quilts for the Waits family. Every shred of their clothing and bedding had gone with the terrible wind.

The drouth and the big depression hung on and on. There were more dust storms, with the unearthly darkness that came on hours too soon; but after the first one we knew it wasn't the beginning of the Judgment Day. Sometimes the dust came on howling winds in the night but, night or day, it seeped into the house and piled in drifts on the window sills and in front of the doors. No house could keep it out. Red, yellow, black, or white, depending on the direction it came from, everybody scooped it up and carried it out when the winds died.

Throughout the big dust bowl, pastures grew shorter and shorter. In many places they were finally as bare as a floor, sometimes for miles and miles; and where there was a little grazing, the forage was coated with dust, with seldom so much as a shower to wash it clean. Cattle and sheep died of "dust-bowl pneumonia," and when the carcasses were posted the stomachs and lungs were full of *mud*.

In the sandhills, where the drouth and the insane winds probably did less damage than anywhere else on the plains, there was always grass, short and drouthy though it was. In the meadows the ranchmen could still cut hay, even though the little lakes dried up entirely and the big ones shrank to swamps or scummy ponds.

Thousands of ranchers and farmers went broke before the rains came again, but for us it was not so bad. Bert had sold all his cattle the year we went to Oregon, when the very high prices of 1927 and 1928 were near their peak. After we came back, he stocked the ranch with the best of cows, bought at the lowest prices in almost half a century. As long as he had enough feed, he couldn't lose.

It was one of those hot summers, after we came back to the hills, that Bert made his one and only try at driving the Chevvy. He wanted to go up to Huffmans, and for some reason or other he wanted to go in the car, rather than on horseback. I had had a major operation the month before and the doctor had told me not to drive the car for six weeks. But Bert said if I'd drive across the north pasture and through the first gate, he'd take it the rest of the way.

He did all right, too, until we came to the second gate. There he became mixed up someway and didn't get stopped in time.

He stepped out of the car and looked at the wrecked gate and the torn front tire in disgust. Then he pulled the cut tire off the wheel and hauled out the jack and the spare tire. But the valve on the spare had stuck and it was flat, too. He threw both tires in the trunk and told me he'd fix the gate while I turned the car around and headed it the other way. We'd have to go home on the rim, he said, and from now on he'd know enough to let driving alone. A man could generally figure out what a horse was going to do in a tight spot, but he couldn't tell about a darned car.

In the summer of 1937, when the drouth and depression seemed to be tapering off, Mike David celebrated the opening of his fourth, and last, new store. The big, modern building bore no noticeable resemblance to the tiny sod store that had been its beginning, but Mike was as handsome as ever in his good black broadcloth.

More than 1,200 people turned out for the big opening, and Mike made a little speech, thanking them all for their patronage over the years. In thirty-four years of business at the same location, he had seen a good many changes, he said. Gas and oil now made up a good share of his trade, while calls for buggy whips and kerosene lamps were few and far between. There were more speeches, by little Dr. McGraw and some senators and judges, and music and dancing and singing and readings. Then Mike and Mrs. David and their daughters served lunch to the whole crowd, and afterward there was a ball game on the Tryon diamond.

Mike loved big affairs like that. When the girls, Mable, Eva, and Mary, were married he broadcasted an open invitation to all his friends in four counties—and near two thousand of them turned out every time. The weddings were a lot like the big store opening, with speeches and a program and all, except that the color and beauty of the Greek Orthodox ceremonies made them seem like something out of a storybook.

About a year after the store opening, Mike's oldest son, young David David, was killed in a road accident in a blinding snowstorm. A few months later, Mike, looking years older, sold the store to his daughter Eva and her husband, young Taft Haddy, and moved his wife and youngest daughter Helen to Sioux City, Iowa.

But as long as he lived, Mike's big heart was in the sandhills, and when Helen married he took a three-day lease on a Sioux City hotel and restaurant and invited all his Nebraska friends to the wedding.

Chapter Fifty

WHEN McPherson County celebrated its Golden Jubilee, in October, 1940, the population had dwindled from the 1910 high of 2,470 to 1,175. The county's one bank, the Tryon State, like thousands of others across the nation, had closed its doors. But, unlike most of the others, it had paid its depositors every cent. However, its closing had made one more thing the county was without. It had always been without a railroad, a river, and a saloon. Now, again, it was without a doctor, a lawyer, or a bank.

For the McGraws, after fighting sandhill weather and roads for nearly twenty years, had moved to North Platte. But not before the little doctor had become a celebrity, having her life's story told in a well-known national magazine, and having been Eleanor Roosevelt's guest in the White House.

Mr. Huffman had died, leaving the hills the poorer for his passing. At his funeral I remembered the time, years back, when Bert and little Jake Rupp, now a dozen years dead, had had "words" over something. Jake had gone to Mr. Huffman with his tale of woe, and the good old man had told him, "Now, Jake, you mustn't pay any attention to what Bert said. He was just mad when he said it, and he didn't mean a word of it."

And Glenn Miller, the nice-looking, polite little boy

of the Kinkaid days, had made himself famous with his gay music and big-time orchestra. By then we had a big radio, one with A batteries and B batteries and many tubes, and a bell-shaped loudspeaker that sat on top of it. Miles had put up a tall tower, topped with a windmill wheel, a "windcharger" that kept the B batteries full so that we never had to miss a Glenn Miller broadcast. A few years later, the grim news that Glenn's plane had gone down in the English Channel, another casualty of another World War, came to us over that same radio.

On a Saturday in January, 1936, the mail had come to the ranch for the last time; and when the mail carrier bounced away over the rutted road that day, Lilac joined the hundreds of other little "dead" post offices that had once served the frontiers of the "West." From then on, when the weather and roads weren't too bad, a carrier made daily trips from Sutherland to Lena and back, and we picked up our mail from a box on a fence post, down by the cottonwoods old man Matthews had set out around his shack so many years before.

The Golden Jubilee was as big a success as the old Kinkaid picnics had been. In 1900, the first county census had listed 517 men, women, and children, and 62 of those early settlers were on hand for the Jubilee. Mike and Mrs. David were there, and the McGraws. Even old Gale Patterson, the settler Bert had bought our valley from, came out from Omaha for the day. There was the usual turnout of senators, congressmen, and judges to make speeches, and a big free barbeque in the evening —"1200 sandwiches, 200 pounds of baked beans, and 40 gallons of coffee being consumed by a crowd estimated at between 700 and 1000 people," according to the *Tryon Graphic.*

But, due to the long depression, the dream of good

roads in the sandhills was still mostly that—just a dream.
Back in 1934, the great "Lincoln Highway," the first
all-weather road across the continent, had been completed.
It had been twenty-one years a-building across Nebraska,
from both edges toward the middle; and the final link,
joining the two ends of the whole continental highway,
was the strip across Lincoln County. The same stretch
where we had dragged, hub-deep, through oozing mud
between Maxwell and North Platte on our way to the
Birdwood, thirty-five years before.

A year or two later, McPherson County finished its
first strip of real pavement, the sixteen-mile stretch from
the south county line to the north side of the new courthouse. The north end of the road was Tryon's only
paved street. It came into town from the east, passed
directly in front of Mike David's store, and ended at the
west corner of the courthouse fence. But the north-south
main street was still deep sand, now and then overlaid
with straw or old hay.

That sixteen miles of sandhill pavement was something
new in the way of hard-topping. The engineers had
mixed native sand with thick black oil and spread the
tarry mess in an inch-thick mat on the shallow grade.
Packed and dried, it stood up very well; except for its
first summer, when the weather was so hot that the tar
softened and big truck wheels broke through, leaving
bad ruts and holes. Even so, it was by far the best road
anywhere around and McPherson County was proud of
it. When the weather cooled off a little, a bit more
sand and oil would fix the ruts.

So, when we read in the *Tryon Graphic* that, "Now
and then some one pulls into Tryon and inquires if the
road to the north (which we must remember is also a
'state highway') is as bad as the road between North

THE "GRAPE QUILT," ONE OF MY ORIGINAL DESIGNS

This picture was taken at the International Exposition in New York in 1950. One of the exposition judges, center; my daughter, Bertie Elfeldt, at right.

"BIRD OF PARADISE" QUILT, ANOTHER OF MY ORIGINAL DESIGNS

This, too, is an International Exposition picture. Mrs. Edith Smith, the woman in charge of the booth, sits on the left

Platte and Tryon," we could understand why the editor was "put out." Let them try that road, or any other leading out of Tryon, he snorted; for by comparison that North Platte-Tryon strip was a super highway, fast as a race track and smooth as a floor.

Later that summer, the editor commented, "We have but little drunken driving in our county; for, other than the highway to North Platte, our roads are in such condition that a sober man can just barely get over them."

To the end of the thirties, the only *good* road in the county was that sixteen miles of narrow pavement from the county line to the west side of the courthouse. Throughout the rest of its near one thousand square miles, the ranchmen were still spreading hay and barnyard manure on the worst spots in the crooked trails that crossed their ranches, and still pleading with the state for something better to travel on. The northeast county area was begging for a road from Tryon to Mullen, a little town on the northern railroad. On the west, we were asking for a highway from Tryon to Arthur. The people south of Flats wanted a road between that place and Sutherland. Then a group from Paxton, the next town west of Sutherland, began boosting for a "Corn to Cattle" highway from Paxton to Flats.

For several years, young Forest Snyder (no relation), editor of the *Tryon Graphic,* had been using his paper in a hard-hitting fight for better roads in the sandhills. When the "Corn to Cattle" proposal came up he wrote, "You people of Flats are to be congratulated. You will have TWO highways to the south and ONE passing from east to west. Well—the more roads you ASK for, the more promises you will get down at the capital. In the meantime you'd better ask the County Dads for a few more loads of straw."

At that a Flats' citizen, referring to Tryon's one bit of pavement, wrote Forest a letter. "We note in our Editor's column that he advises us to ask the County Dads for a few loads of straw instead of new highways. Good advice until we remembered seeing ye editor, knee deep in straw, holding to his mother's hand and trudging up Tryon's main street, where now gleams a $50,000 highway investment."

The editor replied:

We didn't say "ask for straw INSTEAD of roads." We said, "In the MEANTIME you'd better ask the County Dads for a few more loads of straw." It's going to take a LOT of straw to keep your roads in shape between now and the time you get those three highways. Think of all the straw that was used on Tryon's main street between the time when ye editor was a little kid holding his mother's hand—which was about the time Tryon road boosters began ASKING for a road—and a year ago, when it was completed.

At its next session, the state legislature designated the Flats-Paxton trail a "state road." The *Graphic* editor, discouraged by past attempts to get something besides promises for paving, wrote, "This road will connect Highway No. 30 (at Paxton) with the east-west Tryon-Arthur highway—WHEN the Paxton-Flats road is built and WHEN the Tryon-Arthur road is built."

The next week we read in the *Graphic:* "County treasurer Steve Clifford has told this editor that auto registrations in the county, so far this year, are far below those of a year ago. Possibly many car owners have stored their machines; for it has been rumored that our roads are now so bad that many rural folk are unable to get their autos off their places, and therefore feel no need for purchasing new license tags."

The next July, during a long, scorching stretch between rains, a Plymouth car burned up on the road between Tryon and Flats, where a heavy spread of hay covered a particularly bad piece of sandy road. In spite of the hay, the car had stalled and its spinning wheels had dug it down until its red-hot exhaust pipe came against the tinder-dry hay and set both the road and the car afire.

The *Graphic* editor published the news item about the loss of the car, and then added his own comment: "It has been suggested that the big automobile firms place on their proving grounds a stretch of sandhill bunch-grass, a few cat-steps and cow-paths, crossed by some barbed wire fences, the whole well dotted with blowouts and deep sand-drifts. The modern sandhill driver would then know just how efficient the new car he buys would be on such ground."

In the winters, when snow on top of sand piled up our road troubles, the telephone was sometimes our only connection with town or neighbors for weeks at a time. Then, when one neighbor called another to ask, "How're the roads up, or down, or over, your way?" the usual answer was, "There aren't any roads up, or down, or over, this way."

During one long snowbound spell, this item came out in the *Graphic:* "Teams and wagons are not uncommon sights in the streets of our town these days. Traffic goes on as usual on the North Platte highway south of here. If we only had our long promised State highway on north from here, and east and west across the county, travel in the hills would not be completely paralyzed every time we have a storm."

As 1941 drew to a close, the gist of the road news from the capital at Lincoln was that all our petitions and agitating were about to accomplish something. When spring

came again, some real highway work was to get under-
way in McPherson County. But before anything "con-
crete" could come of those plans, a new World War
had put an end to all our hopes for better roads—just as
the first World War had dashed our prospects for a railroad a generation earlier.

Chapter Fifty-One

NATE TREGO died at his town home in Sutherland on the Thursday after Pearl Harbor. He had spent fifty-six of his seventy-four years in the sandhills, and nearly forty of them as a commissioner of McPherson County. "Civic leader, outstanding pioneer, leader of youth, friend to all, beloved citizen," the *Tryon Graphic* and the *Sutherland Courier* said of him, "A man who would long be missed by his county and his friends." For Bert, the place of his oldest and best friend could never be filled.

The following fall we read in the *Graphic* that, "Since main street has been taken over as a football field by the high-school boys (it is needed for little else since the advent of gasoline rationing), there have been frequent interruptions in the electric and telephone service. The boys have kicked the ball into the lines so often that they're nearly kicked off the supporting poles."

Gas and tire rationing, together with the usual bad condition of our roads, kept us home most of the time, too, during the war years. By then Bert's joints were beginning to feel the effects of age and long years in the saddle in all kinds of weather. Often then, instead of saddling a horse to ride off to some pasture to check a windmill, he'd ask me to take him there in the car. I would take my work box along, and if he had to spend some time repairing a well, I sewed a few quilt pieces together. A good many of the blocks in my quilts were put together in the car, in some sandhill pasture, while I waited for Bert.

Five or six years before the war, Bert and I had gone to the Black Hills for a two-weeks' fishing trip, and he found out, that summer, that the ranch *could* get along without him for a while. Every year after that, until the war, we went camping in the Black Hills, or on over in Wyoming. I always took a box of pieces with me on our trips, and while Bert fished I cut or sewed quilt pieces.

Since the early thirties, I had worked mostly with unusual quilts, beautiful appliqued designs, or quilts made of many thousands of tiny pieces. The summer I made the appliqued blocks for my "Covered Wagon States" quilt, we spent some time in Wyoming. And one afternoon, while Bert fished from the barren banks of Lake De Smet, I sewed the black and white pieces for the picture of Father De Smet himself, the priest this long, lonesome lake in the middle of a bare plain had been named for. It had been just one hundred years since the famous "Black Robe" had passed this way. And probably nothing had changed, except that Hereford cattle instead of buffalo came now to drink at the lake, and tourists instead of Indians camped on its treeless banks.

It was during the war years that I pieced most of the rest of my finest quilts, the Mosaic Hexagon with over 50,000 dime-sized pieces, and the Basket Petit Point with 87,789 pieces. And then came the October that the last of my three wishes came true.

Elsie asked me to go to California with her for a family reunion that fall. It was to be our first in a good many years, and I told her I'd go.

While we were in Oregon, the Union Pacific had built

corrals and chutes and shipping pens on its branch rail-road north of Sutherland. The little station, known as Coker, made it much easier for cattlemen in that north-west country to load and ship their cattle.

It was a three-day drive from the ranch to Coker, and Bert and Miles depended on me to start from the ranch each morning and meet them at their noon camp with hot meals for the trail crew. After the first two or three years, Bert gave up going on the drives and sleeping out at night. Instead, he followed in the car, with me and the "grub," and went home with me to sleep in his own bed at night; but we always had to be at Coker on the third day to see the cattle loaded out.

When I told Bert I was going to California, he looked at me as if I had taken complete leave of my senses. "But, Mom," he said, "we'll be shipping then and we'll need you. How'll we get the grub down to the men on the road, and how'll I get to Coker when they load out?"

"You'll do just what you'll do when I'm dead and gone," I told him. "I won't always be around at shipping time, but I expect you'll go on shipping just the same. Hollis (Miles's wife) can drive the car for you, or you can hire somebody to do it. I'm going to California."

So I went to California, and that was the last "ha-ha" party we ever had, with all eight of us together; for three years later Roy died suddenly. It was his heart, the doctor said, weakened by the hard case of pneumonia he'd had, that long-ago winter of the measles.

But while we were together in Fresno, where Ethel and Roy lived, and down in Long Beach, where Nellie and Earl lived, the old pet names, Presh and Heart and Gheet and Dovey, came naturally to our tongues again, and we talked of things that had happened so long ago. Of how we used to go down cellar to take hungry

sniffs of the good smell that stayed in the Missouri barrel,
long after the apples were gone. Of how, if Florry saw
Poppie coming to the house before she had dinner ready,
she'd rush to set the table before he got inside. She had
learned, early, that if the table was set when he came
in he'd sit down and wait patiently, even if she hadn't
peeled the potatoes yet. But if it wasn't, he'd scold, even
if she was within five minutes of putting the meal on
the table.

We laughed about the summer Uncle Jonathan and
Aunt Lib came out from Missouri, when we lived on
the Rowan place, and their Tommy had tricked Dovey
and Presh and Nellie into "going out" with him the first
night. Tommy was eight years old, and they had thought
he was brave and wonderful until they found out he
was as scared of the dark and the howling coyotes as
they were.

Tommy hadn't wanted the grown-ups to know he
was afraid, so he wouldn't ask any of them to go out
back with him. Instead, he told the girls he wanted to
play a new game. Dovey, he said, should stand by the
first porch post, and Presh by the second one and Nellie
at the corner of the house. He warned them not to move
until he told them to, and then he slipped along the wall
to the next corner. After a minute or so he came back
and said he guessed it was too dark to play his game—
"But by then we had caught on, and we felt so cheap,"
Nellie said.

It was that same summer that Florry's "ghost" had
scared poor Dovey clear out of her wits. Poppie and
Mama hadn't any use for ghost stories and would not
stand for anyone telling them around us girls, if they
knew it. But Lily Garner, a second cousin about Florry's
age, who stayed with Grandma McCance a while, had

told us plenty of them. Stories about ghosts rapping on walls in the night, and about dead people whose hair and beards kept on growing until they burst the coffins open, and bodies that turned to stone so heavy that a dozen men couldn't lift them. She told us about a graveyard near her home in Missouri that had to be moved, and how, when the grave movers were digging up one coffin, a man accidentally chopped into the corner of it. An awful black juice had run out of the hole, she said, and within a year every man that had helped with the job was dead.

The stories didn't bother Florry and me very much, except that we didn't dare go outside alone at night all that summer, but they kept poor Dovey shaking in her boots day and night. Then, one hot day, I came in from the field for dinner at about the same time that Stella and Dovey came in from herding. Dovey went on into the little back bedroom, and came flying right out again, her eyes big as teacups. "There's someone *breathing* in there," she whispered.

We all went in to see who was breathing in there, and it was only a window blind. The window was open from the top and the roller blind, drawn down against the hot sun, was moving in and out in the opening with a sighing sound that *was* like breathing. We laughed at Dovey for being such a fraidy cat, but the "breathing blind" had sparked an idea in Florry's head.

That afternoon she rolled up a pillow and put a long dress on it and laid it on the bed in the dark little bedroom. She put two sunflowers on the "head" for eyes, and an old screwdriver handle for a nose. She meant to scare Stell, or me, with her ghost, but when we came in from work it was Dovey, again, who went to the bedroom first. She took one look, then screamed and hurtled through the living room and right on out the door.

When Florry saw what had happened, she ran in and grabbed up her ghost and took out after Dovey, intending to show her the silly thing she was running from. But Dovey was already flying down the road toward Cozad. Florry held out the ghost and yelled, "Dovey, oh, Dovey, look!"

Dovey looked, then screamed again and ran faster than ever.

So Florry dropped the ghost and tore down the road after her, until she could snatch her dress tail and yank her to a stop. Dovey turned and looked at Florry, then grabbed her and sobbed, "Oh, Florry, *I thought that ghost was running away with you.*"

"I shiver yet, when I remember that day," Ethel said.

Of course someone remembered old Bill Sherman, and the time he proposed to me. Then Elsie asked if she had ever told us about the letter he had written to her? She hadn't, and we wanted to hear about it.

"It was the summer after we left the Birdwood," she said, "and there was a one-dollar money order in the letter. He wanted me to come to Sutherland as soon as I could, and the dollar was for train fare. I was only fourteen and I couldn't imagine what he wanted to see me for, unless it was to make his will and leave me all his money. But I knew the folks wouldn't let me go, or keep the dollar either, if they knew about it. So I cashed the money order and never told a soul. I meant to keep my part of the bargain, though, and go see old Bill the first time I went up to Florry's. But by the time I got to the Birdwood again, he had gone bumming to Pennsylvania or someplace, and I never did get to find out what he wanted."

"Whatever it was, it must have been pretty important if Old Bill would part with a dollar for it," I said.

At the end of the two weeks we had planned to stay in California, Elsie decided to stay on a little longer. She urged me to stay, too, but I knew Bert thought I had neglected him and the ranch too long already; and, besides, I saw that this was my opportunity to make my third wish come true.

I had married my cowboy and gone to live on his ranch. I had made quilts far finer than any I had ever dreamed about, back there on the Dawson County prairie. Now I intended to cash in my return ticket on the train and *fly home above the clouds.* I knew Bert wouldn't think much of the idea, but he wasn't there to say anything about it, so I came home on an airliner.

It had been fifty years or more, since I had first felt the *need* to get above the clouds. But that night, sailing along smooth and steady, two miles above the ground, the biggest wonder wasn't that I was *flying*, but that I *should ever have flown at all.* Since then, I have *never* missed a chance to fly.

It was about that time that Miles's little son Jimmie reached school age; and by then the wheel had come full circle. Again, there were no children in our big district, except the little boy on the ranch. The old schoolhouse still stood on the flat five miles away, unused for years and slowly falling apart. As usual, the twelve-mile stretch of road to Tryon was in such shape that no car could hang together long under the wrenching and pounding that strip would give it. The roads leading to schools in any other direction were even worse. So Miles bought a small plane and learned to fly it.

For several years then, he flew Jimmie down to Tryon in the mornings and went after him in the afternoons.

The landing field at the ranch was a level strip of meadow near the little hangar; at Tryon it was a patch of smooth pasture beside the highway a mile east of town. Jimmie kept his little bicycle there, padlocked to a fence post beside the road. When they landed in the mornings, he unlocked the wheel and pedaled off to school. In the afternoons, when he heard his dad's plane coming in from the west, he pedaled back to meet him at the landing strip.

The plane was handy in ever so many ways. Miles flew it low over the windmills to see if they were pumping, and to check on the cattle and fences. When a piece of machinery broke down, it was only a few minutes jaunt to Flats, where he could land right in front of the store to pick up repairs.

I flew with Miles many times; Bert only did so once.

In his younger days, Bert never hesitated to climb onto a bronc, no matter how big and mean; but he had no desire to travel any higher above the ground than the seat of a saddle. All the rest of us rode in the plane as a matter of course, and maybe Bert's pride got to hurting a little. Anyway, when Miles was flying down to the Platte one day, he casually showed up and said he guessed he'd ride along.

I don't believe he enjoyed the flight much, and he never got in the machine again, but he saw to it that everybody knew he had gone, that once, just in case anyone might have thought he was afraid to ride in one of the darn things.

Chapter Fifty-Two

IN THE early summer of 1946, Ira Huffman, plowing his way through the sand from Tryon to his ranch at Lena, died of a heart attack in his car in front of the Flats store. At his funeral, I made up my mind to leave the hills before winter and go where there were decent roads. I had already put in too many years pushing and shoveling through sand and snow, and walking for help in the heat and the cold when I couldn't get through any other way.

Of course Bert didn't want to leave the ranch. It was as much a part of him as his right arm, and just as hard to leave behind.

"If we had decent roads, or any roads at all," I told him, "I would be happy to stay in the hills the rest of my life. As it is, I'm getting out before I'm carried out."

I meant it, too, all of it.

Except for good roads, we had all the conveniences of city life. We had electric lights all over the house, powered by Miles's second big windcharger, and a kerosene refrigerator that did everything the electric models in town could do. We had put in a bath and "running water" and they worked fine, except for a while the first winter. That winter was the coldest and stormiest in many years, so cold that our deep-buried pipes froze and we had to go back to shoveling out the "path" and thawing and priming the old pitcher pump on the back porch.

But roads we didn't have, and it didn't look like we'd be getting any soon, so I bought a nice brick home in North Platte and moved in as fast as I could. Bert stayed on the ranch two weeks longer, then he packed his "war sack" and took his foot in his hand and came down to live with me.

The years have gone fast since then. I pieced and quilted a few more quilts, those first years in town, but most of my big "show" collection are the ones I made during the long, snowbound winters on the ranch, or while I sat with Bert on the bank of some good fishing lake or river.

With one or another of my daughters, I have flown to New York City, to West Springfield, Massachusetts, and to other cities where I have exhibited my quilts at national and international quilt shows. I have won almost enough blue and purple ribbons to cover a bed, and my collection of magazine and newspaper clippings about my quilts fills a good-sized scrapbook.

On my flights from Chicago east, I have seen the top sides of more clouds than ever drifted above the Nebraska prairie in my herding days. Coming down over New York at night, where the millions of city lights turned the thick clouds below to a pink glow, was like sinking into an enormous bowl of strawberry ice cream.

In New York, where the four quilts I showed at the twenty-seventh International Women's Exposition won a fistful of top ribbons, we spent an interesting week of sight-seeing. We rode on the old elevated and the subway, shopped on Fifth Avenue, and visited the Statue of Liberty. We ate in an automat, once, and in seafood restaurants so many times that we began to smell like the ocean. We came away twice happy—once because we had been to New York, and once because we didn't have to live there.

At the Eastern States Exposition, in Massachusetts, my Petit Point quilt, the one of 87,789 pieces, had a room by itself; one of the parlors of the beautiful old Potter Mansion in Storrowton village. As always, people seemed to find it hard to believe the quilt was actually made of separate bits of cloth. One woman looked at it for a long time, and asked all the usual questions: "How long did it take you? Is it *really* sewed? *Where* did you get the patience?" Then, backing out of the room with her eyes on the quilt, she said, "I feel as if I ought to curtsey, or something."

At the Nebraska State Fair in Lincoln, one September, I had the pleasure of seeing eighteen of my quilts hung in a long row in the Fine Arts building. (The nineteenth, an original grapevine design, was in a showcase under the purple sweepstakes ribbon.) A card at the head of the line explained that all eighteen had been made by one woman. Men and women read the card, then shook their heads and asked, "How did one woman ever find time to make them all?"

One man was looking at the "Pilgrim" block in the United States History quilt when his wife asked the usual question. "Because she started in 1620, I guess," he told her. Others decided it was because "she didn't have anything else to do." At the time I made all the quilts in that display, I was still living on the ranch, baking our bread, churning our butter, making my own soap, and raising a big garden every summer, not to mention all the time I spent plowing our roads every time I left the ranch.

But, so far, no one has ever topped the remark made

by a woman at the New York show, after she had looked a long time at the Petit Point quilt. "Of course *that* quilt was made by a feeble-minded person, was it not?" she asked of the lady in charge of the booth where it hung.

I pieced the Petit Point quilt during the second World War, from a lovely flower basket design I found on a china plate. I made it of triangle shaped pieces so small that eight of them sewed together made a "block" no larger than a two-cent postage stamp. The effect is more like needle point embroidery than patchwork quilt piecing. I was sixteen months making the quilt, and I used 5,400 yards of thread in the sewing.

While I worked on the quilt, I often wondered where the lovely pattern on the plate had come from, and also if I was infringing on anybody's patent or copyright or something. So, when I finished it, I wrote to the Salem China Company, Salem, Ohio, the name stamped on the back of the plate, and explained how I had "lifted" their design, and asked where it originated. A personal letter from the company president, Mr. F. W. McKee, came right back. He wrote that the design, one of the most popular they had ever used, had come from an artist in Germany, and that they hadn't heard from the poor fellow since a certain one-time paperhanger over there had stirred things up so. He also said he would like very much to have a good photograph of the quilt.

I sent him the picture he asked for, and he was so pleased with it that he sent me a set of the Petit Point china, a very fine grade, banded in 23-karat gold. The first set was a service for six, but Mr. McKee every now and then added to his gift, until I had a complete service for eighteen, enough, he said, to set my table when all the family came home.

When the war ended, Mr. McKee got in touch with

SOME OF THE RIBBONS AND TROPHIES I HAVE WON ON MY QUILTS
AND SPREADS.

OUR GOLDEN WEDDING DAY, 1953

his German designer again, and then sent his name and address, Wendelin Grossman, Berlin, on to me. I wrote to Mr. Grossman, telling him something of my life, and of the quilt I had made from his beautiful design, and enclosing a picture of the quilt.

He replied, in perfect Spencerian script:

DEAR MRS. SNYDER: I was astonished to hear that the design having been so much in favor of the Salem China Co., was even used for a quilt. The work must be wonderful and I only admire your patience and troubles and I understand quite well that you are proud of the great success in the exhibitions. This being a pleasure for me too, hearing that with my design so many nice things arose. It will encourage me to go on working and to create many good ideas.

Till now I have never been in the United States. Maybe it is my fate to come once over and will not forget to see you. My home town was badly destroyed in the war and the house of my parents completely ruined. Three of my relatives lost their lives and the worst was physical need. During day and night attacks, bombs and fire, of course I could not think of working. Now this time is over and new work makes me forget the hardships we endured.

I am a painter. Although I am well known in my home town we have a modest life. The chief thing is that one can create some good. I am 53 years of age. My wife is 42. Thank God we live in the US zone. We pray to God that He may keep away the Russians. Only if this danger is removed will menkind enjoy a real peace.

I guess you are living in a peaceful, quiet landscape, far off from the town and the sorrow about politics. Only under such conditions you could do such a wonderful work, as you did it with love and repose.

Now, dear Mrs. Snyder, that is the essential about my person and my environs. It is astonishing that men, being so far off from each other, get acquainted by a chance and this time by our work. You have enjoyed us so very much and I will do my best to redress your friendship. I'm sorry to say that we didn't live during the war in such a calm situation like you in your country. Often I remember fearfully the awful nights of terror in that murdering time. Maybe a new war will break out again and then nobody knows how the exit will be.

I do not doubt for a moment that your works enjoy you and the generality. I would esteem it as a great favor if you would have the kindness to send me a book of your works when it is done. I wish you and your dear family health and a good luck for your further

work. Kindly receive my heartily and gratefully greetings and wishes
for a happy time and I hope soon to hear again from you. Yours,
                                        WENDELIN GROSSMAN.

One spring while we were still on the ranch, I held
the lucky number in a "Lincoln County Feeder's Day"
drawing in North Platte. My prize was a registered Hol-
stein heifer calf named "Pansy." When we took the
pretty black and white heifer to the ranch, every Hereford that laid eyes on her straightway stampeded for the
far hills. Even the saddle horses shied and snorted at
sight of her for a week or two. Until then, the livestock
on our place hadn't known that cattle sometimes came
in color combinations besides *red* and white.

The *Tryon Graphic* account of my good fortune had
this additional comment by the editor, "Pansy could receive no better care than will be lavished upon her by
Mrs. Snyder, even to the extent of having a prize win-
ning quilt for a blanket."

Some of the other clippings in my scrapbook are funny,
too. Under such titles as "Quilting to Fame," and "Childhood Hobby Wins National Acclaim," the writers let
their imaginations run wild with the facts I gave them.
One had me piecing my first doll quilt while on the way to
Nebraska in a *covered wagon* at the age of *three*. Another
had me carrying my little box of quilt pieces and herding cattle on the prairie, while still in danger of having
to run for my life from the Indians.

The last quilt I made, or will ever make, was a Princess
Feather. For twenty years I had looked for a special
print for that quilt, a print like that in the lovely calico
dress I ruined when the wicked little heifer chased me
under the corral fence, back on the old homestead. I
finally found it, and made up the unusual quilt. By

the time I finished it, cataracts were beginning to cloud my eyes.

Surgery later restored my sight, but not to the point where I could see to set the tiny stitches that I had learned to make so long ago, the kind of work that made my quilts prizewinners in half a hundred shows and fairs.

For a good many years Bert, too, had had two dreams of his own. One was that there would someday be a good, all-weather road from Tryon to Arthur; the other, that oil would be found under the sandhills. He lived to see his first dream come true, even though he almost had to build the road himself.

The guns of war were barely cool when he took up the good-roads fight again. Day after day, in his high heels and Stetson hat—he never changed his way of dress, except that in town he wore "California" stockmen pants instead of Levi's—he made the rounds of the business firms, explaining the advantages to North Platte in good roads in the hills. His arguments made sense, and after his visit with the editors of the town's daily paper, they backed his drive with an editorial:

Financing of the road construction will be $6,000 per mile. The McPherson county commissioners have alloted $28,000 for this purpose. Any amount of money raised locally by Mr. Snyder, in addition to that subscribed by ranchers favoring the road, will be matched by the government. It is pointed out that . . . large trucks are unable to get into the area between Tryon and Flats and such a road would open up the huge ranch industry in that section to North Platte, and facilitate a large increase in the shipping of cattle to this city.

Bert and others along the proposed route had already donated thousands of dollars to the road fund. He collected several thousands more in North Platte, that first year we lived in town. It seemed, then, that as soon as the state and national road departments came through with their shares, McPherson County could begin to get out of the sand.

But the wheels of government seldom turn fast. Not a foot of new grade had yet been thrown up the summer of 1948, when the Helping Hand Club dedicated its new club house in the Huffman Valley. Nebraska's governor was invited out to make the speech of dedication. To help things along, Miles and Bill Trego, both members of the Better Roads committee, arranged for his plane to land at the ranch. It could just as well have come down on the flat in front of the club house but, in the interest of better roads, they thought it a good idea to give His Honor an automobile ride over a seven-mile sample of the kind of roads sandhillers used all the time.

In his speech that afternoon, Governor Peterson said he felt the bumps in the same places the rest of us did, that he could see why ranchers were taking to planes, and that he would do all he could to see that the sandhills got a priority on the building of new roads. Now, we thought, maybe we'd get some action, come spring.

Chapter Fifty-Three

IF THERE has seemed to be overmuch of weather in this story, it is because there is overmuch of weather in Nebraska, and it still has much to do with what goes on in the big state. Man, with all his inventions to make life easier and better and faster, has come an amazing long way in three quarters of a century. But when Nature whips up something really rough in the way of a storm, men and all their gadgets are stopped in their tracks. And so it was on January 2, 1949, when the worst blizzard ever known in the state roared in for a three-day stay.

The size and savagery of the storm were almost unbelievable. The sixty-mile winds left snowdrifts twenty-five feet high all across the state. Houses, barns, and telephone lines were completely buried, stalled trains were drifted under, and cars were buried on the highways. Thousands of families were trapped in farm and ranch homes, with too little food or fuel or medicine. The total number of travelers stranded in the farmhouses, filling stations, and railroad depots was never known. In North Platte alone, the old canteen, famous around the world in the days of the second World War, opened its doors to several hundred snowbound motorists.

As soon as the big storm cleared, the state, the counties, and the cities put thousands of men and machines to work on streets and roads, but the best they could do was of little use. For almost continual high winds, below-zero cold, and more snowstorms plagued the country for weeks to come. What little the army of workers accomplished in a day of hard labor, the wind undid in an hour. Before even a part of a street or road could be opened through the house-high drifts, the wind filled it in again.

When all Nebraska's resources failed to make any headway toward relieving the desperate state of its people, the Fifth Army of the United States was called in to begin its famous "Operation Snowbound." Nearly two months later, on February 26, when General Pick reported "mission accomplished," $5,000,000 had been spent in freeing 79,454 snowbound people, opening 33,973 miles of Nebraska roads, and "liberating" 1,782,877 head of starving livestock.

Railroad and telephone companies had spent millions more in repairing and maintaining their lines and tracks. Airplanes and helicopters had flown hundreds of mercy missions, dropping mail and food by parachute, carrying doctors in and the sick out. Army weasels had moved hundreds of loads of food and fuel across the snow to buried farms. "Operation Haylift" had dropped thousands of tons of hay to cattle that were starving to death beside snow-buried haystacks. By spring, cattle losses had topped $10,000,000.

The roads, opened time and again by giant army bulldozers, filled in every time high winds and new storms swept across the state. By the time it was all over, damage to the state's highways totaled more than $2,500,000. No state money could be spared for *new roads* for another year or two now, the road department reported. It would take it all just for road repairs.

The whole story of the blizzard, the brave deeds and the suffering and the homely little things, would fill a

book. There was the canned milk, parachuted to a farm
near Hershey to save the life of a small baby. The keeper
of weather records in a small town who reported: "Pre-
cipitation report impossible, rain gage under deep snow."
The woman who, weeks after the blizzard, stood on the
drift that buried her clothesline while she hung her washing on the *telephone line!* The twenty-four travelers
stranded at a farmhouse north of Kimball on Sunday,
the first day of the storm, who sent a call for help to
Scottsbluff. Six men started right out with two snow-
plows, and reached the farmhouse at dark, too late to
try to take the travelers out. By morning they were
snowed in, too. The next Thursday, the snowplow from
Kimball managed to get through to "liberate" all thirty.
Thousands of children all across the state were out of
school for weeks. But one group of thirteen youngsters
had the bad luck to be snowed in with their teacher, at
a ranch house where their school bus had stalled in a
drift. They never missed a class until they were dug out,
a month later.

Around the first of February, some of the ranchers
in the Flats community managed to get a telegram out
to the governor, asking him to arrange a "stay of execution" until they could get out of the hills to file their
income tax returns. In the end, the Department of Internal Revenue granted the whole territory a "stay," since
thousands were unable to get their reports out until late
in the month, nearly two weeks past the deadline for
farmers and ranchers.

In Pierce County, up in the northeast section of the
state, a doctor from a town outside the county was flown
in to deliver seventeen babies within a span of twenty
days—probably a "baby-lift" record. Farther west, on
December 29, a snowplow and two engines had been

derailed while bucking a frozen drift left by an earlier
storm. A second plow and derrick, sent to rescue the
first outfit, was caught and buried in the January blizzard.
Both outfits were finally dug out on February 22.

The big drifts were packed so tightly and frozen so
solidly that, when a Union Pacific doubleheader rammed
a high drift near Stapleton on January 18, its plow
caromed off the icy face of the drift and buckled back
to shear off one side of both locomotives. A trainman
was killed in the accident and it was eight hours before
the workers could finish cutting away the wreckage to
get his body out. In its seven weeks of day and night
battling with the storm, the Union Pacific used 15 of
its biggest rotary plows, 33 wedges, 124 flame throwers,
180 bulldozers and 14,000 men.

Throughout the ranch country, men worked day and
night for weeks, digging cattle out of the never-ending
drifts, trying to get hay to cattle, or cattle to hay, whichever seemed the more possible. As long as their cattle
were freezing or starving, they scarcely stopped to eat
or sleep; and before the long fight with the storm was
over, most of the poor fellows were so thin they could
hardly keep their Levi's up. A flying reporter wrote:
"From a plane the sandhills look like mountainous waves
blown by Paul Bunyon winds with, here and there in
the troughs of the ocean, a ranch like a tiny raft, trailing
streaks of cowpaths."

Two weeks after the blizzard, we saw Miles for the
first time since the storm, when he flew down to pick
up pneumonia vaccine for the sick, freezing cattle. He
stayed a little while to tell us how it had been at the ranch.

The terrible force of the driven snow had scoured the
paint from the north sides of the ranch buildings, he
said, and patches of hide and hair from the poor cattle.

More than sixty head of our yearlings had died in the blizzard, others, with frozen feet and legs, were dying every day. Relief planes had been dropping bread, coffee, and other staples at all the ranches, so they hadn't lacked for necessities. But it was impossible to imagine how much snow there was in the hills, he told us, or how big and deep the drifts were. Until that day, he hadn't had time to clear enough of the head-high drifts from his landing field to get out—and there was no other way out of the hills.

Like the other ranchers, when the wind wasn't whipping up the snow in a "ground blizzard," he had worked all through the days, and most of the nights; for moonlight on the unbroken snow cover made the nights almost as light as the days. One way or another, he was managing to get a little hay across the snow to trapped cattle, trying to keep them alive until trails could be broken out and haystacks uncovered.

He was so gaunt that he looked even taller than his six feet two, and the nightmare of the past two weeks was written plain on his poor hollow-eyed face, where long whisker stubble pinned the peeling skin to his frozen cheeks and chin. Bert and I took him back to the airport, where he hitched his belt tighter around his thin middle before he climbed into his little plane and took off into the cold blue haze above the snowbound hills.

Probably no one was more pleased than Bert when, two years after the Big Blizzard, a new road finally began to curve west from Tryon. By then, construction costs were more than double the $6,000 per mile figure the North Platte paper had used back in 1947. So the money ran out when the road reached to the top of the

big hill on the west side of our valley, less than halfway
from Tryon to Arthur.

Twenty years before, when the possibility of a good
road across the county had first stirred up excitement,
Bert and Nate Trego had walked behind a wagon all
the way from Tregos to the county seat, following the
levelest and straightest route possible for a road west
from Tryon. By counting the revolutions of a rag tied
to a hind wheel of the wagon, they had figured the length
of the road in miles. They had given their findings, on
paper, to the first Sandhills Road Association. Whether
or not anyone ever looked at their report again, they
never knew, but when the new highway, surveyed by a
crew with modern instruments, was finished it followed
exactly the route they had traveled, that long-ago day,
on foot. The distance they had measured with their
turning wheel came out right, too.

For a year or two after the highway was finished
through our valley, Bert and I drove up to the ranch
quite often. We never got over being surprised that we
could make that last eleven miles, from Tryon to the
ranch, in less than twenty minutes. And we never made
the trip without remembering the times we had been
stuck on almost every hill, and in nearly every valley;
or the places where we had pushed with all our might on
a sizzling day, or shoveled on a freezing one, or pulled
bunchgrass to put under the wheels for a little traction.

A year or two later, the state and county put crews
to work on the highway again, and by the fall of 1954
the strip reached Arthur, to meet the end of another
highway that stretched on north the rest of the way
across the state. But Bert wasn't well enough to make
the trip when, on October 26, McPherson and Arthur

counties celebrated the joining of the highways with a big barbecue and "ribbon cutting" ceremony at Arthur.

I went, though, for I remembered that it had been fifty-three years ago, that very day, that I had traveled the north stretch of those hills in a two-wheeled cart behind a team of galloping mules—on my way to Lena to teach my first school.

Miles had taken up the fight for better roads where his father's failing health had forced him to leave off, and the year the road was finished he was president of the Sandhills Chapter of the 92 Highway Association. That day, I watched him and other Association officers, together with a United States Congressman guest, climb into a Model T Ford and drive up to the ribbon, which was then snipped apart so they could drive on through. It had taken all the years since that Model T was new to get that road through the hills.

Another strip or two of the narrow oil-sand hard-top winds through the north hills now. One leaves the Tryon-Arthur highway west of the old Skinner Valley, passes near the Huffmans, and within a mile or so of Eclipse church, before it joins a strip that goes on to Mullen. But the "Corn to Cattle" highway, and all the other highways the *Graphic* editor once "pulled" so hard for, are still blueprints in some dusty pigeonhole. Even the editor, probably gray haired by now, has been gone from the county for years.

Bert and I had the privilege and the joy of celebrating our Golden Wedding Day, with our four children and seven grandchildren all on hand to help us. Old oldest grandson was married that same afternoon, and I wished then that Bert and I had been married on *his* parents' Golden Wedding Day. We had missed it by only a week, but it was fifty years too late now.

Of the many friends who came to call, only a few were among those we had known in 1903. Three or four of Bert's old cowboy friends from Wyoming and Montana came, and John Maline and Jennie Cox, Bird Huffman and his sister Mable, and Mrs. Trego. "You know," I said to her, "I was riding your side-saddle the day Bert proposed to me."

"That was a good saddle." She laughed. "I was riding it the day Nate proposed to me."

I am eighty now, and Bert is gone, and the old ranch house too, torn down to make way for a new one for one of Miles's boys. The "big tree" still stands in the old yard, although a dozen younger cottonwoods have long since outgrown it. Near where the old south porch used to be, my yellow rosebushes still bloom in June. I was so happy when I finally got those bushes to thrive on the ranch; for they are descendants of the roses that bordered Poppie's old home in Missouri a hundred years ago. The old windmill and milk house that stood so long by the side of my big garden are gone, too, and the garden has long "gone to grass" again.

Miles's big house, built of logs hauled down from the Black Hills, has already stood twenty-five years on the ridge west of our old yard, and Miles and Hollis are grandparents now. Hangars and planes and tractors fill the space where Bert used to keep his hay machinery, and there isn't a team on the place. But there are still good saddle horses. Though Miles and Jim check windmills and ride pasture fences in a plane, there are some jobs on a ranch that can only be done with a horse. A row of tall black poles carries REA power lines to the ranch now, and enormous commercial cattle trucks now pull up to the loading pens and scales and chutes beside the old corrals.

Only the hills around our valley look the same as they did when I came to the ranch, a bride, sixty years ago.

Sometimes now, in summer, I go to stand in the old yard. Above me, the cottonwoods grieve under every light breeze that stirs their leaves, and it seems to me that I can see the old house, and all of us as we used to be. Bert, forever busy with his cattle; Nellie trying to do her work with her nose in a book; Miles tinkering with a radio in his every spare minute; Billie in her brother's cast-off hat and boots and overalls, riding her pony over the hills like an Indian; little Bertie petting the chickens and carrying baby frogs in her wee apron pocket.

Such busy years, when I baked our bread, churned our butter, raised a big garden and canned all our vegetables, cured our meat, made all the girls' clothes on the sewing machine I had bought with the orphan calf, helped in the hayfield, and still found a little spare time for piecing quilts.

I have seen all of my big wishes come true. Bert lived to see one of his fullfilled, and I may very well see the accomplishment of the other; for half a dozen outfits are drilling for oil in the sandhills this spring.

I couldn't have asked for a more wonderful eighty years to live in. They have reached from the days when old Mr. Wicklund used to drive his oxteam past the homestead, to the day that John Glenn rocketed three times around the world in the space of a forenoon—and through them all I have been blessed by having no time on my hands.

Epilogue

When Mother finished telling me her life story—back in 1962—
we could not know that she had another twenty years to live—or
what busy years they would prove to be. We had shown her
magnificent quilts at many quilt shows and special occasions
throughout Nebraska and their fame had grown and spread.
Bonnie Leman and her husband had come from Denver to
photograph them in color for their *Quilter's Newsletter.* By
request, the quilts (fifteen of them) had hung one winter in the
big main room of the Museum of the Prairie Pioneer in Grand
Island and two summers in the House of Yesterday in Hastings.
Then Lew Cole of the Prairie Pioneer had photographed them in
color, added pictures of Mother—her tintype baby picture, her
likeness at sixteen, her wedding picture, and many others,
making a splendid documentary tape and slide show, complete
with musical effects, to portray her life story, "The Three Dreams
of Grace McCance Snyder," through her ninety-first year. The
tape-slide program has proved very popular over the years and
many copies have been sold in almost every state in the Union and
in Japan, Holland, Australia, and Quebec as well.

Stories and pictures of Grace Snyder and her quilts have
appeared in many quilters' magazines from coast to coast and in
the August 1984 issue of *Better Homes and Gardens.* The quilts have
been shown in huge quilt shows in Texas, Virginia, California,
Washington, Tennessee, Lousiana, Michigan, Kansas, Colorado,
Iowa, and Utah. Five of them were featured at a special quilt show
in the Sheldon Art Gallery at the University of Nebraska–
Lincoln some years ago, and the Flower Basket quilt hung for
three weeks in the place of honor in the great Meadow Brook
Hall, the hundred-room Dodge Mansion in Rochester, Michigan,
in 1983.

Crowds have always gathered before the Flower Basket quilt, to gape in unbelief at the fantastically small pieces that make up the lovely work of art. Probably the finest tribute of all was paid it by a man who looked at it for a long time, from all different angles, then finally turned and said to me, "That is the Stradivarius of all quilts."

Traveling with the quilts was interesting. Since we didn't dare risk them on the planes as luggage, the quilt show people bought two seats on the plane, one for the quilts and one for me, as I rode "shotgun" for them wherever they went. Many people were very curious about what was in the big box that rated a seat of its own on the plane. Wherever they are shown they are the prima donnas of the exhibition. Many people have told me that when they saw that Grace Snyder's quilts were to be shown, they traveled long distances just to see them.

I came home from each show with so much to tell Mother about what folks said of her marvelous work. She always listened eagerly, her face beaming, then said, "That's wonderful. But when I was having such a good time making them, I didn't dream that someday so many other people would enjoy them, too." That seemed to please her most, that others found pleasure in just looking at them "live" rather than in pictures. When the Flower Basket quilt was judged best of show in one of the big California exhibits and was awarded the thousand-dollar grand prize, my first thought was of telling Mother—but I couldn't tell her. She had left us the winter before. The famous quilt hangs now in the Nebraska State Historical Society Museum in Lincoln, Nebraska, in a case designed especially for it where it will be treasured, protected, and enjoyed by all quilt lovers.

It seems that Grace Snyder had a part in the great quilt revival that has swept the world. When she made her last quilt, "the Princess Feather," in 1953, quilting appeared to be a dying art. Then, after *No Time on My Hands* was published in 1963, she began to receive letters from women who told her they had read her book and were busy starting quilting clubs. A large group of Lincoln women wrote to ask if they could come to her home in North Platte for a special showing of the quilts. They went home inspired and organized a club that grew rapidly and is still very active in quilting circles. Many men caught the bug, too, and became well-known designers and makers of fine quilts. All seemed to look up to Grace Snyder as the quilter par excellence, inspirer of dreams. In 1980, at ninety-eight years of age, she was honored by induction into the Quilters' Hall of Fame by the National Congress of Quilters of Arlington, Virginia, a most exclusive group made up of the world's best quilters.

In 1981 Molly Newman of Denver came to North Platte to interview Grace Snyder. She also purchased a copy of *No Time on My Hands,* read other quilting books, and interviewed other quilters. The result was the play, *Quilters,* by Molly Newman and Barbara Damashek, which made its debut in 1982 and has since toured from coast to coast and to Scotland and Ireland. This moving play was based partly on Grace's life and its success has been astonishing. *Quilters* promises to become an American classic, to be seen and loved down through the ages.

As the years passed, Mother became very frail, though still alert and interested in her family, friends, and current events. Her first great-great-grandchild was born in her ninety-first year; others followed until, including Miles and Hollis's twin grandsons, they numbered fifteen. That same year she asked to go back to the ranch and ride a saddle horse again. With the help of devoted grandsons she proudly mounted the horse and posed for her picture.

On April 23, 1982, she celebrated her one hundredth birthday. By then she was living with her daughter Billie in the handsome new home Billie and her husband had built on North Platte's southernmost street, where the wide windows looked out on the timbered river. The big house was filled all afternoon with family and friends who came to congratulate her on achieving the century mark. Her pleasure in the day was unbounded, but from then on she seemed to fade slowly. By Thanksgiving she was very weak and on December 8 she passed quietly away in sleep. A gallant, lovely lady who saw her three big dreams come true, she rests now beside Bert "Pinnacle Jake" Snyder in the North Platte Cemetery.

Nellie Snyder Yost
August 1985